ESSENTIALS OF CHRISTIAN COMMUNITY

Daniel W. Hardy

ESSENTIALS OF CHRISTIAN COMMUNITY

Essays for Daniel W. Hardy

Edited by
David F. Ford and Dennis L. Stamps

to Ann Nickson,

with great respect

Dan Hardy

T & T CLARK
EDINBURGH

T&T CLARK LTD
59 GEORGE STREET
EDINBURGH EH2 2LQ
SCOTLAND

First published 1996

ISBN 0 567 08502 3 HB
ISBN 0 567 08503 1 PB

British Library Cataloguing-in-Publication Data
A catalogue record for this book is available from the British Library

Typeset by Fakenham Photosetting Ltd, Fakenham, Norfolk
Printed and bound in Great Britain by Biddles Ltd, Guildford

Contents

Contents

Preface

This is a book which might well be read by starting with the Postscript 'A Magnificent Complexity' and only then moving forward from the Introduction. The essays on a range of major issues about Christian community have been offered to Dan Hardy in celebration of his sixty-fifth birthday in November 1995 and have elicited from him his most extended treatment of this theme to date. He has taken up most of their main points in a critical and constructive way. That is often the task of an introduction, and some may find it valuable as such. On the other hand, readers may want to repeat our experience as editors. We read the essays as they arrived, forming our own judgements, and only then received the fascinating, unforeseeable response.

On behalf of all the contributors, we congratulate Dan Hardy on his birthday, offer our immense gratitude for all he has been for us and look forward to our continuing life together in academic and church communities.

David F. Ford
Dennis L. Stamps

Acknowledgements

The publishers gratefully acknowledge permission to reproduce extracts from the following works in chapter 3:

Patrick Kavanagh, 'Canal Bank Walk', *Collected Poems* (London: Mac-Gibbon & Kee, 1964). By kind permission of the trustees of the Estate of Patrick Kavanagh, c/o Peter Fallon, Literary Agent, Loughcrew, Oldcastle, Co. Meath, Ireland.

Brendan Kennelly, 'Ambulance', *A Time for Voices* (Newcastle upon Tyne: Bloodaxe Books, 1992).

Michael O'Siadhail, 'Freedom', *Hail! Madam Jazz* (Newcastle upon Tyne: Bloodaxe Books, 1992); 'Invitation', *A Fragile City* (Newcastle upon Tyne: Bloodaxe Books, 1995).

Richard Wilbur, 'The Beautiful Changes', *New and Collected Poems* (London: Faber & Faber, 1989). In the USA and Canada: Harcourt Brace & Co.

ix

Introduction

The Architecture of Life with God

DAVID F. FORD

AN obvious essential for Christian community is people. This book is by a group of people who are all members of the Christian community and who in addition have two things in common. We are theologians (if Micheal O'Siadhail will agree that his quotation from Patrick Kavanagh about poets being theologians permits us to include him in that category), and we want to honour Daniel Wayne Hardy (Dan to his friends) as a fellow-theologian.

It was clear to us that the best way to honour him was to do theology on some basic question as well as we could and then to invite him to respond. For many years he has been developing a concept of the faith and the church in the contemporary world which is quite unlike any other. It therefore seemed right to try to stretch ourselves in fresh thinking on this theme, many of us having already been in dialogue with Dan Hardy for years about aspects of it, and to elicit in reply a foretaste of the books he is preparing on it. Right from the start the project has had a serendipitous feel to it, as nearly everyone invited accepted with alacrity and produced their contributions promptly. This enabled Dan Hardy to read them before writing his culminating piece. The eagerness and promptness are themselves a tribute: the content of the chapters and the strikingly diverse way in which they show their indebtedness to Dan's theology reveal the fruitfulness and capacity for intellectual hospitality that has marked his career in a way that is hard to parallel in Britain or USA.

To focus on Dan Hardy in this introduction is an appropriate way into the essentials of Christian community. Christianity is a faith inseparable from its embodiment in particular people living in community, beginning with Jesus and his first fellow-Jewish disciples. It is learnt best in community with contemporary followers, and it is a considerable advantage in treating the title theme of this book to be able to look at one such follower. My main concern will be Dan's theology as it is interwoven with his multiple involvements in church, academy and society.

I. A THEOLOGICAL BIOGRAPHY

Dan Hardy is one of the least autobiographical of people – he very rarely talks about himself in that way, and this is matched by his theology not giving a prominent place to narrative. I will use his biography in a low-key way in this section in order to try to give cumulatively some notion of the dimensions of his theological work and especially to characterize the reconception of the field of theology and religious studies that it advocates and exemplifies.

(a) Early life

He was born in New York in 1930 into a family to which his eventual vocation as a priest and theologian came as a surprise. He was educated in good private schools and colleges, culminating with Haverford College. This is a Quaker foundation which was then still in touch with its origins, and attending Quaker Meeting for weekly worship made a deep impression, as did the presence of the Quaker thinker Douglas Steere.

Anglicanism had first made an impression through its liturgy at school. Later, after Haverford, his decision for ordination led to training in General Theological Seminary in New York and then to become Assistant Minister in Greenwich, Connecticut. While there he had considerable influence on the design of a striking new church building, St Barnabas. I have worshipped in it and talked to those who remember his key role in the construction of the first church in modern style in that area. He coordinated lengthy consultations with the congregation and put together the architect's brief. His other main task in Greenwich was leading a youth group at the other church, Christchurch. This was fifteen strong when he arrived; by the time he left four years later it had a hundred and twenty members focused on a programme of discussion and worship.

Two crucial developments happened during this period. He met and married Perrin (Kate Perrin Enyart), the relationship which has remained at the heart of his life ever since. And he became clear about the fundamental need for theology. He said much later that his late start in academic theology was because he spent so many years finding out just how deeply it is needed. This led to his return to a teaching post in General Theological Seminary, where Perrin and he had Deborah, their first of four children. The other three, Jennifer, Daniel and Christopher, were to be born in England.

The next move was to Oxford for four years to study with Ian Ramsey and others. This was an ambivalent time, allowing for wide-ranging thought in theology, philosophy and other areas but also exposing serious deficiencies in the theology on offer and the horizons within which academic discussions went on. Its main feature was a rigorous pattern of study for about nine hours a day which was a first immersion in sustained, cumulative thinking. This period came to an end in 1965 when he was offered two posts, one in the USA and one in the Department of Theology in the University of Birmingham, and chose the latter. That began what was probably the most important period in his theological formation, the twenty-one years in Birmingham.

(b) Birmingham – teaching and Jubilate

The key element in this formation was the immersion in modern theology and philosophy that he undertook in order to create new courses. He read widely in primary sources, considered the rationale for studying theology in a secular university (and in particular for doing anything that might count as positively Christian), and developed the first course in an English university to treat eighteenth, nineteenth and twentieth-century theologies thoroughly and in relationship to each other. The comprehensive reconception of courses, programmes and ways of studying has remained a feature of his procedure ever since.

I joined the department in Birmingham in 1976, half-way through his time there, and shared the teaching course he had devised. We shared lecturing and supervising, attended each other's lectures, and constantly discussed the issues. It was the most stretching period of my own education, engaging with one theologian after another, with different periods, and with the whole range of doctrines and methodological questions, and with constant conversation with Dan about the issues and their implications for church and society. If I were singling out one thing above all as most valuable it would be the appreciation of what is involved in adequate theological judgement – the complexity of factors, the interplay of disciplines, the range of historical reference, the interpretation of scripture, and the often startling use of a recent work on quantum physics or economics or philosophy. But perhaps the most striking thing about his way of doing all this was the sense it conveyed of the endless richness of truth and of the corresponding impossibility of ever resting in a 'position'.

That is worth pausing to consider. A 'position' is the last thing one thinks of in relation to this nevertheless very systematic thinker. There is a never-ending reworking going on. What might seem like a satisfactory statement is the next day refined, reconceived, or even left to one side in order to come at the matter from a very different angle. I never ceased being amazed by (and was never able to imitate) the rewriting of every lecture every year which I witnessed. Immense intellectual energy and wide further reading went into these lectures year after year. The same passion for reworking was evident in his writing and is part of the reason why he has not published more. At the heart of it is a pursuit of truth that is deeply aware of the interconnectedness and dynamic complexity of reality and of the relationship of everything with a God who constantly stretches our minds. Our knowing, the creation and the God of abundant truth, beauty and love are all involved in an infinitely rich interrelationship, and any 'position' is a temporary vantage point and an inadequate articulation of some part of that. Within theology every doctrine – God, creation, salvation, church and so on – can be reworked from within each of the others and also in relation to a range of disciplines and to an indefinitely larger number of life issues.

I recognized something like this recently in a description of the sculptor and artist Alberto Giacometti as he ceaselessly returned to his key themes and faces, never remotely satisfied with what was produced because the creative engagement itself opened up more and more. His biographer quotes him: 'Art interests me very much, but truth interests me infinitely more. The more I work, the more I see things differently, that is, everything gains in grandeur every day, becomes more and more unknown, more and more beautiful. The closer I come, the grander it is, the more remote it is.'[1] In Dan Hardy's work the closest analogy to the figures in Giacometti's sculpture and painting is perhaps in the area of conceptuality. The labour of thought frequently results in coining or borrowing some dense, summary concept or network of concepts. The production, refining and relating of such intellectual distillations is a continuous feature of his theology. It is no accident that in recent years he has so often in his writing and preaching used the poetry of Micheal O'Siadhail, where he has recognized an intensity of language that resonates with his own practice of conceptual creativity.

Parallel with the courses for undergraduates in Birmingham there was an ever-increasing number of postgraduate students to supervise. The testimonies to his abilities in this role are numerous and well represented by some of the contributors to this book. His generosity with time and ideas, his frighteningly perceptive reading of drafts, the astonishing range of the literature to which he referred students, the high standards together with endless patience and encouragement, the seemingly paradoxical combination of his own definite understanding with his ability to liberate students to follow their own paths, and perhaps above all the ever-renewed discovery in conversation with him of what living theology is – all that and more was the experience of a succession of students.

My own experience in co-authoring *Jubilate: Theology in Praise* (USA title, *Praising and Knowing God*)[2] with him in Birmingham was analogous. Indeed, joint authorship with a senior colleague in this way must be the ideal post-doctoral education. We set aside Thursday mornings to work on the book. They were invariably feasts: hours of talking theology, much 'shorthand' possible because of the course and conver-

---

[1] James Lord, *Giacometti: A Biography* (New York: Farrar, Strauss and Giroux, 1985), p. 474.

[2] London: Darton, Longman & Todd, 1984; Philadelphia: Westminster, 1985.

sations we were already sharing, time for extensive detours, freedom to pursue ideas wherever they led us, no need to worry about inadequacies or being unable to support something or respond to objections, constantly feeding in fresh reading and other experience, and no deadlines (we took several years). The book is my own favourite on my bibliography, only partly due to the happy association that it was a factor in bringing me together with his daughter, Deborah, who became my wife. But compared to the richness of those mornings in conversation the book sometimes seems like leftovers served the day after the feast. In fact, of course, writing and conversation are somewhat like distinct art forms, and we entered a very different stage later as we discussed and revised the drafts of chapters. But the process of generating the main ideas of the book explains why it has always been impossible to attribute them to one or the other of us – many of them, indeed, occurred while talking. One effect on the theology of both of us was to establish praise, worship and blessing as a key relationship within which to know God and as the most helpful dynamic through which to appreciate the 'ecology' of God, people and the rest of creation in interaction. Typically, Dan has gone on rethinking the ideas ever since, and some of his recent work shows the results of that, notably in 'Worship as the Orientation of Life to God'[3] and the entry on 'Worship' in the *Dictionary of Theology and Society*.[4]

(c) Birmingham – the nature of theology

The Birmingham department was headed by Prof. J. G. Davies, with whom Dan worked very closely on departmental policy. There were some basic differences in approach to the discipline in the department, some wanting to see it shift towards American-style religious studies. One way of posing the question was in terms of a choice between confessional theology and non-confessional religious studies. Dan wanted a third option, harder to label but crucial to understanding what he had worked at for over thirty years in academic life. His conception of theology has been developed and refined since then, but it was in Birmingham that it received its basic shape. How is it to be described?[5]

It is a conception that stretches the available options beyond the limits

---

[3] *Ex Auditu* 8 (1992), pp. 55–71.
[4] Forthcoming (London: Routledge).
[5] The description which follows is based on: unpublished reports and policy papers produced by Daniel Hardy for the Center of Theological Inquiry, Princeton; 'Epilogue: The Strategy of Liberalism', in *The Weight of Glory. A Vision and Practice for Christian Faith: The Future of Liberal Theology. Essays for Peter Baelz*, eds. D. W. Hardy and P. Sedgwick (Edinburgh: T. & T. Clark, 1991); 'The Future of Theology in a Complex World', delivered to a Symposium on Christ and Context in Dunedin, New Zealand, 1991; 'On the Agenda for Theology and Religious Education', delivered to a conference on religious education in Durham, 1994; and innumerable discussions over many years.

within which they are comfortable. Confessional theology is found inadequate in various respects. It tends to fix on certain periods, sources and authorities and to have a 'repetitive' and past-oriented attitude to theological truth. For theology to be true to itself, this option is inclined to say, the intellectual habits of the past are normative, and faith therefore is discussed and affirmed in ways that are marginal to modern life. Those theological courses which do adopt modern methods and engage with a range of disciplines are often still constricted by conventions about periods and sources which survive from a more purely confessional approach. The choice of confessions, traditions, periods or authorities inevitably seems arbitrary and even discriminatory in a bad sense. And in addition, they often fall into the trap of thinking that theology results from the interplay of disciplines – historical, linguistic, hermeneutical, sociological, philosophical or political – as they deal with this material. The more strictly academic forms of confessional theology easily become absorbed in the professionalism of the 'guilds' of different specialisms, and the strong attractions of academic respectability leads to a bracketing out of larger or more fundamental questions which relate to theology as a search for wisdom. Overall, there is a greater or lesser avoidance of the full implications of questions about the truthfulness and practicability of any tradition for today. It is not that what is studied is unnecessary; rather, confessional theology typically mistakes what is necessary for what is sufficient.

Religious studies opens itself to a variety of religions and approaches, which is to be welcomed. But it is constricted in other ways. Without even the confessional concentration on certain definite materials the way is open for a dazzling array of methods set to work on an increasing diversity of religious phenomena. Religion is seen as primarily historical and cultural, and the categories of historical and cultural description and analysis become dominant. Questions about continuities in the rational grasp of reality, let alone specifically theological questions such as those about the truth of God, are left untouched. The required academic stance is ideally that of the empathetic but neutral observer. That has its strengths, but it separates the student from the illumination which occurs for the reason of religious believers in active relationship with God, such as in prayer and worship. The combination of dominant historical/cultural categories with a stance which is on principle disengaged from the dynamic relationship in which believers relate to God results in a deficiency in both objectivity and subjectivity. If, for example, a phenomenology claiming to be without normative assumptions sees doctrine and worship as just two among several elements in the experience of 'religion', the effect is twofold:

It severely limits the determining role of active relation to God in worship, and the reconfiguration of human life in the world which that requires, and in its place elevates religious experience. And it reverses the role of fundamental beliefs and practices in religion. From conclusions derived – often through centuries-long painful struggle, from the intelligent worship of God which transcended the possibilities afforded by current intellectual endeavour, they are transferred to the position of reflections on human experience which are subject to the categories of thought available in particular cultural circumstances. The effects are very drastic for the configuration of religious theory and life, removing its two most fundamental determinants from their central position.[6]

Study of religion as one form of cultural study cannot, for all its value, do adequate justice to the seriousness, range and complexity of the issues with which theology must deal. Faith cannot be disengaged from its relationship with intelligent understanding:

> Where religion/theology is studied in public institutions, it is supposed that the question of the truth of faith should not be addressed; it is sufficient to catalogue the phenomena of religions, as if they were all equally valuable. That is supposed to be the strategy for preserving the place of religious study in public institutions, or in places where there is disagreement about the value of different traditions. Such an approach mirrors the blandness and vacuousness of much life in the West, where there is nothing but appearance and all appearances must by definition be equal. 'Plastic life' is what it's called in California.[7]

The tendency in academic institutions in the USA, Britain and many other countries is for religious studies approaches to encroach on theology, usually under the pressure to conform to standards and fashions of the various disciplines. Perhaps the most serious casualty is the pursuit of a wisdom that attempts a convergence of understanding on important matters and interweaves that understanding with issues of practice.

Dan Hardy's third way has already been emerging through his critique of the other two. It takes seriously the positive concerns of confessional theology but attempts to be both more open and more critical. It takes seriously the range of approaches and phenomena in religious studies but aims to spend more time on fundamental questions of truth and practice and in particular to locate them in relation to God. There is no necessary tension between commitment to reason and commitment to God. The

---

[6] See note 5 above.
[7] 'The Future of Theology', p. 13.

God affirmed by Dan is one who empowers and expands the capacity for rational comprehension and critical judgement. The prejudice (found in all types of theology and beyond) that belief in God cannot live with full rationality, that faith means suspending the critical faculty, and that therefore one who believes is somehow not able to treat theological topics with academic integrity, is insidious – it misconstrues faith, reason and God. Or perhaps it would be better to say that it is a general statement which presupposes specific and questionable concepts of faith, reason and God.

This discovery that there can be no neutral adjudication of the nature of this discipline points to one of Dan's recurrent themes: that methods, or ways of studying reality, cannot be separated from substantive issues of content. There are basic theological questions implicit in the dispute about the field of theology and religious studies. Dan's refusal to bracket out any of the biggest questions about thinking *God* in relation to being, truth, wisdom, goodness and beauty is hospitable to most of what goes on in the field but is also awkwardly persistent in exposing its limitations. I will illustrate this in his treatment of liberal and contextual approaches to theology.

In his epilogue to the Festschrift for Peter Baelz entitled 'The Strategy of Liberalism',[8] he typically redescribes liberalism so that its positive features accord with what he himself sees theology aiming to do. He sees liberal Christian theology

> looking for the possibility of a deeper Christian faith through modern understanding, in which the possibilities of faith are enriched through modern ways ... The purpose of liberal thought is not to compromise Christian faith, but to rediscover the means of maintaining it in the modern world ... The allegiance is not to the 'givenness' of certain statements of faith ... but to a tradition which revivifies itself in creative appropriation.[9]

It resists dogmatism and moral absolutism and also the 'cumulative over-specification' of belief and practice. Its tradition-recreating labours seek the right kind of liberality, God's liberality to all creation. This involves the aesthetic and imaginative, worship, the cognitive and the practical, and all these as inextricably connected. But Dan also discerns a fundamental weakness in much liberalism: the scant attention given to the character of God, partly due to the tendency to adopt the norms of a post-Kantian 'turn to the subject'.

In New Zealand in 1992 he addressed a symposium on the explosive

[8] See note 5 above.
[9] 'Strategy of Liberalism', p. 301.

issues of 'Christ and Context' and spoke of the future of theology. His interpretation of 'context' was in line with its etymology, a braiding, weaving or connecting together. Cultures themselves are dynamically intertwined. He conceived the agenda for theology for the future in these terms:

(1) The first question is this: In a world where the possibility of deep unity between peoples, that which is based on their service of a common good, has been lost in the welter of the conflicting claims of self-interested groups, how are we to recover the intertwining of cultures and peoples? (2) And the second question is: How, in the braiding together of cultures and peoples in a dynamic unity, is God himself present? How, indeed, does God's life appear in the service of a common good? (3) And the third question is: How are we properly interwoven with nature? How does God's presence appear in our proper interwovenness with nature? What, then, is the identity of the God who so appears?[10]

There follows a wide-ranging critique of the common ways of doing theology and religious studies, with a plea for a form of wisdom more complex than any of them usually offers. The positive vision of theology is as a creative, intelligent *poesis*. In line with the refusal to separate form from content, this is articulated through a consideration of the resurrection of Christ, what it generated and what that shows of the character of God. It all amounts to an understanding of 'the proper form of the interwovenness of human beings and the way in which God is present in it'.[11]

The passionate ethic of theological responsibility that pervades this vision was stated in the opening of the same address:

[U]nless theology is simply a curious study of religious thoughts and practices, you and I and we need to be reminded that in what we say we are morally responsible for the future of theology. Not only in what we say, but in the manner in which we deal with the questions and disagreements with which we will be concerned, we are exemplifying theology and fashioning it for the future. It used to be said that theological statements are self-involving, and that is true enough. But theological statements are also God-, community- and world-involving; each statement enhances or destroys God, others

---

[10] 'The Future of Theology', pp. 6–7.
[11] 'The Future of Theology', p. 32.

and the world. It is facile – if not irresponsible – to suppose other-wise.[12]

The logic of ever greater involvement was carried over into the institutional locations of theology. In Britain, Dan's two main national arenas were the Church of England (discussed below) and the Society for the Study of Theology. People often find the latter hard to categorize. It is largely Christian but not confessional (in the sense of the Society of Catholic Theologians); it is not largely 'religious studies' in approach; it is not academic in any restricted sense: many members are from university departments or theological colleges, but more are theologically educated members of other occupations; it is largely British but has specially close links with Ireland and Holland and has held annual meetings in both those countries. One reason for this character is that Dan has been one of its formative members. For years he sat on its committee and helped to shape conference topics; he was its Treasurer and its President; he delivered several papers and at annual meetings he regularly sits up after midnight deep in theological conversation. Perhaps the most striking contribution has been in the discussions of papers from 'the floor' – usually late interventions that go to the heart of what has been said, identify key issues and make the sort of constructive statements that call for another paper. In the USA he has been a member of the American Academy of Religion for decades, and in particular has shaped and contributed to its long-term group on nineteenth-century theology.

(d) Birmingham – education and church

In the late 1960s in Britain plans were made for a Bachelor's degree in Education (B.Ed.) uniting educational and specialist subject studies in a four-year degree. There were sixteen colleges in the Birmingham region which taught theology as part of this and Dan offered to co-ordinate the new degree. It meant syllabus construction, inspection visits, examining, participation in staff appointments and persuading colleagues in the University to take part in relation to their fields. He joined the Board of the Faculty of Education and became Chairman of the Board of Examiners for the B.Ed. in all subjects. He tried to create courses which interwove the basic concerns of education and theology. After some years of this immense labour it was recognized that he was carrying an extra job, and a new post funded by the B.Ed. was created in his field – I was the first to hold it.

Birmingham during his time was also a centre for passionate debate about a controversial syllabus for Religious Education in state schools.

---

[12] 'Future of Theology', p. 1.

Dan was not involved in making it, but took part in the debates afterwards as one of its leading opponents. As he saw it, the syllabus opted for 'generic religious education' which could never do justice to the reality and depth of any particular religion and in its approach had flaws similar to those of religious studies in universities.

Exercising his priesthood in a parish setting was also an integral part of the time in Birmingham. He was Honorary Curate for seventeen years in St Mark's Church, Smethwick, a largely working class Black Country parish. He regularly preached and celebrated the Eucharist and did a considerable amount of pastoral work (some of which has continued from a distance). There is a room in the parish buildings named after him.

Beyond the parish he was involved in the Diocese of Birmingham in several ways. He was on the Bishop's Council and Diocesan Synod; was a member of almost every diocesan committee concerned with education – in schools, for adults and for Readers (a form of lay liturgical ministry). When a Needs and Resources Commission was set up to rethink the operations of the dioceses he was a leading member and did much of the drafting of the report. He was also the main architect of a Charitable Trust for Anglican Chaplaincy in the University of Birmingham.

Beyond the Diocese, he was called upon increasingly to serve on central Church of England bodies. He helped devise policy for training Readers and was on the central Board of Education. But his major contribution was to the most radical restructuring of syllabus and assessment in theological education for ministry in the Church of England this century. It has been a quiet revolution, and part of the story is told in this volume by Brian Russell, who also played a leading role in it.

In the mid-1980s Dan found himself in a series of key roles focusing on the initial training of clergy. He was a Moderator of the General Ministerial Examination taken by ordinands, and he chaired the examiners; he was on the committees that dealt with the overall shape of theological education and with the content of the syllabus; and he was on the working party which inspected colleges on behalf of the Bishops. It became clear that the syllabus and forms of assessment were unsatisfactory, and a working party chaired by Dan was set up to produce a report. After a year of monthly meetings he largely drafted the final report. It was later published as ACCM Paper No. 22 (see below for Brian Russell's account and Peter Sedgwick's reference to it). It is a document which is, I think, unparalleled in the Church of England for its combination of asking clear basic questions, doing fundamental, high quality theological thinking about them, drawing coherent practical implications and recommending a workable form of implementation and follow-up. It was astonishing how this radical (in the true sense) report was accepted so smoothly by the Bishops and the other relevant Church bodies. It was one of those rare fulcrum times in an institution when someone prepared in the right way could, with the help of others who recognized the need of the moment, produce a considerable change with relatively little power or conflict.

One further initiative in theological education was the Simon of Cyrene Theological Institute, also mentioned by Brian Russell below. It was the outcome of a series of 'Young, Black and Gifted' conferences, aimed at enabling black candidates to train for the ministry in the Church of England. Dan spent a long time helping to develop the concept, was influential in persuading the Church of England to sponsor it, and then served on its board.

(e) Durham – Canon and Professor

In April 1986 Dan became Van Mildert Professor of Divinity in the University of Durham and Canon of Durham Cathedral. Within a term he was also Head of the Department of Theology, responsible for co-ordinating a complete curriculum revision. His number of graduate students multiplied (he was supervising twenty-four by the time he left) so that he used to teach five days a week, morning and afternoon. It was a time of intensive multiple responsibilities, and a great deal of theological thinking went into the curriculum and the supervising.

There were two major, interconnected new developments. The first was the experience of integrating cathedral with university through his canon professorship. In Birmingham church affairs had been a personal addition to a post in a self-consciously secular university. In Durham active church life was at the heart of the post, and he led worship, preached and played a full role in the Cathedral Chapter with Peter Baelz as Dean. He gave an immense amount of attention to his sermons which are one of the best sources for his theology of this period.

The other development was his course on Church, Ministry and Sacraments. He had never taught these subjects in Birmingham, but having taken over the course from his predecessor, Stephen Sykes, he set about rethinking the topic. The result was what he considered a breakthrough in grasping the foundations of ecclesiology. Ecclesiology became the focus for new dimensions of his previous thought on theology, on other doctrines and on a range of concepts such as sociality, 'diversitarian' forms of explanation, God's dynamic order as the condition of a social dynamic order, and the dynamics of church structures, responsibilities and sacraments. One published outcome has been his contribution to *On Being the Church*,[13] 'Created and Redeemed Sociality', but neither in

[13] Edited by C. E. Gunton and D. W. Hardy (Edinburgh: T. & T. Clark, 1989). Cf. also his essay 'God and the Form of Society', in *The Weight of Glory*, pp. 131–44.

Durham nor since then has he yet had the opportunity to pursue this topic in anything longer than a paper.

(f) Princeton – fully interdisciplinary theology

In 1989 a 'search' by the Center of Theological Inquiry (CTI) in Princeton for its second Director in succession to James McCord led them to offer the post to Dan Hardy. It is easy to see the attraction of CTI. It is a small, reasonably well-endowed, independent institution set up to sponsor advanced theological work, especially in relation to major contemporary intellectual inquiries and discussion. It houses about twelve members at a time, giving them all the facilities they need, including accommodation for themselves and their families and, if necessary, a stipend. They usually stay for periods between six months and two years, and have the use of library and some other facilities of Princeton Theological Seminary and Princeton University. Durham had been an institutional culmination of Dan's decades of doing theology through both university and church. Princeton was a culmination of his parallel commitment to doing theology through a thorough engagement with a wide range of academic disciplines and current issues.

He took up his new post in 1990 and at the time of writing is still there. During that time CTI has been reorganized in its administration and admission procedures, increasing numbers of leading academics have been applying for membership, more funds have been raised and the support of major foundations obtained, and an array of colloquia, collaborative projects and institutional links established. At the heart of it is a programme of long-term consultations, and Dan's conception of these, laid out in various CTI paper and reports, which reads like a manifesto for theology heading into the next millennium. The consultations focus on five areas: the natural sciences; the formation of society, institutions and community; human nature and the quality of personal life; the formation of culture; and the interplay of religions.

In these years the 'ecology' of CTI has changed considerably (before his arrival it had largely become a place where scholars of a more or less conservative bent spent sabbaticals), as has the perception of it in the academic world. One cost has been that there has not been time to write the books which are waiting to be written. The original conception of the post as involving between forty and fifty per cent of the Director's time spent on his own research and writing proved impossible to realize. This is partly because of the comprehensiveness of the reformation which Dan has set in motion. But it is also due to a wider American difficulty which has two aspects. First, the idea of a type of theology that is not confessional or religious studies/history of religious thought is very hard to grasp in a setting where most institutions in the field are committed to one of those options. Second, the American pattern tends towards having deans who are expected to run an institution but not at the same time carry on research. It seems that both the Board of CTI and most of its members have treated him as some sort of dean. Nevertheless, the output of these years in papers, reports, sermons, lectures, articles, dictionary articles and addresses has been considerable (see Bibliography), and at least two books are also there, largely conceived and partly written, awaiting sufficient time to be completed.

There is much else in his life which would be worth discussing, not least because each aspect could be related to his theology. Family life, music, architecture, economics, management, money, politics, pastoral care and counselling, history, archaeology, Pentecostalism, feminism, race relations, social justice – the list of matters with which he has been involved could go on. But it is time to conclude with a more direct look at his own theology.

II. THEOLOGY ITSELF

Dan Hardy has been a most productive theologian, but one whose work does not fit into the main category by which the work of academic theologians is usually measured: single author books. So far he has not written one of those – several await his retirement from CTI. He and his wife have built a retirement house in Cambridge and he is already General Editor of a new Cambridge University Press series, Studies in Christian Doctrine, for which he is himself contracted to write a book on the church.

Monographs have not, so far, been a top priority because of the sort of theologian he is. Some of the factors that contribute to his particular character as a theologian have already been mentioned – a passion for reworking, lifelong institutional commitments, giving personal work with students and colleagues a high priority, and ceaseless rethinking of theology in relation to other disciplines. The slowness of his start was also important – his first university post was at the age of 34; and then followed the build-up of the Birmingham years, as he worked through Calvin, Descartes, Locke, Spinoza, Kant, Schleiermacher, Hegel, Kierkegaard, Troeltsch, Barth, Rahner and others, and constructed pioneering courses.

There are other factors interwoven with those. One is to do with the sort of thinker he is. As I learned during the years producing *Jubilate*, he thinks primarily in concepts. Intellectual imagination sometimes works mainly through words or images, but Dan's basic currency seems to be condensed ideas with multi-levelled relationships to each other. They are articulated first in notational form, and the transition into words is often slow and painful. Words are felt to be confining rather than liberating, and there is endless dissatisfaction at the inadequate transpositions of concepts into language. Yet this is far more so in writing than in conversation with its possibilities for mutuality, improvisation and puzzling away at an idea for as long as it takes to clarify it for that partner or group. Most of his writings contain some generative concepts which need a great deal of unpacking, and one of the most common comments on his theology is that it is (for better or for worse) 'dense'. Examples of these concepts include: energized relationality; dynamic order; dynamic non-equilibrium; theology as empirical-theoretical and performative-normative; created and redeemed sociality; diversitarian as opposed to strongly unified explanation; an understanding of history in terms of the emergence of significance within and from contingent particularities; kinds of subsidiarization in the concept of the self; underdefinition and overdefinition in theology; the largesse of God in language. In addition, the constant reworking means that such concepts do not necessarily reappear in later works but are supplanted by fresh ones. Yet through all the wrestling with language the writing has flowed more in the Durham and Princeton years than ever before, as the Bibliography in this volume and the companion volume of selected works indicate.

Another factor is that his commitments to institutions, disciplines, students, colleagues and other people cumulatively embody an idea of what theology is. Theology is primarily *mediated* through all that work and communication. Perhaps theology has its best results when it is not separately identifiable between the covers of a book but has contributed to transforming a community, illuminating an issue, educating a person, informing worship, or shaping a field of inquiry. The metaphor of interconnection, interweaving, or dynamic interrelationship recurs, and this entails the inextricability of one person's contribution. There is a paradox here which has analogies with the activity of God in the world and the reality of incarnation: thorough mediation involves hiddenness and unrecognizability. One thinks of the hours Dan has spent doing theology in mediated forms to which his name is never attached. His own theology is endlessly reworked in the context of being given away.

This is closely connected with another feature of his theology, its *exteriority*. By that I mean its orientation to others – people, societies, nature and God in order to bring them to their fullest life, truth, goodness and beauty. Subjectivity and interiority figure very little as interesting in their own right, and his own subjectivity least of all. This goes with his manner of relating, which blends great warmth with a certain reserve and formality. He flourishes best in a conversational mode that is concerned with matters of some weight, enabling the partners to be taken up into a movement of joint exploration beyond themselves. There is a clear concept of the self, both as 'focused' and as 'distributed' in dynamic interaction with others through all those orientations. The appropriate accompanying theology is one in which thought is complexly interwoven with all areas of life before God, and 'thinking God' is continually renewed in the process.

There is a large body of non-monograph works, many of whose characteristics should already be clear from the above description of his conception of theology. He has attempted in them a good deal of what he recommends for theology in general. I will simply survey his writing on a few topics, with the help of representative quotations, introduced by what I consider the most fundamental concept.

The concept that pervades his theology is undoubtedly that of the Trinity understood in dynamic and relational terms. Time and again he returns to the impossible task of articulating in fresh terms how the reality of God and creation can be conceived. Ideas from many disciplines, from scripture and Christian tradition, from poetry and from his own intellectual *poesis* are used to rethink the character of God in relation to one topic after another. Since they are impossible to summarize, it is worth quoting at some length just one statement about the Trinity. It is taken from an unpublished paper on 'The Question of God in God's Action in the World', delivered to the CTI Consultation on Theology and Science in June 1994:

Christian theology has – potentially at any rate – a very rich set of conceptions of the nature of God and God's active relations with the world, and develops these through the discernment of a Trinitarian God who is himself through the economy of his presence in the world. This God maintains the consistency of his life in an ordered but energetic congruence with his world, through self-restructuring in a controlled response to the perturbations (constructive or destructive) which occur in that interaction and in those with whom he interacts.

As regards the 'immanent Trinity', God in himself, his own unity is that of a dynamic consistency of his self-structuring in self-sameness. Such an explanation of the immanent Trinity provides for an energetic (Spirit-driven) unity in the Godhead which is yet true to its own initial conditions (what we designate by the word 'Father') and ordered in its interactions (that which we call 'the Son' or the 'Logos'). But this is not so much an explanation of a 'state of affairs' in God as it is an explanation of the energetically consistent congruence with the world by which God remains himself. Here, 'energetic' refers to the operation of the Holy Spirit, 'consistency in following initial conditions' refers to the Father and 'congruence with the world' refers to the Son. This is a 'fierce and excited contingency', in which the Spirit 'excites' the fulfillment of initial conditions through an ongoing self-structuring in which there arises a true congruence with the world in love. To use more formal words, God is a dynamic structured relationality in which there is an infinite possibility of life ...

What occurs in the life of the Trinitarian God is an outpouring of energy through which the initial conditions of God are fulfilled, and this fulfilment is in God, but occurs also through the congruence of God with the world – by which God is himself. What occurs in God, therefore, is a self-enhancement, but this occurs also in both his constitution and active sustenance of the interwovenness of the world. Words for this are difficult, but the language of 'blessing' and 'glorifying' may be best, for they signify the intensification of *ordered life* (the combination of words is significant) which occurs in God and from God in the interwovenness of the world. So far as God himself is concerned, it brings a concentration of energy in the initial conditions by which God is himself and which are manifest in the fullness of ordered relationality in God, and also with the world in the Logos. Thus, from the implicit relationality of 'the Father', the Spirit can be seen to generate the fullness of the Father through the Son and through the Son's work in the world.

What are the *marks* of the activity of the Trinitarian God in the interwovenness of the world? It is the active source of interweaving, constituting and shaping for the future. At the same time, with this interwovenness, the Trinitarian activity of God sustains a complexity of particularities, establishing 'relativities' with their own integrity in full interweaving.[14] And the 'relativities' or 'particularities' are linked into active and contingent ways, in the fashion appropriate to an actively self-ordering God.

This passage continues by quoting two poems of Micheal O'Siadhail,[15] interpreted as making clear

the active bestowal by its source of the highly contingent complexity of all being and activity, in which are interwoven nature and God's

---

[14] [Note in the text of the original paper] This is to be sharply distinguished from the post-modernists' notion of particularism, which opposes a false universalism by a false particularism. Their notion of particulars rests on privileging, and the supposition of the inaccessibility of others with whom we are interwoven/related. These are over-statements, understandable for those who need to recover their particularity from submersion in a monolithic world, but fundamentally a denial of the wider interweaving which is the condition of the world.

[15] The first two poems from 'Perspectives' in *The Chosen Garden* (Dublin: The Daedalus Press, 1991), also published in *Hail! Madam Jazz* (Newcastle: Bloodaxe Books, 1991).

action. It is that very contingency which opens freedom for each element of nature, while also providing the scope and parameters within which it may operate. At the same time, this freedom is activated and energized by the free ordering of God, by which it is blessed/enriched.[16]

Such dense explorations of trinitarian reality abound in his writings. The above is representative in including a typical range of terms and spheres of reference. Other articles, papers and sermons do something comparable through discussing worship, language, history, sociality, covenant, the church, sacraments, rationality, ethics, the gospel story, salvation, human being and eschatology. The appearance of the companion volume of his theology makes it unnecessary to attempt the next-to-impossible task of saying how this many-faceted trinitarian theology works out in each case, but it is worth asking finally what sort of a theological achievement this represents.

'Theology is the architecture of life with God.'[17] A major aspect of Dan's theology has been the effort to get the architectonics of the discipline right. A parallel might be with an architect or engineer who is, of course, concerned about the details of the life that his building might enable, but whose way of showing that is through working hard at the complexities of foundations, structures and the loads they can bear, the shaping of space and the long-term practicability of the building for living. Whatever the details, if the structure collapses or the space proves to be too confined or the uses of it too limited then the possibilities are foreclosed by these fundamental matters. There is a sense in Dan's theology of a capacious conceptual building in which the most diverse life can be carried on. Key concepts are like rooms which are not so much meant to be looked at and admired for themselves as to be places where many people can get on with theological work. There is a curious self-effacing and even elusive quality to his thought. It does not draw attention to itself by 'positions' or 'lines' or confrontations or demolitions, nor does it assist in categorizing itself by following some tradition, school of thought, philosophy or confession. Rather it goes about constructing spaces where a remarkable freedom of theological living is enabled. To design the spaces sensitively it is necessary to understand the basic forms of the activities that are to go on in them. For Dan, this means inquiry into intellectual, aesthetic and practical activities, and trying to come up with concepts that not only describe them as they have been and are but that also enhance them, enrich them and bring a blessing to them. That very notion of blessing is one which he has characteristically rethought,

---

[16] Pp. 6ff.
[17] Dan Hardy, in conversation with the author, 1994.

and it is appropriate to end with a quotation which shows him doing that in the context of a discussion of the activity of worship which is, above all, the one which his theology tries to appreciate. It comes at the end of his article 'Worship as the Orientation of Life to God':

> We recognized that worship is the most embracing act of life for Christians, the primary means by which we locate ourselves in the fundamental activity of God toward humankind in the world – by blessing the God who blesses us. We set out to consider how worship, both its importance and its practice, could be relearned amid the diversity, distraction, and dissipation of modern life – the very circumstances which seem to make it inconceivable and impracticable for people today. And we found ways by which human beings in the very diversities of their existence limited themselves through concentration of various kinds – acts of attention and particularization in the modalities of human existence – even bringing distortion and alienation from each other, from the world around them, and from the very source and pattern of their existence, God.
>
> The very act by which they redress these distortions is, like the Ancient Mariner 'blessing unawares', the relearning of blessing, the participation in spiritual truth which is activated by the life of God himself. We do not, in other words, learn blessing as if we had never known of it; when we 'bless unawares' we are already participating in God's blessing. It is this which we complete when in worship we give God the glory. We 'perfect perfection', by our expression perfecting what is already perfect through God's activity. By so doing we find ourselves, through God's activity in us, recovering the ability to bless the Lord in the 'strange land' of our diversity, distraction and dissipation. Then the circle within which we stand when we bless God for his blessing – which had been disrupted by our distractions – is complete. Even then, however, as in any human particularization, it is only conditionally complete, only an anticipation of the universal and the eventual, and always looks to the place and time when all humankind in the world, in all of its modalities, is incorporated into God's blessing as Father, Son and Holy Spirit.
>
> The practice of worship should relocate us in the fundamental activity of God towards humankind in the world. It must therefore be so ordered as to achieve this. It must enable us to relearn our participation in the active spiritual truth which is the life of God in the world. And, lest this be detached from the modes of our ordinary life, it should provide opportunities for concentrated attention to the blessing of God which occurs in and through all the particularities and contingencies of our existence; for it is by this blessing that they are joined and given meaning.

By these means, worship provides the concrete opportunity by which we participate in our redemption, which is the form which God's blessing takes for those as much affected by alienation as we are. In worship we are redeemed from the alienations to which we have become captive, as these distort our situation in the world, ourselves, our relationships with each other and with God. Of course, such worship requires us to recognize in very clear and particular terms the ways in which we are caught in sin. Even more, it requires that we allow ourselves to be opened and refashioned by the powerful, cleansing, fulfilling blessing of the Spirit of the Lord Jesus Christ, the Son of God. And that also reconstitutes us as the Church which calls to the whole world:

Let every thing that hath breath: praise the Lord.[18]

[18] 'Worship as the Orientation', pp. 68f.

PART ONE: WORSHIP

I

Theology through Music: Tavener, Time and Eternity

JEREMY BEGBIE

AMONG the most valuable of Professor's Hardy's contributions to the theological task has been his consistent promotion of the interaction between theological and non-theological disciplines. Many readers of this volume will bear testimony to his extraordinary ability to 'think together' different modes of inquiry (and enable others to do the same) in ways which result in reciprocal enrichment and growth in wisdom. The interaction between theology and music-theory (of considerable interest to Professor Hardy) has been largely overlooked by twentieth-century theologians. The hills may be alive with the sound of music but the departments of systematic theology are generally not. In some respects this is puzzling, given the saturation of our culture by an enormous range of music, the intense interest shown in music by many philosophers past and present, the growing literature on the politics, sociology and psychology of music, the recent emergence of ethnomusicology, and the intriguing deployment of musical metaphors by a number of natural scientists. Not only surprising, the relative neglect of music by theologians is also regrettable, for as I hope to show below, music possesses considerable power to generate fresh and fruitful resources to articulate and enact theological insight. Jacques Attali, in his remarkable book *Noise*, declares that 'Music is more than an object of study: it is a way of perceiving the world. My intention is ... not only to theorise *about* music, but to theorise *through* music'.[1] Attali's principal interests are in the social economics of music, yet his words prompt the question: what would it mean to theologize not simply *about* music but *through* music? This paper is a tentative attempt to indicate something of what such an enterprise might entail. It is offered in full awareness that a methodological tightrope is being walked – anthropomorphism and idolatry are never far away – but, as Daniel Hardy has shown repeatedly, such tightropes are not only worth treading, but must be tread if the theological understanding is to be significantly advanced.

[1] Jacques Attali, *Noise*, trans. by Brian Massumi (Manchester: Manchester University Press, 1985), p. 4.

23

I. JOHN TAVENER'S MUSIC

We shall concentrate on one major dimension of music, musical time, and use as a point of entry the work of English composer John Tavener (b. 1944). The immense popularity of Tavener's music amongst a very wide range of listeners has been a prominent feature on the landscape of British music in recent years, especially since the appearance of his best-selling piece for cello and string orchestra, 'The Protecting Veil' (1987). On one level Tavener presents an enigma, not least to his detractors. Reared in the 1960s and then exploiting the multiple dissonances and eccentricities of that period, he can now unashamedly employ an ecstatic, almost intoxicating harmonic language (though not all his recent music is as accessible as 'The Protecting Veil'). Moreover, his techniques are drawn largely from the idioms of Byzantine and Russian Orthodox church music. None of this would seem an obvious recipe for success in the concert arenas of the 1990s. Further, his music is no isolated phenomenon – the Polish composer Henryk Gorecki (b. 1933) and the Estonian Arvo Pärt (b. 1935) write in a similar vein and are enjoying a vogue in Britain quite unparalleled by any other serious composers of the last thirty years.

On another level, arguably, matters are not quite so mysterious. In the first part of this paper, it will be suggested that this music's success is less remarkable when set against the horizon of some prominent modern and postmodern attitudes to time. With this in mind, I shall go on to explore the relation between divine eternity and created time implied by Tavener's project, and then contend that this relation can be more instructively illuminated by rather different musical strategies than those adopted by Tavener.

(a) Tavener's musical time

Tavener, like most of us, has inhabited a culture in which music of the modern European tradition has predominated. Such music has generally, though not exclusively, operated according to teleological principles. That is, it possesses an integral order which is sensed or perceived as directional. Through patterns of tension and resolution – in rhythm, harmony and volume – implications are established in the music and expectations set up in the listener giving rise to a characteristically forward momentum. The quintessential expression of directional music in the West is the 'tonal system', fully developed around 1680 and enduring (in the concert/operatic tradition) until the end of the nineteenth century.

Four typical features of tonal music can be usefully highlighted here. First, *organic development and elaboration*. For example, a theme may be sounded and its character then drawn out in some manner, decorated, augmented, or perhaps inverted. The opening of Beethoven's sixth symphony (the 'Pastoral') provides a good example: every note of the first movement derives from the organic expansion of material from the opening eight seconds. Second, *large-scale tension and resolution*. Along with the numerous micro-tensions and resolutions in a piece, there can be tensions which are resolved over many minutes (as in the move from the storm of Beethoven's 'Pastoral' symphony to the radiant last movement) or even hours (as in Wagner's opera *Tristan and Isolde*. Third, *clearly defined beginnings and endings*. There is no ambiguity as to when a Rachmaninov concerto starts and stops; we know when to hush ourselves and when to clap. Fourth, *long-term continuity*. Typically, at almost any point in tonal music it will be possible to explain how one moment relates to what has preceded it and what will follow. Of course, there can be, and often are, deliberate discontinuities, but they will normally be integrated into deeper continuity at a more fundamental structural level.

These are by no means the defining or sufficient conditions of Western tonal music but all four contribute to that sense of directedness so characteristic of it. As far as John Tavener is concerned, though in many respects he stands in the tonal tradition, by means of various carefully controlled musical devices the four features just mentioned are consistently subverted. With regard to the first, one finds little elaboration of themes and motifs in Tavener's recent music. Much more typical of him are strictly symmetrical, reversible structures – e.g. ABC/CBA. So, for instance, a theme might be played and then immediately played backwards: a technique called palindrome, the opposite of organic growth. His best-known choral piece, a setting of William Blake's poem 'The Lamb' (1985), is a sophisticated exercise in symmetry. As for large-scale tension and resolution, this too is virtually absent. There is no ecstasy after thunder here: indeed hardly a cloud fills the sky. In one of his more outrageous pronouncements Tavener asserts: 'I dislike the way that *angst* got into music through psychology at the turn of the century. I think the composer should deal with his *angst* in the composing room, not in the score.'[2] The conventional rhetoric of musical opening and closure is also avoided. Much commoner than strong initiating gestures are sounds emerging out of silence – as in the 'The Protecting Veil'. Similarly, endings can be hard to predict; frequently the music drifts seamlessly into silence. And the kind of long-term continuity typical of classical tonal music is also rare. Tavener much prefers constructing a piece in discrete blocks of sound, self-contained units of internally coherent material with often only the loosest connections between them. The impression is not so much of a musical argument but of moving from one icon to another.

---

[2] As quoted in *The Guardian*, 20 July 1992, p. 18.

The iconic allusion is deliberate. For though other composers of this century have attempted to stifle goal-orientation using these (and a host of other) techniques, what sets Tavener apart from many of them is that, like his mentor Olivier Messiaen, he does so chiefly for theological reasons. Although in contemporary aesthetics there are those who regard reference to a composer's intention as at best irrelevant and at worst obstructive, I would contend that at least some serious insight can be gained by recalling that since his conversion to Russian Orthodoxy in 1977 virtually all Tavener's music has issued directly from this spiritual environment. It is not only the titles of his pieces and their overt ecclesiastical intent which make this clear. The fact that his beginnings are like processes and that his endings simply give way relates to his belief that the music of heaven sounds inaudibly 'before' the arrival of earthly sound and 'after' its cessation. He speaks of his pieces as sonic icons of eternity (hence the frequent use of the world 'icon' in his titles[3]), and it is an eternity he appears to conceive almost as the negation of created time. The ambience of timelessness and stasis is intensified by his fondness for writing music of extreme slowness, often coupled with the erasure of pointed accents, stress or metric pulse.[4] It is also an eternity of simplicity. From 1977 his music exhibits a steady diminishment of plurality and diversity: decorative melodies are pared down, the sonic palette restricted, instrumentation reduced.

(b) Tavener, time and culture

The extent to which Tavener is being faithful to the Russian Orthodox tradition is a complex issue beyond my competence to address. What I would wish to contend, however, is that insofar as his music is taken to be an evocation of God's eternity it indicates rather more about our own culture's unease with time than about the triune eternity whose life is made accessible in the advent of Jesus Christ. In following up his much-read study, *The Condition of Postmodernity*, David Harvey has spoken of postmodernism as a wide-ranging set of phenomena constructed against the background of 'time-space compression'.[5] Part of what that means is that through the communications revolution and the resultant

---

[3] E.g. *Ikon of Light* (1982), *Ikon of St Cuthbert* (1986), and so on. In his recent large-scale work, *We Shall See Him As He Is* (1990), virtually every movement is given the title 'Ikon'.

[4] Two qualifications are necessary here. First, clearly, in music you can never reach complete stasis; notes follow notes – there has to be some movement. Second, stasis does not always mean motionlessness. There are pieces of Tavener which contain fast, highly active sections. Nevertheless, the majority are slow in tempo and very few exhibit large-scale goal-orientation.

[5] David Harvey, 'Looking Back on Postmodernism', in *Post-Modernism on Trial*, ed. A. C. Papadakis (London: Academy Editions, 1990), pp. 11f.

collapse of spatial and temporal barriers inwards, new and intense experiences of time as a tyranny have emerged – the sense of being driven or hounded by many temporalities – and this has led to profound disorientation such that 'the world sometimes seems to collapse inwards upon us'.[6] If there is any truth in this, we might venture to suggest that Tavener offers a kind of musical de-compression, an aural space amidst a temporally compressed culture, and that this might account, at least in part, for some of his popularity and success. He gives us a place to expand, an unhurried, stable cavernous arena in which we are free to breathe. And, we could add – bearing in mind his move towards increasing musical simplicity – in a society overloaded with multiple and contradictory communication systems and messages, Tavener offers a unified, relatively singular and undifferentiated space.

In suggesting this, I am not reading Tavener's music as a calculated response to the postmodern sensibility (assuming there is such a sensibility). Nor am I attempting a totalizing explanation of his music. My intention is more circumscribed: to focus attention on Tavener's use of musical time and suggest that in much of his work we are witnessing, in effect, a musical spatialization of time. Musical space is constituted by pitch, sound quality (timbre) and volume. In Tavener's music – and here he is by no means alone in the twentieth century – there is a tendency for these to become ends in themselves.[7] In tonal music, pitch, sound quality and volume have traditionally been subjected to temporal patterns of tension and resolution. But if these patterns are blurred and loosened, with propulsion and direction suppressed, sound is explored for its own sake. Sound structure can emerge as an independent abstraction.

Inasmuch as our society knows time as an oppressive force, one of the many benefits of Tavener's music is to provide, so to speak, a cool cathedral in a hot and overcrowded town. But I suspect he has rather less to offer when it comes to walking back on to the streets, to engaging with conflict within time and forging a hope within and for the world. It could be contended that the appeal of this kind of music trades to a certain extent on our inability to inhabit contentedly and to come to terms with the temporality with which God has endowed the world.[8] And, we should add, insofar as this music is to be taken as a window on to eternity, it is an eternity of the negation of time. It is as if proximity to God depended on developing an immunity to time's opportunities and

---

[6] David Harvey, *The Condition of Postmodernity* (Oxford: Blackwell, 1989), p. 240.

[7] For a fascinating and sensitive discussion of this in twentieth-century music, cf. George Rochberg, *The Aesthetics of Survival* (Ann Arbor: University of Michigan Press, 1984), pp. 71–147.

[8] Cf. Colin Gunton, *The One, the Three and the Many: God, Creation and the Culture of Modernity* (Cambridge: CUP, 1993), ch. 3.

threats. Though it would be extremely foolish to press Tavener too tightly into a theological schema, the impression given by this music (and by his stated theological intentions) does not seem to be far from an outlook which would assume a very close link between time and fallenness. If Tavener's music does proffer intimations of the incarnation, it is of a divine timeless presence inserted into time rather than of a transformative interaction within created time geared towards the redemption of all things *in*, and not despite, their temporality.

II. TEMPORALITY, CREATED TIME AND ETERNITY

In the second section of this paper, we shall pose two questions. First, might it be that one of music's most valuable contributions is to enable us to come to terms with created time in a more positive and fruitful way, to demonstrate concretely that fallenness is not intrinsic to temporality? Second, taking this matter further, might it be that there are other forms of music which supply more faithful sonic parables of the meeting of divine eternity and created time than those we find in Tavener?

(a) Music and living in time

In attending to the first question, a good place to begin is with Augustine's many-sided discussion of time in Book XI of the *Confessions*. Augustine is deeply impressed by the radical contrast between God's timeless simplicity and the anguished human experience of dispersion (*distentio*) in time. If Gerard O'Daly is correct, the chief problem for Augustine is not so much 'what is time?' but 'how can we measure time in the face of the fragmentation of our past, present and future, in the face of temporal discontinuity?'[9] The conception of time which arises in Augustine and the assumptions on which it is based have been subject to much criticism in recent years.[10] Undoubtedly there is in Augustine a strong stress on the mind as the measurer of time[11] – unlike Plotinus, time is not grounded in God's eternity. And there is certainly equivocation about the extent to which the temporal realm is a place of order and

---

[9] Gerard O'Daly, *Augustine's Philosophy of Mind* (Berkeley: University of California Press, 1987), ch. 6.
[10] Cf. e.g., Gunton, *The One, the Three and the Many*, pp. 82ff.
[11] 'So it is in you, my mind,' he cries, 'that I measure periods of time' (*Confessions*, XI.27.36). The past is *there* only *in* someone's memory – whether God's or ours; the future is there only in someone's anticipatory consciousness; the present is not only in the mind but also for the mind.

goodness. Nevertheless, it is not insignificant that in his search for a solution to the problem of continuity he makes reference to the recitation of a poem (26.33), a hymn by Ambrose (27.35) and a psalm (28.38). And he treats these, for all intents and purposes, as musical phenomena.[12] Without pressing the point too far, it is as if he were aware that music manifests something at least approximating to continuity in temporal successiveness, a time-bridging present, a sequence of elements experienced as a differentiated unity. Supporting this are some earlier reflections in *De Musica* where the same hymn of Ambrose is cited and music is said to be able to lead the mind upward, re-collecting our fragmentation and drawing us toward the divine unity.[13]

What Augustine may have glimpsed has been massively amplified, though in ways sharply contrasting with Augustine's general outlook, by the Austrian musicologist, Victor Zuckerkandl.[14] His argument focuses on the Western tonal tradition of music and hinges on what he calls the 'dynamic quality' of notes. Music consists not merely of individual notes but also of their dynamic interrelationships with one another, and these are irreducible to psychological or strictly acoustical analysis. When we hear a melody, in one sense, all we hear is a stringing together of static tones. But, in line with a number of psychologists of music, Zuckerkandl also wants to say that a dynamic field is established: there are tensions and balances set up between notes. Hence a note is internally related to what precedes it and what follows it: in every note, there is a pointing-beyond, a demand for completion. According to Zuckerkandl, it is time which reveals itself to the ear as a function of the interrelationship between notes: 'The function of time here is ... no longer that of the empty vessel, which contains the tones, or the bowling alley down which the tones roll ... Music is a temporal art not in the barren and empty sense that its tones succeed one another "in time"; it is temporal art in the concrete sense that it enlists the flux of time as a force to serve its ends.'[15]

There are complexities and, I suspect, weaknesses of Zuckerkandl's argument which we shall have to leave on one side. But if his central contention about the inner continuity of musical process is correct, a number of striking implications arise for a Christian doctrine of creation. Three can be mentioned here. First, it would seem that one of music's greatest strengths is its ability to grant us a peculiarly profound experi-

---

[12] It is to be borne in mind that poetry and what we call 'music' were much more closely associated in Augustine's day than now.
[13] *De Musica*, VI, 2. Cf. Robert O'Connell, *Art and the Christian Intelligence in St. Augustine* (Oxford: Blackwell, 1978), pp. 65ff.
[14] V. Zuckerkandl, *Sound and Symbol: Music and the External World* (London: Routledge & Kegan Paul, 1956); *Man the Musician* (Princeton: Princeton University Press, 1973).
[15] Zukerkandl, *Sound and Symbol*, p. 181.

ence of time – not absolute time, nor a time solely contributed by the mind, but time as a function of the interrelationship between physical realities, and thus as an intrinsic aspect of created being. Second, Zucker-kandl implicitly undermines the distrust of time which supports both the tendency to treat time as a tyranny and the response to that tyranny evident in those such as Tavener. Consistency and construction are con-crete possibilities in time; change and order can go together. Because something takes time to be what it is does not thereby render it meaning-less or suspect.[16] (Something of this lies behind Karl Barth's dedication to Mozart: he heard Mozart's music as an articulation of the consistency of the totality of creation, voicing creation's praise without leaping out of temporality and finitude.[17]) The upshot is, third, that music has the power to declare a possibility about inhabiting peacefully and interacting fruitfully with the time God has granted his creation.

(b) Music, eternity and time

Matters become more intricate and hazardous when we move from the doctrine of creation to the vexed question of the interaction of divine eternity and created time. Here we proceed with extreme caution: the battlefield is as active as ever. The following is only offered out of the conviction that music has a place on the battlefield. Arguably, music can supply striking parables in sound of the interaction of eternity and time, and in ways which are more faithful to both God's eternity and our time than Tavener's music would suggest.

We have been arguing that it is plausible to conceive music as a physical process in which the *distentio* of our past, present and future, which so haunted Augustine, is capable of at least a measure of healing. Insofar as that occurs, it comes intriguingly close to what has sometimes been called 'redeemed time', in which the alienation and disruption of our future, past and present is healed. Is it not this, according to the tradition, which has been realized, enacted and opened up to us in the life, death and raising of Jesus: authentic temporal existence re-estab-lished in our midst? Wolfhart Pannenberg, in one of his rare brushes with music, picks up from where be believes Augustine left off, arguing that music is one of a number of ways in which we experience time-bridging duration. As such it can be, as he puts it, 'a remote inkling' of and a form of participation in eternity, the dawning of God's eschatological future in the existence of creatures.[18] Here Pannenberg owes much to Karl Barth.

[16] Gunton, *The One, the Three and the Many*, p. 81.
[17] K. Barth, *Church Dogmatics*, III/3 (Edinburgh: T. & T. Clark, 1960), pp. 297ff.
[18] W. Pannenberg, *Systematic Theology*, I (Edinburgh: T. & T. Clark, 1991), pp. 409f.

Despite his opacity,[19] Barth is clear in his desire to link a vision of redemption as the integrating of past, present and future with the dynamic interrelatedness of God's triunity. Refusing to define eternity apart from the particular temporality of Jesus, Barth specifies the particular eternity of the triune God as 'pure duration', in which beginning, succession and end do not fall apart, in which there is no conflict between source, movement and goal, but rather mutual co-inherence. The configuration of divine eternity, the trinitarian structure of movement and interplay, is perichoretic not only in itself but also in its reception of history. The economy of salvation thus frees and liberates our history for the perichoresis of eternity without dissolving its character as created being.[20] In this connection, some remarks of George Steiner come to mind. Impressed with the resistance of music to human understanding and analysis, and thus with its potential to grant intimations of a source of being outside human making, Steiner provocatively claims: 'The time which music "takes" and which it gives as we perform or experience it, is the only *free time* granted us prior to death.'[21]

(c) Recapitulation and premature closure

We now turn to some particular musical phenomena which are especially instructive as examples of bringing forth in sound the enfolding of created time in eternity. Two may be briefly examined: recapitulation and premature closure.

It has long been recognized that repetition lies at the very heart of musical process, and one of the most significant strategies of repetition is the device known as 'recapitulation' in the classical sonata or symphony. At the outset of Mozart's 'Jupiter' symphony, to take a familiar instance, a theme is heard and about eight minutes later, after secondary themes have been introduced and after considerable elaboration of both the original and subsidiary theme, the first theme reappears, played in full. Let us ask: what might be the resonances between this device and the Eucharist, traditionally regarded as a pivotal encounter of Christ's eternity with our time?

In musical recapitulation of the sort just mentioned, *the particularity of the first appearance of the theme is not erased*. The initial sounding of the theme is distinctive to its musical time and place. Recapitulation is

---

[19] 'No topic in Barth interpretation is more in need of clarification, and none more requires working with the *Church Dogmatics* as a whole, than this one', George Hunsinger, *How to Read Karl Barth: The Shape of his Theology* (Oxford: OUP, 1991), p. 14.
[20] Barth, *Church Dogmatics*, II/1 (Edinburgh: T. & T. Clark, 1957), pp. 608–40. It is arguable that many standard criticisms of Barth fail to take this multidimensional perichoreity of eternity into account; cf. Hunsinger, *How to Read Karl Barth*, pp. 14ff., 291 n. 5.
[21] George Steiner, *Real Presence* (London: Faber & Faber, 1989), p. 197.

not a case of extracting the theme from that situatedness, as if we could wrench it from past into present. It is embedded in a field of particularities. It is not the instantiation of a separable timeless truth or form; its position in that specific context – at the opening – is part of what it is. Thus this becomes an analogy for the classic Protestant concern for the particularity of Christ's work. Further, the theme is particular in its circumscription and boundedness (at least in this piece of Mozart's). The recapitulation is not a continuation of the initial theme, nor an attempt to prolong it – the parallel here being with eucharistic theologies which trade on metaphors of extension.

Further, *the distinctive particularity of this recapitulation of the theme is also crucial.* For the theme recapitulated is distinctive to *its* musical time and place. Musicians talk of 'returning to the theme' but by this they mean the return of the theme *to us*, not our return to a theme; it is not a case of pulling ourselves out of our time into another time. Indeed, the new location of the theme is part of the reason why recapitulation is never dull. As the performer will tell us, a recapitulation never feels the same the second time round, for it is now heard in a new set of temporal relations. The theme acquires new depth in this setting – after five minutes of thematic and harmonic struggle – without relativizing its first appearance. Likewise, in the Eucharist, our time and place is not abrogated; we are met amidst all the contingencies of this time and this place, and these contingencies are given new depth in a way which does not downplay the decisiveness of Christ's death.

Nevertheless, having conceded all this, *there is a profound, interactive continuity between first and second appearances of the theme.* Bearing in mind all we have observed about the time-bridging power of music, could we not here speak of an energetic interplay between the two appearances of the theme: perichoresis(?), a particularly intense conveyance of a kind of time in which past and present co-inhere while retaining their particularity? There is still a structure of before and after, a dependence of the second upon the first,[22] but the first is not allowed to remain locked in ever-receding remoteness but is encountered afresh in our time. We might even say we are recalled by and to the theme. Is this not something of the dynamic generated in the Eucharist when we are united through the Spirit to the ascended Christ so as to share here and now in his time? The 'distance' between our time and Christ's must not be absolutized – the tendency of much eucharistic theology which then has to make frantic (and artificial) efforts to pull past and present together. Faced with this very problem, Calvin sought to dispense with

---

[22] We are not effacing an 'order' of before/after, indeed, upon this the power of recapitulation hinges. Recapitulation depends on directionality between this appearance of the theme and that at the beginning of the piece.

any understanding of the sacrament as essentially *our* act in calling upon God, insisting that it is Christ who calls us to share in his life and time, in all that he was, is and will be. Musical recapitulation offers an intriguing concrete parable of this very process.

I am not pretending that every stumbling block in eucharistic controversy evaporates in the presence of music, but enough has been said to suggest that music might be of singular assistance in freeing us from some conceptions of time and eternity which have often disfigured the debates. And it can do this concretely, through something we all experience every time we listen to a symphony, or indeed, hear a song for the second time.

But what of the future, which must surely be integral to any eucharistic theology? Christ's advent in the Eucharist entails our present being opened to his future, the final destiny of creation. And that possibility rests on the *telos* of creation having been anticipated in the raising of Christ crucified. It is here that another musical procedure can be especially enlightening: the premature closure. In Mozart's 'Jupiter' symphony (1788), a beguiling example occurs in the middle of the third movement. Immediately after the end of the minuet section we are greeted with a 'perfect cadence', an unambiguous, universally recognizable gesture of closure. Indeed, if it was not for the reduced orchestration, we might think it was a reiteration of the ending we have just heard. But it turns out to be the beginning of an entirely new phrase. This 'ending' constitutes a new start. Mozart plays on the ambiguity between closing gesture and opening process – analogous to the crowds on the day of Pentecost: 'is this the end or a beginning?' Furthermore, we find this closing profile becomes the chief ingredient out of which the following thirty seconds of music are generated. An 'ending' becomes the initiative and the material for a series of novel developments – as with the work of the Spirit, post-Pentecost. And all this takes place *in the midst* of the third movement. Into the middle Mozart introduces an atmosphere rife with fertile rumours of the end – surely a sonic parable of the grace of the Kingdom in our midst. Mozart was a theologian of eschatology *par excellence*, in ways that not even Barth understood.[23]

But even here, though they are gestures of ending, we are not given direct anticipations of an end which is eventually attained. For an intriguing instance of this we turn to Beethoven again, to the first movement of his last string quartet, written towards the end of his life (Op. 135). Some thirty seconds into the first movement a grand closing gesture appears, of the kind one would normally associate with the end of a piece. (Later we discover that this is the way the whole movement closes.) The music continues, although now we are hearing a present whose

[23] For a fascinating discussion of this (and the Mozart example cited earlier), cf. Jonathan D. Kramer, 'New Temporalities in Music', *Critical Inquiry* 7 (1981), pp. 539–56.

future we have already experienced. The past is not merely past for us but lies before us. We recall Heb. 1.2: 'in these last days he has spoken to us by his Son' – reminiscence becomes implication. A few minutes later, another grand closing gesture greets us, and then the piece continues to unfold as before. In fact, the movement 'ends' three times. Furthermore, in the middle of the movement these closing gestures are woven into the musical argument and become integral to a rich and prolific development. In this movement of multiple temporal subtleties we are granted a broken, but concrete, parable of the transformation of our time by the eternal God. 'In my beginning is my end ... in my end is my beginning' – a misapplication of T. S. Eliot's words perhaps, but the invocation is irresistible, especially since it comes from one of *his* Quartets.

2

The Liturgical Shape of the Christian Life: Teaching Christian Ethics as Worship

STANLEY HAUERWAS

I. BEGINNING AT THE BEGINNING

IN Texas we love to tell an apocryphal (maybe) story about the head coach of a not very good high school football team. As is well known Friday night high school football is the most significant liturgical event in Texas.[1] This coach's team unfortunately found itself behind 75–0 at half-time. Rather than begin with the pep-talk or the 'chewing out' that is usually expected at half-time, this coach, holding a football in front of him, said: 'Boys, I think we need to begin at the beginning – this is a football'.

There is nothing like being completely trounced to force teams, communities, or traditions to get back to the basics, to rediscover those elementary habits and practices that make them intelligible to themselves. I am not suggesting that Christians and, in particular, theologians are rediscovering the centrality of worship for Christian life and thought because we are currently being trounced, but I do think it is no accident that as a people who are beginning to realize they are in a conflict what Dan Hardy and David Ford describe as 'praise of God'[2] turns out to be

---

[1] This is documented in H. G. Bissinger, *Friday Night Lights: A Town, a Team, and a Dream* (New York: Harper Perennial, 1991). Bissinger's wonderful book is about one football season of the Odessa Permian High School – the winningest high school football team in Texas history. Bissinger wrote what he thought was an appreciative, if not loving, portrayal of the young men who play and the townspeople who support this rather bizarre practice. He was shocked to discover that the town was, as we say in Texas, 'none too pleased' with his account. In fact some school members threatened to kill him. They take their high school football seriously in Texas. 'Friday night lights' refers to the lights that illumine the football fields on Friday nights that can be literally seen for miles in Texas.

[2] Daniel Hardy and David Ford, *Jubilate: Theology in Praise* (London: Darton, Longman & Todd, 1984). The significance of Hardy's and Ford's argument concerning the significance of praise for the grammar of Christian theology, I believe, has not been appropriately appreciated. This book is a goldmine of suggestions not yet fully exploited in contemporary theology. One of my favourite insights in the book is their claim that 'Dante can set his own

a battle cry. Hardy and Ford advance the extraordinary claim that praise is the very character of Jesus' relationship with the Father, so they are making not 'just' an empirical generalization but a full-blooded metaphysical claim.

Yet the theological metaphysics they develop I believe is crucial for a church that finds it is in a fight and already behind 75–0 at half-time. For a church so situated nothing could be more salutary than being reminded that what makes Christians Christian is our worship of God.[3] Of course the praise of God cannot be limited to 'liturgy', but it is none the less the case that Christians learn how to be praiseworthy people through worship.[4] The account Hardy and Ford provide of praise, if it does nothing else, reminds us where Christians necessarily begin.

In order to suggest what I take to be the fruitfulness of Hardy's and Ford's reflections, I want to report on how I have tried to teach the basic course in Christian ethics at the Divinity School at Duke for the last ten years. I realize it is a bit odd to write a supposedly scholarly article to honour Dan Hardy by reporting on a course. Such a report is not the normal way to do 'theology'. But Dan Hardy's life as much as his work has taught us that theology abstracted from those activities integral to the

---

autobiography in a story which embraces the whole of the known universe. The modern predicament is typically that of a dichotomy between contemplating the universe and one's own life in it', p. 50.

[3] See, for example, Hardy's and Ford's extraordinary account of the threat of 'stoicism' as the most appealing alternative to Christianity in the past as well as today. They suggest the problem is not simply that 'stoicism' threatens Christianity, but that we now have largely a 'stoicized Christianity'. 'The nation state is delighted to welcome a religion that is so timid and orderly, leaving the passions free for economics, war and collective sport. In Britain today the civic religion might be described as stoicism with the Christian influence. It is full of rectitude, good patterns and principles, but it is being challenged by more exciting and extreme creeds to which it seems at present to have neither the daring nor the moral, intellectual and political creativity to respond', *Jubilate*, p. 144. They quite rightly suggest that the joyful Christian worship has prophetic importance as an alternative to stoicism.

[4] Liturgy in its broadest meaning simply means the work that the church, or any community, does for the public good. The church impoverishes itself when it excludes from its liturgical action business meetings to consider whether the church building needs a new roof. How such business is conducted, however, finds its *telos* in the praise offered by the community gathered in word and sacrament. For a powerful account of how the 'business' of the church in such matters as 'binding and loosing' as well as how authority works in the church is integral to church's worship as well as her politics see John Howard Yoder, *Body Politics: Five Practices of the Christian Community before the Watching World* (Nashville: Discipleship Resources, 1992).

The recognition of the political character of worship is extremely important in order that worship not become 'aesthetics' in the modern sense. Terry Eagleton has rightly reminded us that the construction of the very category of the aesthetic reproduces the class presupposition of modernity. 'Art' was 'depoliticized' to serve the politics of a commercial class.

life of Christians too often turns out to be systematically elegant but empty.[5] By focusing on a course I hope to exhibit why we Christians insist it is hard to distinguish between what we think and what we do – particularly as both what we think and what we do are constituted by God's praise.

I had taught seminarians at the University of Notre Dame, but since I was not Catholic I thought it inappropriate for me to teach their basic course in moral theology. So I had not really been challenged to ask myself how a basic course in Christian ethics should be structured until I came to the Divinity School at Duke.[6] I was sure that it did little good to teach seminarians Christian ethics as a series of alternative positions – e.g., Reinhold Niebuhr stresses the importance of sin and/or Calvinists concentrate on the importance of covenantal relationships. While no doubt such teaching gives students some quite valuable information, it seldom initiates students into the activity of moral reflection by which they acquire skills necessary for their ministry.

It occurred to me that whatever else the ministry may be said to be about the one thing ministers clearly do in an embattled church is lead their congregations in worship. So in consultation with my colleague, Professor Harmon Smith, we designed a course in Christian ethics shaped around worship.[7] Our task, after all, is to train seminarians for ordination for the church's ministry. It is no doubt true that many churches are currently unclear about what power ordination confers which results in the ennui and cynicism that currently grips the lives of so many in the ministry. We thought a course constructed around worship might counter some of the lack of clarity surrounding the ministry to the extent that the course embodied the presumption that there is literally nothing more important for the Christian people to do than praise God.

We also hoped by patterning the course on the liturgy we could defeat the dreaded 'and' as in 'theology and worship'. That *and*, of course,

---

Eagleton argues, however, that the 'aesthetic' can now provide a powerful challenge to current dominant ideological norms. My argument entails an argument similar to Eagleton's, but given my ecclesiological presuppositions my politics is obviously different. For Eagleton's argument see his *The Ideology of the Aesthetic* (Oxford: Basil Blackwell, 1990).

[5] At stake here is the very question of how theology is to be done today as well as its most appropriate genre. I do not pretend to have great insight about such matters though I am sure that when theology becomes academic in a manner such that theologians write mainly for other theologians something has profoundly gone wrong.

[6] The Divinity School at Duke is predominantly Methodist though we have a wide range of Protestants from other denominations in our classes.

[7] Professor Smith is an Episcopal priest but since Duke Seminary is predominately Methodist we followed the Methodist order of worship. We taught the course together the first three years, but due to the retirement of one of our colleagues we had to begin offering the

reflects the current irrationalities of the theological disciplines enshrined in seminary curriculums. As a result, students who suffer the disadvantages of seminary education are left with questions such as 'what is the relation between systematic theology and preaching?' This is particularly a problem for those of us who 'do ethics' since 'ethics' too often is understood by 'theologians' and 'ethicists' alike as what you do after you have gotten the theoretical issues straight in theology. This results in a convenient peace treaty that defines turf – i.e., the theologian does not have to be concerned with 'ethics', and the 'ethicist' does not need to do any theology. Through the liturgical shape of the course, we hoped that students might learn that part of the problem facing Christians is found in those practices that make the distinction between theology and ethics appear intelligible.[8]

The course begins with lectures that are meant to help the student understand why the course is shaped by the liturgy. These lectures contain everything that will be said over the whole course, but I have learned that you cannot repeat yourself too often. Indeed I try to help the students understand that the reason why repetition is intrinsic to worship is because the God we worship requires repetition exactly because our God is a God of surprises. As Hardy and Ford observe:

> God is free and one cannot make rules for how he may speak and act. Yet the complementary point is that God is faithful and consistent, the sort of God who takes part in liturgies as well. The further perspective that embraces both these is that God is above all to be praised, and that he is well able to guide individuals and communities to do so.[9]

Through the introductory lectures I challenge many of the presuppositions of political liberalism that are the basics for the widespread assumptions that 'ethics' and 'politics' can be distinguished. That distinction, moreover, reinforces the widespread assumption that ethics is primarily about 'quandaries' and/or decisions rather than the formation of virtuous

---

course independently. Yet much of what I do in the course as well as the way I report on the course remains indebted to Professor Smith. I have included a syllabus of the course as an appendix to this paper.

[8] One of our difficulties in developing the course is that no readings exist that fit the structure of the course. That no such literature exists is not surprising since the very disciplinary divisions that the course is meant to challenge ensure that such a literature does not exist. There are a few books that deal in general with the theme of worship and ethics, but the very existence of the 'and' reproduces the presupposition we wished to challenge. We used Karl Barth's *Church Dogmatics* III/4 in some of the first offerings of the course. We have each continued to change our readings often since nothing seems quite 'right'.

[9] Hardy and Ford, *Jubilate*, p. 21.

people. Yet the formation of Christians through the liturgy makes clear that Christians are not simply called to do the 'right thing', but rather we are expected to be holy. Such holiness is not an individual achievement but rather comes from being made part of a community in which we discover the truth about our lives. Such 'truth' cannot be separated from how such a community worships since the truth is that we are creatures made for worship.

Fergus Kerr rightly contends that:

> It is because people exult and lament, sing for joy, bewail their sins and so on, that they are able, eventually, to have thoughts about God. Worship is not the results but the precondition for believing in God. Theological concepts are rooted in certain habitual ways of acting, responding, relating, to our natural-historical setting. It does not follow that the idea of God has a place in the conversation simply because we enjoy singing hymns: but if we cannot imagine what it is to observe rites, enjoy singing hymns and the like, the nature of religion is bound to remain opaque.[10]

The focus on worship is a constant reminder that knowledge of God and knowledge of ourselves is interdependent and that interdependence is what 'ethics' is about.

Accordingly any account of truthfulness as well as the rationality of theological convictions cannot be abstracted from worship. Through worship we not only come to know God, but we are changed by our knowledge of God, 'not only morally but also rationally'.[11] Once theology is liturgically shaped we hopefully can recover the theology as a tradition determined craft in contradiction to the ahistorical accounts of truth and rationality so characteristic of modernity.

Hopefully students begin to get a hint that worship is not something Christians do to make them 'moral', but rather worship and the holiness of life intrinsic to worship cannot be related as cause to effect. Rather they are activities that have no consequence exactly because they are purposefully directed to God. Exactly because worship puts all that we do before God, we are made part of God's praise and joy. That is why the first task of the church is not to make the world more just, but to make the world the world. For the world can only know it is the world through its contrast with the church that rightly knows the joy of worshipping

---

[10] Fergus Kerr, *Theology after Wittgenstein* (Oxford: Basil Blackwell, 1986), p. 183.
[11] Hardy and Ford, *Jubilate*, p. 113.

the true God.[12] Insofar as ethics has a task peculiar to itself it is to assemble reminders from the training we receive in worship that enable us to rightly see the world as well as how we continue to be possessed by the world.[13]

II. FROM GATHERING TO SENDING FORTH

The course is organized around the basic movements of the liturgy. To so structure the course challenges the presumption that ethics is about how general principles or concepts, such as love or justice, should be 'applied'. If our lives are shaped through the worship of God any abstraction that requires application indicates something has gone wrong.

That Christians must be gathered to worship, for example, in itself is a 'morality'. Gathering indicates that Christians are called from the world, from their homes, from their families, to be constituted into a community capable of praising God. The basis for such a gathering derives from the great commission given in Matt. 28.16–20. The church is constituted as a new people who have been gathered from the nations to remind the

[12] I therefore refuse to privilege the distinction between 'personal' and 'social' ethics since I assume that distinction derives from practices foreign to the church's narrative. If the church's first task is to make the world the world, that is its fundamental social and political task. Such a claim is often resisted because it sounds so intolerant, which of course it is, but it is an intolerance based on charity that would have the world saved by knowing it is the world. If the church does not worship rightly how can the world know it is the world exactly to the extent it does not willingly glorify God? As Yoder puts the matter in *Body Politics*, p. ix, 'stated very formally, the pattern we shall discover is that the will of God for human socialness as a whole is prefigured by the shape to which the Body of Christ is called. Church and world are not two compartments under separate legislation or two institutions with contradictory assignments, but two levels of the pertinence of the same Lordship. The people of God is called to be today what the world is called to be ultimately ... The phrase found in the title, *body politics*, is of course partly redundant. Yet each term does say more than the other would alone. 'Politics' affirms an unblinking recognition that we deal with matters of power, of rank and of money, of costly decisions and dirty hands, of memory and feelings. The difference between church and state or between a faithful and an unfaithful church is not that one is political and the other not, but that they are political in different ways.'
[13] The emphasis on the relation between church and world is a correlative of the strong eschatological theme running through the course. I argue that the attempt to display Christian ethics in terms of nature/grace or creation/redemption often results in a failure to appreciate the eschatological character of Christian convictions. For example, it is interesting to note that ethics based in nature/grace and creation/redemption schemes often only refer to the church as an afterthought. That such is the case, I suspect, betrays the ahistorical character of such theologies. For example, I think it is telling that such theologies while appearing Christologically orthodox in fact leave Jesus behind once they begin to 'work out the practical implications'.

world that we are in fact one people. Gathering, therefore, is an eschato-logical act as it is the foretaste of the unity of the communion of saints. Such a unity is possible only for a people who worship the true God.

The focus on gathering makes it impossible to divorce Christian ethics from ecclesiology. A. MacIntyre rightly argues that every moral philos-ophy characteristically presupposes a sociology, but from the perspective of the gathered church the church determines what counts as the 'socio-logical'.[14] That eleven o'clock on Sunday morning remains the most segregated hour in North Carolina has a different significance once the necessity of gathering is acknowledged. For the segregated character of the church is not problematic because it offends democratic egalitarian presumptions, but because a church so constituted is not gathered and therefore not able to properly worship God.

Such an account of the gathered church, I argue, renders problematic E. Troeltsch's well known characterization of church, sect, and mystical types, as well as H. Richard Niebuhr's famous 'five types' of the relation of Christ and culture. Such typologies not only derive their intelligibility from quite doubtful epistemological assumptions, but, more troubling, their very heuristic power tempts us to forget that even the 'church type' is gathered. Such typologies are arguments disguised as sociological analysis that presuppose the practices of liberal Protestantism. Schooled by such intellectual habits Christians lose the skills derived from our worship to see well the world in which we live.

Under the influence of Troeltsch and Niebuhr, Christians can lose any sense that the way they think about the world is different than how others may think about the world. In particular, Troeltsch and Niebuhr underwrote the assumptions that Christian ethics should be an ethics for anyone since such an ethic was a necessary correlative to the presumption that Christianity is a civilizational religion. In contrast I argue that the very fact that Christians must be gathered to worship suggest that the audience for Christian ethics must be those who have been shaped by the worship of God.

Obviously Christians think what we have learned from our worship about how to live well is true for anyone. That is why we have the obligation and joy of witnessing to what God has done for us. But the very notion of witness means we cannot presume that those to whom we witness already have learned what we have learned by the necessity of our being gathered.

I have some students, usually quite conservative evangelical students or ones who have had in their undergraduate training a bad introductory

---

[14] Alasdair MacIntyre, *After Virtue* (Notre Dame: University of Notre Dame Press, 1984), p. 23. The 'twist' on MacIntyre's suggestion obviously owes much to John Milbank's arguments in *Theology and Social Theory* (Oxford: Basil Blackwell, 1990).

course in philosophy, that begin to be worried about the 'relativism' they think implied in this approach. I try to help them see that the very description 'relativism' depends on epistemological presuppositions that must be questioned if God is the God known through worship.[15] Moreover 'relativism' is far too kind a description of the world which requires that God's people be gathered from the nations.

Gathered Christians greet one another in the name of the Father, Son, and Holy Spirit. Accordingly, I remind my students that any account of the Christian moral life begins and ends with the question of the God we Christians worship. The God Christians worship is known through initiation into the practices of a tradition that are necessary to know how rightly to name God. That God is a name challenges the anthropological starting-point so prevalent in Christian ethics. Christian ethics as a 'field', particularly in America, was the child of the liberal Protestant theological presumption that theological language works primarily as a provocative account of the human condition.[16] The liberal tradition assumed Christianity names insights about 'life' that should be compelling for anyone, but liberals forgot that such 'insights' are empty when divorced from worship of God.

After greeting one another in the name of the Trinity, Christians confess their faith by reciting the Creeds as well as confessing their sins. The structure of such confessions is classically seen in Isa. 6.1–13. Awed by

---

[15] I often draw on the work of MacIntyre in order to help the students understand the philosophical issues intrinsic to the Christian ethics I am developing. In particular I try to help them see that once one recognizes the traditioned character of rationality then the difficult question is not how to defeat something called 'the problem of "relativism"', but rather from what position is one standing to even know how to characterize relativism. Too often the so-called 'relativist challenge' presumes a standpoint outside all tradition. MacIntyre rightly suggest that the 'sociology' that seems to make 'relativism' such a challenge is the creation of cosmopolitan cultures that give certain individuals the presumption they are standing in different traditions at the same time. That many are so positioned today is without question. Nor should it be surprising that many of us who count ourselves as Christians are so located. What is crucial for Christians to recognize is that any response to relativism cannot come from a theory of rationality, but rather must be found in practices, such as the Eucharist, that embody a unity that makes it possible for our different positions to become more than the sum of our parts. For MacIntyre's reflections on perspectivism and relativism see his *Whose Justice? Which Rationality?* (Notre Dame: University of Notre Dame Press, 1988), pp. 349–69.

[16] Hardy and Ford in their account of liberalism put the matter just right, I believe, when they note, 'the only safe forms of Christian liberalism are those which live a basic existence of praising and knowing God within the other three streams of Christianity. Without this praise and knowledge liberals lose Christian credibility, and distort the very content of the freedom which they champion. As soon as freedom is seen as not primarily something given by God to be fulfilled in free praise and love of God, then the whole ecology of life is polluted. When liberalism of this sort refers to God it tends to become agnostic and vague, and loses the ability to know or proclaim much that is definite about him', *Jubilate*, pp. 143–4.

the God that greets us as we gather and in whose name we greet one another, Christians confess their sins to one another. The confession of our sins is possible through the training we received through worship. Sin, therefore, is a theological issue requiring the practice of confession, reconciliation, and forgiveness. Such practices require an account of the virtues and corresponding moral psychology in order to suggest the complex relation Christians insist pertains between 'acts' and 'agents' for the upbuilding of the Christian community.

The practice of confession of sin, forgiveness, and reconciliation is an appropriate context to introduce the students to the history of 'Christian ethics'. Drawing on Matt. 18.15ff. I introduce the history of penitential practice in order to show the importance as well as the variety of casuistical reflection in Christian tradition. The loss of penitential practice in Protestantism helps account for the abstractness of Protestant 'ethics' and why, as a result, Protestants are so tempted to sentimental portrayals of Christian existence devoid of judgement. For example, many Christians think racism is a sin because it is unjust, but they are not all sure if they want to call adultery or abortion sin. Through the practice of confession Christians are trained to confess that racism and adultery are equally sinful since they have learned that sin, at least for Christians, is a more determinative notion than injustice.

The centrality of scripture and preaching for worship provides a wonderful opportunity to develop the importance of authority in general for Christian practice and in particular for moral argument. The Christian practice of hearing the scriptures read and preached as good authority challenges the presumption in liberal cultures that all authorities are authoritarian. Preaching 'ethically' is not just when explicit ethical issues are addressed, but rather the very practice of preaching is an ethic to the extent preacher and congregation alike are trained to stand under the Word. Moreover, that the church is directed to preach on the same texts year after year challenges the modernist assumption characteristic of fundamentalism and historical criticism that the text of the Bible has *a* meaning.[17]

Those called to exercise authority through the ministry of the Word must have the character necessary for such ministry. Such a ministry is not just another profession in which the performance of the function can be abstracted from the person performing the function. Those called to ministry are given a power through their ordination that I as a layman do not have. The exercise of that power means, for example, the church rightly should expect them to have the virtues of constancy and patience so that the joy of the ministry will not be lost.

[17] For a more developed account of this position see my *Unleashing the Scripture: Freeing the Bible from Captivity to America* (Nashville: Abingdon Press, 1993).

43

Exploring questions of 'ministerial morality' opens up more general issues associated with an account of the virtues. Questions of the relation between the moral and intellectual virtues, how the virtues are acquired, the individuating of the virtues, whether the virtues can conflict, and in what sense they are a unity can be dealt with in a manner that make them something more than just 'theoretical'. For example, whether humility, a virtue unknown to Aristotle, is a virtue intrinsic to the Christian life can be investigated as well as how the naming of such a virtue requires the display of the complex relation of narrative, practice and tradition.

Christians respond to the proclamation of the Word through the waters of baptism. I assume that just as Christian worship builds on itself, the course at this point recapitulates everything that has gone before, since baptism is the necessary presupposition for the very existence of the church. Accordingly an account of the 'sacraments' can now be given as those 'summary' acts that bind the church's life to the life of Christ. Though obviously Christological themes have run through the course from the beginning, I now deal with them explicitly in the hope my students will see how questions about Christ's nature are not just 'speculation' but rather required by the gift of baptism. We are, after all, only able to baptize because Jesus is our resurrected Lord.

Since in baptism we are baptized into his death, I finally take up matters the students recognize as 'ethical' – e.g. suicide, abortion, marriage, and sex. This is the crucial time in the course where students either begin to 'get it' or give up on what I am trying to do. Hopefully, they will begin to appreciate why suicide and/or abortion are descriptions of practices incompatible with a community constituted through baptism. Moreover by discussing these topics in the context of baptism the students hopefully will begin to appreciate how the Christian understanding of suicide may be quite different from that of the wider culture.

For example, given the presupposition of individual autonomy underwritten by most liberal societies, it is hard to understand what is wrong with suicide or even why you would want to continue using such a description. In contrast, for Christians the very description 'suicide' is produced by our being a people formed by a baptism through which we learn our lives are not our own. The use of this kind of example is meant to help students see baptism is a politics in the same way that the church in liberal society is able to maintain the practices that make the description, 'suicide', work. We are thus reminded that Christians must be willing to expose our bodies, particularly when they are in pain, to one another as a way to avoid the necessity of suicide. The difference such a view of the body might make for how Christians think about medicine and the development of 'medical ethics' I think is quite illuminating.

It may seem odd to treat matters of marriage and sex in the context of baptism, but if baptism constitutes our true family then the question of

44

what marriage means as well as why Christians marry must be considered. One of the most distinguishing aspects of the early church was the discovery of singleness as a necessary way of life among Christians. Christians do not 'need' to marry since their true family is the church. It is only against the background of such presumptions that marriage becomes a calling that must be tested by the community. That two people may be in love is therefore not a sufficient condition for their marriage to be witnessed by the church since the church must be convinced that such a marriage will contribute to Christ's body. Moreover the Christian understanding of marriage as a lifelong monogamous fidelity only makes sense against the background of our baptismal covenant with one another. Any attempt to develop a 'sexual ethic' abstracted from the churches' practice of singleness and marriage cannot help but be unintelligible. Furthermore it is only in the context of those practices that the prohibition against abortion makes sense since there simply can be no 'unwanted' child born among Christians.

Irenaeus' image of Christ 'summing up' all of Israel's history is one I like to use for how the eucharist 'sums up' all that we have done in praise of God that now leads to the 'great thanksgiving'. Without all that had gone before eucharist could not take place, but that it takes place gives purpose that would otherwise be missing to all that we have done. The Eucharist provides a wonderful opportunity to develop further Christological issues and in particular questions concerning the atonement. The attempt to develop a 'doctrine of atonement' in a manner that separates Jesus' person and work is, I believe, the result of theology being separated from worship. Sacrificial doctrines of the atonement too often result in the eucharist being understood as a sacrifice God demands rather than God's sacrifice for the sake of the world in which we are graciously included.

Questions of capital punishment take on quite different shape when situated in relation to the sacrifice of the eucharist. The Christian objection to capital punishment is not that it is cruel or inhumane, though such reasons are not unimportant, but because human sacrifice has been ended for all times through Christ's cross. Moreover by discussing the question of capital punishment eucharistically, it becomes not just a question of taking life but why the church has a stake in limiting the state's power to punish. Eucharist again turns out to be a politics that reminds Christians that we are not of 'this world'.

Reflection on the eucharist is also a 'natural' place to consider economic questions and the ethics of war. If eucharist is about the sharing of Christ's body such a sharing should have implications for how Christians understand their relation to 'ownership'. We come bringing our 'offerings' that hopefully challenge the widespread assumption in capitalist societies that the distinction between what is 'mine' and what is 'yours' is problematic. 1 Corinthians 11 and the Book of Acts become surprisingly powerful when read against our current economic practices. How the unity discovered through eucharist is not equivalent to liberal egalitarianism insofar as the latter only reproduces capitalist practices remains one of the most difficult but also one of the most important issues with which I deal.

The peace necessary for eucharistic celebration creates the condition necessary not only for questions of the ethics of war but for exploring the question of why war should be distinguished from murder. The peace of the eucharist is not the absence of violence or the violence that often appears as order, but rather it is the peace that comes from being made friends with God and with one another. For example, I ask the students to consider whether Christians can get up from the meal in which Jesus has been the host and begin to kill one another in name of national loyalties. The eucharist, therefore, becomes the necessary background for understanding why Christians who feel called to participate in war bear, as the just war tradition presupposes, the burden of proof. At the very least by so situating a 'just war theory' it becomes a mode of Christian casuistry rather than predetermined justification for what the state is going to do anyway.

Just as suddenly as Christians have been gathered they are sent forth with God's blessing. I again return to Troeltsch's and Niebuhr's typologies to suggest that the church being sent out means that the church can never be a 'sect'. For Christians it is never a question of whether to serve the world, but how they are to be of service in the world. We can never forget that worship is the way God has given us to serve the world. Historical considerations are again introduced, as here it seems important to treat Augustine's account of the two cities, Luther's understanding of the two realms, as well as the Calvinist understanding of a holy commonwealth. Too often such accounts become predetermined justifications for Christians to be loyal to a 'state'.[18] Rather what is needed are the kind of discriminating judgements about this or that state or society which Christians must negotiate with all the skill acquired through their worship of God. Such skills are exactly what I hope the students will discover they have acquired through the practice they have been put through in the course.

III. ENDING WITH THE BEGINNING

I have obviously not tried even to mention every issue I take up in this

---

[18] I spend at least a lecture on the church and the Third Reich in this context. The example of the church under Nazi Germany can be too comforting for American Christians as they think they live in a political system that makes Fascism impossible. Such a presumption,

course.[19] The stress I place on the narrative character of worship and ethics, the ongoing polemic with the presuppositions and practices of liberalism, the conversation with other 'ethicists' – all these obviously have more prominence in the course than is apparent from this report. Moreover any attempt to display, much less defend adequately, the many claims and assertions I have made above would take at least a book and quite a long one at that. I have rather tried to suggest how structuring a course in Christian ethics around worship can provide the means to renarrate familiar Christian commitments in a manner in which they take on new power.

From the beginning to the end of the course I make it clear I have no interest in teaching students about theology and/or ethics. Rather I hope to transform my own and their lives that we all might live the life of praise more faithfully. Such transformation is an ongoing task as our very familiarity with the language of the faith becomes a mode of domestication of God. Yet it turns out that God will not be domesticated forcing us to see what we had looked at far too long and not seen at all. So hopefully as we come out for the second half we will have learned the importance of where Christians always began – in praise of God.

---

however, makes it particularly important to challenge the assumption that 'democracy' is the form of government and society most congenial if not required by Christian worship.

[19] I have not, for example, dealt with the importance of hymns and music as well as prayer as intrinsic to Christian worship. Such themes are not only underdeveloped in this essay, but in the course. It is tempting to defend their absence by claiming that one simply cannot be expected to do everything in one course, but I do not think such a defence adequate. The truth of the matter is that I think the importance of music and prayer have been undervalued in much of contemporary theology, mine included, apart from the outstanding example of von Balthasar. Nor should Patrick Sherry's *Spirit and Beauty: An Introduction to Theological Aesthetics* (Oxford: Clarendon Press, 1992) be overlooked. Sherry makes a striking suggestion 'that the transfiguration of the cosmos is being anticipated now in the Spirit's work of creating beauty is similar to the claim that the Spirit's present work of santification is an anticipation of our future glorification and life of holiness', p. 165. This strikes me as an extremely suggestive claim that could help us understand the relation between eschatology and sanctification in worship.

Appendix: A Syllabus for Teaching Christian Ethics
CHE 33   Professor Stanley Hauerwas
Fall 1993

1. Required Reading

Anne Tyler, *Saint Maybe* (New York: Knopf, 1991).
John Howard Yoder, *Body Politics* (Nashville: Discipleship Resources, 1992).
Leslie Newbigin, *Foolishness to the Greeks* (London: SPCK, 1986).
Sharon Welch, *A Feminist Ethic of Risk* (Minneapolis: Fortress, 1989).
Stanley Hauerwas, *The Peaceable Kingdom* (London: SCM, 1983).

2. Course Structure

Worship and Life
Gathering and Greeting
Confession and Sin: Race, Class, Gender
Scripture and Proclamation: Virtues and the Ministry
Baptism: Marriage, Sex and the Family
Offering, Sacrifice, and Eucharist: Economic Justice, War and Peace
Sending Forth

3. Course Schedule

Weeks 1–2 Worship and Life
Readings: 31 Aug.–3 Sept.: Tyler, *Saint Maybe*
                   7–10 Sept.: Yoder, *Body Politics*

Weeks 3–4 Gathering and Greeting
Readings: 14–17 Sept.: Newbigin, ch. 1–2
                   21–24 Sept.: Newbigin, ch. 3–6

Weeks 5–6 Confession and Sin: Race, Class, Gender
Readings: 28 Sept.–1 Oct.: Welch, Parts I–II
                   5–8 Oct.: Welch, Part III

Weeks 7–8 Scripture and Proclamation: Virtue and the Ministry
Readings: 12–15 Oct.: Hauerwas, ch. 1–4
                   20–22 Oct.: Hauerwas, ch. 5.

Weeks 9–10 Baptism: Marriage, Sex, and the Family
Readings: 26 Oct.–5 Nov.: Hauerwas, ch. 6–8

Weeks 11–13 Offering, Sacrifice, and the Eucharist: Economic Justice, War and Peace
Readings: 9–24 Nov.: Yoder, *Body Politics*

Week 14 Sending Forth
Preceptorial: 3 Dec.

3

Crosslight

MICHEAL O'SIADHAIL

WHAT is a poet doing in a Festschrift for an eminent theologian? 'O unworn world, enrapture me ...' My only excuse is the delight with which Daniel Hardy and David Ford laced *Jubilate*[1] with the poetry of Patrick Kavanagh alongside Herbert, Hopkins, Dante and other 'secretaries of praise'. But it is not simply the vested interest of a poet that rejoices in this infiltration of modern theology. After all, as *Jubilate* reminds us, 'man as poet and priest of creation' is an ancient concept and what extraordinary poets the authors of the Psalms or the Song of Songs must have been: 'My beloved is mine, and I am his: he feedeth among the lilies'. There is also the joyful attention paid by the authors of *Jubilate* to a poem. That standing in the presence of a poem, in the tension of the images, accepting metaphors not as rhetorical devices but rather as a mode of saying. So often literary criticism veers towards trivialities of technique or show-off comparisons and misses the point of all that energy and imagination searching for 'the light supreme'. At least, Kavanagh, with his dictum that a poet is a theologian,[2] might not be too surprised!

At first glance Kavanagh's remark may look easy and off-the-cuff. But there was nothing easy or unearned about his journey. I am sure he had understood worship instinctively and at the deepest level of his being:

> Leafy-with-love banks and green waters of the canal
> Pouring redemption for me, that I do
> The will of God, wallow in the habitual, the banal
> Grow again with nature as before I grew.
> The bright stick trapped, the breeze adding a third
> To the couple kissing on an old seat,
> And a bird gathering materials for the nest of the Word
> Eloquently new and abandoned to its delirious beat.
> O unworn world enrapture me, enrapture me in a web
> Of fabulous grass and eternal voices by a beech
> Feed the gaping need of my senses, give me adlib
> To pray unselfconsciously with overflowing speech

[1] Daniel W. Hardy and David F. Ford, *Jubilate* (London: Darton, Longman & Todd, 1984).
[2] Patrick Kavanagh, *Self-Portrait* (Dublin: Dolmen Press, 1964), pp. 27–8.

For this soul needs to be honoured with a new dress woven
From green and blue things and arguments that cannot be proven.

I thank you and I say how proud
That I have been by fate allowed
To stand here having the joyful chance
To claim my inheritance
For most have died the day before
The opening of that holy door.[4]

In a recent article Edward Farley[5] has attempted to tease out the underlying connection between literature and theology. He points to how, ideally, poetics is 'a distinctive embodiment of the paradox of the universal and the concrete'. By this he means that, just as in the language of facts 'the world is brought to a stop – summarized, featured, evidenced, generalized', 'the literary artist also brings the world to a stop, not by featuring it, but by writing it, and what is written is the concrete'. Then, 'paradoxically, the concrete is what is most universal'. At the heart of religion is also a paradox, 'the paradox of the concreteness of acts, beliefs, traditions, symbols and the like, and the necessary absence of the sacred'. The question then arises as to how the sacred as absent can be worshipped, spoken, celebrated? Farley answers that in the case of believers 'their worship, their relation to the sacred, can only take place in the experience that preserves the absence, that refuses to reduce the mystery or tame the transcendence ... Absence, mystery, and the refusal of explanation are just what we have in the aesthetic mediation of the concrete. Absence and the concrete, absence (mystery) and reality itself are correlates. This is why it is not accidental that religious faiths not simply *use* but *are* a kind of aesthetics as they move to expression.'

I suppose we're always drawn towards what is our own ideal. In many ways, much of what I admire most in Daniel Hardy's work is his engagement with modernity in all its manifestations. Although I claim no knowledge of theology, I suspect that the temptations for a theologian are either, at one extreme, to withdraw entirely from modernity into a pure traditionalism or, at the other extreme, to reinterpret a religion in terms of a modern secularity. Daniel Hardy seems to me to stand at some point of intersection where he is fascinated by how a religious tradition and modernity in its various scientific, sociological and cultural expressions throw light on each other. Nether subsumes the other and both are richer caught in the crosslight:

---

[3] Patrick Kavanagh, 'Canal Bank Walk', in *Collected Poems* (London: MacGibbon & Kee, 1964), p. 150.
[4] Patrick Kavanagh, from 'Thank You, Thank You', in *Collected Poems*, p. 193.
[5] Edward Farley, 'The Place of Poetics in Theological Education: A Heuristic Inquiry', *Theological Education* 31/1 (1994), pp. 133–48.

I wove the web of colour
Before the rainbow
The intricacy of the flower
Before the leaf grew.

I was the buried ore,
The fossil forest,
I knew the roots of things:
Before death's kingdom
I passed through the grave.

Times out of mind my journey
Circles the universe
And I remain the first day.[6]

Apart from the deep and historical bonds of literature and faith, in our culture there may be parallel dilemmas. It is just that these terribly brittle worlds of word and metaphor so often face similar temptations. Poetry's reaction to any crude cultural positivism has so often been either to retreat into Romanticism (and I follow Charles Taylor[7] in regarding an excessively individualistic 'modernism' as a successor to Romanticism) or to adapt to the needs of cultural consumerism until any sense of 'saying the unsayable' is lost. We often find ourselves pulled between the poles of a poetics of private piety and that of an excessive postmodernist irony. Of course, I am outlining extreme positions and there are all the gradations between. And I should also say I am speaking of an ideal poetics, for, as always, the corruption of the best is worst. The shadow of Foucault passes over us reminding us all too clearly that a poetics can simply serve to bolster a dominant regime. For my own part, I want to stand in the crosslight, to stand where all we can grasp of the world around us, scientifically, sociologically, culturally, can still be seen and spoken of with wonder and compassion. I am no 'Renaissance man'. I could not compare my own interests with the breadth of Daniel Hardy's knowledge and clear-sightedness. Even more important than the breadth of his vision is his extraordinary gift for seeing the interconnectedness of things. It is this overall vision which I always find so refreshing in these days when so many of our universities have become polyversities. Although we can never again have a specialized knowledge of all fields of knowledge, surely there can be something of the excitement of a Renaissance, a relishing and tolerance of the complexity and interwoven richness of our world?

I am sure there are all kinds of comparisons between the world of faith and art: the weight of tradition and community, the role of memory, the

---

[6] Kathleen Raine, from 'Northumbrian Sequence 1', in *Collected Poems* (London: Hamish Hamilton, 1956), p. 111.
[7] Charles Taylor, *Sources of the Self* (Cambridge: CUP, 1989), chs. 25 and 26.

self-abandon, the need for apprenticeship, metaphor as a vehicle of thought and feeling, the inadequacies and longings. But I must concentrate on my own delight in poetry and let any other likenesses be merely implicit; partly for fear of the charge of idolatry, partly because I reckon this cobbler should stick to his last and can only hope that revelling in the marvel of language and poetry may reflect something of the ultimate fullness.

The joy of art, it seems to me, is its invitation and its gift. Its claim on us to lose our dominion and simply to behold. It has often been said that music is the purest form of contemplation. Certainly, it enters me unbidden like a perfume. But beloved poetry can have the same bodily pleasure of rhythm and metre, the moods, the precision and the silence. Then, there is the dimension of concept and metaphor which music evades. The endless intrigues, delights, insistences and inadequacies of language. The vagaries of words.

I remember how surprised I was when I took some lessons in classical harmony how mechanical and arithmetic it seemed. All those octaves, fifths and fourths, the desirable intervals, harmonics, the series of progressions by which you homed to the tonic. I know these rules and regulations were artificially distilled from one period of European music, but it is beautifully mathematical. I could feel the enthusiasm of Pythagoras halving the length of a vibrating string to raise its pitch by an octave or reducing its length by a third to raise its pitch a fifth. And so on, as the intervals work in ratios. Quite amazing to think of the magnificent soaring expression of the great composers fashioned from the ordered relationships of ratios. Naturally, in taking harmony lessons I was doing it the wrong way around because my apprenticeship in culture means that at some subconscious level at least I can guess where the line of a hymn or a folksong is leading. It is precisely that subconscious level that I find so marvellous. But, of course, I should not have been so surprised at this subconscious arithmetic. After all I had trained in philology and in generative grammar and knew how one dimension of language also operates at a similar subconscious and almost mechanical level:

> I have found my music in a common word,
> Trying every pleasurable throat that sings
> And every praisèd sequence of sweet strings . . . [8]

It is by no means necessary for a poet to be aware of the dynamic layers of language rules and developments, no more than a musician need be a mathematician or a sculptor a geologist. Yet it fascinates. Perhaps all those laws and sound-shifts triggered and patterned subconsciously over

[8] Gerard Manley Hopkins, from 'The Alchemist in the City', in *Selected Prose and Poetry* (Harmondsworth, Middlesex: Penguin, 1953), p. 5.

time reflect our deep and endless desire to order and re-order, this ballet of symmetry and arrangement highlighting our universal and inherited potential for syntheses and learning. Nor is it simply in the past. It is unpredictable and it keeps on happening. I remember how when I was young older people pronounced *garage* with the second syllable stressed (the way Americans still pronounce it, showing its French origins). I stressed it on the first syllable which reduced the second syllable to *-idge* as in words like *cabbage* or *porridge*. It would have sounded silly for someone of my generation to pronounce it like older people. On the other hand, I was brought up stressing the first syllable in the words *primarily, harass* and *controversy* and now I notice people all around me accenting the second syllable. The great unpredictability of deviation and re-configuration which has over thousands of years shaped and re-shaped language into language. A model of contingency and continuation. But I do not want to dwell too much on this constant re-arranging on the level of pronunciations and inflectional paradigms.

What is most interesting is the shifts which take place at the semantic level, how words connect and shade from one meaning to another. Just think of a word like *trust* which is borrowed from Old Norse *traustr* meaning 'confidence', 'firmness' with its origins in an Indo-European root **deru* 'to be firm', 'solid', 'steadfast'. (In its more specialized sense it means 'wood', 'tree' or certain objects made of wood such as 'tray', 'trough'.) The implications and ramifications of its variants and borrowings from language to language are wide. It is connected with, for instance, 'true', 'truth', '(be)trow' and 'truce', and through its cognates with Latin *durus/durare* whose English derivatives give us a word like 'endure'. In German *trost* or in Norwegian *tröst* comes to mean 'consolation', 'comfort', 'solace'. Even the French *triste* is thought to be derived from the Old Norse verbal form of the same word, so a triste is 'a place where one stands trustingly'. It begins to read like a meditative poem on the theme of trust. To know that some truth endures and stands like a tree to believe and console us and to give us somewhere we can stand with confidence:

> Now I am here, what wilt thou do with me
> > None of my books will show:
> I reade, and sigh, and wish I were a tree;
> > For sure then I should grow
> To fruit or shade: at least some bird would trust
> Her household to me, and I should be just.[9]

I never cease to be amazed by this choreography of words. A lovely and

---

[9] George Herbert, from 'Affliction' (1), in *The English Poems of George Herbert* (London: Dent, 1974), p. 67.

especially English word is 'worship'. As a noun it expresses the quality of having worth (and therefore to be revered). I often think it is a pity that its spelling does not show its almost transparent make-up: *worthship* that is *worth* and *-ship*. However I am a little late with my regrets as Middle English had *worschipe* and we have to get back to Old English for *weorthscipe*. What a rich and layered world! The ending *-ship* we know from words like *horsemanship* or *scholarship* where it signifies the state or condition of having the quality of a horseman or what pertains to a scholar. (The ending has in itself an interesting background; it's a collective suffix connected to the word *shape* which provides other Germanic languages with their word for 'create', for instance, Norwegian *skape*). But the central idea here is *worth*. This is believed to be derived from a root **wert* which means 'to turn', 'to wind' which we see in English 'in*ward*', 'to*ward*' etc. The verb is common in other German languages, for instance, *werden* 'to become' (from 'to turn into') and has a cognate in Latin *vertere* 'to turn' from whose compounds many English words such as 'convert', 'invert', 'avert' are derived. The word 'worth' apparently derives from **werthaz* meaning 'toward', 'opposite' and therefore 'equivalent', 'worth' and the noun clearly associates value and worth with the idea of equivalence. Perhaps it's fanciful but in that sequence of subtle semantic shifts maybe there's a hint of some link between what is opposite and equivalent and what is worth. We touch here on the whole philosophical idea of accepting what is opposite, turned towards and facing us, as having the equivalent needs and rights as ourselves. The well-known *thou* of Martin Buber, or less symmetrically, the command of the other's face in Emmanuel Lévinas. My own associations are with that revelation of Dorothea Brooke in George Eliot's *Middlemarch*[10] that her husband Casaubon 'had an equivalent centre of self, where the lights and shadows must always fall with a certain difference'. There are all sorts of implications of worship and otherness. At any rate, the word 'worship' is a unique development in English and trust Gerard Manley Hopkins with his love of Anglo-Saxon words to pick it up:

> To man, that needs would worship block or barren stone,
> Our law says: Love what's love worthiest, were all known;
> World's loveliest men's selves. Self flashes off frame and face.[11]

All the slippage and overlappings of words. Maybe these ambiguities and finesses, these ambivalences and paradoxes reflect much about what's most captivating and mysterious in our dealings with others. Room for change and subtlety and tension. Music holds us poised, expectant and agog, on a diminished seventh chord in the crosslight between tonalities.

[10] George Eliot, *Middlemarch* (Harmondsworth, Middlesex: Penguin, 1965), p. 243.
[11] Gerard Manley Hopkins, from 'To What Serves Mortal Beauty', in *Selected Prose*, p. 58.

And room for transcendence and playfulness. So much of our fun is based on double meanings, homonyms and puns. I think of John Donne at his most boisterous in the virtuoso 'To his mistris going to bed':

> Come, Madam, come, all rest my powers defy.
> Until I labour, I in labour lie.
> The foe oft-times having the foe in sight,
> Is tir'd with standing though he never fight.
> Off with that girdle, like heaven's zone glistering,
> But a far fairer world incompassing.

> Licence my roaving hands, and let them go,
> Before, behind, between, above, below,
> O my America! my new-found-land,
> My kingdome, safliest when with one man mann'd,
> My myne of precious stones, My Emperie,
> How blest am I in this discovering thee!'[12]

I do not wish to labour the word play! That rumbustuous and swaggering youth! Listening carefully you could almost guess that the intensity of that temperament would issue in 'Ask not for whom the bell tolls, it tolls for thee'. But there are quieter, fine-drawn uses of language's ambiguity. Richard Wilbur's 'The Beautiful Changes' in a book of the same title published when he was only twenty-six allows the mystery of ambivalence to enter in to us. Does the beautiful change or are the changes beautiful? Or both?

> The beautiful changes as a forest is changed
> By a chameleon tuning its skin to it;
> As a mantis, arranged
> On a green leaf grows
> Into it, makes the leaf leafier, and proves
> Any greenness is deeper than anyone knows.

> Your hands hold roses always in a way that says
> They are not only yours; the beautiful changes
> In such kind ways,
> Wishing ever to sunder
> Things and things' selves for a second finding, to lose
> For a moment all that it touches back to wonder.[13]

Yet I wonder if it is not this equivocal quality, the slippage and polysemy which sometimes drives us to despair of language. The terrible

[12] John Donne, from 'Elegie xix To His Mistris Going To Bed', in *Complete Poetry and Selected Prose* (London: The Nonesuch Press, 1990), pp. 96–7).
[13] Richard Wilbur, from 'The Beautiful Changes', in *New and Collected Poems* (London: Faber and Faber, 1989), p. 392.

inadequacy of words always falling short of desire. The ungraspable joy, the uncommunicable sorrow. And even here there's another paradox. The drift and shortcomings of language which causes us to fail again and again are also what urge us to begin afresh, poem after poem, generation after generation. This inexhaustible hankering after the absent. The necessary absconding of the sacred.

> You are for me now
> The mystery of time
> i.e., of a person
> Changing and the same,
>
> Who runs in the garden
> Fragrant after the rain
> With a ribbon in your hair
> And lives in the beyond.
>
> You see how I try
> To reach with words
> What matters most
> And how I fail.
>
> Though perhaps this moment
> When you are close
> Is precisely your help
> And an act of forgiveness.[14]

For all its shortfalls, the property of words to have more than one meaning is at the core of language. For reasons of economy there have to be limits to the number of sounds and words and a deal of doubling-up of meanings. This in turn makes it necessary for a word's meaning to be dependent on the context. You can often only understand what a word means from the whole sentence and context. In a poem, where you cannot question the author as you could in a conversation, there is the possibility of ambiguity and misunderstanding. Donne's word plays exploit the tension between the equivocality of the word 'discover' ('uncover', 'undress' or 'explore previously unknown territory') and the unambiguous meaning in the overall context. In Wilbur's 'The Beautiful Changes' the spell is in the veiled ambiguity which remains at the level of the sentence and context. It is the magic and power of underdeterminancy. Milosz, for his part, is coming to terms with the fact that we must live with the mystery of the elusive otherness. In spite of our best efforts in language, at some level every other human is forever a stranger. Communication without the forgiveness of love always falls short.

[14] Czeslaw Milosz, from 'A Photograph', in *Provinces* (New York: The Ecco Press, 1991), p. 35.

But polysemy, this property of words to have more than one meaning, has an even more significant role. I am not thinking here of scientific language where the aim is to totally eliminate polysemy and where it employs metaphor to tie down the context to one narrow meaning in the interests of argument. Scientific language is, of course, necessary and complements the ordinary language of communication. It is in our efforts to heighten and deepen our perception, however, that the ability of words to have more than one meaning comes into its own. We approach the use of metaphor as the exploitation of polysemy at the ever-expanding boundaries of language.

Many of us, including myself, were schooled in the rhetorical tradition where we learned a long list of various figures of speech: hyperbole, oxymoron, irony, synecdoche, metonymy, simile, metaphor, and so on. Unless we have had particular cause to look them up afterwards, most of us have probably forgotten how they are defined. The most unfortunate outcome of this tradition was in fact to make you think of all of these figures of speech as ornaments, a sort of decoration to make our language high-flown. The result is especially regrettable in the case of metaphor and leads to what is called a substitution view of metaphor. Take Brendan Kennelly's short poem 'Ambulance':

Shrieking on its mercy mission,
The white hysterical bully
Blows all things out of its way,
Cutting through the slack city
Like a knife through flesh.
People respect potential saviours
And immediately step aside,
Watching its pitch and scream ahead,
Ignoring the lights, breaking the rules,
Lurching on the crazy line
Between the living and the dead.[15]

So easily we're trained to think that the poet uses 'the white hysterical bully' when, of course, he means the ambulance. We just need to substitute 'ambulance' for 'the white hysterical bully' and we're back to square one. Happily, there is a series of thinkers (among them I. A. Richards, Monroe Beardsley and Max Black) who have abandoned the idea of metaphor as something stylistic and devoid of content. Janet Martin Soskice's definition of metaphor as when 'we speak about one thing in terms suggestive of another' gets nearer the mark.[16] The real wonder is

[15] Brendan Kennelly, 'Ambulance', from *A Time for Voices* (Newcastle upon Tyne: Bloodaxe Books, 1992), p. 121.
[16] Janet Martin Soskice, *Metaphor and Religious Language* (Oxford: Clarendon Press, 1985), p. 54.

that metaphor blurs the usual logical boundaries and uncovers new like-nesses. There is a whole spectrum from the dead metaphor which has become an entry in the dictionary, as say, 'the hands of the clock', all the way to referring to 'the white hysterical bully' in a poem describing an ambulance. And indeed the so-called 'dead metaphor' may not be with-out its effect on our way of viewing reality as shaped by our language. To quote the philosopher Paul Ricoeur:

> our concept of likeness as the tension between sameness and differ-ence has the extraordinary power of redescribing reality ... the strategy of discourse implied in metaphorical language is neither to improve communication nor to insure univocity in argumentation, but to shatter and to increase our sense of reality by shattering and increasing our language ... With metaphor we experience the meta-morphis of both language and reality.[17]

An ambulance rushing through the city streets will never look the same again!

Our sign system is finite but the potential for growth in meaning is infinite; we stand in the crosslight of structure and freedom:

> Freedom. We sang of freedom
> (travel lightly anything goes)
> and somehow became strangers
> to each other, like gabblers
> at cross purposes, builders
>   of Babel
>
> Slowly I relearn a *lingua*,
> shared overlays of rule,
> lattice of memory and meaning,
> our latent images, a tongue
> at large in an endlessness
>   of sentences unsaid.[18]

And just as in language and metaphor, tradition and innovation are held in tension, so too in literature. There is both the desire to absorb the canon and to interrupt and subvert it. Edward Farley puts this paradox succinctly: 'Poets thus both destabilize – by historizing the general, the

[17] Paul Ricoeur, 'Creativity in Language: Word, Polysemy, Metaphor', in *The Philosophy of Paul Ricoeur: An Anthology of His Work* (Boston: Beacon Press, 1978), pp. 132–3.
[18] Micheal O'Siadhail, from 'Freedom', in *Hail! Madam Jazz: New and Selected Poems* (Newcastle upon Tyne: Bloodaxe Books, 1992), p. 111.

sedimented, the enduring, and stabilize – by becoming an enduring part of the community's (or individual's) *anamnesis*. Through that, poetics contribute to the traditioning and remembering the community needs simply to exist as that community.'[19]

I began by inquiring what a poet was doing in a theologian's Fest-schrift. Once in an interview the American poet Richard Wilbur was reminded that both he and Robert Lowell had said that all poetry of the highest quality is religious. The interviewers then asked in what sense did he mean that. 'I think there are various ways you could argue for that position', he replied.

You could say that all poetry, however much it may be irrational, moves towards clarity and order, that it affirms all that is clear and orderly in the world, affirms the roots of clarity in the world. Then, you might say that poetry is given not only to saying that this is like that, as in the simile; it is given also to saying that this is that, to affirming rather nervily that prosaically unlike things are to poetry's eye identical, co-natural. I think that there is a natural disposition of the poetic mind to assert all things are one, are part of the same thing, that anything may be compared to anything else. And if anything can be compared to anything else, the ground of comparison is likely to be divine.[20]

The soul shrinks
 From that it is about to remember,
From the punctual rape of every blessed day,
And cries,
 'Oh, let there be nothing on earth but laundry,
Nothing but rosy hands in the rising steam
And clear dances done in the sight of heaven'

 Yet, as the sun acknowledges
With a warm look the world's hunks and colours,
The soul descends once more in bitter love
To accept the waking body, saying now
In a changed voice as the man yawns and rises,
 'Bring them down from their ruddy gallows;
Let there be clean linen for the backs of thieves;

[19] Farley, 'The Place of Poetics in Theological Education', p. 136.
[20] Richard Wilbur, from 'Richard Wilbur: An Interview with Robert Frank and Stephen Mitchell', in *Conversations with Richard Wilbur* (Jackson and London: University Press of Mississippi), pp. 24–5.

> Let lovers go fresh and sweet to be undone,
> And the heaviest nuns walk in a pure floating
> Of dark habits,
>   keeping their difficult balance'.[21]

Following his explanation of how poetry of the highest quality is religious, Wilbur described that poem as 'against dissociated and abstracted spirituality'. Keeping the difficult balance, indeed. And all the traditions with their names for the task: Greek poet 'the one who makes', Irish *file* 'the one who sees', Icelandic *skáld* 'the one who narrates', Welsh *bardd* 'the one who praises'. To acknowledge some source of the great plenitude of order, energy and life. The extraordinary strata of richness and complexity found in language, which in turn are just a glimpse of the fullness and diversities of various aspects of our cosmos and our culture. Music, physics, sociology, biology, genetics. The abundance of it! 'O unworn world, enrapture me, enrapture me in a web . . .'. A source in the light of everything around us. Everything around us in the light of a source. To make some sense of it, to be a seer, a narrator, a praiser in the crosslight. Dare I say a lover? The wonderful and bewildering paradoxes and complementarities, the constant change and becoming. The threat of chaos, the leaps to greater intricacy. And running though it all, some irrepressible richness:

> Anywhere and always just as you expect it least,
> Welling or oozing from nowhere a desire to feast.
>
> At Auschwitz Wolf hums Brahms' rhapsody by heart
> As Eddy, thief turned juggler, rehearses his art.
>
> Fling and abandon, gaieties colourful and porous.
> The Mexican beggar's skirt, an Araner's *crios*.
>
> Irresistible laughter, hiss and giggle of overflow.
> That black engine-driver crooning his life's motto:
>
> 'Paint or tell a story, sing or shovel coal,
> You gotta get a glory or the job lacks soul.'
>
> Abundance of joy bubbling some underground jazz.
> A voice whispers: Be with me tonight in paradise.[22]

---

[21] Richard Wilbur, from 'Love Calls Us to the Things of this World', in *New and Selected Poems*, p. 233–4.
[22] Michael O'Siadhail, 'Invitation', in *A Fragile City* (Newcastle upon Tyne: Bloodaxe Books, 1995).

PART TWO: FAITH AND LOVE

4

The Trinitarian Dynamics of Belief

STEPHEN PICKARD

INTRODUCTION: LOSS AND RECOVERY OF TRINITARIAN BELIEF

THE tendency of Christian belief to collapse into a undifferentiated form of monotheism has been a recurring feature of the Christian tradition. Karl Rahner's observation in this regard is most apposite:

> despite their orthodox confession of the Trinity, Christians are, in their practical life, almost mere 'monotheists'. We must be willing to admit that, should the doctrine of the Trinity have to be dropped as false, the major part of religious literature could well remain virtually unchanged.[1]

More recently Jürgen Moltmann, among others, has drawn attention to the impact of this loss of trinitarian belief within the wider socio-political and ecological contexts of modern life.[2] The roots of this trinitarian slippage are varied and complex and have their traces in the formative stages of the Christian tradition.[3] However, it is also the case that the rationalistic temper of European Enlightenment thought contributed to, if not accelerated, the drift from a distinctive trinitarian form of belief into more diffuse and abstract notions of the presence and action of God in the world.[4]

This problem has intensified from the nineteenth century under the impact of the Feuerbachian critique of religion.[5] As a result the church

---

[1] Karl Rahner, *The Trinity* (London: Burns & Oates, 1970), pp. 10f.

[2] See e.g. Jürgen Moltmann, *The Trinity and the Kingdom of God* (London: SCM, 1981), esp. ch. 6; and *God and Creation: An Ecological Doctrine of Creation* (London: SCM, 1985), esp. pp. 94–8.

[3] For a recent discussion see Colin Gunton, *The Promise of Trinitarian Theology* (Edinburgh: T. & T. Clark, 1991), ch. 3.

[4] This problem is highlighted in John Locke (1632–1704), *The Reasonableness of Christianity* [1695], ed. and intro. by G. W. Ewing (Washington: Regnery Gateway, 1965). A highly reduced form of Christian belief is proposed – belief in one God and in Jesus as the Messiah – in relation to which the doctrine of the Trinity cannot but appear as a marginal and metaphyiscal irrelevancy.

[5] The de-objectification of God has led to a radically immanentist account of divine reality. As a result God becomes the sum total of human spiritual ideas. An example is Don Cupitt, *Taking Leave of God* (London: SCM, 1986).

has had to face more directly the challenge of recovering the fullness of Christian belief in order to nourish and sustain ongoing discipleship in the modern world. This has constituted a major agenda for the church in the twentieth century and is evidenced in important attempts to relocate Christian belief and practice within a fuller trinitarian framework.[6] This suggests a new effort to identify in a comprehensive and rich way that which is more distinctive in the Christian tradition.[7] This development raises, indeed provokes, questions to do with the dynamics of belief that is self-consciously trinitarian in form, e.g., how is the God believed in present for faith, initiating and sustaining human believing? To what extent is it possible to embody the object of belief in statements of belief? By what process does belief come to full form? How significant is the ecclesial nature of Christianity for belief? What is the function and purpose of belief? Ultimately, such questions have to do with the foundation and dynamic of discipleship witnessed to in Christian belief. In many respects Christian theology has failed to show how belief and practice of faith nourish and stimulate each other. This has contributed to the inner dissolution of the trinitarian form of Christian belief. Ultimately it would be of great practical benefit for the Christian community to understand what it means to live in the Spirit of the God of Jesus Christ.

The following discussion of the dynamics of Christian belief falls into three parts. Part I locates the impulse and source for Christian belief in the triune character of God. Part II examines how the impulse and source of Christian faith impacts upon the process by which human beings formulate their statements of belief. Part III considers some important aspects of the ecclesial nature of trinitarian belief. In short what is distinctively *trinitarian* in the dynamics of belief will be woven into a discussion of the strategies and environment that attend faithful response to God in the community of Jesus Christ.

I. Trinitarian Belief: Its Impulse and Source

Uncertainty over the presence of God in the world and human society has had a major impact on Christian belief. Specifically, it has become unclear whether distinctive Christian beliefs 'reach back' to, and thus mediate, the presence of God witnessed to in the community of Jesus

---

[6] Gunton, *Trinitarian Theology*, ch. 1, notes the important developments in the doctrine of the Trinity in Barth (Reformed), Rahner (Roman Catholic), and Lossky (Orthodox) as well as in more recent theology.

[7] Jürgen Moltmann, *History and the Triune God* (London: SCM, 1991), p. xi states: 'The doctrine of the Trinity has become important in the last ten years because it is the way in which the distinctive feature of Christianity is formulated'.

Christ.[8] As a result the long-held conviction that the Christian disciple already dwells in the truth as it is in Jesus (Eph. 4.21b) has become problematic. It can no longer be taken for granted that Christian belief gives expression to a fundamental bond in the Spirit with the God of Jesus Christ. The problematic nature of the 'whence' of Christian belief reveals itself in the range of options in theology for identifying the source and impulse for belief.[9] An option at one extremity evidences a conventional or hard objectivism. This usually involves appeal to a strong formal authority for belief in terms of biblical warrant and/or its authoritative interpreter. In this context belief is reduced to assent to propositions. This mode of belief is usually underpinned by the assumption of a strict one-to-one correspondence between word and object.[10] Attention is necessarily transferred from what is primary to its intermediate forms. Although a form of trinitarian faith may be vigorously espoused, it is unclear how a trinitarian dynamic actually operates in such belief. Whilst belief may come in some sense *from* God, the *way* such belief is held raises suspicions of a malfunction in the dynamic of belief. Unsurprisingly such believing usually generates a form of uncreative repetitive discourse.[11]

As a counterpoise to conventional objectivism the other extreme of the theological spectrum locates the impulse for belief within the realm of human religious subjectivity. Thus for Schleiermacher, belief arose from an inner relation to the redeemer: Jesus Christ.[12] To state such belief was to give linguistic expression to the religious self-consciousness as formed by the 'impression' of the redeemer. Belief was thus a response to piety and only *indirectly* a response to God. Primary belief was that which could be identified as an immediate utterance of the religious self-consciousness. On this view, Christian belief had no intrinsic trinitarian structure; since the triunity of the being of God was not, in Schleiermacher's view, an immediate utterance of the religious self-consciousness.[13]

---

[8] For further see Edward Farley, *Ecclesial Man: A Social Phenomenology of Faith and Reality* (Philadelphia: Fortress Press, 1975), ch. 1.

[9] The question of the source and impulse for Christian belief is implicit in George Lindbeck's discussion of the cognitivist, experiential-expressivist and cultural-linguistic approaches to Christian doctrine. See G. Lindbeck, *The Nature of Doctrine: Religion and Theology in a Postliberal Age* (London: SPCK, 1984).

[10] See Lindbeck, *Nature of Doctrine*, p. 80.

[11] This is at the heart of Karl Barth's critique of the fundamental articles of faith tradition in Protestantism. Here Christian belief becomes codified in certain 'irrevocable' articles of belief which are simply repeated but no longer able to be reconstituted by the Word of God; see *Church Dogmatics*, I/2 (Edinburgh: T. & T. Clark, 1975), pp. 863–6.

[12] Friedrich Schleiermacher, *The Christian Faith* (Edinburgh: T. & T. Clark, 1928), p. 56; cf. 'original impression' (p. 125); 'image' (p. 56) and 'influence' (p. 49).

[13] Schleiermacher, *Christian Faith*, pp. 738–51.

Both the above options imply different answers to the question of the impulse and source of Christian belief. In the first option the content of belief is codified in a manner that thwarts the dynamic of belief appropriate to the triune God. The latter form struggles to avoid the collapse of Christian belief into a *form* of Sabellian modalism.[14]

Important attempts have been made to recover the fullness of Christian belief and avoid the above problems. Here the *possibility* and *content* of belief is located more directly in what is 'given' for faith to apprehend.[15] Thus for Karl Barth belief is a graced response to an encounter with the Word of God, incarnate in Jesus Christ, witnessed to in scripture and proclaimed afresh in the church.[16] The impulse and source of Christian belief is located in the prevenient activity of God revealing Godself in such a way that faithful response is made possible. The possibility for belief rests here in the free and loving will of the revealer to be present for human beings, revealing the identity of the hidden God.[17] This makes possible a faithful response toward God through the power of the revealedness of God *from the side of the human being*.[18] The threefold form of God as revealer, revelation and revealedness, corresponding to Father, Son and Holy Spirit, is both *what* is given for faith to apprehend and determinative for the *way* human beings can respond.[19] In this trinitarian dynamic, belief is both a gift from God and a free human response of trust in God.[20] This dynamic in faith involves both a closure of 'the circle of divine judgement and grace' in Jesus Christ and a corresponding opening of the 'closed circle' of the human being.[21]

For Hans Urs von Balthasar belief that corresponds to the being of God involves aesthetic considerations. The mystery of Christianity has an inner form to be discerned by the light of faith as it attends to what is given.[22] Christ constitutes the 'fundamental form'.[23] The *visio Christi* –

---

[14] See e.g. William Hill, *The Three-Personed God: The Trinity as a Mystery of Salvation* (Washington: Catholic University of America Press, 1982), pp. 90f.

[15] Thus Barth, *Dogmatics*, IV/1, p. 742, can say: 'Faith stands or falls with its object ... It [faith] simply finds that which is already there for the believer and also for the unbeliever'.

[16] For Barth's discussion of the object and act of faith see *Dogmatics*, IV/1, pp. 740–79.

[17] Barth, *Dogmatics*, I/2, p. 245.

[18] Barth, *Dogmatics*, I/1, p. 451: 'God Himself becomes present to man not just externally, not just from above, but also from within, from below, subjectively. It is thus reality in that He does not merely come to man but encounters Himself *from man*' (my italics).

[19] The significance of Barth's pneumatology in this dynamic of faith is discussed by Philip Rosato, *The Spirit as Lord: The Pneumatology of Karl Barth* (Edinburgh: T. & T. Clark, 1981), pp. 60–5.

[20] See Karl Barth, *Dogmatics in Outline* (London: SCM, 1966), pp. 17 and 139f.

[21] Barth, *Dogmatics*, I/2, p. 743.

[22] Hans Urs von Balthasar, *The Glory of the Lord: A Theological Aesthetics*, vol. 1, 'Seeing the Form' (Edinburgh: T. & T. Clark, 1982), p. 156, refers to faith as 'the light of God becoming luminous in man, for, in his triune intimacy, God is known only by God'.

[23] Balthasar, *Glory of the Lord*, vol. 1. p. 576; cf. p. 153.

'the material heat and centre of his theology'[24] – is manifested in the 'transparency' of ecclesia's mediate forms (e.g. worship, ritual, creeds and confessions, forms of discipleship) which receive their form from the form of Christ.[25] Thus in statements of belief what 'shines forth' is 'Jesus Christ and his invisible truth'.[26]

Barth and von Balthasar express, in their own ways, a common answer to the question of the whence of belief. Christian belief is 'capacitated' by God. However, the correspondence implied here can never be isomorphic, for it is a correspondence with the plenitude of God's being.[27] Both theologians exemplify an effort to allow full freedom for the content of Christian belief to be determined by God in God's self-revelation. Significantly this approach has fostered richly textured patterns of belief consistent with believing that seeks faithfulness to 'the eternally rich God'.[28] The presupposition here is that God is present in the believing such that belief is Spirited along in a manner which honours the God of Jesus Christ. Belief here is derived from a source that is involved not only in the content of belief but also in the process of believing. What is believed and how it is believed are thus related through a dynamic intrinsic to God's own being.[29]

II. TRINITARIAN BELIEF: A COMMUNICATIVE PROCESS

When the accent is on belief as the *response* of faith, belief has the character of a communicative activity in which the founding reality of faith receives more concrete and determinate forms. This embodiment occurs through a variety of mediums including religious practices (e.g. worship and religious rites; services and care) and explicit articulations of faith (e.g. creeds and confessions, doctrine). When such belief is understood as merely a *product* of reflection upon what is given in the divine-

---

[24] Remark made by Donald Mackinnon in his intro. (p. 4) to the English ed. of von Balthasar's *Engagement with God*, trans, J. Halliburton (London: SPCK, 1975).

[25] Balthasar, *Glory of the Lord*, vol. 1, p. 252.

[26] Balthasar, *Glory of the Lord*, vol. 1, p. 242.

[27] See e.g., Balthasar,*Glory of the Lord*, vol. 1, p. 552. Von Balthasar's notion of the 'evermore' of the trinitarian event is discussed by Gerard O'Hanlon, *The Immutability of God in the Theology of Hans Urs von Balthasar* (Cambridge: CUP, 1990), pp. 124–30. For Barth see the discussion of simplicity in the text below.

[28] See Barth, *Dogmatics*, I/1, p. 763.

[29] This feature of belief is precisely what is missing in Alister McGrath's inquiry into the *genesis* of doctrine. See *The Genesis of Doctrine: A Study in the Foundations of Doctrinal Criticism*, Bampton Lectures for 1990 (Oxford: Basil Blackwell, 1990).

human relation the nature of belief, as a response from *within* a relation to God, is easily obscured. Christian belief cannot, on this latter view, be reduced to a merely interpretative activity somewhat secondary and distant from the founding reality of faith.[30] A more adequate view regards the believer's interpretative response to the gospel as an activity intrinsic to the dynamic of Christian faith and as the means for its enrichment. In this process the reality of Christian faith is brought to its full strength at the level of religious consciousness.[31] Furthermore, precisely because the response of faith occurs from within a genuine relation to the plenitude of God's own being, specifications of the content of that relation will have a necessarily provisional character. Thus an expectation is raised in faith of an ongoing communicative effort in which the full truth of the bond of believers in Christ (Gal. 3.28; cf. Col. 3.11) is continually and critically uncovered in myriad contexts. This points to the importance of the actual process and strategies by which Christians formulate their beliefs. Attentiveness to this process will reveal the deeper dynamics of the trinitarian impulse and source of belief.

(a) The search for foundations

The search for foundations has been an important recurring and controversial strategy initiating faith's attempt to deepen understanding of life in relation to God.[32] The search for, and identification of, the axiomatic substructure of belief has offered the possibility of fixity, permanence and definiteness for Christian faith. The danger of this strategy is that it tends to overstabilize the dynamic of faith's response to God and can result in the conventional objectivism in belief identified earlier. The search for a more adequate hermeneutic of foundations will have to take account of both the contingent nature of faith and the nature of that fundamental relation between God and human beings generative of Christian belief. It is difficult to depict fully this relation because in the Christian tradition this relation is characterized, in its divine aspect, as one of plenitude. This is concentrated in Jesus Christ (Col. 1.19, 2.9), richly dispersed in the Spirit (Rom. 5.5) and experienced by humankind as God's superabun-

---

[30] For an example, see Daniel Hardy's discussion of John Hick in 'Theology through Philosophy', in *The Modern Theologians: An Introduction to Christian Theology in the Twentieth Century*, 2 vols., ed. David Ford (London: OUP, 1989), vol. 2, pp. 54–9.

[31] For Bernard Lonergan, *Method in Theology* (London: Darton, Longman & Todd, 1972), pp. 295–334, doctrine is not an alien intrusion but rather a product of the 'differentiated consciousness'. What is not so clear is how this activity might contribute to the fullness of God's presence for the believer.

[32] For an important recent discussion see Colin Gunton, *The One, the Three and the Many: God, Creation and the Culture of Modernity*, the 1992 Bampton Lectures (Cambridge: CUP, 1993), pp. 129–35.

dance of grace, faith and love (1 Tim. 1.14). It is precisely this fullness of the being of God which has funded, among other things, a recurring trinitarian pattern in the history of Christian belief. This kind of plenitude is richness in perfection; the maximal concentration of 'God's expanding perfection'.[33]

Faithful response to a foundation construed in the above manner will generate ever deepening and lively belief and fresh possibilities for Christian discipleship. An interesting example here, from within the Christian mystical tradition, is the eighteenth-century Anglican, William Law (1686–1761).[34] In Law's later Christian life he rediscovered the soul-presence of the triune God. His reappropriation of the foundation of faith generated interior renewal, animated the fundamental beliefs of Christianity – incarnation and redemption – and broke the conventional forms of stating Christian belief in the church. For Law Christian belief was essentially a response to the 'outflow' or 'overflow' of God who was 'All Love'; in whom there could be no wrath.[35] Yet the response of faith belonged, for Law, to the movement of God's own vivifying presence in the believer, propelling faith into free-flowing abundant speech. The linguistic unravelling of this reality was the way in which praise of God found its precision and wisdom.

Law is but one example that testifies to the fact that foundations rooted in God are foundations with the capacity to disrupt what is stable and conventional in favour of fresh and surprising orderings of reality. The dynamic operating in Law's believing represented the logic of God's outward-directed movement of love, incarnate in Jesus Christ and continued in the regenerating activity of the Spirit. Believing within this trinitarian dynamic drew the believer deeper into the divine reality.

(b) The appeal of simplicity

Implicit within the search for foundations is an appeal to simplicity. The concept of simplicity is implied in any critical reduction in belief, a fact clearly evidenced in the important discussion in Protestantism of the 'essence of Christianity' and the appeal to certain fundamental articles of Christian belief.

At a practical level simplicities in the faith are important (e.g. catechesis, credal statements, worship, apologetics). However, the issue

[33] The notion of God's expanding perfection is discussed in Daniel Hardy and David Ford, *Jubilate: Theology in Praise* (London: Darton, Longman & Todd, 1984), pp. 63 and 161–7. See also above n. 27.
[34] The high point of Law's later works is *The Spirit of Love* reprinted in *The Classics of Western Spirituality*, ed. Paul G. Stanwood (London: SPCK, 1978). In particular 'The First Dialogue', pp. 391–427, is a good introduction to Law's mystical theology.
[35] Law, *Spirit of Love*, p. 429.

is of more than practical interest for at the heart of simplicities in Christian belief is a question about the simplicity of God. The concept of God as pure simplicity has been a dominant feature of the doctrine of God from early in the Christian tradition. As Karl Barth noted, theological talk of God has meant essentially 'only the simplicity of God and not the richness, at best the simplicity of riches, but at bottom only the simplicity'.[36] In Barth's discussion of the perfections of God he redeveloped the concept of simplicity in relation to plenitude as the characteristic relation of the Lord of Glory:

> Consideration of the divine attributes can but move in circles around the one but infinitely rich being of God whose simplicity is abundance itself and whose abundance is simplicity itself.[37]

Consequently, for Barth, God's simplicity was not 'poverty': 'On the contrary, God is one in the fullness of His deity and constant in its living vigour'. In this way the doctrine of the Trinity as co-inherence of plenitude and simplicity is the Christian doctrine of God.[38]

This discussion suggests that faithful response to the kind of God referred to above will generate communicative patterns of belief that evidence an ongoing dialectic between highly concentrated statements of belief and extended forms of discourse. Something of this dynamic is present when the writer of the letter to the Ephesians asks the church to pray 'that whenever I open my mouth, words may be given me so that I will fearlessly make known the mystery of the gospel' (Eph. 6.19). The point here is that the gospel of God's creating, redeeming and sanctifying love may not be simple but *it may be put simply*. However, as the writer suggests, finding the wisdom of simplicity in stating the gospel requires a community of intercessors seeking the fullness of the *communio* of the triune God. When the criterion of simplicity operates to thwart ongoing enlargement of faith, belief has ceased responding out of the fullness of God's presence. Within a trinitarian framework simplicity can not be an end in itself, but rather a *recurring moment* in the communicative dynamic of Christian faith.

(c) The emergence of hierarchy

When the dynamic of Christian faith is operating in a free and disciplined manner the search for foundations and the appeal of simplicity contribute to a grading in Christian belief. This grading of Christian belief

---

[36] Barth, *Dogmatics*, II/1, p. 329.
[37] Barth, *Dogmatics*, II/1, p. 406.
[38] Barth, *Dogmatics*, II/1, pp. 326f.; cf. pp. 445f.

represents a practical effort to prioritize for the purpose of communicating the more central matters of faith. However, to the extent that hierarchy emerges as a response to complexity *per se* – indicative of an attempt to assign relative values, to select and differentiate in order to avoid what is trivial – more substantive issues are involved. From this perspective, hierarchy in Christian belief is a way of responding to the richly differentiated form of God's presence. In this sense grading of belief is what happens as faith is *formed by*, and comes to form *in relation to*, the quite distinctive and particular presence of the God revealed in the Judaeo-Christian tradition. This dynamic in Christian belief has its roots in the long-held conviction of the essential unity of Christianity. This conviction was generated out of the early church's experience that 'God was in Christ reconciling the world to himself' (2 Cor. 5.19). A consequence of this was the affirmation of one Lord, one faith and one baptism (Eph. 4.5). This one faith, encapsulated in the early church's confession of the Lordship of Christ (e.g. Acts 2.36; Rom. 10.9; 1 Cor. 1.23) required a fresh appropriation of an inherited Jewish monotheism.

The new and surprising relation to God through Jesus Christ in the power of the Spirit was the catalyst and guide for the reconstitution of the doctrine of God in the early centuries of Christianity. The intense conflicts that attended the development of the trinitarian pattern of Christian belief indicated just how difficult and necessary it was for the early church to state what was of critical importance in order for belief to remain faithful to the presence of God in Jesus Christ. The 'simple' solution of Arius, for example, generated a mistaken hierarchy of belief in relation to the Father and the Son that undermined the fullness of Christian redemption.[39]

Underlying the emergence of hierarchy in Christian belief is the presupposition that God's presence and action is not marked by sameness but by rich variety, evoking a response of praise as this presence is discerned and indwelt. In particular, it has been the church's experience of the crucified and risen Jesus present as life-giving Spirit that has provided the energy and direction for ecclesial existence. Discipleship formed and motivated by such a focus on God is one that evidences an emergent cruciform and transformative pattern (Phil. 3.10). This points to a reciprocal relationship between the inner dynamic of Christian discipleship and fundamental Christian beliefs. Properly focused and graded belief ought to find embodiment in forms of discipleship that honour God's Christ-like presence and action in the world. The ongoing nature of this

---

[39] Thus in Athanasius' view the attribution of a creaturely status to the Son negated the possibility of full salvation, i.e., deification and full immortality. For a contemporary discussion see Francis Young, *From Nicaea to Chalcedon* (London: SCM, 1983), ch. 2.

activity points to the emergent and unfinished structure of Christian belief.[40]

The above discussion suggests that the content of belief emerges into full form through a dynamic process requiring the active engagement of the human subject. Key elements in this participation were identified in terms of the search for foundations, the appeal to simplicity and the emergence of hierarchy. A distinctively trinitarian dynamic was discerned in this process of belief formation. It was a dynamic characterized by an essential interwovenness between what is believed, how it comes to form, and the One from whom believing takes its cue.

III. TRINITARIAN BELIEF: THE ECCLESIAL FORM

Insofar as the dynamics of belief are trinitarian they are *necessarily ecclesial*. What is being identified here is a fundamental axiom of trinitarian theology: communion generates communion. This arises from the fact that *faithful* response to the God identified in the economy of salvation as the God constituted eternally as a communion of persons ought ideally to be a response that finds embodiment in a new communion of persons in society and the wider creation.[41]

The position adopted here suggests that it is inadequate to identify the church as mere *context* for Christian belief. There is a critical interplay between the church's own worship and mission and its attempt to express the truth of its life in the form of specific beliefs.[42] This suggests a reflexive relation between ecclesia and Christian faith. In ecclesia the truth of the bond with Christ in God receives determinate form: ecclesia is the place in which the truth of the gospel of God is embodied and maintained.

(a) Guarding the truth in the church

An important implication of the foregoing argument is that the church's attempt to state its belief becomes a critical means through which the deepest reality of its life is organized, expressed, argued about, and thus guarded. In this respect it is possible to identify the dynamic by which the ecclesial community's primary beliefs are developed and maintained. Important here are 'governing doctrines': those principles and rules

[40] See e.g. Dietrich Ritschl, *The Logic of Theology* (London: SCM, 1986), p. 122.
[41] See Gunton, *The One, The Three and The Many*, pp. 210–31, for a recent discussion of the question of Trinity and sociality.
[42] For further see Stephen Sykes, *The Identity of Christianity: Theologians and the Essence of Christianity from Schleiermacher to Barth* (London: SPCK, 1984), ch. 11.

which guide a community in the articulation of its fundamental beliefs.[43] The eighteenth-century Anglican, Daniel Waterland (1683–1740), identified fourteen such rules. He considered most of them faulty because their application could not generate a trinitarian form to the Christian covenant.[44]

Governing doctrines guide the community of faith but such rules belong to a richer dynamic through which the right focus in Christian belief is maintained. The Reformation doctrine of justification by faith is an instructive example in this respect. Luther's focus on the justification of the sinner before God provided the hermeneutical clue for the reappropriation of the dogmatic tradition concerning Christ and the Trinity. In this sense the doctrine of justification identified the dynamic by which the incarnate Word and the Spirit effected human transformation in relation to God. The doctrine was clearly more than a governing rule, identifying how persons in the church were reconstituted in the truth and righteousness of the triune God.[45]

The actual history of the Christian tradition indicates that the operational doctrines of Christianity, i.e. those that identify the dynamic of revitalized faithful believing, can and do vary. In this respect the Lutheran theologian, Jaroslav Pelikan, has suggested that the doctrine of the church has become 'the bearer of the *whole* of the Christian message for the twentieth century, as well as the *recapitulation of the entire doctrinal tradition* from the preceding centuries' (my italics).[46] Pelikan offers here a highly programmatic statement for the reordering and presentation of the gospel message. How might it be true? Within the Christian tradition it would be necessary to show how central Christian affirmations concerning the economy of God's salvation through Christ in the Spirit might be developed in relation to the rich reality of ecclesial life – its worship, confession and discipleship in the world. Significantly, it is precisely the interweaving of a doctrine of God in relation to the church that can be discerned in important theological efforts across the ecclesial spectrum of the late twentieth century.[47]

[43] Governing beliefs are discussed by William Christensen, *Doctrines of Religious Communities: A Philosophical Study* (New Haven: Yale University Press, 1987), pp. 2, 11, 219–21, 230.
[44] See Waterland's 'Discourse of Fundamentals', in *The Works of the Rev. Daniel Waterland*, 6 vols. (Oxford: OUP, 1843), vol. 5, pp. 77–104.
[45] For further see Jaroslav Pelikan, *The Christian Tradition: A History of the Development of Doctrine*, 5 vols. (Chicago: University of Chicago Press, 1971–88), vol. 4, pp. 156ff.
[46] Pelikan, *The Christian Tradition*, vol. 5, p. 282.
[47] See e.g. John Zizioulas, *Being as Communion: Studies in Personhood and the Church* (London: Darton, Longman & Todd, 1985). From a more practical ecclesial perspective see the 1994 report by the Doctrine Commission of the Uniting Church in Australia: 'Ordination and Ministry in the Uniting Church in Australia'. Here a doctrine of ministry is developed within a trinitarian framework.

Recognition of the ecclesial nature of Christian belief has provided conditions conducive to a renewal of trinitarian theology and its correlatives, a Christology of the humanity of Christ and a doctrine of the Spirit as life-giving presence. This renewal in the form and content of Christian belief corresponds to the contemporary search for forms of Christian discipleship patterned after the humanity of Christ and enlivened by the Holy Spirit.[48] The church's truth concerns are best guarded, it seems, as they receive embodiment at the level of concrete practice of faith.

(b) Christian belief as a public deed

The fact that Christians seek to guard the truth of the gospel, and in doing so state what they believe, is evidence of the rather obvious, but not to be overlooked, fact that the Christian community has an active and important part to play in the formation of its beliefs. In this activity the bond in Christ *formative* of the community now appears as a *product* of the community of faith. Through this externalizing of the community's bond in Christ, the church's memory of the narrative of creation and salvation, and its hope for the final consummation of the world, can endure in the form of corporate public expression. This gives a particular enduring significance to the ancient Apostolic and Nicene creeds, especially in the context of Christian worship. Public belief of this kind strengthens the self-understanding of the Christian community in its calling to live a life of reconciliation and compassion patterned after God's pilgrimage of reconciliation and perfecting of creation in Jesus and the Spirit. The emergence of new forms of community in the unlikeliest places thus bears witness to the character of the God worshipped in the Christian community and identified in its primary public beliefs.

(c) The ongoing dynamic of Christian belief

The desire for a global form of public faith has persisted in Christianity. It is evidently a deed worth pursuing, notwithstanding the conflicts and challenges that attend it. The persistence is expressive of a desire to identify communal faith that has authority as normative Christian belief. The irony, of course, is that this ideal actually provokes as well as resolves conflict. In this sense it might make more sense to speak of an unfinished consensus in what constitutes Christian belief. The provisional status of such belief is not simply a negative one, the result of the inability of frail human beings to agree together. Rather, the question of

[48] See e.g. Colin Gunton's discussion of the theology of Edward Irving, in *The Actuality of Atonement: A Study of Metaphor, Rationality and the Christian Tradition* (Edinburgh: T. & T. Clark, 1988), pp. 128–37.

the unfinishedness of Christian belief is a 'given' of the mystery of the gospel which is, by its very character, both resistant to full thematization and generative of a rich variety of authentic Christian responses. This points to the fact that there is an abundance of 'play' in the matrix of ecclesial belief that is constrained by the love of Christ and embodied in myriad contexts of human life. Christian belief remains a deed in process.

The above discussion suggests that Christian belief cannot be *simply* repeated. Merely to repeat the deed entails both a rejection of its contingent status and a dangerous sacralizing of a past particular statement of faith. Pure repetition is thus a sign of infidelity to, rather than security in, the gospel. An ongoing faithfulness in Christian belief will require a fresh discernment of the presence of the triune God in newly emergent contexts. Within a trinitarian dynamic what is required is a creative repetition in belief in which *freshness through sameness* is the ideal sought. Such communication corresponds to the creativity of God's threefold action in the economy of salvation.

Clearly, continuity and identity in the faith cannot be construed simply, either in terms of over-formalized statements of belief or of a radically relativized faith unassimilated to the tradition. From an ecclesial point of view such manoeuvres are indicative of a falsely stabilized institution, either through neglect of contemporaneity or rejection of its own history. In the former, stability is over-reached, in the latter it is under-achieved. Both strategies are expressive of the lure of simplicity in a complex world. At a deeper level such developments are the result of a loss of the trinitarian dynamic of belief. Belief that is formed from, and informed by, God's Christ-like work through the life-giving Spirit operates quite differently. It is a Spirit-informed belief that finds its delight dwelling in, and probing further, the 'depth of brightness and precision of wisdom'[49] of the God whose light has been made to shine in the face of Jesus Christ to give the light of the knowledge of the glory of God.

---

[49] The phrase can be found in Hardy and Ford, *Jubilate*, p. 55.

5

'Orthodoxy' and 'Liberalism'

STEPHEN SYKES

INTRODUCTION

THIS may be the moment to state publicly that in the late 1960s a group of theologians teaching in English universities began to meet with a fair degree of regularity in support of one another. Dan Hardy, then Lecturer in Theology at Birmingham, was the group's most senior member.[1] Although of widely differently theological stances, the group shared a knowledge of the story of modern German theology, and a concern that the systematic, philosophical and hermeneutical problems faced by Barth, Bultmann and their successors should be understood in the then somewhat flaccid English theological context. The group had a variety of literary and other ambitions, most of which came to nothing. But from a vantage point some thirty years later it is not too strong to point to an almost complete transformation of the atmosphere of English theology, in which it is now possible to speak confidently and unselfconsciously of the task of systematics within English universities in a way unthinkable thirty years earlier. Dan Hardy's contribution to this process has been a major one, especially in his sustained commitment to the Society for the Study of Theology. Here, as elsewhere, he has constantly reminded his hearers of the deeply-laid metaphysical presuppositions behind the sometimes superficially conceived disputes about Christian doctrine.

Paramount within Hardy's contribution has been his delineation of the transformational potential of God's presence within the social order; could the church but do proper justice to it on understanding and practice. In this essay, which links three Van Mildert Professors of Divinity, it is proposed to argue for a dynamic understanding of 'orthodoxy'. By this is meant a way of inhabiting the Christian tradition which involves hard conceptual work. To be orthodox is not a matter of lazily repeating the decisions and arguments of the past to meet each new critical proposal. The transformational dynamic of orthodoxy is only in evidence where theologians fully accept the contemporary task of uncovering presuppo-

---

[1] The other members of the group were Dr Rex Ambler, the Revd Robert Morgan, Dr R. W. A. MacKinney and myself.

sitions, analysing arguments and engaging in vigorous dialogue. This has been Hardy's outstanding gift to the contexts in which he has worked, and this essay is written in acknowledgement and gratitude.

I. THE PROBLEM

The problem with which this essay proposes to deal is the imprecision in both the terms 'orthodoxy' and 'liberalism', when used in theological contexts. Conceptual imprecision, of course, can be dealt with by stipulative definition: 'when I use the word "orthodoxy"', I could say, 'what I mean by it is such-and-such'. And so long as you were willing at least to allow that I had some right to offer a definition, and if I were reasonably consistent in my use of the term, the problem would evaporate. But language is not really like that, because there is no way of erasing from the memory all the other usages of the term 'orthodoxy' to which we have been exposed. Even a rigorous prescriptive definition could hardly escape the impact of other meanings, seeping into the discussion and contaminating it. Because of this porosity in our language it is safer, and in the end a more satisfactory method of approach, to start with ordinary language with all its imprecision and ambiguity, and by analysis and discussion to work towards an elucidation.

On this account it is *because* the terms 'orthodoxy' and 'liberalism' are imprecise that they are frequently used in a polarized sense to denote mutually exclusive and antagonistic theological styles and commitments. Polarization is, in fact, a sociologically conditioned by-product of the process of secularization. Precisely because of the speed of change, it is impossible to be absolutely conservative. Os Guinness put the dilemma of the conservative in the following way:

> To defend conservatism well, they [sc. modern conservatives] must do it in a progressive way; to fight for tradition, they must use weapons which are modern. Like democrats condemned to become illiberal in the process of defending pluralism or humanitarians who become inhuman in defence of humanity, modern conservatives are caught in a double bind ... They will resist change to the death, but in the struggle for tradition not a single feature of their familiar world will be left unchanged.[2]

Precisely because of this necessity their instinct is to sharpen the boundaries between themselves and those whom they oppose. The process is exacerbated by the modern media which particularly relish passionate

---

[2] Os Guinness, *The Gravedigger File* (London: Hodder, 1983), p. 184.

opposition. In the process of simplification which the media require, those with a differentiated analysis come to realize that a polarized view is the price of their admission to the public forum.

The consequence is that the terms 'orthodoxy' and 'liberalism' which are not antithetical by any kind of inherent necessity become antithetical in use. In this respect they are like the terms 'Catholic' and 'Protestant'. A moment's thought will reveal the fact that no Protestant would accept for a moment that she or he was not a member of the universal church. Only if 'Catholic' or 'Protestant' were to be the name of a member of a particular denomination would the usage be clear. The moment it is used adjectivally to signify the profession of particular kinds of beliefs, it ceases to be exclusive. A person can be a catholic Protestant without obvious self-contradiction. (For this reason it makes absolutely no sense to say that because, for example, of the decision to ordain women to the priesthood the Church of England has 'ceased to be catholic'.)

Similarly, though not in precisely the same way, the terms 'orthodoxy' and 'liberalism' are not self-evidently antithetical. What *are* antithetical are the terms 'orthodoxy' and 'heresy'; or (more problematically) 'liberalism' and 'conservatism'. But precisely because liberalism *are* not self-evidently heresy, one would have hoped that, at least in intellectual contexts, a measure of precision would make controversialists hesitate.

One episode in recent theological history is instructive. Karl Barth self-consciously set himself to oppose the theological novelties of his own teachers, beginning with the famous church historian, Adolf von Harnack. But when his work began to be known in the United States it elicited an outburst from a Calvinist fundamentalist, Cornelius van Til, who designated Barth's theology a 'new Modernism'.[3] A more frequent term for Barth's endeavour, however, is 'neo-orthodoxy'. Apart from illustrating the uncertain character of these labels, van Til's self-proclaimed defence of orthodoxy, in his case the beleaguered post-Darwinian Protestant orthodoxy of high Calvinism, demonstrates the uncertainty of that term. The problem is, indeed, imprecision; we need to advance beyond slogans.

II. THE CLASSIC THEORY OF ORTHODOXY, AND AN ALTERNATIVE

The category of 'heresy', the logical antithesis of 'orthodoxy', was refined

---

[3] Cornelius van Til, *The New Modernism: An Appraisal of the Theology of Barth and Brunner* (Philadelphia: Presbyterian and Reformed Publishing Co, 1946). For an enlightening account of this episode, see Philip R. Thorne, *The Reception and Influence of Karl Barth in American Evangelical Theology* (PhD thesis: University of Cambridge, 1993).

within the first two hundred years of the church's existence. For a description of the standard patristic view of heresy, and a sophisticated alternative to it, we can turn to Professor H. E. W. Turner's neglected classic, *The Pattern of Christian Truth*, Bampton Lectures for 1954 (delivered while he was Lightfoot Professor of Divinity in the University of Durham).[4] Turner was one of the very few English theologians to give an extended account and criticism of Walter Bauer's *Rechtglaübigkeit und Ketzerei in ältesten Christentum* (first edition 1934; second edition 1964; translated into English in 1971 as *Orthodoxy and Heresy in Earliest Christianity*[5]). This work had fundamentally questioned the appropriateness of the concepts of orthodoxy and heresy in the light of the great variety of doctrinal views of early Christian writers. Bauer's argument had a great and continuing impact in Germany, especially in Protestant theological circles. As in earlier generations, its failure to achieve major status in the British Isles can be attributed to the combination of a failure to read German scholarship in the original, and the existence of a competent refutation in English. In the case of patristic study one must also take account of the astonishing dominance of a textbook, J. N. D. Kelly's *Early Christian Doctrine* (first edition 1958), which, though it claimed not to have attempted 'to define the intrinsic nature of orthodoxy',[6] nonetheless gave a very different account of the development of theology in the early church from that offered by Bauer, to whom reference is nowhere made.

But Turner was no mere reactionary. Like Bauer, he was unconvinced by what he called 'the classical theory of the origin of heresy' offered by the church fathers of the early centuries. According to this, the church had kept unsullied the teaching of Jesus and his apostles, from which heresy is simply a departure and an offshoot. The existence of heresy is not surprising because it was prophesied. Moreover the heretics are motivated by pride and the spirit of factiousness. Whereas the truth is one, heresy is infinitely diverse and self-contradictory. Unlike catholic truth, heresies are merely local phenomena. Finally, they represent a dilution of pure Christian teaching with philosophies of pagan origin.

Turner recognizes that as an account of the history of the early church this will not do. Early Christian thought was much more fluid than the picture of a fixed and static norm suggests. The New Testament itself contains 'a considerable variety of theological traditions'.[7] He recognizes that the writings of the sub-apostolic period cannot be reduced to a

---

[4] H. E. W. Turner, *The Pattern of Christian Truth: A Study in the Relations between Orthodoxy and Heresy in the Early Church* (London: Mowbray, 1954).
[5] Eds. R. Kraft and G. Krodel (Philadelphia: Fortress, 1971).
[6] J. N. D. Kelly, *Early Christian Doctrine* (London: Black, 1958), p. v.
[7] Turner, *Pattern*, p. 9.

'single doctrinal common denominator'.[8] Different parts of the Christian world developed different traits in their approaches to theological problems. Turner accepts the fundamental thesis of Freidrich Loofs that orthodoxy was a 'fruitful fusion of theological traditions' independently incapable of doing justice to the fullness of that truth. One should note that the contemporary biblical scholar, Raymond Brown, holds precisely this view in relation to the strands of Johannine and Pauline Christianity, whose fusion he regards as the basis of so-called 'early Catholicism'.[9] Turner's examples are drawn from a later period, but amount to the same general structure.

Furthermore Turner argues that a student of early Christianity has to accept some theory of actual development in the early centuries to account for the fate which befell the reputations of both Tertullian and Origen in later times. Doctrinal tendencies which had passed as orthodox at an earlier stage 'were superannuated in the light of later developments'.[10] He concludes:

> Orthodoxy in the second century must be differently interpreted in the fourth and fifth. If orthodoxy itself certainly antedated the achievement of fixed doctrinal norms, it begins to wear a different aspect after the process of doctrinal formulation had got properly under way. Even at the same period standards of orthodoxy might differ in different fields.[11]

From this it is apparent that Turner is now obliged to offer an alternative theory of orthodoxy. He makes clear that he is unwilling to accept the radical theses of Harnack, Martin Werner and Rudolf Bultmann. He discusses and disputes the thesis of Walter Bauer to the effect that orthodoxy is the late creation of a minority group under episcopal leadership, which eventually triumphed and rewrote the early history of the church. No more is a staunch Anglican Canon of Durham likely to accept the theory of John Henry Cardinal Newman concerning the 'Development of Christian Doctrine'. Indeed in a certain sense we may say that what Turner is confronting is the problem which Anglicans have had since 1845, when Newman joined the Roman Catholic Church.[12] What

---

[8] Turner, *Pattern*, p. 10.
[9] See, for example, his *Biblical Exegesis and Church Doctrine* (New York: Paulist, 1985), esp. the essay, 'The New Testament Background for the Emerging Doctrine of "Local Church"', pp. 114–34.
[10] Turner, *Pattern*, p. 14.
[11] Turner, *Pattern*, p. 16.
[12] The problem is partly addressed in the Anglican-Roman Catholic International Commission's Final Report of 1982; but there are still considerable difficulties to confront. See S. W. Sykes, 'Newman, Anglicanism, and Fundamentals', in *Newman after a Hundred Years*, eds. I. Ker and A. G. Hill (Oxford: OUP, 1990), pp. 52–99.

understanding of development can Anglicans offer which is able on the one hand to account for the facts of early church history, but is not simply a legitimation of the outcome of subsequent theological disputes in favour of the dominant parties to them?

A brief sketch of Turner's positive theory of orthodoxy is now required. In due course I will offer a discussion of it in the light of Mariological doctrines, the Immaculate Conception and the Blessed Assumption.

Turner argues that what a modern theologian must give is an account of development which does justice at once to the 'fixed' and to the 'flexible' elements of Christian theology and their interaction. There are three aspects to the fixed elements, the church's grasp on what he calls 'the religious facts themselves', the biblical revelation, and the Creed and Rule of Faith. By the 'religious facts themselves' Turner intends to draw attention to such phenomena as the singing of hymns to Christ as God, spoken of by Pliny, or the opening words of 2 Clement, 'Brethren, we must think of Christ as of God'. Christians, he claims, 'lived Trinitarianly long before the evolution of Nicene orthodoxy', citing as evidence baptism in the threefold name. Likewise, in the realm of eucharistic theology Turner perceives a 'realistic experience of the Eucharist' long before formally articulated theological accounts of consecration or conversion. Turner constantly returns to this phrase 'the religious facts themselves', but the explanation is not precise. The claim, however, is a strong one; to embrace these 'facts' is to have 'a relatively full and fixed experimental grasp of what was involved religiously in being a Christian'; they form 'the instinctive basis for [the] exercise of Christian common sense'; they make possible 'instinctive spiritual discrimination'. In this connection Turner invokes the Latin tag, *lex orandi*, provided it is not understood as implying something too static. As one of the 'fixed' elements 'the religious facts themselves' are capable of a variety of expressions.[13]

The second element is what Turner terms 'the Biblical Revelation'. Even before the completion of the canon of the New Testament, Turner observes to what an extent early theological argument turned on proof texts from the Old Testament. Despite the often strained and unconvincing form of patristic exegesis, Turner adduces this as evidence of the desire to 'maintain at any cost the Biblical basis of Christian theology'.[14]

Finally, the Creeds and the Rule of Faith constitute evidence going back into the apostolic period itself for a continuous concern for what Turner eventually calls 'an Agreed Syllabus'.[15] Here the references include several to J. N. D. Kelly's 1950 publication, *Early Christian*

[13] Turner, *Pattern*, p. 28.
[14] Turner, *Pattern*, p. 29.
[15] Turner, *Pattern*, p. 475.

Creeds, which itself had drawn upon C. H. Dodd's highly influential *The Apostolic Preaching and Its Developments* (1936). Kelly's view was that though there was no substance in the myth of a meeting after the Ascension at which each of the Apostles contributed an article of the Creed, the conviction that the 'rule of faith' had been inherited from the Apostles 'contains more than a germ of truth':

> Not only was the content of that rule, in all essentials, foreshadowed by the 'pattern of teaching' accepted in the apostolic Church, but its characteristic lineaments and outline found their prototypes in the confessions and credal summaries contained in the New Testament documents.[16]

It is apparent from this whole account that Turner is ready to acknowledge considerable internal variety within what he calls the 'fixed elements'. But they are explicitly contrasted with so-called 'flexible elements', which include differences in Christian idiom, such as a contrast between the eschatological and the metaphysical modes of interpreting Christianity, differences in philosophical background and terminology, and differences in the characteristics of individual theologians.[17] The subsequent bulk of the book, after an account and criticism of Bauer's more radical theory, amounts to a thorough examination of the patristic period with a view to testing the new theory. In these chapters Turner is at pains to do proper justice to the plain facts of partial understanding, disagreements, and developing ideas, whilst at the same time defending a theory of the 'autonomy' of orthodoxy evolving from a common starting-point in the biblical tradition, engaged in a running battle with heresies of various kinds, and enjoying to a greater or lesser extent cross-fertilization from independent theological traditions. Fundamental are the 'Biblical facts', the mighty saving acts of God, mediated through the *lex orandi*, developing through the Rule of Faith towards an intellectual formulation in various centres of Christian thought by a process of what Turner calls 'Catholic thinking'. The sources of orthodoxy are Scripture, Tradition and Reason, though not independently of each other. The pattern of Christian truth 'unfolds', he believes, as the three strands of it converge upon one another. The 'Christian facts themselves' constantly resist the imposition of an alien framework, and an instinctive rejection of heresy constantly comes to view in Christian history. Behind it lies what Turner designated 'a kind of Christian common sense exercised at all its levels within the Christian Church, which is merely another name for the guidance of the Holy Spirit leading

[16] J. N. D. Kelly, *Early Christian Creeds* (London: Black, 1950), p. 29.
[17] Turner, *Pattern*, p. 31–5.

the Church into all truth'. Such guidance is never automatic, and is consistent with the continuing presence of sin, blindness and error. To speak of 'infallibility' would be 'a misuse of categories'.[18]

Together with this classic modern defence of orthodoxy written in the 1950s, it is instructive to take Turner's 1976 essay in the Report of The Doctrine Commission of the Church of England, *Christian Believing*.[19] On the Commission were theologians of a much more radical turn of mind, especially Professors Wiles (who was the Chairman), Evans, Lampe and Nineham. 'This has not been an easy report to write', was the understated opening sentence of the Chairman's Preface.[20] The contrast between Turner's essay and those of Lampe or Wiles makes this abundantly clear. What is also apparent is the fact that, confronted with a radically different attitude both to New Testament criticism and to the interpretation of the patristic period, Turner was unyielding. Here the same three factors are defended, the self-revelation of God recorded in biblical data, the Catholic Creeds, and a commitment to the defence of ontological trinitarianism in theology. The focal point in both religion and theology is the incarnate Lord. The Virgin Birth and the Empty Tomb, inescapable parts of the evidence as a whole, 'set the boundary limits of the incarnate life which lies between them', the miracles depending on the mystery not the mystery on the miracles.[21] Although some of the characteristic phrases of *The Pattern of Christian Truth* are no longer repeated, the essential standpoint is unchanged. There is an obvious tension between Turner's essay and the implications of the jointly signed report, which makes the Creeds a kind of dialogue partner, in an ongoing theological discussion within the church, albeit the senior partner.

It is not my intention to discuss Turner's theory in any detail. Its major rival in contemporary theology is Edward Farley's important methodological study, *Ecclesial Reflection*.[22] Farley likewise studies and rejects the classical theory of orthodoxy. Although he lacks Turner's patristic knowledge, he brings to his reconstruction of the working of what he terms 'ecclesial reflection' a philosophical acuteness sharpened by sophisticated consideration of phenomenology. He is therefore sensitive to social processes at work in the performance of the tasks of theology, processes which intellectual historians sometimes neglect. But the subject-matter of history is plainly provided by the problem with which Newman, Walter Bauer and Turner are all concerned, namely tracing patterns of continuity in Christian theology into the modern period. If

[18] Turner, *Pattern*, p. 498.
[19] (London: SPCK, 1976).
[20] *Christian Believing*, p. xi.
[21] *Christian Believing*, p. 120.
[22] Edward Farley, *Ecclesial Reflection: An Anatomy of Theological Method* (Philadelphia: Fortress, 1982).

his language and many of his conclusions are much more radical, we are discernibly on the same territory. Turner's contribution in the defence of a conservative alternative to the classic theory of orthodoxy deserves recognition as a major effort and commands respect. We must now examine its relation to 'liberalism'.

III. LIBERALISM

We are constantly being warned, and rightly, about the danger of '-ism' words in intellectual history. They are constructs. They are shorthand and tend to obliterate important distinctions. They are often coined for the purpose of dismissing or ridiculing beliefs or doctrines worthy of more careful examination. They do not escape the charge of coming loaded with unexamined intellectual content, masquerading as neutral categorization. All these things are true of many pejorative uses of the term 'liberalism' in contemporary theological controversy. Turner himself scarcely uses the term. It is not even deployed in his account of Harnack. On the contrary, for him (Turner) Liberalism (with a capital 'L') is said to be 'deeply committed to the ontological idiom', and constitutes an opposite pole to eschatological thinking in Christian theology.[23]

The term 'liberal' contains etymologically that sense of the word 'free' which sets itself in antithesis to slavery or unfreedom. Not all freedom, however, needs to be defined as 'freedom from'; important and long-developed themes in Christian theology draw equal attention to the existence of 'freedom for'. Nonetheless atonement theology has, from the first, embedded 'freedom from bondage' to the devil, to death, to law and to sin in the basic metaphorical collection of Christian ideas of atonement. To be liberal in the sense of being free in open-hearted generosity is also a biblical usage, found in the King James Version of Isa. 32.5.

Freedom from constraints can have both negative and positive connotation in ordinary English. On the one hand the seventeenth-century controversialist, Henry Dodwell, is said to have been so liberal in his discourse in London that a gentleman threatened to bring him into danger. On the other hand 'liberal opinions concerning the duties of kings' would be, in Gibbon's mind, views which were free from narrow prejudice, open-minded or candid.[24] The burgeoning use of 'liberal' and eventually 'liberalism' in both religious and political contexts is the coinage of the early nineteenth century. John Henry Newman's *Apologia pro Vita Sua* (1864) and John Stuart Mill's 1859 essay *On Liberty* stand,

---

[23] Turner, *Pattern*, p. 496.
[24] Examples from *The Oxford English Dictionary* (Oxford: OUP, 1989), art. 'Liberal'.

therefore, in the middle of the process of defining how the term is going to be used, and have rights to a certain classical status. In Newman's work it is the case that, as Stephen Thomas' research has clarified, to call a person a liberal is the worst thing you could say.[25] By 'liberalism' he simply means 'the anti-dogmatic principle and its developments'.[26] The following is his considered view:

> Whenever men are able to act at all, there is the chance of extreme and intemperate action; and therefore, when there is exercise of mind, there is the chance of wayward or mistaken exercise. Liberty of thought is in itself a good; but it gives an opening to false liberty. Now by Liberalism I mean false liberty of thought, or the exercise of thought upon matters, in which, from the constitution of the human mind, thought cannot be brought to any successful issue, and therefore is out of place. Among such matters are first principles of whatever kind; and of these the most sacred and momentous are expecially to be reckoned the truths of Revelation.[27]

From this it is absolutely apparent that Liberalism wherever and whenever it appears is false, a stipulative definition with a vengeance. This way of viewing the matter is not merely somewhat idiosyncratic as Professor Owen Chadwick and Professor Nicholas Lash have asserted. It simply functions as a name for a bag of views opposed to the Christian faith as he (Newman) understood it. It marks a boundary between true and false liberty of thought, but it tells us nothing about where that boundary lies. It does not help us, for example, in determining how the exercise of thought may be conducted in a way consistent with revelation, which is, after all, the whole point of Christian theology. We are simply told, prescriptively, that there cannot be such a thing as liberal Christian thinking. But, as Nicholas Lash justly points out, the opposite of what Newman calls 'liberalism' is, in fact, that conservative ideology, beloved of clerics and the religiously neurotic, to which Bernard Lonergan gave the name 'classicism'.[28] That Newman himself was sensitive to 'all manner of complexity, uncertainty, diversity and darkness' in theology and religious life',[29] that he saw the necessity of change both in religion and politics, that he accepted the (liberal) notion of a free church in a free state, is all evidence of the necessity of not taking his definition simply at

[25] John Henry Newman, *Letters and Diaries*, vol. II (Oxford: OUP, 1979), p. 317, cited in Stephen Thomas, *Newman and Heresy* (Cambridge: CUP, 1991), p. 2.
[26] Newman, *Apologia*, ed. M. J. Svaglic (Oxford: OUP, 1967), p. 54.
[27] Newman, *Apologia*, pp. 255f.
[28] N. L. A. Lash, 'Tides and Twilight: Newman since Vatican II', in *Newman after a Hundred Years*, p. 460.
[29] Lash, 'Tides and Twilight', p. 461.

face value to cover all forms of what might plausibly or historically be counted as 'liberal' thought.

Nonetheless there is a case to answer, and it is right to take the warning of Newman (and, of course, many other subsequent theologians, including Barth and Turner) seriously. Standard presentations of the intellectual ancestry and content of liberalism, in its political or social aspect, raise complex questions. One example may be cited:

> Liberalism is the culmination of a development that goes back to the Hebrew prophets, the teachings of the pre-Socratic philosophers, and The Sermon on the Mount, from all of which there emerged a sense of the importance of human individuality, a liberation of the individual from complete subservience to the group, and a relaxation of the tight hold of custom, law and authority.[30]

The theologian is at once alerted to the oddity of citing sayings of Jesus of the form, 'You have heard what our forefathers were told, but what I tell you is this . . .' (Matt. 5.33–34), as evidence of the relaxation of the hold of authority. Moreover to speak of liberalism as encouraging a 'liberation of the individual from *complete* subservience to the group' immediately suggests the existence of forms of group-consciousness or group-authority which do not amount to *complete* subordination. Once again, in other words, we hear the sound of boundaries being drawn, without precise indication of where and how, but this time from within the liberal citadel.

The role ascribed to the Christian religion by those who research the origins of the classical liberalism of John Stuart Mill and his successors is equivocal. On the one hand Christianity is credited with having emphasized, if not invented, the doctrine of the sacredness of each individual human being. On the other hand Christianity is generally seen as antipathetic to worldly success and material abundance, which is the reward of individual progressive endeavour. Critics of liberalism tell another story. In a broadside against liberalism's collusion with colonialist intolerance, Professor Bhikhu Parekh, Professor of Political Theory at the University of Hull, depicts non-liberal societies in positive terms as resting on what he calls a 'theory of overlapping selves':

> Those bound together by familial, kinship, religious and other ties do not see themselves as independent and self-contained ontological units involved in specific kinds of relationship with 'others', but rather as bearers of overlapping selves whose identities are constituted by and incapable of being defined in isolation from these

[30] 'Liberalism', art., *Encyclopaedia Britannica* (1977), 10: 846.

relationships. Individual and self are distinct and their boundaries do not coincide, so that naturally distinct individuals may and do share their selves in common.[31]

This bears more than a slight relationship to a Pauline doctrine of membership in the Body of Christ. At the very least, therefore, the Christian religion has sponsored elements both in liberalism's formation, and also in what might be seen to be its alternative.

It follows that it is simply not possible for Christian theologians to adopt a categorical stance over liberalism, either by way of endorsement or root and branch opposition. This is not just because of the conceptual imprecision of the term, which our inquiry has illustrated. It is also because in the nature of the case it is impossible for a Christian either to be for, or to be against, all the various guises which authority has taken in the history of Christian thought and life. Two examples illustrate this beyond dispute. The first is the history of biblical criticism and the second is the history of feminism. Biblical criticism is not a homogeneous movement based on the anti-dogmatic principle. One cannot either embrace or reject new theories of authorship, date, or historical veracity on principle. There is no alternative but to consider them one by one, and weigh the evidence on which the various proposals rest. There is no possibility of simply resorting to theories or answers maintained in earlier generations or centuries. As Raymond Brown, the distinguished Roman Catholic exegete, puts it:

The future lies not with a rejection of the historical-critical method (which I regard as a permanent contribution to knowledge), but in a refinement of the method, so that it will answer appropriately posed questions even more accurately, and its contributions to the larger picture of biblical interpretation can be seen in better perspective.[32]

Similarly with feminism. There is no one position called 'feminism' which *per se* is, on principle, either contrary to, or required by Christian theology. But no one who has taken the trouble to study what was once taught authoritatively, and reinforced in canon law, to be the place assigned by God to women, can seriously doubt that the contentions of those who oppose those long-established traditions have to be considered one by one. Even the meeting of arguments advanced by biblical critics and feminists imposes on conservatives the use of weapons which are modern, as Os Guinness has asserted. A classic example is the historical

---

[31] B. Parekh, 'Superior People', in *Times Literary Supplement*, 25 Feb. 1994, No. 4743, p. 12.
[32] Brown, *Biblical Exegesis*, p. 25.

defence of the doctrine of the Empty Tomb. The'trial' of the witnesses of the resurrection, or the inquiry into 'who moved the stone', are modern devices to respond to the charge of historical discrepancies in the existing narratives. The very nature of the arguments acknowledges the necessity of taking historical evidence seriously. Only a principled rejection of the whole procedure would correspond to the stance of the tradition which did not allow that contradiction could arise in scripture.

Nor is the authority of the church in any better case, as the example of the 'Johannine comma' shows. In 1897 the Holy Office declared that the Vulgate text of 1 Jn. 5.7 (which had been interpolated to read 'there are three who testify in heaven') was genuine, and that no Catholic student of scripture could think otherwise. But as Raymond Brown, who had discussed all the relevant manuscript evidence, bleakly puts it in his commentary, 'all recent Roman Catholic scholarly discussion has recognized that the Comma is neither genuine nor authentic',[33] that is, neither written by the evangelist, nor even authentically part of scripture, as the subsequent declaration of the Holy Office proposed in 1927. A celebrated test-case for detecting an unacceptably liberal cast of mind simply collapses before the burden of particular pieces of evidence carefully scrutinized. The term 'liberalism' simply does not help us at that level of detail.

IV. MARIOLOGY AS A TEST OF ORTHODOXY

We must finally offer a brief discussion of Marian doctrine, which figures in Turner's work as a reason for, and an example of withholding consent from Newman's doctrine of development. The central question which Turner invites us to consider is how the admitted silence of scripture in relation to the Immaculate Conception and bodily Assumption of the Blessed Virgin Mary is to be interpreted. He will not allow that neutrality on these dogmas is adequate in the light of what he claims to be Jesus' active dissociation of his mother from himself in relation to his specific mission in the world.[34] It is, he claims, the unacceptable tendency of Marian doctrines to approximate the theological status of Mary to that of Christ. Mariology, he holds, gains its plausibility from the exaggerated transcendentalizing of the person of Christ, and a loss of organic wholeness in the doctrine of incarnation. This is a case of 'addition to the subject-matter of orthodoxy in the supposed interests of a coherent

[33] R. E. Brown, *The Epistles of John* (London: Chapman, 1983), p. 781.
[34] Turner, *Pattern*, p. 490.

whole of faith and life, purchased at the expense of its true scriptural balance',[35] and it must be resisted.

Turner, of course, wrote before the Second Vatican Council's sober sections on the Blessed Virgin and the church were composed.[36] The 'duties and privileges of the Blessed Virgin' are said always to refer to Christ 'the source of all truth, sanctity and devotion'. Despite this, even ARCIC in the Final Report treats Anglican reticence about the Dogmas of Immaculate Conception and the Blessed Assumption as a problem, and openly suggests that the failure to define these dogmas at a Council is one obstacle to Anglican acceptance of papal authority.[37]

The point at issue, as far as Turner is concerned, has three aspects: first, whether there is explicit biblical support for a development; secondly, if not, at what subsequent date the development manifested itself (the test of antiquity); and thirdly, where the development impairs or distorts important biblical principles or insights. The first two of these points might be said to raise the historical question in a particularly modern way. And it would be in exactly that same evidential vein that the question of belief in the Virgin Birth itself would be raised by exegetes. Raymond Brown explicitly discussed and addresses this question, how the church moved 'from the evidence that in the New Testament only two evangelists mentioned the virginal conception and the likelihood that it was known to a minority of New Testament Christians to an affirmation that historicity of the virginal conception is part of the direct revelation about Jesus Christ'.[38] Brown's answer is that what historical-critical study is bound to leave open, for lack of evidence, the church is in a position to resolve. He goes further, in the context of a reply to Dr John McHugh:

A frank confrontation with the kind of evidence uncovered by an intelligent use of the historical-critical method can bring Catholic students to appreciate the need for a teaching church ... This is far healthier than pretending, as some would have us do, that our status as Catholics enables us to find more historical information or evidence in the literal sense of the text than can our Protestant brothers and sisters.[39]

What is undeniable about this phrasing of the issue is its modernity. Neither the evidential value of precise historical information, nor the

---

[35] Turner, *Pattern*, p. 491.
[36] *Lumen Gentium*, Second Vatican Council, 21 Nov. 1964, paragraphs 60–5, and 66–7.
[37] *Final Report. ARCIC I*, 'Authority in the Church' II, para. 30.
[38] Brown, *Biblical Exegesis*, p. 36.
[39] Brown, *Biblical Exegesis*, p. 73.

question of the church's right to resolve an issue which was not resolved in that way earlier, would have been formulated in this way in earlier centuries. Not merely is the question new; the answer is likewise new, and, though its conclusion is consistent with the verdict of antiquity, the reasoning has changed. In this way, I believe, it is a distortion of the truth to suggest that what is available to a modern student of Mariology is a choice between liberalism and orthodoxy. The defence of orthodoxy requires, in my analysis, the deployment of argument which implicitly acknowledges that an appropriate challenge to the tradition has been offered. It may still be possible to identify within the arguments assumptions which imply, for example, the impossibility of miracle or divine self-disclosure. But this will have to be done with care and in detail. The mere asking for proper historical evidence does not itself constitute the vice of liberalism.

A similar situation arises over the entirely proper feminist questions about Marian doctrines. In this regard Ann Loades' verdict is particularly instructive:

> If we could retrieve from the tradition the association of 'virgin' with autonomy, and *without* the abasement of a woman's visual image, and associate autonomy with the affirmation and not the negation of what women discover themselves to be, then we might be able to re-connect 'Mary' to the needs of twentieth-century woman.[40]

Here again one is faced by a choice. Either 'traditional orthodoxy' in the sense of the later definitions of Marian doctrine is to be challenged in the name of a 'biblical orthodoxy' – in which case modern theological work has to be done. Or the Marian doctrines need the kind of interpretation which they have never previously been given – in which case, again, modern theological work needs to be done. In neither case will the terms 'liberalism' or even 'heresy' shed any light independent of what is said to be the criteria of orthodoxy, which in both cases will have to be explained. Of the two, indeed, the term 'heretic', because it is more obviously related to orthodoxy, and thus directly to the standards of theological authority, is to be preferred, since its use makes the clash of criteria inescapable.

---

[40] Ann Loades, *Searching for Lost Coins* (London: SPCK, 1987), p. 83.

6

Healing the Damaged

ALISTAIR McFADYEN

I. LOSS AND RETRIEVAL OF INITIAL CONDITIONS?

M Y three-year-old son was watching an animated fantasy in which a world had become distorted, disfigured and dysfunctional through the operation of a malevolent power. When good had triumphed over the evil witch under whose spell it had been cast, my son was ecstatic with wonder, joy and delight: 'Look, Dad! It's gone back to how it was before!' In a situation that falls under the power of such terrible and systematic distortion that its original, good state is barely recognizable, one naturally judges the present by contrasting it with its past. The evil of the present is seen as consisting in the damage, distortion or loss of the original state. Healing then appears to consist in the return to a good which has been lost, suppressed or distorted, in a return to initial conditions, so that it is as if nothing bad had ever happened: going back to how it was before.

To speak of damage and healing in terms of loss and retrieval of an original state carries the assumption that the order of perfection is backward-looking and static – a given, against which deviation is to be measured. But is speaking of damage and healing in this way adequate either to its lived reality or to what is required in order to heal it?

Frances Young raises a related question when she finds herself wanting to resist the suggestion that salvation for her mentally handicapped son (Arthur) will mean 'restoring' him to an ideal state which he has never known in life – transformed 'back' into what he 'should' have been.[1]

In terms of the dualism in which some forms of Christianity find expression, this would mean retrieving the eternal and immaterial soul from the damaged body in which it has been trapped, but through which it has not sustained any real damage. And that is tantamount to saying that fundamental personal identity is untouched and unshaped by the

---

[1] Frances Young, *Face to Face: A Narrative Essay in the Theology of Suffering* (Edinburgh: T. & T. Clark, 1990), pp. 61ff.

various factors conditioning our lives or by the way in which we shape our lives in relation to their conditionality.

It is true that she is here considering the healing which might take shape in Arthur's final salvation, rather than that which might be hoped for in the here and now. But the theological criteria by which she judges the former also apply to the latter. At bottom, what she articulates is a refusal to accept that the eschatological healing of Arthur can be so inattentive to the lived particularities of his life as effectively to replace the concrete, handicapped Arthur with a perfect, heavenly form. It is not that Young has a vision of heaven which merely eternalizes handicap. It is more that she rightly rejects the notion of idealized human essences which are more real than our concretely lived particularities. And the corollary of such a view must be that what we 'essentially' are, even in relation to salvation, is worked out in concretely lived existences in which there can be fundamental distortions and dysfunctions of our being. And healing, even – or perhaps especially – the healing of salvation, must somehow involve a working through or re-shaping of the identity which has concretely taken shape through life. And that must mean beginning with the damage, not eliminating or ignoring it.

II. The Power of Abuse

In order better to discern the nature of damage and the requirements of healing, I shall concentrate on the concrete situation of child sexual abuse.

(a) Damaging relationality

It is tempting to think of sexual abuse primarily in physical terms, since sexual activity is its defining characteristic. And so our attention might be drawn exclusively to the physical, inviting us to think of abuse and subsequent damage in physical terms: as sexual acts with a child which might be physically injurious to him. It is the case that much sexual abuse does take the form of physical acts (and that some sexual abuse is accompanied by violence), and that some of those acts can, by their nature, lead to physiological damage.

It is, however, a mistake to make the physical the primary and controlling factor in understanding sexual abuse and the damage it can cause, not least because that would exclude from consideration those forms of sexual abuse which involve no tactile contact between abuser and child.[2] Such a concentration on the physical aspects of abuse and damage carries the further implication that abuse (including most non-invasive physical acts) which does not result in direct physical damage might not be damaging at all. The physical aspects of abuse and subsequent trauma are significant aspects among a complex of others[3] which interweave to produce more or less damage to the survivor of abuse, and there is no simple and direct correlation between physically painful or damaging acts and the level of non-physical trauma (damage to the person) associated with the abuse.

It is much more helpful to see the basic dynamic of abuse and of damage as primarily related to the distortion of relationality, of which certain physical transactions (which may of themselves be physically damaging) may be a constitutive element. The sexual abuse of a child effects a distorted form of relationship, which can neither be based on nor oriented towards a genuine mutuality and reciprocity, not least because of the differentials in power, status, knowledge and understanding between abuser and victim which are exploited by the abuser.

It is more appropriate to understand sexual abuse in relational terms,[4] rather than in act categories, such as assault. The distorted intimacy of sexual abuse establishes a relationship between abuser and victim which endures even after abuse has stopped and they are not in physical proximity. It rarely approximates to a one-off act;[5] it effects some kind of bond between abuser and victim. There is a sense in which the abuser (especially through threats concerning disclosure, the possibility of future abuse or traumatic memory) is present to the child even

[2] Examples would be an abuser exposing himself to a child; masturbating in front of the child or invoking the child to masturbate in front of him; exposing the child to pornography. For an extensive definition, see Carol R. Harman and Ann W. Burgess, 'Sexual Abuse of Children: Causes and Consequences', in *Child Maltreatment: Theory and Research on the Causes and Consequences of Child Abuse and Neglect*, eds. Dante Cicchetti and Vicki Carson (Cambridge: CUP, 1989), pp. 95–128.

[3] Such as age-difference, abuser's sex, number of abusers, psychological and familial factors, time over which the abuse takes place, relation to abuser, and so on.

[4] There is a 'politically correct' resistance to the language of relationship, however, not least because it is often invoked by abusers to present the abuse as consensual or based on mutuality and reciprocity, even love. That the abuser is able to distort the language of relationship to defend abuse is itself an indication that it is relationality which is here being distorted. It is only if we take relationship to be a term indicating always a positive quality of connection that we have reason to avoid it here. But since the word is qualitatively neutral, there is no reason to avoid it. Indeed, avoiding it because it is used by abusers to redefine abuse (so it looks as though there is a clear choice in terming what is happening as abuse or relationship) inhibits understanding abuse as initiating a dynamic which overflows into all relationships, including that to self.

[5] Even one-off acts of abuse committed by strangers whom the child never meets again are not necessarily better understood in terms of act or event rather than relation, particularly if the abuser 'closes' the event with injunctions to secrecy.

when physically absent. Even after the abuse has stopped (at least for now) the child has to manage and cope with it, has to organize himself and his life in light of it, and so remains related to it and to the abuser.

(b) The bonds of secrecy

When children are sexually abused, they are almost invariably enjoined to secrecy (implicitly, if not explicitly). This injunction to secrecy closes off the immediate context of abuse from other contexts and isolates the child in the relation to the abuser from all other relationships. Enjoining her to secrecy, the abuser weakens her bonds of relation to other people and contexts of meaning and communication; simultaneously, he strengthens the bonds between her, the abuse and himself. And this applies, even if she never sees him again.

Secrecy obviously interdicts the passage of information from the context of abuse to other contexts and frameworks of meaning. But this also means that the child is prevented from processing that information herself, since the resources for doing so are unlikely to be in her command already, and access to external resources is inhibited by the social isolation effected by the secret. So the 'information' she has is unlikely to be understood by her fully or without distortion, even though (or, rather, for that very reason) it may be profoundly informative for her being.

The secret does not merely isolate her from the companionship, solace and assistance of others, then, but from the processes of public meaning, communication and exchange through which the meaning and significance of the abuse may be processed. She is isolated from the social means for comprehending and interpreting reality, including the reality of an abusive sexual relationship. She is locked into the reality of abuse with only the 'rationality' deep within the dynamic of the abuse and that used by the abuser to explain, justify and comment upon it. The abuse and the abuser become the sole reality by which the abuse may itself be understood.

This enclosure of the child in the reality of abuse effects a substitution of the rationality of abuse for the child's own rational structures and resources, along with those available in his general situation. By that means the behaviour of the child is eventually (if not from the outset) controlled internally – the rational structures of the child are sequestered by abusive rationality. So the child's own willing, thinking, horizon of possible action and meaning are bound to the abuse. Abuse becomes the reality which all action has to take as its base-line, the unalterable fact to which all else must relate itself (a 'properly basic fact', functioning in relation to will, intentionality and action as a 'properly basic belief' does in relation to the language game of a belief system). Abuse becomes normative for the child's willing, intentionality, and action.

This does not necessarily and simply mean that the child comes to will to be abused, to enjoy it or even to regard it as otherwise than abuse (although all of this can, indeed, happen). But it does mean that all the child's resources for survival not only permit the abuse to carry on, but have the effect of confirming and more deeply embedding its reality. All strategies for psychological survival are also in effect accommodations to the abuse and the requirement of secrecy.[6] They can be nothing else, since it is not in her physical, psychological, emotional or social power effectively to resist the abuser or to leave the situation, and there are powerful inhibitors on disclosure.

(c) Internalizing damaging energy: restructuring identity

Surviving therefore has an immense cost, and appears almost inevitably to involve an internalization of abusive meanings from the situation. Since the conflicts and confusions attending abuse cannot be resolved through recourse to frameworks of public meaning, they can only be survived by turning them inward in a series of rationalizations in the form of deep-seated, distorted beliefs concerning his identity and value ('I am dirty'; 'it is my fault'; 'I let this happen'; 'I am evil' and so on).

The child cannot free himself from the effects of abuse, primarily because he cannot be free from what he must do to survive it. The dynamic and rationality of abuse are totalitarian: capturing the child and all his energies for living and surviving the abuse, and disabling the instrusion of any competing rationality, set of norms, energy or information. Abuse insinuates itself into the child's way of being, relating to, interpreting and communicating in every context of interaction. It distorts the deepest structures of personhood and therefore his whole ecology and economy of relating.

Abuse is a highly energized information event. It presents the child with new, confusing and disturbing information (especially about what is right and acceptable). It confuses and disturbs him because it conflicts with norms of interaction operating elsewhere, implied by the injunctions against disclosure, even if other norms are not directly available to him. He is, however, unable to process this information because of the blocks on communication which inhibit exchange of information, the capacity to be informed and transformed through the exchange of energized information.

The information communicated in the abuse cannot be de-energized or dissipated, since it cannot be combined with that which is presently

---

[6] Cf. Karin C. Meiselman, *Resolving the Trauma of Incest: Reintegration Therapy with Survivors* (San Francisco: Jossey-Bass, 1990), p. 90.

informing the structure of identity (pattern of relating to oneself and others), nor with information from contexts external to the abuse. It therefore creates a traumatic disequilibrium in the present structure of identity. Who he understands himself to be; how he relates to himself, to others and to reality as a whole – all is knocked out of equilibrium.

Because the child is isolated from other contexts of communication, other relationships and other resources, the abusive energy is confined in its field of force to the child. It remains concentrated and focused, and therefore highly potent and active. Anything that the child does to survive (even strategies employed during abuse, such as dissociation), all his own energies which are brought into play in order to re-establish structural equilibrium, effect a further concentration and intensification of the damaging power of abuse. In order to avoid psychological fragmentation, a new structuring of identity is necessary, a new equilibrium has to be found and maintained. Yet, as we have already seen, that has to be an organization of identity around the basic reality of abuse which becomes the prime informant of identity, and yet does so in a hidden and distorting way because it cannot be properly processed. And so all the energies of survival have to be invested in this new structure of abused identity which, whilst enabling psychological survival, actually more deeply embeds the abuse. The child's own energies of will, intentionality and rationality have to work with and redouble the power and energy of abuse to create more damage – to himself and to others.

The generation of a new equilibrium in identity structure is a way of converting the kinetic energy of abuse into potential energy, and so of resolving the dynamic of abuse into rest, or so it seems on the surface at least. (It is misleading to consider this change of form as a de-energizing of the abuse, since potential energy is that which the abuse still has by virtue of its core relation to the structure of personal identity and relation, which is now patterned around the reality of abuse.) What this indicates is that the new equilibrium must be static; the new structure of identity, closed. The dynamic equilibrium (as well as the disequilibrium which it would constantly risk) of a structure open to new information (to being informed by different norms and codes of relation) hazards the transformation to kinetic energy once more. The managing of abuse requires a structure of identity robust to new information, to disconfirmation.

This is why the dynamic of abuse traps in ever more constricting bonds and why it has the capacity to invade and distort the entire ecology of relating. It presses the survivor to re-confirm the distorted identity he has structured in order to survive the abuse in every relationship (incorporating deeply internalized beliefs about worth, blame, guilt and what can be expected from others), even those which are potentially and perhaps intentionally therapeutic. This happens most obviously in patterns of revictimization or future abuse,[7] but also in patterns of heightened empathy and attunement to others' needs to the point of sacrifice of self (so an active abuser is not strictly required) which arises, not out of a positive sense of relation to another, but as a strategy to protect oneself in a situation of felt alienation from others.[8]

It is not just that survivors are so damaged that they lack the energy, trust or hope to respond to the call to be in relation in a way which is not distorted by the damage they have sustained. It is rather that the structure of identity is so rigid that disequilibrium threatens disintegration, and thus a great deal of energy must be invested in maintaining its non-dynamic order; any relationship or interaction which threatens that order must be withdrawn from or resisted.

Relationships cannot be sustained where they appear to require a transformation of present identity structure. Worse, relationships which require the repetition of the structure of identity which is damaged and

---

[7] This tends to fall out in gender-related patterns, with revictimization more common among women survivors; propensity to become an abuser (not necessarily sexually, and not exclusively of children) more common among men. See: J. Miller, D. Moeller, A. Kaufman, P. DiVasto, D. Pathak and J. Christy, 'Recidivism Among Sex Assault Victims', *American Journal of Psychiatry* 135 (1978), p. 1103f.; D. Finkelhor and K. Yllo, *Licenced to Rape: Sexual Violence Against Wives* (New York: Holt, Rinehart, 1985); D. Russell, *Rape in Marriage* (New York: Macmillan, 1982); *idem, Rape, Incest and Sexual Exploitation* (Los Angeles: Sage, 1984). Finkelhor's study in *Child Sexual Abuse* (New York: The Free Press, 1984) failed to find a statistically significant connection, but offers possible explanations for that, pp. 193f. On the evidence of sexual abuse in the history of male abusers, see Finkelhor, *Child Sexual Abuse*, pp. 181ff; and for statistical data, see M. De Young, *The Sexual Victimization of Children* (Jefferson, NC: McFarland, 1982); P. Gebhard, J. Gagnon, W. Pomeroy and C. Christenson, *Sex Offenders: An Analysis of Types* (New York: Harper & Row, 1965); N. A. Groth, W. Hobson and T. Gary, 'The Child Molester: Clinical Observations'; in *Social Work and Child Sexual Abuse*, eds. J. Conte and D. Shore (New York: Haworth, 1982); N. A. Groth and A. W. Burgess, 'Sexual Trauma in the Life-Histories of Rapists and Child Molesters', *Victimology* 4 (1979), pp. 10–16; R. Langevin, L. Handy, H. Hook, D. Day and A. Russon, 'Are Incestuous Fathers Pedophilic and Aggressive?', in *Erotic Preference, Gender Identity and Aggression*, ed. R. Langevin (New York: Erlbaum Associates, 1983); T. Seghorn and R. Boucher, 'Sexual Abuse in Childhood as a Factor in Sexually Dangerous Criminal Offences', in *Childhood and Sexuality*, ed. J. M. Samson (Montreal: Editions Vivantes, 1980).

[8] In relation to this alienated form of empathy, N. D. Feshbach's findings concerning the physical abuse of children are undoubtedly transferrable to sexual abuse. See his 'The Construct of Empathy and the Phenomenon of Physical Maltreatment of Children', in *Child Maltreatment*, pp. 349–73. Meiselman, *Resolving the Trauma of Incest*, p. 35, and Emily Driver, 'Through the Looking Glass: Children and the Professionals Who Treat Them', in *Child Sexual Abuse: Feminist Perspectives*, eds. Driver and Droisen (Basingstoke: Macmillan, 1989), pp. 112, 116–19, both suggest a gender differentiation in the construction of empathy amongst survivors of sexual abuse. Both empathy and its opposite (abusing others in some way) are regarded as ways of escaping from the sense of isolation, alienation, hopelessness and powerlessness inflicted through abuse, either through a mirroring form of attachment to others' needs, involving a distancing from oneself, or an enacted dissociation or isolation from others' needs in order to enact oneself in one's own power over others.

damaging (in relationship – both to oneself and others) will prove attractive and will serve to re-concentrate the energies of damaging distortion because the order of the relationship provides confirmation of identity. It is a measure of how deep the damage is that the lack of dissonance in an abusive or oppressive relationship may be experienced as powerfully reassuring, as a concentration of the energies of selfhood. Damaged identity is non-dynamic; the structure is incapable of sustaining itself across a varied range of interactions. It can only replicate itself by setting up or entering relationships which invite repetition. So the good will be encountered as threat, not as potentiality for healing.

III. REDESCRIBING DAMAGE

I opened this paper by asking whether it was appropriate to conceive of damage as disaffection from an initial, functional state, to regard initial conditions as definitive of good and proper functioning and therefore of damage and healing also. From such a perspective, the sexual involvement of adults with children might be judged to be damaging, to constitute abuse, because it effects physiological, social, psychological or developmental dysfunction – a falling away from initial (or programmed, developmental) conditions.

But is the standard of initial conditions (or normal development from them) the appropriate standard of reference against which sexual abuse is to be judged as damaging and healing sought? Is the standard of reference against which abuse is judged to be abuse, to be damaging, limited to such a restricted conception and norm of human well-being as absence of dysfunction? And is healing to be construed as the restoration of these initial, stable conditions? Does this not work, in fact, to constrict the full reality of the abused person? Does it not undercut the possibility of seeing herself, and being seen and treated by others, as oriented towards and constituting a richer, deeper, more abundant and more particular reality than may be characterized by the retention of normal functioning in a stable state? If so, then such a standard of normative reference parallels just that constriction of her reality which she encounters in the abuse and operates with a restricted conception of what energies of transformation might be available.

It is not just that the restoration of initial conditions, as if nothing had happened, is an unrealistic hope which fails to take the reality of abuse seriously. On its own, that is a counsel of despair (or at least of stoic acceptance) against any hope of meaningful healing for damage so severe that it takes flight from the risks of healing. If such a despairing view, that taking damage seriously cancels the possibility of healing, appears realistic, that is because we suppose that the resources available for healing, even for healing construed as restoration of initial conditions, are therapeutically inadequate. The view that damage and healing represent loss and restoration of initial conditions and the 'realism' which feeds a counsel of despair both rest on a deficient notion of the good which human beings are always related to. And it is only from the perspective of this relation to the good therefore that we may assess both damage and the possibilities for healing. For damage is a disaffection, not simply from a past, static equilibrium, but from the possibilities of healing. In theological terms, it is resistance to and distortion of salvation as well as of creation, or, rather, of the energies active in both.

And so the questions 'in what does damage consist?' and 'whence comes the power of healing?' are to be answered in relation to the triune God: damage is a blocking of the energies of dynamic relationality communicated to us in God's creative and saving presence and action, through the trinitarian dynamic of transcendence and immanence. It is only in relation to the healing action of God that we understand both what is necessary to put the damage right, and also what damage actually is in the first place (indeed, we come to see also that initial conditions are not static). The healing activity of God defines the damage in the act of healing it, in the act of going through the resistance of damage to healing; of taking the damage, including its resistance to healing, into itself.

IV. THE TRIUNE GOD AS HEALER

Were God a simple unity, then we might expect God to impose a fixed, static order on the world which corresponds to the fixity of the divine being. That correspondence would then be the basis of God's relationship to creation. Given that the order of being and relation are both fixed, a severe restriction is here implied in God's capacity to respond to any departure from the static equilibrium of the initial conditions of creation and its relation to the creator, since God could not endure the disequilibrium involved in maintaining active relationship with a creation which has fallen out of the equilibrium of its own internal order and of relation to God. Healing, then, would be a backward-looking restoration of initial order. But, since creation and creator are not in this view dynamically interrelated, it is hard to see how even this re-ordering could be energized. In its disaffection from proper order, the world loses relation to the order of God, and so, in effect, closes itself from the energies of this singular God. But, in any case, such a God would be incapable of developing new order from disorder by the healing communication of new energy or the excitement of creaturely energy into new structure and order. The world would be left with its own limited supply of energy, because neither God nor the world nor the relation between them is dynamically ordered.

(a) Damage and dynamic order

The triune God, however, is a dynamic order of relationality which resists description in static categories of being. One might say that this God is more like a verb than a noun, both within Godself and in relation to the world, where dynamic categories also have to be employed. Order and structure in and of the world which the triune God creates are themselves dynamic, and that world is dynamically related to God. Perhaps it would be better to say, God is the source of the dynamic order of the world. The world is caught up in the dialectic of transcendence and immanence which is constitutive of God's reality.

Dynamic order indicates the capacity of a system to reorder and restructure itself through interaction and relation with other systems and its environment: to change. So the equilibrium of a structure must itself be dynamic and open to the future, capable of refocusing its energies, of reorganizing itself through disequilibrium. This understanding effects a radical shift in the construal of damage. For the proper order of something may not now be defined in terms of a given essence, state or equilibrium which is to be preserved. The teleological aspect of reality is instead much more appropriately conceived in the language of calling than preservation – calling into a future development of, an increase in, dynamic order through relation to that of others, to self and to God in the concreteness of one's situation. This implies an increase in the freedom of a structure which, far from being a dissafection from or damage to its own ordered particularity, is actually an intensification of it.

If this is the case, then damage and disequilibrium cannot be synonyms, since periods of disequilibrium are necessary to dynamic order. Damage must instead relate to a dissipation of energies of dynamic order, of self-structuring in open relation: a dissipation of energies of relation and participation which effects either a collapse in identity in relation to others, or else, in a desperate attempt to concentrate the energies of self-organization in the face of possible collapse, turns it into a static structure, stabilized against change, against otherness, transcendence and futurity. In dynamic order, however, energy may only be concentrated by avoiding over-stabilization.

Childhood naturally encompasses stages of disequilibrium as an identity structure takes shape within the concrete contingencies of psychological, familial, social, cultural, economic and other conditions. Sexual abuse of children can be profoundly damaging, not only because it effects a particularly traumatic disequilibrium, but because it also inhibits the possibilities of organizing a new equilibrium in identity structure which is dynamic and open to growth, change and challenge; open, that is, to otherness, to transcendence. In a sense, abuse threatens to leave the survivor stuck in and oriented to the abusive past.

What is damaged and distorted by sexual abuse is the child's relationship to the energies of dynamic order (which, through the creative activity and ordering presence of the triune God, are available to human beings through 'natural' forms of sociality). Abuse threatens to distort her encounter with the enriching, empowering, energizing, life-giving, transforming source of overflowing plenitude and abundance. It threatens to turn her face away from God and from those forms of relation with others which may be mediators of this dynamic, overflowing, abundant life. It blocks transcendence in every way and at every level. So sexual abuse is a constriction of and resistance to the richness of life before God and others. Sexual abuse is abuse because it encapsulates and encloses the child in a highly restrictive and distorting reality and in a resistance to the healing and transforming power of God. For that reason it is sin also, not merely with reference to what the abuser does, but in the effects it has of so enclosing the child in its reality that she adds will and intentionality to the abuse, giving it more power, and finding herself unable to separate herself from it effectively.

And so the energy of relating to the abundant resources for living humanly in relation to herself, others, the world and God are sequestered and her capacity for joyful encounter with herself, others and the world distorted. Abuse is abuse of capacity for joy, or, in theological terms, of praise, of the possibility of standing in the proper economy of praise of God, which requires dynamic self-affirmation and openness to others in love. It is the joy of praise which human beings are made for, which is our vocation, and in which we receive our true being and freedom. Joy in and through God is more primary, primordial even, than communication, action, cognition, and intentionality. Our being is not neutral and then put into motion through intentionality, action, relation. Our very being is found in the movement of praise and joy in the dynamic order and ecology of relation.

(b) Healing

Damage is to be conceived in terms of the de-energizing of dynamic order, the dissipation of the energies for structuring an identity in relation which is open to others, to God, to transformation and to futurity. Healing must therefore be construed in terms of the re-energizing of the means of dynamic order in relationships. Healing then means neither returning to a past equilibrial state (initial conditions) nor a stoic resignation to the damage. Both these options involve a problematic sense of temporality and embodiedness. The first suggests both that the proper order of human identity is static and that, once that order falls into disequilibrium, it is possible to regain it (the essence may be uninformed by damage 'in the flesh'); the second assumes that, because damage is a reality which one cannot move backwards from, all that is possible is a serene acceptance of present conditions. Both have inadequate notions of the resources for healing which human beings may be in touch with and in relation to: that which healing represents as a refocusing of the energies of relation in dynamic order which liberates present structures of identity to draw the history of damage into a new future. Interaction with the dynamic being of God calls into being new dynamic order, a call through which all that has happened in the past is related to in a new way.

There is an ongoing interaction and relationship between the world and God which sustains the dynamic order of the rest of the world and so makes energy available for transformation and healing 'naturally'. But God also acts on, in and towards the world in ways which make available new energies for transformation which may then become a means for focusing naturally available energies for future transformation – and God acts precisely at the points of most damage, where energy for the achievement of free, dynamic order is most dissipated. This brings the concrete possibilities of restructuring and reordering in dynamic ways which open up new futures in situations which would otherwise have been closed to any future other than one which replicates the past and is overdetermined by it. This is not a freedom *from* the past, which sets it aside in order to recover initial, stabilized conditions, a non-contingent future; more a freedom *through* the past, which finds a way of taking this past up into a new future which is highly contingent on, although not overdetermined by, it.

Primarily, we see this release of energy for new dynamic order in the resurrection of Jesus. The resurrection was absolutely not a reconstitution of initial conditions in relation either to Jesus or to God's relationship with humanity, neither did it involve an escapist fantasy about the incapacity of particular, concrete events and relationships to effect serious damage. Jesus is not resuscitated to a life which still has death before it; the killing of Jesus is taken absolutely seriously, not undone, but worked through. And the total collapse of humanity into sin is also taken absolutely seriously; it is met with a radical measure which, again, works through the reality and, instead of restoring initial conditions, pours out the possibility of and energizes a more abundant life than before.

How are human beings incorporated into the transforming activity of God? How is participation in the energies of transformation effected and mediated? The initial consequence of Jesus' resurrection was the re-concentration and focusing of the energies of community which had been altogether dissipated on Jesus' death; initially amongst the first disciples, then more expansively. This consequence is, in fact, absolutely inseparable from the event itself. Why does Jesus appear again; why does he not immediately ascend? Is the reality of resurrection not in essence an event only between the Son and the Father which excludes us? Were that the case, then the appearances would be merely revelatory, rather than constitutive, of the reality of resurrection. But the appearances partly constitute that reality by incorporating people into its offer of reconciliation and forgiveness, a new structure of corporate and personal identity and relationality. The re-energizing sociality of the church is part of the event itself. The community-building and transforming acts of repentance and forgiveness are the medium through which we participate in God's act in Jesus' cross and resurrection and which concentrate the energies of dynamic order free for the future.

Healing therefore requires a way of forgiving and of being reconciled to the past which draws it into relationship with future possibilities of transformation.[9] It is not so much that this can only happen in Christian community, but worshipping Christian community draws on and mediates the energies of such transformation in dynamic order through a conscious relationship with the dynamic order of God. And it is only in relation to such a relationship that the nature of damage and of resistance to it may appropriately be discerned.

[9] Two particularly vivid, non-theological, portrayals of the need for reconciliation with and forgiveness of an abused past may be found in Meiselman, *Resolving the Trauma*; and Penny Parks, *Rescuing the Inner Child: Therapy for Adults Sexually Abused as Children* (London: Souvenir Press, 1990). I am grateful to Peter Sedgwick for drawing my attention to the latter.

7

Love in the City

PETER SELBY

INTRODUCTION

SINCE love is one of Paul's 'three things that last' it should make no difference where it happens. If it can last through time, it ought also to be able to make its dwelling anywhere. Urban and rural loving should be much the same. In fact, many ideals of love seem to reflect a kind of suburban background in any case, the suburb being a kind of no-place and any-place.

Yet cities are not generally felt to be very loving places. To take a theme from Dan Hardy's seminal paper to the Society for the Study of Theology, their *sociality* seems to be rather more fallen than either created or redeemed.[1] They are lively, certainly, but not easy places for many aspects of human flourishing. They are places for exploiting, and for escaping if people can afford it, where the sheer fact of having too many human beings in too close proximity to each other produces the same results as are found in overcrowded rat populations. For village dwellers a visit to the city can be a scary business, and the bigger the city the worse it is. Often people from Newcastle visiting London complain about the scale and the dirt and the noise, and then are surprised to learn that many rural Northumbrians make the same complaints when they pay visits to Newcastle.

Yet the visitors still come, and even when they are at home in the country or the suburbs they still orient their lives around things that can only be had because there are cities. Maybe too many people in one place at one time makes for stress, for the transport and the drainage as well as the other people. But how else shall we make our theatres and restaurants viable, how else deal with distributing the range of commodities and artefacts that have become the necessities for living and which mean that whether we like it or not we are all urban now?

And if love can exist anywhere, cities certainly cannot. They are built where rivers or railways made commerce possible, or where natural

[1] See Daniel Hardy, 'Created and Redeemed Sociality', in *On Being the Church: Essays on the Christian Community*, eds. C. E. Gunton and D. W. Hardy (Edinburgh: T. & T. Clark, 1989), pp. 21–47.

barriers made them defensible against prospective enemies and invaders. Love may seem to be the same wherever it happens, but again cities are not: they display in unavoidable starkness the economic character of their society and the social pressures under which it labours. Like the sun shining through a magnifying glass, they focus the strengths and achievements, the history and the prospects of nations; though like the sun shining through a window pane they show up the dirt as well.

So to speak of love in the city is to bring together the timeless and the historical, the potentially ubiquitous and the inevitably local, so as to bring out all our strong ambivalence towards urban living. We cannot live without cities; that applies just as much to those who could not themselves bear to live in them. Yet sustaining urban life in a loving and humane manner seems always to elude us. We perceive a conflict between the values of the gospel, which we seek to express in every time and every place, and the demands of historical conditions and the pressures of the locality. In that conflict it generally seems that the timeless is almost bound to lose. The demand for 'realism' (a term which only begs the question of what reality commands our first loyalty) excludes anything but a passing nod in the direction of 'vision'; though realism without vision is bound to lead to desperation or complacency.

Somewhere here there seems to lurk an error, a kind of docetic conception of love that confines it to the realm of religion or romance, and denies it the possibility of any real appearance within the world of time. To expect to see love within the operation of the market or the campaigns of politicians and within the power structures and arguments that are demanded for the regulation of the city's life is actually to expect incarnation, of course, and that has always been a difficult conviction to hold on to.

Addressing that incarnational conviction implicit in the notion of 'love in the city' seems to require that we build time into love, that temporality becomes not something love has to take into itself, but that which love itself contains and presupposes. Then, and only then, does it become possible to speak of love in the city without seeming to be joining together two essentially incompatible ideas, the eternal character of God with the historical character of social living. If love is itself temporal, however, then the Christ begotten before the foundation of the world represents the constant orientation of the creating and redeeming love of God towards the historical flux and constant ambiguity that characterize the social intercourse of human beings. This paper is concerned therefore to speak about the intrinsic temporality of love, and then to illustrate that in relation to one of the most pervasive, and probably explosive, realities of contemporary urban living, namely the ever larger mountain of debt which we seem to need to build and sustain our cities, but which also overshadows them.

I. LOVE'S HISTORY

It is of the character of love to transport lovers out of history into ecstasy, and it is of the character of our history that it threatens our love with the invasion of disturbance and cares. The capacity for ecstasy is dimmed, even destroyed, by the damage of the past, the pain of the present and the fear of the future, and all loving is thus vulnerable to the passing of time and all that time brings. Yet the ecstasy itself engenders the hope that love will last through the passing of the years, and participate in the quality of endurance which is recognized as the key alike to the loyalty of friendship and the faithfulness of a marriage covenant; both thrust lovers into shared history, that for which in their ecstasy they long. Yet the history which the lovers long to share needs to be experienced as the fulfilment of their ecstasy, not its enemy.

Rightly, Anders Nygren in his classic *Agape and Eros* resists the tradition that makes *agape* a merely moral quality, cut off from its roots in the relationship of God with the world.[2] 'Paul is assuredly not a theologian of the Enlightenment, for whom religion "is revealed as plain unvarnished morality"', he remarks in opposition to Harnack's exposition of Paul's 'Hymn to *Agape*' in 1 Corinthians 13.[3] On the other hand *agape* does not become the love that lasts by being love for God rather than neighbour:

> Whether human love is one of the things that pass away, or one of those that abide, depends not on whether it is love for one's neighbour or love for God, but on whether it is merely human love or a love born of God's own and in its image. If it is the latter, then it belongs to the things that abide, no matter what its object may be. It is not of this kind or that kind of Agape, but of Agape as such, of all Agape whatsoever as proceeding from God, that Paul says, 'Agape never faileth'.[4]

Love is therefore to reflect the divine love which is its origin, and that is to apply to love of neighbour as well as love of God. What is seen in that reflection is the quality of endurance and commitment which is not and will not be dependent on the changes of circumstances which inevitably accompany the lives of people and communities. Love is to survive, transcend and transform the occasions of failure and even betrayal which are the observed features of human relationships; that survival, through

---

[2] Anders Nygren, *Agape and Eros*, trans. Philip S. Watson (London: SPCK, 1982), pp. 133ff.
[3] Nygren, *Agape and Eros*, p. 137.
[4] Nygren, *Agape and Eros*, p. 141.

repeated acts of forgiveness, secures not merely the continuance of the relationship as though by cancelling a debt, but its enhancement by bringing new creation to pass when disaster threatens. In that way love repeats the dynamic of God's relationship with the elect people.

Love's most significant effect, therefore, is to provide an environment of security in which the unknown future of society can be faced. Life together requires a security in relation to that future, since what is quite certain is that the history which lies ahead will contain the same occasions of possible disaster as the past. The character of love is such as to enable the future to be entered into even in the expectation that love's demands will not be met, and the high hopes to which love gives rise will be radically disappointed.[5]

This is the aspect of love which comes through most clearly in the famous discourse on the character of love in the New Testament, presented by St Paul in his correspondence with the Corinthian church. It is true, as David Ford writes:

> ... here precisely where [Paul] is describing a 'still more excellent way' than service through various gifts of the Spirit in the Church he resonates most deeply with the best in the general wisdom of his culture. Far from cutting the vision of 'common sociality' off from the specifically Christian, Paul sets a standard for the Church by it.[6]

Yet the characteristics of love, and particularly the way in which they contrast with the gifts of the Spirit, turn out to be ones which build on a specifically divine history. In that sense they have something to offer to society both then and now. What love offers according to this picture is space for the unknown future:

> Love does not come to an end. But if there are gifts of prophecy, the time will come when they must fail; or the gift of languages, it will not continue for ever; and knowledge – for this too, the time will come when it must fail. For our knowledge is imperfect and our prophesying is imperfect; but once perfection is come, all imperfect things will disappear. (1 Cor. 13.8–10)

Seen in the light of love's openness to the future, the words Paul uses in

---

[5] I have written elsewhere on the significance of the possibility of radical disappointment for urban living; see Peter Selby, 'Saved through Hope', *Christian Action Journal* (Summer 1986), pp. 17–26.
[6] David F. Ford, 'Faith in the Cities: Corinth and the Modern City', in *On Being the Church*, p. 243.

his 'Hymn to Agape', though they parallel descriptions of love offered by many of his contemporaries, take on a quite new significance:

> Love is always patient and kind; it is never jealous; love is never boastful or conceited; it is never rude or selfish; it does not take offence, and is not resentful. Love takes no pleasure in other people's sins but delights in the truth; it is always ready to excuse, to trust, to hope, and to endure whatever comes. (1 Cor. 13.4–7)

What love does not do is focus on one's own achievements in the past (*boastful, conceited*), or the past failings of others (*pleasure in other people's sins*); it is not defensive of one's own present position (*rude, selfish, take offence, resentful*); it does not identify or fix one's own future by reference to what others already have (*jealous*). By contrast, what love does do is make space for the unknowable possibilities which the future holds for those who know the history of love as revealed in the dealings God has had with God's people (*patient, kind, ready to excuse, to trust, to hope, and to endure whatever comes*).

We are to be towards one another as those who do not know our own or each other's future, except that it is in the hands of the One who has proved trustworthy in the past:

> When I was a child, I used to talk like a child, and think like a child, and argue like a child, but now I am a man, all childish ways are put behind me. Now we are seeing a dim reflection in a mirror; but then we shall be seeing face to face. The knowledge that I have now is imperfect; but then I shall know as fully as I am known. (1 Cor. 13.11–12)

So as God has revealed it, and in contrast with the gifts which were so greatly esteemed in Paul's Corinthian audience, love has a history, can face any history and will endure through all history. It is the way God keeps human history open.

In Paul's mind, this perception has enormous implications for the character of the Christian community; it is a community which can only be understood and whose essential character can only be lived out on the basis of a clear eschatology. Rightly, David Ford points to this severe lack in the Church of England's engagements with urban issues as epitomized in the theology which undergirds its most significant and effective report on this subject in recent decades, *Faith in the City*.[7] For all of its value

---

[7] *Faith in the City*, the Report of the Archbishop's Commission on Urban Priority Areas (London: Church Information Office, 1985). Cf. Ford, 'Faith in the Cities', pp. 225–30, 246–9, 254ff.

in showing up clearly the grievous injustices faced by those living in urban priority areas and expressing the Church of England's commitment to the inner city, the report is constrained by the ball and chain of the perpetual difficulty an established church has in taking the eschatological dimension of faith seriously.[8] Ford suggests that while it may be adequate to ground an address to the nation in the general moral requirements of justice and compassion, the report's address to the churches would have needed a far more explicit eschatology and a clearer statement of the church's character.

Yet even to address the society in which we live on the subject of what it would mean to love in the city requires an attention to the way in which Paul roots the concept of love in the history of God's people. If the gospel is not only for the church but also for the world, the common cultural understanding of love requires the clarity of a specifically Christian critique. If the possibility of life together in a wholesome and sustainable setting depends on the city's foundation being love, then Dan Hardy is right to say, to society as well as to the church:

> It is of great importance, therefore, that the foundations of the possibility of society be intelligently grasped, and the possibility thus revealed acted upon. Only thus may the direction of society be identified and pathological deviations discovered and remedied. To address this task is to ask about the position of society in the Doctrines of Creation and Redemption from which the issue of society has come to be disconnected.[9]

It is to one of the most profound signs of that disconnection and its resultant pathological deviations that we now turn.

II. Debt: the Binding of the Future

Among the economic statistics that are eagerly awaited each month is the level of consumer debt. A significant increase in consumer debt is regarded as a sign that the economy is reviving, and is greeted with appropriate exultation by those responsible for the direction of economic policy. This is in some ways odd at a time when in other areas 'Victorian values' are in vogue: evidently thrift and prudence are not necessarily high on the list. Yet the reason for this very positive attitude to consumer debt is that it is regarded as a reasonable index of public confidence:

[8] See Selby, 'Saved through Hope', pp. 23f.
[9] Hardy, 'Created and Redeemed Sociality', p. 22.

people will only borrow more, so the argument runs, if they are more confident in the future, if they expect their jobs to be secure and the property market buoyant. This very positive view of debt does not extend to public debt, government borrowing, which is regarded as a very negative phenomenon. It applies only to private debt, the debts of individual consumers. (It is worth noting in passing that the use of 'public' and 'private' in relation to debt is a particularly flagrant example of the individualism that accompanies a failure to identify the 'direction of society' and remedy its 'pathological deviations'; after all, how many individuals' debts does it take, and how large do they need to be, before they cease to be 'private'?).

It needs first to be pointed out that a large proportion of personal debt is not voluntary 'consumer debt' at all, and therefore in many cases the view that debt is a sign of renewed confidence in the future is (in the derogatory sense of the word) a myth. Persons in receipt of benefit do not borrow from the social fund out of a sense of renewed confidence in the future but because of desperate need in the present. (In this respect the debts of the poorest members of society resemble the indebtedness of the countries of the two-thirds world.) Furthermore, the escalating indebtedness of students does not betoken the sense they have of their steadily improving career prospects on graduation but of the necessary price of higher education. Any talk of indebtedness as a sign of confidence masks the large areas of society where it is simply a sign of desperation.

Yet a critical examination of indebtedness which confined itself to its effect on the poorest sections of the community would be too limited. For surely as important as the causes of indebtedness are its effects. A rising level of personal indebtedness in effect mortgages the future of the whole of society: it is itself the creator of social needs and the producer of great shifts in social attitudes. On the one hand, all of us who contract debts for whatever purpose limit our future freedom of action: the pattern of our future life is largely determined if we have considerable debts to pay off. On the other hand, since we borrow against the hope of a rising standard of living and against the expectation of a steady increase in the price of property, those expectations *must* be met and those results *have* to be produced. As a result it is likely that whatever a government does in pursuit of those goals will be willingly accepted, whatever may be the accompanying costs in civil liberty or social justice. The current policies of lending money to the poorest and increasing student loans will have many effects, but a principal one will be social control: what chance of students being in the vanguard of social criticism if they all have huge debts to pay off?

To make this point is not to mount a doctrinaire attack on all forms of borrowing and lending, but to draw attention to the fundamental dynamic involved when the ideology of debt and the amount of it pass without examination. That dynamic is revealed in that original transaction by which those without food entered slavery:

> When that year was over, they came to Joseph the next year, and said to him, 'We cannot hide it from my lord: the truth is, our money has run out and the livestock is in my lord's possession. There is nothing left for my lord except our bodies and our land. Have we to perish before your eyes, we and our land? Buy us and our land in exchange for bread; we with our land will be Pharaoh's serfs. But give us something to sow, that we may keep our lives and not die and the land may not become desolate.' (Gen. 47.18–19)

The slavery which is the background to the Exodus and thus to the history of redemption results not from invasion or colonization, but from debt. Whether as a result of that folk memory or because of other experiences, the Bible enjoins stringent controls on debt, on rates of interest, on the lengths to which creditors might go in seeking repayment, and on the length of time during which a debt could remain in force. Behind this is certainly the recognition of the dynamic of power that is involved in involuntary indebtedness, and more seriously still the effect that it has on the future freedom of action of the debtor. All the efforts of the ancient equivalent of social policy were directed at ensuring that debt was not a means to exploitation or to depriving others of their freedom for the future.

Thus the presentation of Christ as *redeemer* was not simply created out of the imagination, but was drawn from the deepest memories and contemporary experience of a people who knew what debt could accomplish and saw it as the reverse of the freedom which new life in Christ was intended to be. Lending and borrowing can, when the transaction is undertaken by two voluntary and equal participants, facilitate the best use of available resources; but it can only do that if its highly dangerous capacity to bind the future and impose the will of the creditor on the debtor are recognized and controlled. The point has a particular importance in a situation where most who enter credit transactions do so in the fond belief that they are doing so voluntarily: the pressures of an economy based on acquisition are such that the avoidance of debt is almost impossible, and the constraints of indebtedness on the future freedom of the debtor are so grave as to be something we hardly dare notice.

Ahead of us in the pursuit of the sociality symbolized by escalating debt is a society composed of two more or less clearly defined sections. On the one hand there are those with so much to lose and to protect that their capacity to see their own future as an open sphere of freedom is severely diminished; and on the other hand there are those whose indebtedness has been forced to a level far beyond anything they might be expected to repay – they will be those with nothing to lose, whose future is simply a continuation of the bondage they already experience, and whose investment in society's good and society's laws will become minimal. Such is the effect of unrestrained debt on the very possibility of maintaining the fabric of anything called society.

III. Love and the Freedom of the Future

The nature of debt comes to the surface very quickly in any game of 'Monopoly': the possibility of buying and selling in fantasy the names of famous city streets is one that some find exhilarating; but it is not so easy for losers to have that same sense of power – rows of upturned property cards marked 'mortgaged' are hardly ever the sign of a player with confidence in the future or much chance of surviving. (Such 'games' can also be 'played' in a way which demonstrates the way in which world trade works.) The game surely survives because it is easier to relish the fantasy of large winnings than to savour the bitter fruits of bankruptcy.

Such a game is of course a caricature, a bringing into high relief of the reverse of that 'social transcendental' of which Hardy speaks. Any attempt to propose that a city might be built upon some other foundation, some form of social relation other than that between debtor and creditor, will immediately be branded either as sheer idealism or as the attempt to re-establish some form of repressive socialism long presumed dead. Such objections reveal the degree to which the economy now prevailing over our urban life rules in our minds and commands what amounts to worship. That economy and its rules constitute a social transcendental other than God, an object of worship made by human beings, an idol chosen instead of the possibility represented by the Christian picture of love.

We have already noticed how close is the relationship between ancient cities and idols – gods made by men – because they bear the same names. It is precisely by this creation of idols that the city closes herself up to God. Now she has her own God – the gods she has manufactured, which she can hold in her hands, which she worships because she is master over them, because they are the surest weapon against any other spiritual intervention.[10]

What Paul teaches, and what God has offered in Christ, is indeed a

[10] Jacques Ellul, *The Meaning of the City* (Grand Rapids: Eerdmans, 1970), p. 54.

social transcendental which is in direct contrast to what such idols offer. It is a love which opens history up towards the future instead of locking the future up in an unequal distribution of power and resources by the fantasy of unlimited possibilities of affluence. For if that is the future in which the city chooses to lock itself, it has indeed defended itself well against any possibility of 'spiritual intervention'. Such a 'society' is defended against all change except the unlikely one of revolution or the already evident signs of internal disintegration wrought by crime and social disorder. The links between acquisitiveness and crime, especially in the ambitions of young men, are well displayed by the example of Beatrix Campbell's account of 'joyriding':

> Joyriders' communication systems were built around the community on the one hand and technology on the other ... Radio scanners gave the joyriders greater knowledge of police manoeuvres than the police could reciprocate.[11]

And she makes the point that only a fundamental consideration of the *meaning* of car crime and the way in which it connects crime and personal wealth will have any effect:

> In the absence of any challenge to the connections between the car cult, the potency of its pleasures, and their very identity as men, the criminal justice system was unlikely to impinge on these young offenders.[12]

The attempt to speak of love in the face of such realities runs the severe risk of sounding like a retreat into romanticism. The fear engendered in many parts of our urban environment, the places where nobody dares go, is such that it is hardly surprising that love is separated in our minds from anything that might be expected to be known in society, and the effects of those ideologies which have attempted to achieve sociality by planning and then imposing their plans is hardly encouraging. As Hardy writes:

> Given the ideologies and events of modern times, one might readily doubt whether there could be a transcendental sociality in the real world which was either Godly or fully human.[13]

Yet it is in the face of that fact of our modern world-view that Paul

---

[11] Beatrix Campbell, *Goliath: Britain's Dangerous Places* (London: Methuen, 1993), p. 257.
[12] Campbell, *Goliath*, p. 269.
[13] Hardy, 'Created and Redeemed Sociality', p. 28.

writes to the Corinthians of a way of being together that opens up the possibility of a new history. He speaks of a sociality that has to be real, to be practical; it starts, in the mind of Paul, with the church as the community brought into being on the basis of the love revealed in Jesus, one that redeems those who were enslaved and whose future was constrained as a result of their indebtedness to false socialities. Paul's vision is of a society in which we shall 'owe no one anything but to love one another' (Rom. 13.8).

If the social transcendental called love is to begin with the church, it cannot end there; and the social project called 'church' has to be based on ideas and processes which might have the capacity to undermine that alternative sociality operative in society at large. In constructing our life as church we have to take account of the pressure upon the church's members to conform to the life of the world and participate in its social reality. One of the realities which we may assume, therefore, is that our congregations will be composed of people who know something about love – and who also know a lot about debt.

So a start would be to talk about that reality openly and begin to see how any possibility of being responsive to the call of God's future has been constrained for us all by the ways in which we have placed the future Christ offers in bond; we might even discover that more significant than the agenda created by the loss of the Church Commissioners' millions would be the agenda created by all the years when they gained – at whose expense?

And while we do that, we shall also need to carry out another part of making the social transcendental a practical reality. We require the rehabilitation and control of the economy of debt: to bring it within the bounds of mutuality, equality and concern for its effects. We must support those institutions like credit unions which enable the needy to borrow without thereby losing their freedom of action and/or their ability to speak out and question the roots of their impoverishment.

It is doubtless fruitless to speculate whether Jesus taught his followers to pray to have their debts forgiven as they forgave their debtors (Matt. 6.12), or to pray to have their sins forgiven as they forgave those who sinned against them (Lk. 11.4) or both. What is beyond doubt is that those who experienced the social reality he created found that they could only describe it as a place where people who had previously been burdened by a debt they could never meet found themselves the recipients of treasure beyond price. There were others too who observed that new society; they decided such a world would be too hard to control.

PART THREE: SCRIPTURE

8

The Bible in the Church

JAMES D. G. DUNN

A RECURRENT concern of biblical scholarship throughout the post-Enlightenment period has been that the Bible should be seen and heard to be relevant in the church. The clearest example of this, understandably, has been with regard to Jesus.[1] It was because the Jesus of Christian dogma seemed so unhuman, so remote from the everyday life of the church, that the quest of the historical Jesus was undertaken in the first place – the attempt to recover a Jesus who was meaningful to 'modern' Christians. In nineteenth-century Liberalism the concern was that the Bible should be heard to speak meaningfully to those for whom religion focused in the inner life and in ethical conduct. In Martin Kähler's reaction the concern was that 'the historic biblical Christ' not be replaced by a humanly constructed historical artefact.[2] In the Barthian reaction the concern was for the words of the Bible to be heard again as the word of God and not be lost in the detail of historical analysis.[3] And in the Bultmannian reaction the concern was that the kerygma be heard in and through the biblical myth and not remain imprisoned therein or lost when the myth was removed.[4] So too the more recent flight from the historical-critical method has been motivated by a concern that its results were so minimal and so controverted that the function of the text as communication of meaning was being lost.[5] The contemporary concern to find meaning 'in front of' the text rather than 'behind' the text, in the interaction of reader and biblical text is motivated by the same desire that

---

[1] For the quest of the historical Jesus see now, e.g., C. Brown, 'Historical Jesus, Quest of', in *Dictionary of Jesus and the Gospels*, ed. J. B. Green *et al.* (Downers Grove, IL: InterVarsity, 1992), pp. 326–41.

[2] M. Kähler, *The So-Called Historical Jesus and the Historic Biblical Christ* (1896) (Philadelphia: Fortress, 1964).

[3] Note the much quoted lines in the preface to the second edition of K. Barth's *Romans* (London: Oxford University Press, 1933), particularly p. 7.

[4] R. Bultmann, 'New Testament and Mythology' (1941), in *Kerygma and Myth*, ed. H. W. Bartsch (London: SPCK, 1964), pp. 15–47; *idem, Jesus Christ and Mythology* (London: SCM, 1950).

[5] Expressive of the mood and influential in biblical circles has been the brief treatment by W. Wink, *The Bible in Human Transformation* (Philadelphia: Fortress, 1973).

the Bible should be heard to speak with relevance and effect to the contemporary church and world.[6]

All this hive of activity and burden of concern presupposes the importance of the Bible as the church's book.[7] That is not to deny that the Bible can be read and valued outside the church; the Bible is not the church's exclusive property – a factor in the overall role of the Bible to which we must return. But there is a symbiotic relationship between the Bible and the church without regard to which the Bible's importance cannot be clearly, let alone fully appreciated. The point focuses particularly in the New Testament (NT). For though the church preceded the NT; the NT consists of its teaching and liturgical materials.[8] Yet, at the same time, the NT is itself the primary statement of the gospel, by responding to which the church came into existence, and out of which the church grows. The mutuality of interdependence between NT and church means that the one cannot be properly comprehended without reference to the other. What this means in practice will also, hopefully, become clearer as we proceed.

For the purpose of this brief reflection the role of the Bible in the Church can perhaps be summed up most conveniently under the three heads, Information, Definition and Inspiration.

I. INFORMATION

Any religion needs some statement about its beliefs (faith) and practice, for its own self-understanding as well as to explain itself to others. Here it is important to remember that Christianity is not constituted by a statement of timeless truths, or by a code of practice which could be transmitted in brief written form or in a regulated system. It is constituted rather by a series of stories, about God who created, about God choosing a people and giving them rules to live by, about that people's ups-and-downs in their relationship with God, and not least, about Jesus of Nazareth, and about its own establishment and initial expansion and consolidation.[9]

---

[6] See e.g. the two large-scale reviews of the debate by A. C. Thiselton, *The Two Horizons* (Exeter: Paternoster, 1980); *idem*, *New Horizons in Hermeneutics* (London: HarperCollins, 1992); and F. Watson, ed., *The Open Text: New Directions for Biblical Studies* (London: SCM, 1993).

[7] I am referring here, of course, to the Christian Bible; the problem that the *Christian* Bible includes as its Old Testament the *Jewish* scriptures will be touched on later.

[8] See e.g. W. Marxsen, *The New Testament as the Church's Book* (Philadelphia: Fortress, 1972).

[9] This feature of the biblical text has become very important in recent literary criticism of the Bible; see e.g. those referred to in Thiselton, *New Horizons*, pp. 479–86; and N. T. Wright, *The New Testament and the People of God*, vol. 1 (London: SPCK, 1992), ch. 3.

Of course, the story (of Christianity) continues beyond the Bible, and that continued story is also important for giving content to the name 'Christianity'. But there is a particular fascination about the period of birth and early childhood. As the stories of a person's early years often help to explain features of the person's present character, so it is with Christianity. There is a similar fascination about one's immediate ancestors, since they too may help explain features and traits which an individual's conscious memory cannot recall. Correspondingly, the church simply needs to know these stories which embody its own pre-history and early history, otherwise it cannot properly know itself.

A central characteristic of most of these stories is that they claim to have taken place in history. To be sure, the Bible can properly be said to include stories which are essentially mythical, particularly with regard to its beginning and ending chapters (early Genesis and Revelation). These are stories which go beyond recordable history and which, consequently, are not amenable to scrutiny by historical techniques. But the great bulk of the stories in between claim to be historical. More to the point, *their theological significance for the church is bound up with that claim*. For they claim to be recounting the ways and means by which God revealed himself and acted in history, the ways and means by which God was encountered or experienced by people living fully within the flow and eddies of the moving stream of history.

This is also to recognize that God revealed himself within the contexts, contingencies and relativities of historical situations, events and processes – where insights granted are always in greater or less degree personal and context-related, expressed in the language (Hebrew, Aramaic, Greek) and idiom of the time – where truths expressed are always contingent and context-conditioned, however much they may also transcend historical particularities – where most texts (not all, but most) are so embedded in the thought and social world of their time, rooted there by their very terminology and syntax, interwoven into the fabric of their time of composition by innumerable tendrils of taken-for-granted usage and subtle allusion, that they cannot be pulled free from that context without inflicting on them serious damage.[10]

Consequently, the bulk of this information thus provided in the Bible *is* amenable to historical scrutiny. A Christianity which makes such claims about events and people in history, by reference to such texts, and which understands itself in large part in terms of that history and these texts cannot and should not wish it otherwise. For Christianity to take refuge in a system of esoteric signs or mystical visions or technical terminology

---

[10] See further my 'Historical Text as Historical Text', in *Words Remembered, Texts Renewed*, Essays in Honour of John F. A. Sawyer, eds. J. Davies, G. Harvey, and W. G. E. Watson (Sheffield: Sheffield Academic Press, 1995), pp. 340–59.

or traditional ritual praxis as a way of escaping such scrutiny would be to make a decisive change in its own character. In contrast, however, Christianity by telling such stories places itself in the public forum; its information is subject to public scrutiny.

For some, that thought opens up the fearful prospect of Christian teaching as constantly prey to sceptical historical method. That, of course, is a danger. But it is not a danger which the church should shy completely away from. On the contrary, it is an inevitable consequence of a story in which God in his self-revelation in and through the man Christ Jesus puts himself at the mercy of history. The Bible's vulnerability to historical scrutiny, like Jesus' vulnerability to historical processes, is simply part of Christianity's character. Moreover there is an up-side to this down-side. For it is precisely the Bible's public character which enables it to claim a hearing in the public forum, which makes it possible for it to communicate with those who have not been trained in Christian terminology or conditioned by experience of the Christian mystery.

We are here, of course, caught up into the ongoing theological tension between faith and history. But this again is a tension which is constitutive of the biblical witness – the tension in theology between a God who acted decisively once-for-all in history (the Exodus, Good Friday and Easter) and the Baals of Canaanite fertility cults or the mystery deities who competed with early Christianity. However, it is a tension which has become particularly acute for Christianity since the Enlightenment, when history became an autonomous discipline. It is the issue underlying the brief description of the opening paragraph of this paper. Suffice to say, once again, that it is a tension which cannot be escaped, given the nature of the Bible's testimony. To seek to escape into an area of faith totally separate from and invulnerable to historical scrutiny once again would undercut Christianity's character, just as it would pervert Christianity to reduce it solely to phenomena, events and processes within the historical sphere, and so render it vulnerable without remainder to historical scrutiny.[11]

The point is that a church caught up in such public debate needs its skilled practitioners to help direct and carry forward that debate. It needs its professionals trained in understanding and interpreting the Bible; from the first, teachers, expounders of the tradition, have been integral to the church's function.[12] Today that means, for one thing, professional theologians and scholars who can both prosecute the historical inquiry within the community of faith and engage with the church's intellectual despisers at the most scholarly level when necessary. For another, it means trained practitioners who know where the fruits of generations of

[11] See further n. 28 below.
[12] E.g. Acts 13.1; 1 Cor. 12.28; Gal. 6.6.

historical scrutiny have been harvested (in lexical commentaries, text-books and fundamental studies), and who, thus equipped, can handle inquiries (everything from dealing with textual variants and choice between translations, to clarifying Jesus' teaching on the kingdom and Paul's teaching on the atonement) and retell the stories in an informed and lively way.[13]

This does not make the professional theologian or minister the sole authoritative voice in explaining or expounding the Bible. For we are speaking only at the level of the first function of the Bible – to provide information. And in this role within the church those with professional expertise are simply functioning as part of the community of faith, exercising their charisma and calling within the church. Any religious community needs those whom it sets aside and depends on to be well informed on its tradition and stories and to explain their complexities and continuing relevance. All it means in the church's case, given the nature of the Bible as telling stories of people and events in history and in languages and idioms of bygone ages, is that such professionally qualified individuals are essential if the church is to be able to maintain its own self-respect and integrity within a world which similarly depends on other such professionalisms.

It is also important to remember that this role is not only directed toward the world outside the church, in apologetic or persuasion. It is also a role important within the church. For the church in its successive generations constantly needs to be reminded not only of the content of its foundational documents, but also of their character and of the character of the stories which they recount.[14] A God who has made his self-revelation so vulnerable to history, in the first place to historical processes, and in the second to the subsequent need for historical scrutiny, is a God who is content that all formulations and practices are integrally contingent and who thus also warns against making any formulation or practice into an unconditioned absolute, into an idol.

But this brings us already to the second function of the Bible within the church.

---

[13] It is regrettable that in the twentieth-century ecumenical movement the intensity of focus on *sacramental* ministry as the distinctive feature of *ordained* ministry has diverted attention from this crucial professional role, and that the theological *teacher*, as distinct from the ordained minister, has no formal role within the traditional and still current structures of most churches. Contrast the role of the rabbi in Judaism and the imam in Islam.

[14] The challenge of Christian education as an ongoing process is one which the churches, particularly in Britain, need to address with increasing urgency.

II. DEFINITION

A second and more important role of the Bible in the church is to provide definition of what Christianity is or should be. The Bible constitutes the founding or foundational documents of the church. Its function on this point is analogous to that of the constitution of the United States – an indispensable reference point by which subsequent statements of policy or practice must be measured, a basic statement of the principles by which the corporate body of the United States defines and recognizes itself. Of the three functions of the Bible in the church this is the most problematic and so requires fuller treatment.

With regard to the Bible this role is seen most clearly, once again, in reference to Jesus. For Jesus is *the* distinguishing feature of Christianity – in particular, the claim that the revelation determinative for Christianity was embodied in the life and ministry, death and resurrection of the historical figure Jesus of Nazareth. This claim ties Christianity to a specific historical figure to an extent true of no other religion. Of course it is Jesus *himself* who is the defining feature of Christianity. But for that feature to serve as definition makes the church wholly dependent on the biblical documents which tell us who this Jesus was, which tell us both the content and character of the revelation he embodied. It is true that some might want to put all the weight on Jesus' death and resurrection, as theologically rather than historically evaluated, and to sit light to the records of Jesus' life and ministry; but the church has generally resisted attempts to separate Jesus of Nazareth from the crucified and risen Lord, the 'historical Jesus' from the 'Christ of faith', incarnation from exaltation.[15] This is in no way to deny that there have been subsequent lives of Jesus, subsequent statements of his significance, including, of course, credal, confessional and dogmatic statements. The point is, however, that *all of these subsequent statements are dependent on and derivative from the NT accounts.* There is no independent source apart from the NT, the Gospels in particular, for information about that defining historical person. These accounts therefore are themselves definitive because they alone provide access to the definitive historical person and events.

This function of the Bible in the church throws up a number of troublesome corollaries which in the last generation no one posed so sharply or effectively as Ernst Käsemann. One is the *diversity* of the biblical witness. Thus Käsemann:

---

[15] Whether the original separation attempted in Gnosticism or the Kierkegaardian limitation of the defining focus to the mere historical thatness of Jesus' existence; witness the response of the new questers to Bultmann, particularly E. Käsemann, 'The Problem of the Historical Jesus' (1951), in *Essays on New Testament Themes* (London: SCM, 1964), pp. 15–47.

The New Testament canon does not, as such, constitute the foundation of the unity of the church. On the contrary, as such (that is, in its accessibility to the historian) it provides the basis for the multiplicity of the confessions.[16]

The point can be illustrated by reference to the Bible's testimony to Jesus himself. For it should never be forgotten that the Bible contains *four* Gospels and not simply one – four *different* Gospels, with differences both subtle (between the Synoptics) and obvious (between the Synoptics and John's Gospel). This means that the church which acknowledged these four Gospels as canonical thereby recognized, if only implicitly, that the story of Jesus (and the defining revelation embodied therein) could be told in different ways, with diverse emphases, or, alternatively expressed, that the story of Jesus could not be limited to a single definitive telling. The information which historical study can provide to illuminate the historical reasons for this diversity (Section I above) can help explain much of the why and the what of that diversity (Gospels directed to more Jewish or more Gentile oriented churches, or seeking to engage with and counter a more gnosticizing expression of the gospel, or whatever). But the definitional (or canonical) significance of a diverse fourfold gospel is to warn the church against imposing a too narrow conformity on the contemporary expression of the gospel.[17] Of course, that in no way validates a limitless diversity: in recognizing four Gospels the early church disowned other documents bearing the same title.[18] Not a few retellings of the story were unacceptable. Nevertheless, it is still important to remember that the normative forms of the story are themselves marked by a significant degree of diversity. In sum, the canon canonizes diversity as well as unity.

More problematic is the fact that the church does not recognize everything in the Bible as equally definitive. To be considered here above all is the problem of the Old Testament (OT). For the OT consists of the Hebrew scriptures of Israel, of Judaism. As such they do not function as

---

[16] E. Käsemann, 'The Canon of the New Testament and the Unity of the Church', in *Essays on New Testament Themes*, pp. 95–107, here p. 103; see also my *Unity and Diversity in the New Testament* (London: SCM / Philadelphia: TPI, 1977, 1990²).
[17] Cf. O. Cullmann, 'The Plurality of the Gospel as a Theological Problem in Antiquity', in *The Early Church: Historical and Theological Studies* (London: SCM, 1956), pp. 39–54.
[18] For the non-canonical Gospels see W. Schneemelcher, *New Testament Apocrypha*, Vol. *1*, ed. R. McL. Wilson (Cambridge: James Clarke / Louisville: Westminster, 1991). Despite arguments to the contrary by H. Koester, *Introduction to the New Testament*, Vol. 2 (Berlin: de Gruyter / Philadelphia: Fortress, 1982) and others, the judgement of the early church on the unhistorical as well as non-canonical value of these Gospels cannot be lightly disregarded.

definition directly for the church. The church, for example, does not regard prescriptions regarding circumcision and sacrifice, food laws and sabbath (as such) as of continuing validity. But neither can we speak of the NT simply as superseding the OT. Rather we must speak of a pre-definitional function, of the OT as background to, preparatory for, explanatory of the revelation in and through Jesus. Since Jesus was a Jew and Christianity began within early Judaism, the OT plays a crucial role in giving content to and even helping define the definition. The God of Jesus and of the first Christians is the God of Israel, the God already defined as one, unseeable, 'the Lord merciful and gracious, ...' (Ex. 34.6–7). In his fundamental character as Messiah/Christ the content of the definition of Jesus is in large part determined by the OT. And so on. The NT can only function as definition when understood in the light of the OT.[19]

Even more problematic is the question of whether the NT as a whole is definitive, or equally definitive across its pages. Is Revelation of equal authority for Christians as Matthew, 2 Peter as Romans? It is not enough to conclude that the NT is the primary authority within the Bible, the NT as canon within the biblical canon. Do we not have to speak also of a canon within the canon with reference to the NT itself[20] – whether Christological (it preaches Christ,[21] or Jesus the man become Lord,[22] or the Jesus-kerygma[23]), or 'justification by faith',[24] or, going outside the NT, 'the rule of faith'[25]? Given the time-conditionedness of the NT's witness, and that some of its teaching is more closely context-related than the rest,[26] by what yardstick is the definitional weight of any text to be recognized or evaluated?

The problems posed in the preceding paragraphs are simply particular examples of the larger hermeneutical problem, which now features so largely in contemporary discussion of the Bible and its continuing value.

[19] See particularly the sustained concerns of P. Stuhlmacher, e.g. *Vom Verstehen des Neuen Testaments: Eine Hermeneutik* (Göttingen: Vandenhoeck, 1979); *Versöhnung, Gesetz and Gerechtigkeit: Aufsätze zur biblischen Theologie* (Göttingen: Vandenhoeck, 1981); *Biblische Theologie des Neuen Testaments: Band 1. Grundlegung von Jesus zu Paulus* (Göttingen: Vandenhoeck, 1992).
[20] Here too Käsemann's work has been most stimulating and provocative; see his *Das Neue Testament als Kanon* (Göttingen: Vandenhoeck, 1970).
[21] The famous criterion of Luther; see e.g. W. G. Kümmel, *The New Testament: The History of the Investigation of its Problems* (London: SCM, 1973), pp. 25–6.
[22] My own attempt at formulation in *Unity and Diversity in the New Testament*.
[23] S. M. Ogden, *The Point of Christology* (London: SCM, 1982), pp. 51–63, following W. Marxsen.
[24] Käsemann's own characteristically Lutheran position in *Kanon*, p. 405; similarly S. Schulz, *Die Mitte der Schrift* (Stuttgart, 1976), pp. 429ff.
[25] Classically in Irenaeus and Tertullian.
[26] The issue of Christian women wearing head covering in the worshipping assembly in Corinth is the standard example (1 Cor. 11.2–16).

How do we discern meaning in and from the Bible (as from any text)? Part of that discussion leads us into our final section. Here we remain focused on the definitional meaning of the text in its historical context, which follows from the definitional character of the person and events to which it bears witness. But even here the question of what the text meant remains open in one degree or other. This is why it is not enough simply to assert dogmatically that the Bible is inspired and therefore authoritative. The question still stands: even so, in regard to particular texts, what is their inspired meaning? Nor will the Reformation confidence in the perspicacity of scripture necessarily help much beyond the great 'truths of salvation', since those passages whose meaning is 'clear' to some (by which they determine the meaning of the 'unclear' passages) are unclear to others (hence Käsemann's point about the NT validating the diversity of the denominations). The uncomfortable fact is that apart from the great saving truths the definitional meaning of the Bible on many an issue is disputed.

The historic answer to this problem is that the definitional value of scripture has been determined by the tradition of the church, which, within the Catholic tradition, means the magisterium of the church. There are many, of course, who recognize a wider catholicity – tradition as including all that has maintained continuity with the apostolic gospel, the *sensus fidelium* which includes all the faithful; but they too have to acknowledge the importance of tradition in relation to the Bible. On so many issues of faith and living the questions have moved far beyond those which the biblical authors addressed; so any church which seeks to speak to its contemporary world (and which believes in the Holy Spirit) is bound to recognize the necessity to draw out truths and principles from the biblical witness and develop them well beyond what is actually said in the Bible or can be uncovered by critical exegesis as such. Apart from anything else, the ecumenical creeds in their definition of the faith already go well beyond what the Bible actually states.

In such cases can we still speak of the definitional role of the Bible? Yes, partly because the biblical witness demonstrates that the truth of God, or at least human perception and expression of it, forms a developing trajectory (God and his Spirit understood progressively more fully through the OT, the significance of Jesus likewise coming to fuller expression through the NT, and so on).[27] So, to that extent at least, the definitional role of the Bible itself validates divinely given truth coming to ever fresh and fuller expression in different language and culture contexts. But yes also, at least to the extent that the church's rulings and practices continue to draw on biblical assertions, themes and precedents; that is, to the extent of providing a primary statement of these assertions,

---

[27] See further my *Unity and Diversity*, pp. 379–82.

themes and precedents, which, despite its historical conditionedness, still remains normative or canonical for the church.[28]

This definitional role of scripture has become increasingly important within Roman Catholicism since Vatican II. Recent years have seen an increasing recognition that within the twofold norm of scripture and tradition primacy must be given to scripture, that the canon must be allowed to function as norm within the twofold norm, that scripture must be recognized to have a critical function vis-à-vis tradition.[29] The unavoidable dependence of the church on its own living tradition to interpret scripture to changing times and questions is not at issue here. But the still more fundamental dependence of the church on the biblical testimony to Jesus Christ cannot be downplayed without changing the fundamental character of Christianity. In the last analysis this means that the historical language, idiom and structure of the biblical witness retain a definitional authority, which in principle and practice must continue to serve in at least some measure as a check and determining factor on what can and what cannot properly claim the title 'Christian'.

III. INSPIRATION

For most Christians the most important role of the Bible in the church is

---

[28] Cf. e.g. R. Morgan and J. Barton, *Biblical Interpretation* (Oxford: OUP, 1988), p. 182, 'The only way to maintain some theological flexibility while retaining the benefits of an authoritative and well-used scripture is to combine hermeneutical creativity with historical controls'. For other balanced critical appraisals of the role of historical criticism within the larger hermeneutical task, see e.g., from a Protestant perspective, P. Stuhlmacher, *Historical Criticism and Theological Interpretation of Scripture* (London: SPCK, 1979); F. Hahn, *Historical Investigation and New Testament Faith* (Philadelphia: Fortress, 1983); and from a Roman Catholic perspective, R. E. Brown, *The Critical Meaning of the Bible* (New York: Paulist, 1981); S. M. Schneiders, *The Revelatory Text: Interpreting the New Testament as Sacred Scripture* (San Francisco: Harper, 1991).

[29] The point was accepted by Cardinal Ratzinger in a positive response to the Protestant critique of *Dei Verbum* (the Vatican II statement on Divine Revelation) in *Commentary on the Documents of Vatican II*, ed. H. Vorgrimler, Vol. III (London: Burns & Oates, 1968), pp. 192–3. See also the statement of the Biblical Commission on *Scripture and Christology* (1985), particularly §§ 1.2.1.1 and 1.2.2.1, with its clear distinction between the language of the creeds as 'auxiliary' language, and the 'referential' language of the inspired writers, which is 'the ultimate source of revelation'; J. A. Fitzmyer, *Scripture and Christology* (London: Chapman, 1986), pp. 19–20, 57; and Schneiders, *Revelatory Text*, p. 86, 'Tradition is the essential context for the interpretation of scripture, but scripture is the norm by which the true and living tradition is discerned'. A striking example of the application of this principle is K.-J. Kuschel, *Born Before All Time? The Dispute over Christ's Origin* (London: SCM, 1992), p. 487, 'The message of Jesus himself and the original proclamation of Jesus as the Christ remain the critical standard for later dogmatic statements' (see also pp. 489–90).

this third role.[30] For their main experience of the Bible is as it actually functions in the church's worship and liturgy: in the psalms and canticles which they sing, in the readings they hear (but why always in such brief extracts?), and in the homilies and sermons which take biblical texts or themes as their subject-matter and which are usually primarily inspirational in purpose and in character. Simply because this constitutes the major everyday use of the Bible in the church we must accord this role due prominence.

It is important to grasp the fact that this role is fundamental to the Bible's character. For what the Bible consists of is primarily the materials of worship, some of which stretch back three millennia. It is an astonishing fact, much dulled for most Christians by long familiarity, that the psalter has provided such continuous vehicle of prayer and praise for so long and for two world religions – that alone attests its inspirational value. Hearing and obeying has always been at the heart of Jewish religion understood as a way of living, and Christianity resonates with that emphasis, even though historically 'faith' has been a more important category for Christians. The NT too had its initial function within the church's worship: the Gospels consisting in large part of reminiscences of Jesus' ministry put together to be read and taught and meditated on; the letters written to be read out within churches gathered to share their common life and for worship; and so on.

We see too a developing tradition of worship, for instance the prayer of Hannah inspiring the Magnificat (1 Sam. 2.1–10; Lk. 1.46–55), or the Shema of Deut. 6.4 re-expressed for Christians in the conjoint confession of one God and one Lord in 1 Cor. 8.6.[31] Or within the NT itself we may instance the Lord's Prayer and words of institution of the Lord's Supper in two different forms and evidencing the effect of liturgical usage (Matt. 6.9–13/Lk. 11.2–4; Mk. 14.22–24=Matt. 26.26–28/Lk. 22.19–20=1 Cor. 11.24–25).[32] Here as with the developing trajectory of Christian doctrine (see section II) we may say that the Bible both validates a developing liturgical practice but also provides materials which continue to be inspirational in their own use and to inspire fresh material. Certainly it can hardly be said that the Bible encourages a uniformity of worship or a rigidity of liturgical tradition.

In addition we must note the extensive history of personal or small group spirituality which equally attests the inspirational role of the Bible. For a whole dimension of Christian spirituality the Bible functions not

---

[30] An alternative term would be 'transformation' as in Schneiders, *Revelatory Text*, pp. 13–14.

[31] See further my *Christology in the Making* (London: SCM, 1980, 1989²), pp. 179–83.

[32] J. Jeremias, *New Testament Theology, Vol. 1, The Proclamation of Jesus* (London: SCM, 1971), pp. 193–6; Dunn, *Unity and Diversity*, pp. 165–8.

merely as the word of God to past generations, but continues to function as the word of God now – inspired in order to inspire (2 Tim. 3.16–17). God is heard still to speak through its pages; it functions as much as the Eucharist as a means of grace, as itself a sacrament, to be cherished and resorted to frequently for that reason. Hence the emphasis in so many Christian traditions on the inescapable interwovenness of word and sacrament, though in fact Christian practice has tended to diverge between a word-centred worship or a sacrament-centred worship. Nor should one forget or soon discount the many testimonies to the converting power of the Bible, of testaments and individual books of the Bible which, coming into the hands of individuals at a fitting time, spoke words of challenge or of grace 'by which they were saved'. The role of the Bible Societies and of Gideon Bibles in lonely hotel rooms indicate the importance of a ministry fulfilled by the Bible whose full effectiveness can never be quantified.

At the other end of the same spectrum we have to speak of the Bible's aesthetic power, that it has the inspiring quality of the great masterpiece which speaks effectively at a less explicitly religious level. This too is part of the public character of the Bible, that in societies shaped by European tradition, biblical imagery and themes have so entered into the warp and woof of their cultural life (art, literature and music in particular), that the springs and streams of that culture are forever suffused with its message, affording, once again, invaluable points of contact between church and wider society. The same is true in diverse measure of the moral principles and humanitarian ideals which have shaped and still inspire the ethos of most western democracies.

All this again highlights an important feature of the current debate on the Bible's meaning – that meaning is not to be found, as it were, solely by quarrying into the text, but also (or always, in greater or less measures) in the interaction of the reader with the text, not just 'behind' the text but also 'in front of' the text. It will not do, then, to limit use of the Bible in the church to the question of what it *meant*; equally, or more important, is the question what it *means*. Is the meaning of the text determined solely by what the original author (where we can speak of such) intended (assuming that it can be discerned)? Is the canonical meaning of the text, that is, the meaning it had for those who determined the content and limits of the Christian canon, not equally or more determinative?[33] And if we believe in the Holy Spirit as a living force within the church today, we must presumably be open to the possibility and indeed likelihood that new insights will be given to and emerge from the

---

[33] Notable here has been the sustained advocacy of B. S. Childs, as most recently in his *The New Testament as Canon: An Introduction* (London: SCM, 1984).

church's contemporary reading of the Bible.[34] Particularly important in the last few decades have been the challenges of feminist readings[35] and readings in the light of liberation theology,[36] which have for many been themselves transforming experiences, liberating from stultifying patriarchal and 'first world' perspectives. 'There is yet more light to break from God's word'.

There is one further matter which ought not to be ignored: that some biblical texts seem to encourage a reading which does not accord or no longer accords with the mind of the church. One thinks, of course, of some of the more bloodthirsty elements in the Psalms (classically Ps. 137.9). There are also the assumptions of biblical writers with regard to such matters as slavery and the status of women, which have been part of the provocation of feminist and political readings and which makes their challenge so serious. But even more pressing in recent years has been the problem that many texts, particularly John's Gospel, seem to encourage a fierce anti-Jewishness and have in fact been used in the history of the church to inspire and validate anti-semitism (classically Matt. 27.25 and Jn. 8.44). What of this inspiring role of the Bible?

For some the answer has been to omit such passages from the lectionary or to alter the translations to avoid encouraging unchristian attitudes.[37] But that answer is not satisfactory; anything that does violence to the text of the Bible will surely not do. Better to keep these passages, rendered as accurately as possible in accord with the Hebrew and Greek of the critically received texts, at the very least as historic witnesses to honest prayer, or culturally conditioned morality, or the intensity of truth inadequately expressed and fought for. Moreover, one of the important corollaries of recognizing the diversity of the biblical witness is the recognition also that there are 'texts for the times' – different texts for different times. The book of Revelation, for example, may not speak with any force or relevance to many churches today; but to churches under persecution and threat to their very existence the inspirational value of the seer's visions could be unquantifiable. 'The Bible in the church' means

---

[34] A fruitful image has been that of the scriptures not simply read in church but 'performed' in Christian community and living; see particularly N. Lash, *Theology on the Way to Emmaus* (London: SCM, 1986), ch. 3, 'Performing the Scriptures'; and F. Young, *The Art of Performance: Towards a Theology of Holy Scripture* (London: Darton, Longman & Todd, 1990).

[35] The classic text is E. Schüssler Fiorenza, *In Memory of Her: A Feminist Theological Reconstruction of Christian Origins* (London: SCM, 1983).

[36] See e.g. C. Rowland and M. Corner, *Liberating Exegesis: The Challenge of Liberation Theology to Biblical Studies* (London: SPCK, 1990); F. Watson, 'Liberating the Reader: A Theological-Exegetical Study of the Parable of the Sheep and the Goats (Matt. 25.31–46)', in *The Open Text*, pp. 57–84.

[37] E.g. N. A. Beck, *Mature Christianity: The Recognition and Repudiation of the Anti-Jewish Polemic of the New Testament* (London/Toronto: Associated University Presses, 1985).

also in the one church extended through time as well as throughout the world. It may well be right, then, for some texts to be set on one side as of less 'word of God relevance' to a church in circumstances different from those envisaged in the text, though even that policy is questionable since who can tell through what text the Spirit may speak afresh the word of God? But rather than modify the text itself, it would surely be better to insure that lectionaries and Bible reading notes add when necessary a gloss which explains the historical circumstances or literary traditions and rhetoric which gave rise to texts which otherwise might cause offence or inspire falsely.

CONCLUSION

It is important to recognize that the Bible has all three functions in the church, information, definition and inspiration, and not to restrict its role, in theory or practice, to one or other. It is also important to recognize that all three functions are interdependent. To focus solely on the first would make the Bible a mere archive and depository of interesting archaeological information. But neither can the Bible's information-function be set aside in favour of the other two, for the accuracy of the information it provides gives the definition shape, and, as we have just noted, the inspiration which ignores the historical character and conditionedness of the information may become the medium of false prophecy. Likewise the Bible's canonical role can hardly be downplayed without Christianity's self-understanding becoming blurred, 'a yacht without a keel'. At the same time, to stress the Bible's definitional role in isolation from the other two would make it difficult if not impossible to handle the 'troublesome corollaries' which we outlined above and would exalt its character as law over its force as gospel. And without the inspirational power of the Bible, the word of God would quickly become a dead letter. At the same time an inspiration divorced from definition becomes a recipe for individual flights of pietistic fancy and the dominance of the charismatic guru.

Alternatively expressed, scripture separated from living tradition speaks in a foreign language; tradition separated from scripture can soon become repressive, merely 'the tradition of men'. Scholarship separated from preaching is more likely to deaden than to make alive; preaching separated from scholarship is likely soon to become ill-informed, superficial or irresponsible. Devotional reading separated from the teaching ministry of the church can leave the individual prey to the 'devil who quotes scripture for his own purposes'; but the church which only teaches but does not inspire is already lost; 'with teaching a community will not die, but without prophecy it will not live'.[38]

[38] J. D. G. Dunn, *Jesus and the Spirit* (London: SCM, 1975), p. 284.

9

Paul's Church and Ours: Re-forming a Biblical Theology of the Church

DENNIS L. STAMPS

INTRODUCTION

THE Bible, Holy Scripture, the Word of God – all these terms designate one of the crucial elements in the life of the Christian community. Christianity has been and continues to be shaped by the written testimony of the 'people of God'. In the early church, the Old Testament was an authoritative voice which spoke of the purpose and promise of God in history, which spoke concerning Christ's ministry and mission, and which spoke regarding the consummation of history. During the period of apostolic ministry, even the writings of the apostles themselves appear to have taken on authoritative status (2 Pet. 3.15); and in the post-apostolic period and beyond it, this status only grew and developed until the New Testament 'canon' was fixed. As a fixed document, the Old Testament combined with those recognized New Testament texts assumed a primary role in shaping the thought and life of the church, a role which was only enhanced by its designation as a sacred text.[1]

So the tale continues as the Christian church, in all its diversity, reads and interprets its sacred text. The Christian community searches for ways to let the text speak and inform its life and praxis. It is at the juncture where there is a transition from text to theology and practice that problems multiply. Theology based on the Bible or biblical theology becomes problematic because it entails interpretation coupled with application within the context of a specific human situation.[2]

It is this move from sacred text to the theological thinking of the Christian community which I wish to explore in this essay, specifically the move from the Pauline writings to a biblical theology of the church. I am very conscious that this exercise is an attempt in doing biblical theology before even defining what biblical theology is and before setting

[1] E. Farley, *Ecclesial Reflection: An Anatomy of Theological Method* (Philadelphia: Fortress, 1982), pp. 47–82.
[2] W. G. Jeanrond, 'After Hermeneutics: The Relationship between Theology and Biblical Studies', in *The Open Text*, ed. F. Watson (London: SCM, 1993), pp. 85–102.

out the philosophical justification and methodology for biblical theology. In that sense this 'doing' of biblical theology is an exploration of or a move towards a biblical theology of the church for the church in the context of a post-structuralist hermeneutics.[3]

The first section will examine the Pauline corpus to see how Pauline teaching about the church corresponds to the historical contingencies each Pauline letter addresses. The second section will suggest a hermeneutical strategy for moving from the biblical text to a biblically informed theology. In the third section some tentative suggestions will be presented as a biblical ecclesiology.

I. THE CHURCH IN THE PAULINE LITERATURE

Before examining the Pauline literature, something needs to be said about the extent of the Pauline corpus which is under consideration. Many studies of the theme of the church in the Pauline writings make essential distinctions based on the premise that Ephesians and Colossians are not authentic to Pauline authorship and that the Pastoral epistles are post-Pauline literature.[4] While the question of Pauline authorship can be an important historical factor for reconstructing the history of the Pauline mission and for tracing the development of theological thought and of early church life, it is not an essential factor for the biblical theology enterprise in general. Canonically, the Pauline corpus includes all those writings which claim to be by Paul. The problem of theological diversity, development, even potential contradiction within this corpus with regard to a particular issue is part of the given. One may evaluate such theological diversity from a historical perspective – such diversity represents different authors at different times and in different situations – or one may affirm such diversity as part of the theological process (however it came to be historically) and as part of the biblical given within the strictures of the canon.[5]

As one surveys (and a brief survey is all that can be offered here) the Pauline literature several facets of the early church experience within the orb of the Pauline mission emerge. This survey will be organized accord-

---

[3] See W. G. Jeanrond, *Theological Hermeneutics: Development and Significance* (New York: Crossroad, 1991), pp. 12–158, for a fuller statement of the present context of the hermeneutical situation.

[4] A. T. and R. P. C. Hanson, *The Identity of the Church: A Guide to Recognizing the Contemporary Church* (London: SCM, 1987), pp. 3–12; J. D. G. Dunn, *Jesus and the Spirit* (London: SCM, 1975), pp. 345–50.

[5] Compare the more perceptive remarks on this point in H. Küng, *The Church* (Garden City, NY: Image Books), pp. 35–46.

ing to several of these facets: the structure and authority of the church, the worship and practical life of the church, the theological issues in the church, and the Pauline teaching about the church.

In order not to flatten out the situational dimension of the Pauline letters when evaluating the biblical teaching on the church, something needs to be said at the outset about their historical specificity. Each Pauline letter presents itself as addressed to either a specific church (Rome, Corinth, Galatia, Philippi, Colossae, Thessalonica) or to a specific individual (Timothy, Titus, and Philemon, though this address also includes the church which meets in his home). The epistle known as Ephesians may be an exception, though a majority of manuscripts and early tradition give the address as 'to the saints in Ephesus'.[6]

In addition, a rapid run through of each letter reveals that besides having a specific address, there were specific circumstances between the sender and recipients which were particular to each letter's situation.[7] In Romans, it is Paul's future visit to this church, one which he had not founded, in order to gain their support for his mission to Spain which motivates a long letter explaining his gospel. 1 Corinthians is a response to oral reports about factions and other problems, as well as to a letter full of questions from the Corinthians. In the epistle to the Galatians, Paul is angry that the Galatians have been confused and persuaded by individuals who have arrived preaching a 'different gospel'. In 1 Thessalonians, the problem of Christians dying before the parousia presents real problems to the Christian believers there. In 2 Thessalonians, a spurious letter and a misunderstanding of Paul's teaching in 1 Thessalonians provokes a clarification of Paul's eschatological teaching. The letter to Philemon is a plea to receive back the converted runaway slave, Onesimus.

The interpretative issue which emerges as one surveys the occasion for each Pauline letter is that the theological teaching of Paul is earthed in a historical situation. Paul's letters are not theological treatises in epistolary form. They are letters of instruction to specific individuals or communities who are within the umbrella of Pauline authority and to specific needs and problems particular to each addressed recipient.[8]

As each letter is addressed to a church or individual connected with a

---

[6] B. M. Metzger, *A Textual Commentary on the Greek New Testament* (United Bible Societies, 1971), p. 601.

[7] Discerning the purpose of the Pauline letters is not as straightforward as the discussion below indicates, but represents assessments of both the texts themselves and recent scholarly discussion. An excellent summary of introductory matters including the purpose of these texts is L. T. Johnson, *The Writings of the New Testament: An Interpretation* (London: SCM, 1986).

[8] A fuller justification of this classification of the Pauline letters can be found in ch. 3 of D. L. Stamps, *The Rhetorical Use of the Epistolary Form in 1 Corinthians: The Rhetoric of Power*, JSNTSup (Sheffield: Sheffield Academic Press [forthcoming]).

church, the letters present a theology of the church. One aspect of this ecclesiology is the structure and authority of the church. First, the Pauline letters, while addressed to a singular locale, recognize that the central social unit for the church in these locales is the individual and separate meetings in many different private households (1 Cor. 16.9; Rom. 16.5, 10, 11, 15; Col. 4.14; Phm 2).[9] It is difficult to determine whether these household gatherings ever met as one large gathering, though this may be the situation behind 1 Cor. 11.17–34 (cf. 1 Cor. 14.23). It seems reasonable to assume that some of the problems of division which the letters address are caused by the distinctive differences between various house gatherings rather than the image of one large church in one place being divided by various interest groups.

The leadership structure for the Pauline churches is complex.[10] The historical ideal of the Pauline churches representing a charismatic and democratic community seems a theological imposition and a neglect of the evidence in the letters.[11] In several of the letters individuals are singled out by Paul in order to endorse and enhance their authority with respect to the church with which they are associated. One of the functions of the large number of personal greetings in Rom. 16 is to recognize certain church leaders who have Pauline approval. In 1 Corinthians, the household of Stephanas is elevated to some larger leadership role with respect to the church in Corinth (1 Cor. 16.15–18). The opening of Philippians includes a specific recognition of leaders, overseers and deacons (Phil. 1.1b). In 1 Thess. 5.12–13 certain persons are recognized as 'over you in the Lord' and as such deserve special regard. The Pastorals, whether coming late in Paul's ministry or in a post-Pauline context, recognize the office of elders (Tit. 1.5), overseers (1 Tim. 3.1–7) and deacons (1 Tim. 3.8–13).

In addition, certain other roles based on a ministry function are recognized in the Pauline church community. The list in Rom. 12.6–8 includes allusions to prophets, servants/deacons, teachers, and leaders/rulers. Similarly, the list in 1 Cor. 12.28 mentions, with some kind of ranking, apostles, prophets, teachers, miracle workers, on down to those who speak in tongues. Likewise, Eph. 4.11 endorses the appointment of certain offices by Christ himself, apostles, prophets, evangelists, and pastor-teachers. Exactly how these various offices or ministries functioned in relation to house-gatherings and the wider church community is not spelled out.[12] As each of these lists are in the context of the dis-

[9] W. A Meeks, *The First Urban Christians: The Social World of the Apostle Paul* (New Haven: Yale University Press, 1983), pp. 75–7.
[10] B. Holmberg, *Paul and Power: The Structure of Authority in the Primitive Church as Reflected in the Pauline Epistles* (Philadelphia: Fortress, 1980).
[11] This theological ideal is found in Dunn, *Jesus*, pp. 259–300.
[12] For one perspective, see Dunn, *Jesus*, pp. 280–91.

cussion of the body metaphor for the church, they probably have a primary reference to each house-church. But this conclusion is complicated by the reference to the office of apostle whose function and authority does not appear to be limited to single house-gathering.[13]

Organizationally, the Pauline churches are governed by another stratum of leadership: the Pauline missionary team. Paul personally asserts his apostolic authority over the churches he has founded and challenges those who usurp his apostolic role over these churches (1 Cor. 3.10, 4.15; 2 Cor. 11.1–5; Gal. 1.8, 4.17–20; 1 Thess. 2.7–9, 19–20).[14] Conversely, he respects the apostolic mission of others (Rom. 15.20). In addition, Paul manages the life of the Pauline churches by the team of Pauline emissaries or envoys which Paul sends in his absence to extend and continue his spiritual oversight[15] (2 Cor. 7.6–7; Eph. 6.21–22; Phil. 2.19–23; Col. 4.7–9; 1 Thess. 3.2): 'For this reason I am sending to you Timothy, my son whom I love, who is faithful in the Lord. He will remind you of my way of life in Christ Jesus which agrees with what I teach everywhere in every church' (1 Cor. 4.17).

In addition, the management of the Pauline churches is affected by the creation of a wider church community. Paul appeals for conformity based on church-wide practice and teaching (1 Cor. 4.17, 7.17, 11.16, 14.33). He suggests there is a wider-church unity and community especially among the Pauline churches (1 Cor. 1.2), an aspect which is made clear by the parties who exchange greetings in the letter closings: 'All the churches of Christ send greetings', Rom. 16.16; 'the churches of Asia send you greetings', 1 Cor. 16.19; 'all the saints send you greetings', Phil. 4.22.

So in terms of the structure and authority of the Pauline churches, the primary emphasis is on the church in each place which is composed of individual house-gatherings. But the Pauline churches also represent a wider-Christian community unified around the apostolic authority of Paul and his missionary team and around a common set of teaching and practice. Besides being under the authority of the Pauline mission, the local churches are structured according to various recognized leaders and according to recognized offices of ministry and leadership.

A second dimension of the church life found in the Pauline letters is the worship and practice of the Pauline churches. The most extensive discussion of this is found in 1 Corinthians: a specific case of sexual immor-

[13] J. H. Schütz, *Paul and the Anatomy of Apostolic Authority*, SNTSMS 26 (Cambridge: CUP, 1975).
[14] For a convenient summary of Paul's view of his authority as an apostle, see Dunn, *Jesus*, pp. 271–80.
[15] M. M. Mitchell, 'New Testament Envoys in the Context of Greco-Roman Diplomatic and Epistolary Conventions: The Example of Timothy and Titus', *JBL* 111 (1992), pp. 641–62.

ality, 1 Cor. 5.1–13; lawsuits among fellow Christians, 1 Cor. 6.1–11; the general issue of sexual morality and marriage, 1 Cor. 6.12–7.40; eating meat sacrificed to idols, 1 Cor. 8.1–13; head coverings during worship, 1 Cor. 11.3–16; the abuse and practice of the Lord's Supper at Corinth, 1 Cor. 11.17–34; the theology and use of spiritual gifts in the worship of the church, 1 Cor. 12.1–14.40. With regard to these church-life issues at Corinth, the Pauline teaching is either general or situation specific depending on the source of the information. Questions from the Corinthians are answered by general paraenesis; oral reports, by specific instructions (instructions which are usually endorsed by a promised follow-up visit by either Paul or one of his envoys).[16] All these problems are set against the backdrop of the larger problem of factions or divisions. Indeed, the Corinthian church was not a model example of a pristine Christian community under the sway of God's Spirit. In fact, it appears things only got worse as one reads between the lines in 2 Corinthians. One could argue that 1 Corinthians was a failure as an assertion of apostolic teaching and authority as it took at least two more letters and several visits by various Pauline parties to sort out the problems at Corinth, at least from Paul's perspective.

As already noted, all the letters, with the possible exception of Ephesians, appear to have some specific issue which prompted the need for an apostolic letter of instruction. In some of the letters the instruction is governed by the need to solve a situation-specific problem or problems. Even where the letters offer some general instruction as found in the household codes (instructions to husbands, wives, children and slaves), specific Pauline principles are being discovered. Paul's desire for the stability and security of the Christian community seems to motivate his application of cultural moral codes to the Christian community, so that slavery remains intact and women assume their cultural role. Similarly, in Rom. 13 the discussion of submitting to secular authorities and paying taxes seems to stem from a perceived need to keep the Christian church from unnecessary and hindering political and social opposition. The general moral principle which seems to cover these cultural matters with regard to the church's life in the world is stated in 1 Thess. 4.11–12, 'Make it your ambition to lead a quiet life, to mind your own business and to work with your hands, just as we told you, so that our daily life may win the respect of outsiders and so that you will not be dependent on anybody.' In Paul's writings, instructions to the individual churches regarding Christian life principles are very much earthed in a particular historical and cultural context.

When it comes to the theological issues and problems found in the

---

[16] For a detailed treatment of the Pauline response to the issues addressed in 1 Corinthians, see Stamps, *Rhetorical*, ch. 6.

church communities which Paul addressed in his letters, a similar historical contingency is operative. For instance, Pauline eschatology is worked out in response to the unexpected death of Christians and to the over-expectant believers who abandon responsibility to await the Lord's return in 1 and 2 Thessalonians. Similarly, much of the theology of the resurrection from the dead and the resurrection body seems to emerge for the first time as Paul answers those who deny the resurrection as discussed in 1 Cor. 15. Paul's view of the Jewish law and justification by faith along with his concept of life in the Spirit and the ideal of Christian freedom emerges from the crisis in Galatia over the invasion of legalistic Judaizers. Similar Pauline theological tenets are worked out in Philippians and Colossians in response to teaching from outside the Pauline mission which Paul considers erroneous: 'Watch out for those dogs, those men who do evil, those mutilators of the flesh', Col. 3.2; 'See to it that no one takes you captive through hollow and deceptive philosophy, which depends on human tradition and the basic principles of this world rather than on Christ', Phil. 2.8.

There are large sections of theological discourse in Romans and Ephesians which seem more abstract, that is loosed from specific historical exigencies. Yet even in these sections the dialogical nature of the discourse anchors it to a specific audience and to the purpose of the letter's argument.

As one evaluates the theological argument of Paul, one sees how he is seeking to discover the theological relevance of basic Christian beliefs and apply them to a host of problems and issues which require theological exposition. J. D. G. Dunn isolates only a few essential Pauline beliefs: Jesus is risen, the death of Christ, an imminent parousia, Jesus as Lord, union with Christ.[17] Yet rarely are those basic beliefs expounded together in any great detail or in any fixed or final form. For instance, in both 1 Cor. 15.3–11 and 1 Tim. 1.15 (cf. 2 Tim. 1.13–14), Paul is stating similar theological tradition, but not in a fixed formula, which then forms the premise of his situation-specific exposition.

It appears that whether Paul is addressing specific theological issues which concern a particular community or whether he is offering a more general theological discourse, he seems to write himself to a conclusion or opinion rather than writing from the stance of an already worked out theology.[18] In each case, the theological discourse is governed by the textual context – the letter convention, and by the historical context – the

[17] J. D. G. Dunn, *Unity and Diversity in the New Testament* (Philadelphia: Westminster, 1977), pp. 21–3.
[18] This view of Paul's writing is explored in D. L. Stamps, 'Interpreting the Language of St. Paul', in *Translating Religious Texts*, ed. D. Jasper (New York: St Martin's Press, 1993), pp. 21–43.

epistolary situation.[19] One may discern certain theological beliefs which remain constant across the spectrum of the Pauline corpus, and one may discern certain theological themes which occur in several different letters. However, it is significant that one does not find in the Pauline literature any statements of beliefs or themes repeated in a fixed form larger than the use of certain phrases and sentences.

One can examine this lack of uniformity with respect to Pauline theological discourse by culling some of the theological themes which appear to have a direct bearing on Paul's theology of the church. There are two main themes which impinge upon an understanding of Paul's ecclesiology. First, there is the use of the term church, *ekklēsia*; second, the use of the body metaphor for the church.[20]

Most of the occurrences of the word, *ekklēsia*, refer to the local congregation gathered in a particular place (Rom. 16.1; 1 Cor. 1.2, 11.18, 22, 14.4, 5; 2 Cor. 1.1). In Colossians (1.18, 24) and Ephesians (1.22, 3.10, 21, 5.23, 24, 25, 27, 29, 32) the use of the term *ekklēsia*, definitely has the sense of an abstract concept which is not necessarily particularized to a place or gathering, what is often spoken of as the 'universal church'. An interesting use of the term is 1 Cor. 1.2, in which the syntax suggests a tension between a wider concept and a particular designation: literally, 'the church of God, the one being in Corinth'. This can be understood as either, 'the church of God at Corinth', or 'the church of God which meets in Corinth'. As one reads 1 Cor. 11.18, 'when you come together as a church', there is a sense in which the church does not exist as some theoretical ideal, but comes to be when the people of God assemble, in this case for the Lord's Supper, and in the case of 1 Cor. 14 for worship. Yet, the limited reference of the word in 1 Cor. 11 and 14 fits the argument of addressing specific problems peculiar to the Corinthian church. Likewise, the abstract and non-particular reference for the word 'church' in Colossians and Ephesians is appropriate to the letter's intent to push the readers into a deeper understanding of the Christian life.

One of the interesting themes found in Paul's writings with respect to the church is the body metaphor. It is only in Colossians (1.18, 24) and Ephesians (1.23, 5.30) that one finds the body motif specifically designated as the church: to quote one example, 'And he is the head of the body, the church', Col. 1.18. Additionally, as reflected in the quote above, in these two letters Christ is designated as the head of the body. These perspectives are not at odds with less specific exposition of the body metaphor found in Rom. 12.4–5 and 1 Cor. 12.12–27. In Romans

---

[19] These terms are defined by Stamps, *Rhetorical*, ch. 2.
[20] On both, I am dependent upon the discussion in D. E. H. Whiteley, *The Theology of St. Paul* (Oxford: Blackwell, 1964), pp. 186–99.

and 1 Corinthians the connection between Christ and the body is equally explicit. Further, in Rom. 12, 1 Cor. 12, and Eph. 4 the body motif is placed in conjunction with a discussion of the gifts of the Spirit. One should not necessarily demarcate the discussions of the body metaphor in Colossians and Ephesians against the use of the metaphor in Romans and 1 Corinthians. It is in the nature of a metaphor that a writer can draw out particular aspects which suit the immediate discussion.[21] The important point is that it is a metaphor which becomes the major focus of Paul's thoughts about the church. To emphasize the metaphor is not to deny that the teaching does not move into ontological assertion as the dense text in Rom. 12.4–5 makes plain: 'Just as each of us has one body with many members, and these members do not all have the same function, so in Christ we who are many form one body, and each member belongs to all the others'. J. C. Beker summarizes the didactic emphasis found in Paul's use of the body metaphor as follows, 'the metaphor of the body expresses ... both our participation in Christ and the mutual dependence of all the various members of one body of Christ'.[22]

As one surveys the nature of Paul's church both in his teaching and in the historical representation found in the letters, the church of the first century CE had many similarities with the church today. There is division and conflict. There are moral problems within the church. There are theological misunderstandings and questionable beliefs and practices. Paul's response is always situationally contingent. There is little, if any, Pauline instruction which is fixed and pre-determined. The church Paul worked with was a church full of problems and very much in process.

II. HERMENEUTICAL FACTORS IN MOVING FROM THE BIBLICAL TEXT TO BIBLICAL THEOLOGY

Having surveyed some of the biblical perspectives on the church in the Pauline corpus, it remains to consider and evaluate this evidence in order to move from the biblical text to a biblical theology. Traditionally within some sectors of the Christian community the sacred scriptures are regarded as a kind of deposit of truth, the word of God, which can in the interpretative process be translated into propositional statements which

---

[21] E. F. Kittay, *Metaphor: Its Cognitive Force and Linguistic Structure* (Oxford: Clarendon Press, 1989), pp. 17–37. See also the relevant discussions in J. M. Soskice, *Metaphor and Religious Language* (Oxford: Clarendon Press, 1985).
[22] J. C. Beker, *Paul the Apostle* (Philadelphia: Fortress, 1980), p. 318.

are authoritative for the thought and practice of the church today.[23] Though this position has a theological system which undergirds it, nevertheless, it rests particularly on the basis that there is some supra-textual referent which has invested the biblical text with special authority.

The critique of 'logocentrism' from the various philosophical perspectives associated with post-structuralism, however, has seriously challenged all traditional theological strategies for proposing the sacred and authoritative nature of the Bible.[24] In fact, in view of the whole post-structuralist critique of traditional epistemology and ontology, the church's understanding of the role and authority of scripture needs serious reconsideration. Such reconsideration will change the way in which biblical theology is constructed.

But as it is not possible in the scope of this paper to offer a reconstructed understanding of the authority of scripture (and I admit I do not even have such to offer), it is still possible to consider how the Bible might inform the Christian community at present. If one accepts the situation in which it is recognized that various interpretative communities recognize the biblical text as a 'classical' text, one can begin to think through the process of moving from the biblical text to a biblical theology.[25]

In an important article, 'Created and Redeemed Sociality', Prof. Daniel Hardy suggests a theological model or perspective which offers a way to maintain a concept of transcendentals which inform the pragmatic and empirical expressions of reality.[26] I will try to explain what I think Prof. Hardy is saying which is relevant to the task of this paper.

After evaluating certain understandings of the doctrine of creation, Prof. Hardy concludes that attempts to consider fundamental operations of human thought and life (like a doctrine of creation) should not be expected to produce perfect results, but should be projects which are capable of self-correction (p. 34). Such self-correction entails that these fundamental projects are a dynamic process which is always contingent. He rejects the criticism that all such projects are simply human constructs based on the retort that such a classification *prejudges* the whole issue of such a project's correspondence with truth.

---

[23] A view which is chronicled in J. Barton, *People of the Book? The Authority of the Bible in Christianity* (London: SPCK, 1993[2]).

[24] Without endorsing his conclusions or theological agenda, see the critique of M. C. Taylor, *Altarity* (Chicago: University of Chicago Press, 1987); *idem, Deconstructing Theology* (New York: Crossroad, 1982).

[25] See the important analysis and application of David Tracy's concept of a classical text to modern theological reflection in W. G. Jeanrond, *Text and Interpretation as Categories of Theological Thinking*, trans. T. J. Wilson (Dublin: Gill & Macmillan, 1988), pp. 13–50.

[26] D. W. Hardy, 'Created and Redeemed Sociality', in *On Being the Church*, eds. C. E. Gunton and D. W. Hardy (Edinburgh: T. & T. Clark, 1989), pp. 21–47. Future references will be given as page numbers in the text.

Prof. Hardy then illustrates this process with the project of establishing a social transcendental (pp. 35–47). Any formulation of a social transcendental should have some correspondence with the truth of sociality, but it must be recognized that human thought fails, 'through irrationality and wickedness', to appropriate a social transcendental which corresponds with this truth (p. 35). This means the postulation of a transcendental is always contingent. It always remains open to the self-correction which might come through new information, knowledge or understanding. He proceeds to show how the process of articulating a social transcendental entails a twofold critical dynamic, affirmative and critical:

As affirmative, it will be a projective realisation of society, and thus a raising of the most basic conditions for this by affirming them in thought and life. Furthermore, it will be capable of generating 'richer and more open-structured forms of order' in a social universe of constantly expanding complexity. As critical, it will identify and negate inadequate conditions based on unsatisfactory categories or particular societies, whether subhuman ... or human. (p. 35)

This process means a transcendental, even in its contingent state, is positively informative in the effort to articulate a practical reality or a corresponding social expression to the transcendental, and it is critically evaluative in the way in which the transcendental critiques practical expressions already operative.

It is possible to apply this dynamic process to the effort to construct a biblical theology of the church. The theological enterprise which is entextualized in the Bible is partially an effort to articulate contingent human formulations of transcendentals and to allow them to inform the pragmatics of Christian experience within the Christian community. The project of constructing a transcendental doctrine of the church in the present can be informed by the record of such efforts in the past. Of course, a problematic dimension in 'listening' to these past witnesses is the need for an appropriate hermeneutic (or interpretative criticism) which allows the text to speak in all its diversity and which prevents the text from dominating the reading community.

Werner Jeanrond in his theory of a theological hermeneutics offers a pertinent comment on this matter:

The insistence on the possibility of criticism in the process of reading signifies here, however, no new denigration of the text but rather the endeavour to allow the text in the best possible manner to speak and for this purpose to orient the individual reader and the reading community in relation to self-criticism and criticism of content ... It is only in this twofold criticism which protects the text against the arbitrariness on the part of the reader and protects the reader against the arbitrariness on the part of the textual effectiveness.[27]

In summary, doing biblical theology is entering into the ongoing critical project of human discovery involved in the fundamental operation of human thought and life. Scripture is a crucial record of that process for the community of faith. As such it entextualizes the contingent dynamic process of postulating transcendentals which expand, inform and critique the empirical practice or praxis of social realities. In order to understand and allow the scriptural witness to inform the present project(s) of the human thought and life, there must be an adequate critical procedure for biblical interpretation which leads to understanding, explanation and assessment.

III. Towards a Biblical Theology of the Church

Whatever one offers at this point with regard to a biblical theology of the church must be tentative. The task is limited because only the Pauline writings have been cursorily surveyed. Even more significant, any reconstruction of the biblical theological project must provide a much more extensive hermeneutical evaluation which can respond to the present situation in terms of literary and social theory.[28]

However, within the circumscribed scope of this study, several pertinent points can be suggested. First, the contingency of Pauline ecclesiology is an essential of a modern ecclesiology. In the situation-specific and occasional letters, Pauline discourse on the church was constantly responding to particular problems which provoked a continual reformulation of prior theological understanding.[29] Pauline theology of the church was never static; it was always contingent as it responded to the conditions of human society which impinged upon the empirical experience of the Christian communities in specific locales. Pauline theological discourse did not attempt 'to maintain the same range of possibilities for social order' (p. 42), but in response to the dynamic process of transcendentals interfacing with social realities, Pauline discourse 'opened up richer possibilities of social order to meet the contingencies to which human beings are subject' (p. 42).

---

[27] Jeanrond, Text, pp. 113–14.
[28] Werner Jeanrond has provided such a constructive evaluation in his books, Text and Interpretation and Theological Hermeneutics.
[29] A similar idea is suggested by D. F. Ford, 'Faith in the Cities: Corinth and the Modern City', in On Being the Church, pp. 236–8.

To evaluate the historically contingent and unsystematic or non-dogmatic formulations of ecclesiology in this vein, is to suggest a positive perspective on the movement within the Pauline literature. The schemes of development which trace a downward development from a democratic and charismatic church to a hierarchical or sacerdotal and dogmatic church, a development based on a historical plotting of the New Testament texts with the Pauline texts embodying the charismatic church and the supposedly post-Pauline Pastorals, the sacerdotal church, suggest a more negative evaluation.[30] The ecclesiology of the Pastorals does not necessarily represent a 'fading of the vision',[31] but may have been the best approximation of the social transcendental the church represents for the historical situation which existed.[32] The ongoing implication is that it is the challenge of the Christian community to respond to its historical contingency in a creative manner which generates 'richer possibilities of social order in a social universe of constantly expanding complexity' (p. 42). Equally, the critical reading of the Pauline formulations may mean that the conservative approach Paul took in affirming cultural norms as a means to keep the Christian community safe from political pressure and persecution may need reassessment. An essential tenet for a modern ecclesiology which stems from the Pauline example is that the church must be engaging with the world as it is and responding in a way which opens up the potential for a new way of being in the world and which critiques the present social order in its weaknesses and failure.

A second aspect which emerges from the Pauline discourse on the church is the suggestive nature of a metaphorically structured transcendental.[33] The Pauline metaphor of the church as the body is an open metaphor which the Pauline ontology of the church based on this metaphor could not exhaust. A present-day ecclesiology may want to explore the potential of a more metaphorically oriented postulation of a doctrine of the church. The popular use of the 'family' metaphor for the life of the

---

[30] See especially, M. Y. MacDonald, *The Pauline Churches: A Socio-historical Study of Institutionalization in the Pauline and Deutero-Pauline Writings*, SNTSMS 60 (Cambridge: CUP, 1988).

[31] As it does in Dunn, *Jesus*, pp. 345–50.

[32] Though Bultmann traces a historical development, this is a point he also suggests, R. Bultmann, *Theology of the New Testament*, Vol. 2 (London: SCM, 1955), p. 99, 'Hence, it is not justified to place the inception and development of church order and church office in such opposition to the sway of the Spirit ... Intelligent conduct which arises from a recognition of what the situation demands does not exclude the possibility that the Spirit is working in such conduct'.

[33] A suggestive discussion is in T. R. Wright, *Theology and Literature*, Signposts in Theology (Oxford: Blackwell, 1988), pp. 129–62, in a chapter titled 'Metaphorical Theology: The Poetry of Faith'. See also a fine example of metaphorical theology, D. F. Ford, 'Tragedy and Atonement', in *Christ, Ethics and Tragedy, Essays in Honour of Donald MacKinnon*, ed. K. Surin (Cambridge: CUP, 1989), pp. 117–30.

church is an example of a metaphorical postulation which has failed because it cannot embrace the alienation of single person family units separated spatially or psychologically from their extended family members. However, there may be unexplored dimensions to the body metaphor which can address the modern contingencies the church faces, and there may be new richer and more open-structured metaphors which the Christian community can present as a way of being in the world today and as a way of critiquing the ways of community in the world today.

A third and final suggestion which stems from Paul's doctrine of the church is the limited theological premise which Paul uses to undergird his ecclesiastical transcendental. The Pauline theological core was primarily Christological and secondarily eschatological. Prof. Hardy has explored the concept of a created and redeemed sociality: 'to ask about the basis of society in creation and redemption is also to ask about the nature and life of the Church, whose witness is to the possibility of a true society in the wider society around it' (p. 22). Biblical theological approximations of the Pauline church have often been constricted by the theological limitations of Paul's thought. Bultmann identified the church as an eschatological community ruled by the spirit.[34] Beker states that Paul's doctrine of the church was anchored in Christology and eschatology.[35] Prof. Hardy, however, by tracing the social transcendental to the 'Logos of God operative in creation' (p. 42) has opened up the possibilities for theological reflection with respect to the sociality of the church. A biblical theology of the church should not be limited to Paul's theological repertoire. A proper biblical theology should attempt to incorporate a fuller engagement with the theological tradition located in the Christian community.

CONCLUSION

The Bible remains an essential part of the life of the Christian community today. But the epistemological and ontological rethinking which is happening at present has severe implications regarding the way in which the Christian community reads and understands this 'classical' text. If the church is going to continue to have a biblical theology which informs its larger theological thinking, it must find a way to move from the text to a biblical theology. Prof. Hardy has explored an exciting possibility of maintaining a belief in transcendentals while allowing them the contingency present hermeneutical suspicion demands. Equally, he has

---

[34] Bultmann, *Theology*, Vol. 2, pp. 95–100.
[35] Beker, *Paul*, p. 303.

opened up the way in which the transcendentals can inform and critique the practice and realities of the Christian community. This dynamic process which he has posited has important suggestions for doing biblical theology.

As I conclude, I am only too aware that there are gigantic issues I have assumed and left not discussed, issues Prof. Hardy would only too quickly point out and request a fuller explanation. But I am ever so grateful for the fact that in private conversation, in public lectures and in publications, Prof. Hardy has forced me to think hard about what it means to be a biblical studies specialist in the context of modern theological thinking. This attempt at doing biblical theology is hopefully one small step in the whole re-forming of biblical theology which will have to occur because the present context of the Christian community in the world demands it.

IO

St John's Gospel, the Incarnation and Christian Orthodoxy

ROBERT MORGAN

I. THE INCARNATION AND CHRISTIAN ORTHODOXY

> Like a mighty army
> moves the Church of God;
> brothers, we are treading
> where the saints have trod:
> We are not divided,
> all one body we,
> one in hope and *doctrine*,
> one in charity.

BARING-GOULD's hymn sounds triumphalist, militaristic, sexist, and ironic in the West today. Unity of faith, expressed in doctrinal agreement, has generally been thought essential to Christian community (and scandalously even imposed), but modern historical study has highlighted the diversity in Christian history. Theological pluralism is warranted by theological diversity with the New Testament itself.[1] 'There can be no normative Christian dogmatics'.[2] Different generations, cultures, even individuals, propose different ways of unfolding Christian faith. If Christian orthodoxy is 'an unchanging set of beliefs',[3] it never existed. But many who know about historical and theological change resist doctrinal relativism and insist that the givenness of the revelation of God in Christ implies a substantial continuity through all true formulations. What counts as substantial continuity is disputed, and orthodoxy or authentic Christianity therefore a contested concept, but theological attempts to define it help sustain Christian community.

---

[1] Cf. E. Käsemann, 'Unity and Multiplicity in the NT Doctrine of the Church', in *New Testament Questions of Today* (London: SCM, 1969).
[2] R. Bultmann, *Theology of the NT, Vol.* 2 (London: SCM, 1955), p. 237.
[3] Quoting John Hick in the Preface to *The Myth of God Incarnate* (London: SCM, 1977, 1993 reprint), p. ix.

In opposition to *The Myth of God Incarnate* the contention of this essay is that rightly understood the *doctrine of the incarnation* provides an adequate criterion of orthodoxy, and basis for Christian community. *The Myth* germinated in Birmingham while Dan Hardy was teaching theology there, and in Oxford where the present writer was also an interested observer. This response expresses gratitude for much learned from Dan during what in retrospect were exceptionally good years for the British university system.

The argument depends on our way of distinguishing between three different ways of speaking of the *mystery* of the incarnation (the alleged divine event acknowledged by faith): in *myth* (a narrative about God or gods); in *theology* which varies with time and place; and in *doctrine* which is more stable. Theology's disciplined reflection on Christian faith is fluid as it relates this to different believers' knowledge and experience; and *doctrine*, summarizing the church's teaching, is the sediment of many generations' life and thought.

The distinctions are hard to draw sharply because many learn doctrine through myth and because doctrine both presupposes and requires theological activity. The terms are also ambiguous; they overlap and are sometimes used interchangeably. Anglicans who find the phrase 'systematic theology' too systematic and 'dogmatics' too dogmatic prefer 'doctrinal theology', but that too is *theology*, whether academic or more practical, exploring further the basic structure of church doctrine.

Except where the word is used purely formally, to identify a topic (e.g. the doctrine of God) doctrines echo their pre-history of theological debate and decision. Thus 'the doctrine of the Trinity' implies some material theological content but remains quite general and in need of theological elaboration to make it intelligible and communicable (e.g. the theological use of the philosophical terms substance and persons). A latitudinarian way of posing the question of Christian orthodoxy today is to ask which, if any, of these *material* doctrines are essential. It is not enough to insist on holding doctrines of God, Christ, salvation, Spirit, church, sacraments, and the end, because these headings are purely formal. The doctrine of the incarnation is different. It also can be interpreted in unorthodox ways (e.g. some Hegelian interpretations) but 'rightly understood', i.e. dogmatically clarified as saying that Jesus is truly God, truly human, it provides a material criterion of orthodoxy, excluding Ebionism and docetism. It requires theological elaboration (e.g. in terms such as natures and person) before it makes rational sense, but this can vary without the doctrine necessarily being abandoned.

The reason for insisting on this doctrine and no other will be clarified by studying the Gospel traditionally ascribed to St John, because that text makes most explicit what all the New Testament (NT) writers presuppose, that in knowing and relating to the crucified and risen Jesus through the Spirit we know and are in relationship with God. The doctrine of the incarnation, which affirms God's self-identification with Jesus, completed (Jn. 19.30) in his death and exaltation, affirms and preserves the saving revelation in Jesus. What the NT says about Jesus and the Spirit points its Jewish monotheism in a direction later formulated in the doctrine of the Trinity but not even John begins to explore the theological questions which led to this. We shall therefore avoid claiming that the NT writers imply the doctrine of the Trinity as they imply (in the sense defended here) the doctrine of the incarnation. John did not reflect, either, on how Jesus can be both human and divine, but the doctrine of the incarnation (as defined here) is not bound to that speculative question in the way that the doctrine of the Trinity is inseparable from its question about three and one. The later doctrine follows from the former (contrary to most textbooks) and is an indicator of orthodoxy, but does not epitomize the NT witness.

Other doctrines whose names mark a claim, such as the Virgin birth, eternal punishment, transubstantiation, and baptismal regeneration, are scriptural or represent conclusions absorbed into church teaching after long theological debate. To reject them is more serious than opposing some particular theology. But if doctrine is supposed to express, preserve, nurture, and protect the essential relationship with God that a religious system mediates, then it should be possible to criticize even large swathes of the doctrinal tradition, provided the one central claim that God is known in Christ remains intact. The question is what is essential to preserve that conviction.

A theologian who has no infallible scripture or infallible magisterium to settle the issue can argue that whatever the answer is it must always have been present in Christianity, at least implicitly. We are therefore driven to echo the famous definition of Vincent of Lerins, 'What has always been believed everywhere by all', whose orthodoxy is generally accepted. No particular *theology* or 'unchanging set of beliefs' will fit that formula, but the *doctrine* of the incarnation may prove loose enough to include all the NT writers and tight enough to exclude deviation from the central affirmation of God in Christ, as witnessed to by the NT, clarified by subsequent theology, summarized in church teaching, and therefore constitutive of orthodoxy.

Our proposal has more in common with the supple, nineteenth-century phrase 'essence of Christianity' than with Vincent himself. Troeltsch explained[4] how that phrase criticizes false developments of

---

[4] E. Troeltsch, 'What does "Essence of Christianity" Mean?', in *Ernst Troeltsch: Writings on Theology and Religion*, eds. R. Morgan and M. Pye (London: Duckworth, 1977).

the tradition. It is not bound to 'essentialism' and can be paraphrased as 'the *identity* of Christianity'.[5]

The point where we come closer to Vincent than to Schleiermacher and Troeltsch is in nominating a doctrine, and one drawn from the tradition which he claims interprets scripture correctly. But no appeal is being made to the authority of Vincent. His phrase can therefore be stretched in accord with the scriptures that he claimed orthodoxy was interpreting.

Vincent's 'what' (*quod*) suggests the faith which *is* believed (*fides quae*) rather than that *by* which (*qua*) it is believed, but his Latin verb *creditur* has a less cognitive flavour than the English 'believe',[6] and his singular *quod* suggests the whole doctrinal structure, not individual items of belief. Christian believing (faith) in Paul and John has more to do with trust and commitment than with the philosophers' justified belief. 'What is believed' refers ultimately to the One who is trusted, obeyed and worshipped; the One who is the way, the truth and the life. Christian doctrine teaches us how to speak of him, but a general assent to that is enough. It may be confirmed by experience, but we can distinguish between that and the strong truth-claim of a theological formulation. The practical truth of the doctrine of the incarnation is affirmed by most Christians, but they do not claim fully to understand the mystery, and may disagree over theological elaborations, while agreeing to reject certain accounts of it.

'Implicit faith' which simply accepts what the church believes without asking too many questions is an appropriately low-key response to doctrines. It sounds disreputable to some Christians who cannot imagine faith without understanding, and to others who are more interested in the living *fides qua*. But faith's personal trust and commitment relates to the One to whom the doctrine refers, and questions of truth arise only in respect of theological content. Doctrines make metaphysical truth-claims only when fleshed out in some theology. As the bare bones of Christian belief they indicate its general shape or form, and only enough content to exclude notorious deviations.

The still to be defined *doctrine* of the incarnation, as distinct from the myth and theologies, can serve as the criterion of orthodoxy in accord with the Vincentian canon. Sharing certain scriptures, identifying with a tradition, repeating the creeds, respecting approved writers, celebrating certain sacraments, and so forth are practices characteristic of orthodoxy. They generate legitimate theological diversity. Only where the identity of Christianity is at stake, as it is in one's assessment of Jesus as the saving revelation of God, are the boundaries drawn more tightly, by dogmatic definitions which exclude some Christologies and clarify the

---

[5] So S. W. Sykes, *The Identity of Christianity* (London: SPCK, 1984).
[6] W. C. Smith, *Faith and Belief* (Princeton: Princeton University Press, 1979).

shape of Christian belief in God, and even here the parameters are generous. Christian doctrine remains more amorphous in the areas of anthropology, soteriology, ecclesiology, and so on, but 'Brethren, we must think of Jesus Christ as of God ...' (2 Clem. 1.1).

How far it is possible to abstract the *doctrine* of the incarnation from the *mythical* forms it receives in popular Christian imagination, or from the *theological* expressions it has received in patristic and subsequent thought remains to be seen. Identifying some thread of doctrinal continuity right through the theological diversity of the Christian tradition(s) would make it possible to test theological proposals against the basic shape of Christian teaching, instead of against alternative (older and dated) theological proposals. The doctrine actually says very little about God and Jesus, leaving that to theology and Christology, but it insists that what Christians say about God and what they say about Jesus condition one another.

All that is true of the doctrine of the divinity of Christ, and this might seem a simpler criterion of orthodoxy in an age when few are likely to deny his humanity. The mythologically-tainted and non-biblical word 'incarnation' is not everyone's choice as 'the article on which the church stands or falls'. But this hallowed word has certain advantages:

1. It refers to both the revelatory *event* and the church's teaching, and so unites the *lex orandi* and *lex credendi*.

2. That link reinforces its symbolic quality as a summary of Christianity.

3. It holds together more of the doctrinal structure, and so combats the atomization involved in listing doctrinal *loci*.

4. It emphasizes the divine initiative and agency better than the static phrase, and is less easily interpreted reductively, to mean perfect humanity.

5. Our knowledge of authentic humanity is imperfect. By speaking also of true humanity the doctrine stimulates reflection and so is more suggestive of what this might mean than are the often banal guesses of historical Jesus research.

6. By speaking also of the true humanity and physical corporeality of Jesus it directs Christian theology to take seriously the materiality of human existence and salvation.

5 and 6 only apply when the doctrine is clarified dogmatically by the *vere homo*. The *idea* of incarnation itself carries with it the dangers of docetism and invites a mythical interpretation. It requires a dogmatic clarification, and received one as early as the anti-docetic 'in flesh' at 1 Jn. 4.2, a precursor of the *vere homo*. Equally the doctrine requires the dogmatic clarification *vere Deus* that insists (like the *homoousion*) that it is truly

God who is encountered in Jesus, not some intermediary being, as apparently Arius thought.

Defining the doctrine dogmatically introduced and risked absolutizing theological concepts which are inevitably inadequate to the mystery, but it has set a bulwark against the threatened dissolution of Christian belief today into deism or Christian humanism. Dogmas provide a protective shell for religious faith. Liberals dislike egg-shells which are sometimes mistaken for the egg, or become empty shells, devoid of religious life and theological thought, but faith's embryo rarely survives many generations without some verbal and institutional protection.

The doctrinal shell defines only the parameters of orthodox Christology. It excludes Apollinarianism and all docetism (and its modern idealist successors that are interested only in the Christ of faith), and Arianism, and Ebionism (and its successors who deny the divinity of Christ), and Nestorianism (and its successors who fail to unite their Jesus of history and Christ of faith in the one Christ).

The conciliar fathers no doubt understood 'true God, true man' differently from NT Christologies and from much modern Christology, but as the phrase was intended to interpret scripture we may read it in the light of our understanding of the NT, not in terms of the traditional attributes of God in some philosophical discourse. That the Jesus they worshipped and confessed was a human who had been executed a few years or decades previously and had been vindicated by God was a shared assumption of all the NT writers, though only the Epistle to the Hebrews made theological capital out of this *vere homo*. The claim that they all implicitly accepted what was later labelled *vere Deus* must now be argued.

Our strategy is to concentrate on the Gospel of John, while understanding it quite differently from the Fathers and their English successors. Many readers have sensed some discrepancy between John's dualism and later incarnational theologies. John gave some support to the gnostics as well as to Irenaeus. His dualism is sharp enough to place a question-mark against his own orthodoxy – though Bultmann is surely right that it is a dualism of decision, not a metaphysical dualism. But it is not John's distinctive ways of talking about the incarnation that are being claimed as normative. It is the *doctrine* implied by his view of *revelation* that is definitive of orthodox Christianity, because being present, though less explicitly, in the other NT writings[7] it satisfies our 'Vincentian' canon.

The reason this account of the orthodox doctrine of the incarnation will seem too hospitable to some is that most definitions of the doctrine

---

[7] Their speculatively reconstructed predecessors and opponents have no claim to be normative or definitive for Christian belief, relevant as they are for understanding the NT writers.

have included some particular theology, usually patristic. Any actual expression of the doctrine requires theology (just as *langue* is always instantiated in a *parole*), but our distinction aims to abstract the doctrine from its detailed theological articulations.

The revelational view of the doctrine adopted here is most clearly expressed by John at 8.19 ('If you knew me you would have known my Father') and 14.9 ('whoever has seen me has seen the Father', cf. 12.45). It makes sense of the Christological use of the wisdom myth in some early liturgical material (Col. 1.15–20, Heb. 1.3, Jn. 1.1–18) and coheres with the other mythological-sounding expressions of incarnational belief in John, where the idea of pre-existence only reinforces the notion of revelation and is not developed speculatively.[8] It is thus quite remote from patristic, scholastic, and Barthian *theology*, but accepts what they were getting at.

Our recourse to John's Gospel also provides an opportunity to unscramble the confusions between myth, doctrine and theology in Christian discourse, because these have been aggravated by the way this Gospel is read by most Christians today, and by the way it was used in patristic theology. Both the emergence of a Christian '*myth* of God incarnate' and early theological arguments about the person of Christ, and the consequent doctrine of the Trinity, owed much to readings of this Gospel which are tangential to the evangelist's own purpose and intolerable to historical sensitivities. Scripture is constantly and legitimately read in new ways, but recourse to what we think were the author's original intentions can today set earlier interpretations in a new light.

II. St John's Gospel and the Incarnation

All four Gospels interpret the life and death of Jesus as a divine saving event. Later Christians have called it the (mystery of the) incarnation. John speaks of it in language which can be called incarnational: Jesus is the pre-existent Logos sent from God, the only-begotten Son sent by the Father and returning exalted to his previous glory. But that distinctive language does not pass the Vincentian test of universality. Even though the early church's Christologies and resulting doctrine were built largely

---

[8] The mythical idea of pre-existence may have to be affirmed in Christology as being implied by the divinity of Christ, but it plays no part in the doctrine of the incarnation as interpreted here. On its relative unimportance for the NT and modern theology, see K.-J. Kuschel, *Born Before All Time?* (London: SCM, 1992).

out of some dubious reading of John,[9] the Johannine raw material is not the *doctrine* shared with every NT writer. It is only a vivid instantiation of that doctrine.

The way John talks abut the incarnation is arguably one-sided, individualistic, dangerously dualistic, and gives rise to mythological accounts of Christianity which many find incredible. Just as the *theology* to which faith gives rise must be distinguished from the post-reflective summary of an institution's teaching in *doctrine*, so it must be distinguished from the *pre*-reflective narrative expression of religious belief in *myth* (usually associated with ritual). It is inappropriate to call John's Gospel (as opposed to much Christian reading of it) mythical, but it draws on myth in the process of projecting Jesus as the revelation of God. What follows will endorse neither John's way of expressing the doctrine,[10] nor the subsequent patristic elaborations. John's incarnational language (certainly metaphorical and arguably mythical in places) presents Jesus Christ as the *revelation* of God. That is what the *doctrine* of the incarnation is saying: that in this man (not his teaching as such) we find the saving revelation of God. In defending only the *doctrine* here we do not wish to criticize the myth, provided it is understood as such. Even the Creeds and collects contain mythic forms of expression: 'He came down from heaven, ascended into heaven; came to visit us in great humility'.

The notion of 'revelation' is often said (as by Bultmann) to be the *Grundkonzeption* of this work, even though the verb occurs only at 12.38 in a quotation from Isa. 53.1. The Johannine verbs 'to make known', 'manifest', 'announce' and 'explain' are relevant, but the Prologue, discourses, and dualistic framework are the main reasons for this judgement. Jesus' heavenly origin and home are what make him on earth the revelation of God. In other words, while John's conception of revelation is expressed in his depicting the 'Christ event' as an incarnation it is the idea of *revelation* rather than the idea of *incarnation* that governs the Johannine theology. It is not (despite 1.14a) that the divine world touches the human and created order (as in classical incarnational theology), or even that Jesus speaks to reveal who he is, the incarnate Son of God (as in some pre-critical proof-texting and popular apologetics), but rather that because he is (as John asserts) the eternal Son, he actually reveals God on earth. The point of Johannine Christianity is not so much what Jesus says, or even what is said about him in Christology, but that in his life and death he *is* the saving revelation of God. All that he is depicted as saying and all that is said about him is intended to make that

[9] See T. E. Pollard, *Johannine Christology and the Early Church* (Cambridge: CUP, 1970), to judge the extent of the dissonance.
[10] Karl Rahner expresses strong reservations about mythological expressions of the doctrine, see K. Rahner, 'Incarnation', in *Encyclopedia of Theology* (London: Burns & Oates, 1975).

claim clear and persuasive. How that revelation is mediated through Christian witness exercises the evangelist both in his practice and at a theoretical level (e.g. 5.30–47). His kerygmatic solution and explanation is itself part of his overall view of revelation.

The way of John's incarnational language subserves his view of revelation suggests how to speak of the incarnation in a way that is in accord with scripture. John's understanding is visible in the Prologue, and more obviously in the discourses. Despite coming before the reference to the Baptist in vv. 6f and the incarnation at v. 14, the light shining in the darkness (v. 5) and enlightening everyone (v. 9) also probably refer at least partly to the incarnation. Light is a powerful metaphor for revelation, both here and in the body of the Gospel (3.19–21, 8.12, 9.5, 12.35f., 46, and perhaps 11.9f). Since revelation is concentrated in Jesus, in his ministry, passion and resurrection, and is actualized by the Spirit-Paraclete in subsequent Christian proclamation, it is hard to imagine the evangelist not thinking of the incarnation in those early verses. However, the main purpose of the Prologue with its talk of pre-existence is to make explicit the divine source of the revelation. Revelation is the main point even here, as is made clear by the final work of the Prologue (v. 18): Jesus Christ, the only-begotten God (or Son) *explained* or revealed God. Elsewhere in the gospel it is even clearer that the myth of pre-existence and incarnation subserves the fundamental idea of revelation. Jesus is the revelation of God. That is what the evangelist believes, and that is what he depicts Jesus revealing.

John's conception of revelation is not clear beyond dispute. Bultmann argued that it was entirely without content – Jesus revealed merely that he was the revealer. That neatly catches its main characteristic. Nothing that Jesus says is actually revelation. But it is not quite right. Hard as it is to specify the content, and inappropriate as it is to 'objectify' it, Jesus is identifiable even in John's Gospel as the man from Nazareth who was crucified. There is more than the naked fact of his life and death here. He is the mysterious stranger from the world above, but he is also the particular man from Nazareth, as Bultmann in effect recognizes when he speaks of God being encountered in the human Jesus. John's claim that Jesus loved his own utterly and that his coming revealed God's love for the world and opened the possibility of salvation specifies that self-giving love as intrinsic to the unique event of saving revelation which Jesus embodied.[11]

Unlike John of Patmos, the evangelist does not use the Pauline and deutero-Pauline word 'mystery',[12] but his understanding of revelation in

---

[11] See John Ashton, *Understanding the Fourth Gospel* (Oxford: OUP, 1988).
[12] On this concept see now Markus Bockmuehl, *Revelation and Mystery* (Tübingen, J. C. B. Mohr, 1990).

Christ is hidden too. John's work can be read as an extended comment on Mk. 4.11, where the secret of God's rule is surely Jesus himself, in whom that rule is secretly present, and given to faith and discipleship. Mark's focus on the man in whom God's rule is already being exercised is made harder and brighter by John, but all four Gospels find God in Jesus. Matthew packs moral guidance into his economical narrative of the son of David – Son of God who will come to judge the world, and even Luke's smoother narrative is about the Lord.[13] Apart from Matt. 18.6 only John makes Christ the explicit object of faith, but the faith in God that Mark also emphasizes is specifically faith in the presence of God's eschatological power in the person of Jesus. When people encounter Jesus they encounter God (cf. 5.19f) and their faith is based on some understanding of Jesus and his significance. Even the more general occurrences of the noun and verb at 11.22–24 are made Christological by their gospel context.[14]

Mark's narrative account of what he (unlike some: 4.12, cf. Jn. 12.40) perceives to be the decisive revelation of God is more true to the historical reality than is the narrative of John, who has been charged, wrongly but understandably, with docetism.[15] Mark's teacher and healer is unquestionably human. Though revealed from heaven as God's Son he is not pre-existent and does not 'come down' from heaven as a divine envoy. The revelation of God that Mark's Jesus discloses by his ministry and passion, or that all four narrate in the light of the resurrection event and hope, is veiled not only by the fact of Jesus' humanity but in addition by Mark's literary devices, commonly bundled together as 'the messianic secret'.[16]

This literary veiling was so appropriate to what Christians see as an actual veiling of Jesus' divine status in his historical life and death that Dibelius interpreted it as an apologetic device by which Mark reconciled his post-resurrection theology with the historical reality. But Mark's design in what Dibelius appropriately called his 'book of secret epiphanies' was probably to prevent these divine epiphanies of God's Son from blinding his hearers and readers to the truly human suffering of the Son of man. Mark's theology of the cross is more realistic than John's, but the

---

[13] On my cautious acceptance of Barbara Shellards' hypothesis that Luke knew John (and Matthew), see my article, 'Which was the Fourth Gospel? The Order of the Gospels and the Unity of Scripture', *JSNT* 54 (1994), pp. 3–28.

[14] Cf. C. D. Marshall, *Faith as a Theme in Mark's Narrative* (Cambridge: CUP, 1989).

[15] See G. Bornkamm, 'Towards the Interpretation of John's Gospel: A Discussion of the *Testament of Jesus* by Ernst Käsemann (1968)', in *The Interpretation of John*, ed. J. Ashton (London: SPCK, 1986), pp. 79–98, which also includes Käsemann's response.

[16] See e.g. W. C. Robinson, 'The Quest for Wrede's Secret Messiah', *Interpretation* 27 (1973), pp. 10–30, reprinted in C. M. Tuckett, ed., *The Messianic Secret* (London: SPCK, 1985), pp. 97–115.

double aspect is present in all four Gospels. John removes the literary veil provided by the secrecy motif, but remains clear that God's glory was revealed in the ambiguity of signs and in flesh and blood that was violently separated on a cross, and that spiritual discernment is essentially a matter of faith (20.8, 28). His insistence on faith (believing) is stronger and more explicit even than Mark's, but to evoke it he writes more directly of the glory of Christ that he and other believers beheld (1.14, cf. 2.11). Like Isaiah he saw (Jn. 12.41) the glory of Christ (which is the glory of God, cf. 7.18, 8.50, 54) and spoke of it. Paul could have said something similar (cf. 1 Cor. 9.1; 2 Cor. 4.6).

Like Mark, John intends (20.31) to elicit Christian faith by projecting the one in whose life and death God was and (through Christian preaching) still is revealing his love for the world. Both evangelists (like Paul, on occasion) are in a sense prophetic or apocalyptic writers, interpreting God's plan for the world by reporting what they have seen and heard and understood (cf. Jn. 12.41) and disclosing the hidden revelation of God in Jesus. But neither Gospel is itself an apocalypse. The revelation has taken place on earth and is known in part by historical memory (cf. Jn. 2.22, 12.16, 14.26) as well as through Christian word and witness. However, just as Mark draws on Daniel and the apocalyptic tradition to speak of the future coming of the transcendent Son of man (Mk. 13.26, 14.62), so too John probably depends far more on this than was realized by nineteenth-century scholars who over-identified 'Apocalyptik' with eschatology.[17] The future hope is largely carried back by John into the present moment of decision for or against the light (e.g. 3.17–21) but what happens in the present is no less divine revelation than what was expected at the end of the age.

John has very little futurist eschatology, despite the possibly redactional quotation of Dan. 12.2 at 5.28f. Even the resurrection 'at the last day' promised at 6.39, 40, 44, 45 (also thought by some to be redactional) was perhaps understood by John in an individual sense (cf. Jn. 14.3). But the Johannine symbolism of above and below, and especially the peculiarly Johannine Son of man sayings about coming down from heaven and going up, may draw on the angelology of Jewish apocalypses. In his understanding of revelation, and in the incarnational language he has forged to present Jesus as the revelation of God, John is probably as indebted to this tradition as any NT writer. This confirms that the Markan 'mystery of the kingdom of God', or the dialectic of a hidden revelation in the earthly Jesus, accessible only to faith and discipleship and communicated by subtle literary strategies, is still visible in the

---

[17] Corrected by C. Rowland, *The Open Heaven* (London: SPCK, 1982). On the history of research see R. Morgan, 'From Reimarus to Sanders', in *The Kingdom of God and Human Society*, ed. R. S. Barbour (Edinburgh: T. & T. Clark, 1993), pp. 80–139.

incarnational language by which John articulates his similar conviction that Jesus is the revelation of God.

John's incarnational interpretation of Jesus is far less destructive of Jesus' historical reality than some ancient theology and devotion or modern parodies of this suggest. The revelation of God in the Son who is identified by his ministry and passion, and proclaimed after his exaltation, remains veiled and accessible only to faith, however plain it is made to the reader or hearer by John's less subtle but more powerful literary strategies. Only the disciples see the manifestation of his glory in the signs (2.11); there is no escape from dependence on John's 'word' of Jesus that reflects Christian proclamation. No less than Luther, Bultmann, and Ebeling, John is a theologian of the Word and faith, and interpreter of the cross as the crux of God's self-involvement with humanity.

This hiddenness of God in the life and death of Jesus is touched on tangentially in the Prologue. 'He came unto his own and his own received him not' (v. 11) and also the preceding verse, 'He was in the world ...' (v. 10), probably refer to the ministry of Jesus. The subsequent flash-back to the event of the Word becoming flesh in v. 14a functions as the climax of the present Prologue, and the Christian response of v. 14b contrasts with the world's rejection at vv. 10f. What John emphasizes is not a public announcement of the incomprehensible, but divine self-concealment comprehensible to faith.

The liturgical reading of John at the carol service, by contrast, refers 'the mystery of the incarnation' to the birth of Jesus. This scarcely accords with the intentions of an evangelist who can only treat such questions ironically (cf. 7.42) or as material for insult (8.41), but both the Christmas interpretation of the Prologue and the Johannine idea of *revelation* throughout the ministry and passion make God the subject of the event and a evoke a response to God by communicating the Christian message in the form of a narrative (which some will call 'myth') about God causing his Son the Messiah to appear. Like Paul's 'kenotic' (1 Cor. 8.9, Phil. 2.7f) and 'sending' (Rom. 8.3, cf. 8.32; Gal. 4.6) texts, they appeal to the imagination.

Most of the confusions surrounding the word 'incarnation' stem from identifying the *doctrine* of the incarnation with 'the *myth* of God incarnate'. Both have roots in John's retelling the story of Jesus' ministry, passion, and resurrection in a way that expresses and advances Christian religious faith. In the discourses, for example, John's Jesus identifies himself with the revelation of God through a series of metaphors and symbols. Thus Jesus is metaphorically identified with bread, light, a door, a shepherd, a vine, and so on. In chapter 6 the Exodus story of the manna provides a type and opens a door to applying the language of descent from heaven to Jesus, but 'myth' is scarcely the appropriate category. It is not the 'coming down from heaven' language of this chapter which accounts for the pervasive sense of incarnation in John's Gospel, and the emerging Christian myth, but rather the *combination* of pre-existence in the Prologue (and occasionally elsewhere), the strong dualism of above and below, light and darkness, and the language of the Father sending the Son and the Son going to the Father (or being exalted, or glorified). John's dualism surely stems from his sectarian Jewish background, and his Prologue, his idea of pre-existence, and his sending language are all intended to present Jesus as the revelation of God. They are each more metaphor than myth, and even the whole can best be described as an overarching metaphor of incarnation. The only trace of what might be called a *myth* of incarnation (and even here not a 'myth of God incarnate') is the language of descent and ascent of the (probably mythic) Son of man figure indicated at 3.13, 6.62 (cf. 1.51).

John's whole story is firmly rooted in history, and the metaphorical language by which he brings out the religious significance of Jesus as the revelation of God does not quite subvert that. Jesus *is* a stranger, whose true home is above and whose true identity is not recognized, but he is also a human being in first-century Galilee and Judaea, whose family is identified and who is executed by Pilate. When we focus on the history it seems absurd to call this narrative *myth*; when we allow the metaphors to play on our imagination it is easy to see how the Christian myth took shape with massive help from this Gospel; when we analyze its thought we can see how its idea of revelation coincides with what the latter *doctrine* of the incarnation is wishing to assert: that in having to do with the crucified and exalted Jesus Messiah, Son of God, believers in John's own day and (10.16; 17.20) subsequently, have to do with God and so have life.

That is not (despite 1.14a) incarnational *theology*, reflecting on God's identification with the material world, or seeking to reconcile believers' confession of Jesus as Lord and God with their monotheism, or trying to make intelligible their belief that Jesus is both human and divine. John clearly was a theologically reflective writer, but these were not the questions he was asking, and he lacked the philosophical conceptuality by which later theologians would articulate them. His affirmations probably developed in controversy within and later outside the synagogue, but his questions and problems arose from the gospel genre itself: how to retell the human historical story of Jesus in such a way as to communicate the Christian message.

His dramatic solution was successful despite or through being doubly misunderstood, as incarnational theology and as history. It contains both, but is rather Christian proclamation, inspired writing by an author who believed the Spirit was leading subsequent disciples such as himself into all truth. He was self-conscious enough to see the main problem of his medium – that it made Jesus seem a self-glorifying monomaniac – and to answer it in chapters 5, 7 and 8 (it is really God or the Spirit who is bearing witness to Jesus in these discourses). Revelation can only be self-authenticating, however much the spirits must subsequently be tested by moral and intellectual criteria to see whether they are of God. But that is the task of theology. Theology follows faith as believers search for expressions of authentic Christianity that are true both to the tradition and to contemporary experience.

A criterion of orthodoxy is only a rule of thumb, identifying the Christianity that binds us to the God of Israel in his Son Jesus Christ our Lord. It proved necessary to insist that this Jesus really was a human being and that it is really God whom we encounter in him. Theology aims to understand enough to communicate that trust, but cannot explain the mystery. The doctrine points us back to the narratives, telling us how to read them and to appropriate them imaginatively. It commits us to a pattern of faith and worship which some call orthodoxy. Our incarnational definition of this is independent of our attitude to myth, which some suspect of falsity, and others find childish or meaningless. That kind of positivism need not intimidate theologians but neither should they cling to myth as a way of avoiding the metaphysical claims staked out by Christian doctrine and justified by theology.

Finding the identity of Christianity in a word that belongs to the realm of religion and myth before ever it is adopted by theology and doctrine corresponds to the reality to which they all refer. The multivalent language of incarnation leads right into the symbolic world of millions whose religious and cultural system hinges on this event, but who spurn the technicalities of theology. Such powerful symbolic language is not to be lightly abandoned, but clarified, qualified and interpreted. The doctrine of the incarnation gives Christian soldiers a compass, pointing them onward and away from back-sliding into Christologies inadequate to their heart's relationship with their King. It is, incidentally, a beautiful antique compass, evocative and precious by long association. It reminds brothers and sisters that they are treading where the saints have trod. In wanting to meet half-way and share this essential of Christian community with friends who have been embarrassed by the myth, and bored by ancient speculations, into teaching a different doctrine, it is still right to celebrate the sense in which we are not divided but confess the same Lord by the same faith and in the same baptism. Pending agreement on this one doctrine along a spectrum of healthily different theologies we can still sing together: 'all one body wee, one in hope and doctoring, one in charity ...'.

PART FOUR: THE CHURCH AS INSTITUTION

11

'How these Christians hate one another ...!': Sectarian Conflict in the Modern World

HUGH MCLEOD

COMMUNITIES survive by providing their members with a place where they feel at home and by offering them a credible vision of the good life. But however comforting communities may be to those inside, they often thrive on the existence of external enemies. Fear of these enemies provides a good reason for clinging together, and an awareness of the faults, vices and errors of those outside may do wonders for the morale of those inside. Christian communities seem to be as prone to these kinds of demonization as any other kind of community, and very often the enemy consists of another branch of Christianity. Some of the most notorious examples of such internecine strife took place in the period of the Reformation and Counter-Reformation, the era of 'Religious Wars'. But there are also many examples in more recent times. In the most extreme cases, members of one Christian confession have killed Christians belonging to another branch of the faith. We are all familiar with the conflicts between Catholic and Protestant in Ireland or between Catholic Croats and Orthodox Serbs. But these are by no means the only examples. For instance, the Swiss civil war of 1847 pitted Catholic cantons against Protestant. In the south-east of France, centuries of violence between Catholics and Protestants continued into the first half of the nineteenth century. And the conflicts between Catholics and Protestants in the 1890s led to claims that Buganda was 'the Belfast of Africa.'[1]

Such examples of lethal conflict are only the tip of a huge iceberg. At many times and in many places less spectacular forms of antagonism between rival branches of Christianity have simply been part of the pattern of everyday life. This was emphatically the case in the nineteenth century, and it has continued to a lesser extent to be the case in the twentieth century.

Not surprisingly, Christians have preferred to treat such episodes as aberrations, although they are really too numerous to be treated in such a way. Meanwhile, others have eagerly seized upon them, and used them as

[1] Geoffrey Moorhouse, *The Missionaries* (London: Methuen, 1973), p. 253.

163

a principal argument in attempts to refute Christianity, usually overlooking the fact that many of the bloodiest religious persecutions of modern times have been inflicted by atheists or militant anti-clericals. Both views tend to be largely or wholly unhistorical, since they posit a Christianity which is always, and by its essential nature, either peace-loving and tolerant, or violent and bigoted.

In this paper I shall focus on western Christendom in the period since the Reformation, and in particular in the period since the French Revolution of 1789. I shall argue that sectarian conflict, rather than being a constant, has fluctuated in scale, intensity and significance, and in the forms it has characteristically taken. In doing this I shall distinguish between three phases of post-Reformation history: first the confessional era; then the denominational era; and finally the era of religious individualism. In the confessional era, running very roughly from the Reformation to the French Revolution, the state attempted to impose a particular form of Christianity on the whole population, and dissenters were subjected to many forms of persecution or discrimination, sometimes very severe. In the denominational era, running roughly from the French Revolution to the 1960s, a considerable degree of religious pluralism existed in many countries, but most people regarded themselves as members of one of the Christian churches, and the larger churches had an extensive public role in such fields as politics, education and welfare. In the era of religious individualism, emerging since the 1960s, the larger denominations have suffered a serious decline in membership, while there has been a growth both in those of no religion and in those adhering to a plethora of new religious movements, both Christian and non-Christian; there has also been a decline in the internal discipline of the churches, as even those who continue to belong to them claim the right to considerable freedom in matters of faith and morals. I shall argue that sectarian conflict reached very high levels during the sixteenth and seventeenth centuries, only to decline somewhat in the eighteenth; that it revived considerably in the nineteenth century, before declining somewhat in the first half of the twentieth century, and then more radically in the period since the 1960s as denominational divisions lost much of their importance, but that other sources of religious conflict have to some extent taken their place.

I. THE CONFESSIONAL ERA

The Reformation and Counter-Reformation divided western Christendom into Catholic, Lutheran, Reformed and Anglican states. Moreover, beginning with the Anabaptists, a variety of new Protestant movements rose, and managed with difficulty to survive without any state backing. Several features of this situation are relevant to my theme. First, with very few exceptions, nearly every state established one Christian denomination in a position of privilege, and penalized, often very severely, the practice of other forms of Christianity. This situation remained normal at least until the later eighteenth century, and often well into the nineteenth century. Second, however, the multiple divisions created in the sixteenth century left behind a general awareness that a variety of different forms of Christianity were available, and that it was possible to convert from one to another. At certain times and places such conversions were quite frequent. More generally however, it meant that Christian denominations defined themselves consciously in opposition to rival branches of the faith, justifying, and often emphasizing the points of difference. The division of western and central Europe on confessional lines, followed by the division of the New World between a mainly Catholic south and a mainly Protestant north, had wide-ranging implications for the development of Western societies in the period from the sixteenth century to the nineteenth.[2]

For instance, confessional identities played a major part in processes of nation-building. The Dutch Republic, which was to be one of the most important economic and cultural centres of seventeenth-century Europe, defined itself as a Protestant nation, formed in the crucible of the long war for independence from Catholic Spain.[3] The experience of war with Spain, and later France, and the memory of Bloody Mary (a persecuting Catholic monarch, married to a Spanish king) also played a central role in shaping English national identity. For several centuries Foxe's *Book of Martyrs* and Bunyan's *Pilgrim's Progress* ranked next only to the Bible among those books which every self-respecting household sought to possess.[4] Meanwhile, Spanish identity was shaped with equal force by the role that country had played in the sixteenth century as champion of Catholic interests. Right into the twentieth century the vision of Spain as a purely Catholic nation continued to exercise a powerful hold on the imagination of Spanish Catholics[5] – thus the uproar caused in 1931 by Azaña's famous speech in which he declared that Spain was 'no longer a Catholic nation', and that the privileged position enjoyed by the church could thus no longer be justified.

---

[2] For an overview of the 'confessionalization' of Europe, see R. Po-Chia Hsia, *Social Discipline in the Reformation: Central Europe 1550–1750* (London: Routledge, 1989).
[3] Simon Schama, *The Embarrassment of Riches* (London: Collins, 1987), ch. 2.
[4] Linda Colley, *Britons: Forging the Nation 1707–1837* (New Haven: Yale University Press, 1992), ch. 1.
[5] Frances Lannon, 'Modern Spain: The Project of a National Catholicism', in *Religion and National Identity*, ed. S. Mews (Oxford: Blackwell, 1982), pp. 567–90.

At the same time, dominant confessions shaped the development of distinctive and contrasting cultures, which at a less conscious level strongly influenced people's way of looking at the world, and emphasized the alien character of those belonging to other confessions. To give a few examples: the much greater wealth enjoyed by the church in Catholic countries than in Protestant in the period from the sixteenth century to the eighteenth left an immensely impressive legacy of religious buildings and works of religious art of all kinds, but also in many cases a tradition of vigorous anti-clericalism; Lutheran and Reformed countries enjoyed at least until the later nineteenth century considerably higher rates of literacy than those that were Catholic; Protestant countries were also initially more strongly influenced by the Enlightenment than Catholic countries – though when the Enlightenment did reach France, it frequently took a bitterly anti-Christian form, which rarely happened elsewhere; Catholic countries were often notable for the strength of popular piety, and the degree to which the church was able to cater for the religious needs of the poor and the uneducated, whereas, by the eighteenth and nineteenth century, the state Protestant churches were tending to adopt a predominantly middle class character, leaving the poor either to sectarian movements, or to forms of devotion that were substantially independent of the church.

In both Protestant and Catholic countries, throughout the period from the sixteenth century to the end of the eighteenth, and often well into the nineteenth century, the church had a dominant role in the provision of education and charity; and it ministered to nearly the whole population at the great turning-points of birth, marriage and death. Also, the parish or local clergyman was potentially a very influential figure, though in practice this influence was limited both by the personal qualities of the man who happened to occupy the office, by his social position, and by the repute or disrepute of the church as a landlord and employer.

Confessional differences thus had immense political and cultural significance. This had a bearing on what happened in the nineteenth century, when, in conditions of relative freedom, there was an enormous growth in religious dissent, and when demographic changes brought members of different confessions increasingly into contact with one another. In the later eighteenth century it had seemed that the confessions were moving closer together. In the 1780s Catholic Austria and France and Lutheran Hamburg all introduced religious toleration, and in Ireland most of the restrictions on Roman Catholic practice were lifted. Some of the British colonies in North America already had long traditions of religious toleration, and in 1791 the first amendment to the constitution of the recently established United States decreed the separation of church and state. In German cities in the later eighteenth century it was said that 'enlightened' Christians regarded denominational distinctions as so unimportant that they would willingly attend one another's churches.[6] In England a notable example of practical co-operation was the Manchester Sunday School, founded in 1784, and managed by a committee which included both Anglicans and Dissenters, and even more notably, Roman Catholics.[7] The persecution of the Catholic Church by revolutionary governments in France in the 1790s also persuaded some Protestants that their enemy's enemy might after all be their friend. For instance large numbers of priests found refuge in England: sympathy for their plight and admiration for the heroism shown by many Catholics contributed to a mood of increased openness to Catholicism on the part of some Anglicans.

Yet much of this was superficial. The new mood of toleration was very largely an élite phenomenon, and had little impact on the thinking of the masses. In the long-term the collaboration of Catholics and Protestants in Ireland's 1798 rising, and the leadership of Wolfe Tone, both a nationalist hero and a Protestant, were less significant than the foundation of the Orange Order in 1795, or the killings of Protestants by Catholic insurgents in the south-east. The Catholic Relief Act of 1778 may tell us less about English Protestant feelings towards the Catholic minority than the Gordon Riots of 1780, which included violent attacks on Catholics and their property. The new spirit of toleration between Catholics and Protestants in France found little echo in the south-east, where the Revolution was seen by many as a continuation of the Wars of Religion.

II. The Denominational Era

In what I have termed the 'denominational era' of the nineteenth century, legal toleration became the norm and, at least in Protestant countries, a wide variety of new religious denominations sprang up. The fact that most states recognized the right to religious dissent, and that religious minorities were beginning to insist on their rights and to take an active part in politics, did not mean, however, that tolerant attitudes generally prevailed among the populace or, indeed, that the state itself behaved with impartiality towards all religious groups. For a whole range of reasons – demographic, political, theological, and so on – the nineteenth century was a period when denominational consciousness was at a high level, and tensions between denominations were often severe.

[6] Lucian Hölscher, 'Secularization and Urbanization in the Nineteenth Century', in *European Religion in the Age of Great Cities*, ed. Hugh McLeod (London: Routledge, 1995).
[7] W. R. Ward, *Religion and Society in England 1790–1850* (London: Batsford, 1972), p. 13.

Tensions between members of established churches and those adhering to Protestant free churches, and especially to newly-established denominations, were at several levels. In the first place, the aggressive proselytism pursued by Methodists, Baptists, Salvationists, and so on, caused widespread resentment. New religious movements won an initial following by methods of propaganda that were noisy and often intrusive, by fierce attacks on cherished customs and forms of recreation, and by pointed criticism of the clergy of more conventional denominations. Not surprisingly, they aroused bitter opposition, and were sometimes subjected to assaults and even murder, with the connivance or open encouragement of those in authority.[8] In the second place, religious differences were often bound up with social and political tensions. And in the third place there were important differences in ethos and life-style between newer and older churches.

In England and Wales, for instance, the split between 'church' and 'chapel' was among the most significant and the most generally recognized divisions in society. In some ways the differences were more profound than those between Protestant and Catholic. For instance, there were important differences in life-style embodied above all in 'chapel' teetotalism. Equally important was the close association between the chapel and Liberal politics. There was a strain of independence, even rebellion, in the world of the chapel, with its defiance of the state church and, equally importantly, of the authority of the squire, or of other powerful figures of secular authority. Especially in agricultural and mining communities, the chapel came to play a crucial role in the development of trades unions. Mutual stereotyping was rife: chapel people were often portrayed as blind fanatics and puritanical killjoys, while church people were seen as snobs, whose belief was superficial, and who merely 'went through the motions'. Like most other religious minorities chapel people had a strong sense of history. They had their heroes (above all, Cromwell) and martyrs, and memories of the persecution suffered by their ancestors remained alive, even when most of them had achieved acceptance and respectability. In 1902, these apparently moribund traditions suddenly became a living reality again, as Nonconformists launched a campaign of 'Passive Resistance' to the Conservative government's Education Act, and some 160 of them went to prison, rather than pay taxes which would support Anglican and Roman Catholic schools.[9]

In Catholic countries, relatively few people left the church of their ancestors, but militantly anti-clerical movements had a role and charac-

---

[8] John Walsh, 'Methodism and the Mob', in *Popular Belief and Practice*, eds. C. J. Cuming and D. Baker (Cambridge: CUP, 1972), pp. 213–28; Glenn Horridge, *The Salvation Army: Origins and Early Days* (Godalming: Ammonite, 1993), ch. 4.

[9] James Munson, *The Nonconformists* (London: SPCK, 1991), pp. 252–89.

ter in some ways similar to that of religious dissent in Britain. Once again, the enormous social, cultural and political role of the church meant that proponents of democratic reform felt themselves forced to challenge the power of the clergy. As in Britain, education was the crucial battle-ground. In the later nineteenth and early twentieth centuries, as most European countries were establishing systems of universal education, no political issue was more generally explosive than the place of religion and the church within these systems. The battles between Catholics and anti-clericals, or between state church and free church Protestants, were not simply a matter of irrational prejudice – though such prejudices no doubt existed in ample measures. Also at stake were conflicting ideas about the nature of education and conflicting visions of the future. These visions tended to be mutually exclusive, as most people still thought in terms of a national system of education, binding the people together in the way that national churches had once done. 'Free' schools might be tolerated, but were scarcely encouraged. Few were yet ready to think in pluralist terms. The country which came closest to pluralism was the Netherlands, where the system of 'pillarization', whereby each religious and political community had its own schools and universities, as well as newspapers, trades unions, and so on, began to take shape in the later nineteenth century.[10] But Dutch pluralism was born of political necessity rather than ideological conviction.

Meanwhile, the centuries-old enmities between Catholic and Protestant were being revitalized as political and demographic changes brought members of the rival confessions into closer contact with one another. The political changes may in fact reflect a certain lack of sensitivity to religious differences and tensions on the part of the generation of aristocratic politicians born in the middle years of the eighteenth century, and brought up on 'enlightened' ideas concerning the primacy of reason, the convergence between religions and the obsolescence of dogma. The Act of Union in 1800 brought the predominantly Catholic Irish into the United Kingdom, and the Treaty of Vienna in 1815 redrew the map of Germany, making many Catholic Rhinelanders reluctant citizens of Protestant Prussia, and many Protestants in Franconia and the Palatinate equally reluctant citizens of Catholic Bavaria. Similarly the Catholic Belgians were incorporated into the Protestant Kingdom of the Netherlands, though the Belgians successfully escaped in 1830. Meanwhile demographic changes, notably the flight of peasants from impoverished rural districts to growing cities and industrial regions, were continually changing the confessional geography of Europe and the Americas. Es-

---

[10] Michael Wintle, *Pillars of Piety: Religion in the Netherlands in the Nineteenth Century* (Hull: Hull University Press, 1987), pp. 62–8; E. H. Kossman, *The Low Countries 1780–1940* (Oxford: Clarendon, 1978).

pecially from the 1830s, the fervently Protestant United States, still in the throes of the Second Great Awakening, faced an enormous influx of Catholic immigrants from Ireland and Germany, later to be followed by Italians, Poles and Mexicans. In the twentieth century the once Catholic nations of Latin America received considerable numbers of Protestant immigrants who, in time, would be reinforced by converts from the traditional faith. Protestant cities like Geneva became predominantly Catholic, and Catholic cities like Cologne or Munich acquired substantial Protestant minorities.

In such situations of proximity, deep-rooted prejudices frequently had a dominant influence on the relations between religious communities. One of the most important manifestations of such prejudice was the taboo on intermarriage between Catholics and Protestants. Opposition to intermarriage between different branches of Protestantism was usually much less. A particularly detailed study of confessional relations in Alsace and Baden in the later nineteenth and early twentieth centuries shows that both Catholics and Protestants regarded mixed marriages as 'treason'. The opposition was strongest in rural areas, and it was common for a man living in a Catholic village to marry a woman from a Catholic village several miles away, although there were Protestant villages that were nearer. Hostile stereotypes were rife. Protestants, referring to the number of Catholic holidays, accused Catholics of laziness, while Catholics both resented the unfair competition generated by the Protestant addiction to work, and pitied the narrowness of life that it reflected.[11] In Ireland, Protestants accused Catholics of drunkenness ('Smell a man's breath and tell his religion'), while Catholics regularly animadverted to Protestant unchastity ('Bastards increase proportionately to the number of Orange Lodges').[12] In northern England in the early twentieth century, Protestants claimed that Catholics were 'scruffy',[13] and in Protestant north Germany to call someone a 'Catholic' was to imply that they were behaving in a stupid or perverse manner.[14]

There were many factors tending to reinforce this powerful sense of sectarian identity. One of the most important was political. In many parts of Europe the period from about the 1860s to the First World War saw the enfranchisement of large sections of the working class, lower

---

[11] Alfred Wahl, 'Confession et comportement das les campagnes d'Alsace et de Bade 1871–1939' (University of Metz doctoral thesis, 2 vols., 1980), pp. 1:388, 614–53; 2:784, 958, 1254–70.
[12] K. H. Connell, *Irish Peasant Society* (Oxford: Clarendon, 1968), pp. 85–6.
[13] Hugh McLeod, *Religion and Society in England 1850–1914* (Basingstoke: Macmillan, [forthcoming 1996]).
[14] Hugh McLeod, 'Building the "Catholic Ghetto": Catholic Organisations 1870–1914', in *Voluntary Religion*, ed. W. J. Sheils (Oxford: Blackwell, 1986), p. 422.

middle class and peasantry. Political parties recognized that the most powerful form of identity that most people possessed was religious, and that the new mass electorate could most effectively be mobilized through the use of religious rhetoric and symbols, the highlighting of religious issues, and sometimes the assistance of religious personnel. At the same time, many of the clergy recognized that politics could be a means of improving the situation of their people and also strengthening the influence of the church. There were Catholic parties and Protestant parties; parties closely identified with religious dissent; and also militantly anti-clerical parties. From about the 1880s there was also a flowing of church-based workers' associations, peasants' associations, trades unions, co-operatives, and so on. In most cases, patterns of religious affiliation and/or practice were a major influence on voting patterns, and probably in a majority of cases they were *the* most important influence. To take two examples, where statistical studies have provided a relative degree of precision: it is estimated that in the 1874 election in Germany 83% of Roman Catholics voted for the Centre Party, and in spite of a subsequent loosening of Catholic support, the proportion was still 55% in 1912; and a study of elections in England between 1885 and 1910 shows that the best predictor of the result was the proportion of Nonconformists in the population.[15] But even where less precise statistics are available the importance of religious variables in elections during this period has been amply demonstrated in countries ranging from the United States to Australia, and from Belgium to Switzerland.[16]

Another aspect of the great popular mobilization during this period was the emergence of numerous nationalist and regionalist movements. Many of these had a strong religious colouring. In so many cases, claims to peoplehood could best be defined in terms of a distinctive religious history, and definitions of national culture drew heavily on religious practices, personalities and motifs. Moreover the clergy were influential and enthusiastic propagators of nationalist ideas. Striking examples of these tendencies would be the strongly Calvinist character of Afrikaner nationalism or the equally close ties between Polish nationalism and the Roman Catholic faith.

---

[15] J. Schauff, *Das Wahlverhalten der deutschen Katholiken im Kaisserreich und in der Weimarer Republik* (Mainz: von Hare & Koehler, 1975), p. 74; K. D. Wald, *Crosses on the Ballot* (Princeton: Princeton University Press, 1983), chs. 7–8.
[16] Paul Kleppner, *The Third Electoral System: Parties, Voters and Political Cultures* (Chapel Hill: University of North Carolina Press, 1979); Michael Hogan, *The Sectarian Strand: Religion in Australian History* (Ringwood, Victoria: Penguin, 1987), p. 152 ; Carl Strikwerda, 'A Resurgent Religion: The Rise of Catholic Social Movements in Nineteenth-Century Belgian Cities', in *European Religion*, pp. 61–90; Urs Altermatt, *Der Weg der schweizer Katholiken ins Ghetto* (Zurich: Benziger, 1972).

But the potential of religion to unite and divide was seen most starkly in areas like the north of Ireland, where two rival nationalisms, rooted primarily in rival religious traditions, confronted one another, each laying claim to the same territory. Protestantism was crucial to the unionist movement and to the ultimate separation of the Six Counties from the rest of Ireland, since the rationale for Partition rested on the claim that the Protestants were a separate people. The Irish nationalist case was ostensibly non-sectarian, since it was based on the claim that the island was one, and that all Irish people, regardless of religious denomination, belonged to the same nation. In practice, however, the great majority of nationalists were Catholics: Catholicism was the most tangible embodiment of the cultural separation of Ireland from the rest of the United Kingdom; the history of oppression to which nationalist orators referred involved to a large extent the oppression of Catholics by Protestants; and the Catholic clergy had a crucial role at the local level in inculcating a nationalist consciousness and promoting support for nationalist politics. Where religion has fused with militant nationalism the combination has often been uniquely lethal. The Catholic hierarchy tried to exercise a moderating role, discouraging assassinations and violent uprisings. But many of the revolutionaries were strongly influenced by their own understanding of Catholicism. Both Patrick Pearse and James Connolly drew an explicit parallel between the sacrifice made by Christ on Calvary and the sacrifice that they were making for the redemption of Ireland, and Pearse presented the cause of 'national freedom' as a religious crusade, indifference or opposition to which was a sin.[17]

On the other side of Ireland's religious divide, there were plenty of Protestants who saw the unionist cause in similar terms. This tradition has been kept alive by those like Ian Paisley, who has repeatedly argued throughout the twenty-five years of carnage in Northern Ireland that the Protestants of Ulster have a special place in God's providence and that the preservation of their heritage against the onslaughts of Catholics, nationalists and Protestant liberals must take precedence over any search for peace.[18]

While political developments in nineteenth-century Europe were tending to stimulate sectarian consciousness and exacerbate sectarian antagonism, equally important was the growing importance in the first half of the nineteenth century of militant and exclusivist versions of both the Catholic and the Protestant faiths. On the Catholic side the key development was the rise of Ultramontanism which began mainly as a grass-

---

[17] F. M. L. Lyons, *Ireland since the Famine* (London: Weidenfeld & Nicolson, 1971), pp. 334–8, 347.
[18] Steve Bruce, *God Save Ulster! The Religion and Politics of Paisleyism* (Oxford: Clarendon, 1986), pp. 268–70.

roots movement, propagated by the parish clergy and by certain religious orders, but treated with considerable suspicion both by most of the hierarchy and by many educated lay people. Under Pius IX, however, Ultramontanism became the official policy of the church, and a series of major pronouncements in the 1850s, 1860s and 1870s, laid down in uncompromising terms the fundamental opposition between the Roman Catholic Church and all those outside. The dogma of the Immaculate Conception, defined in 1854, was unacceptable to Protestants because of its lack of any scriptural foundation. The Syllabus of Errors published in 1864 delivered a comprehensive condemnation of the spirit of the age and of all those Catholics who wanted to adapt themselves to the era of religious and political freedom. The dogma of Papal Infallibility defined in 1870 was not only completely unacceptable to all Protestant and Orthodox Christians, but was also rejected by many Catholics – some of whom left to form such bodies as the Old Catholics and Christ Catholics, but most of whom stayed in the Church and closed ranks with their Ultramontane fellow-believers in the face of the growing mood of anti-Catholic hysteria which developed in the period after the First Vatican Council. On the Protestant side two quite different forms of exclusivism developed in this period, the one evangelical and the other liberal.

Protestants of many different kinds were accustomed to accuse Catholics of idolatry and superstition, to condemn priestly tyranny and above all to repudiate the pretensions of the papacy. Evangelicals especially deplored the downgrading of biblical authority that was implicit in the Catholic insistence on replacing, or at least supplementing, divine revelation with man-made traditions. Especially from the 1830s, eschatological considerations also influenced evangelical criticism of the Roman Church. The Pope was frequently identified as the anti-Christ, and the imminent fall of the papacy was seen as the prelude to Christ's return. The Roman Church was in this analysis not merely mistaken, it was an instrument of Satan, and uncompromising anti-Catholicism was thus a Christian duty. This form of critique was particularly influential in Ireland, where Protestants were very conscious of being a minority and where their sense of their vulnerability was enhanced by the sectarian violence that accompanied the 1798 rebellion in some predominantly Catholic areas. But throughout the Protestant world the second quarter of the nineteenth century was a period when militant anti-Catholicism became a staple theme of Protestant preaching.[19]

In the second half of the century evangelical influence was waning, but liberals were equally severe in their condemnation of Rome. The struggle

[19] John Wolffe, 'Anti-Catholicism and Evangelical Identity in Britain and the United States 1830–1860', in *Evangelicalism*, eds. M. Noll, D. Bebbington, and G. Rawlyk (Oxford: OUP, 1994), pp. 179–97.

between the liberals, self-appointed custodians of the spirit-of-the-age, and the 'dark men' of 'medieval', 'obscurantist' Catholicism was fought out with particular vigour in Germany at the time of the Kulturkampf in the 1870s. German Protestants saw themselves as participants in a centuries-long battle between the champions of individual conscience and the exponents of ecclesiastical authority, between the forces of progress and science and the dead weight of sterile reaction, between the German people and the papacy. With Luther, they declared, 'Here I stand, I can do no other'. They refused to 'go to Canossa'. German liberals were so confident in their historical role that they readily engaged in many forms of coercion in order to keep the forces of Catholic 'medievalism' at bay. Priests were jailed for bringing 'politics into the pulpit'; Jesuits and other religious orders were driven into exile; many dioceses were left without bishops and many parishes without priests. In the Saarland village of Marpingen in 1876, which became a centre of pilgrimage after a group of children claimed to have seen the Virgin Mary, the visionaries were forcibly placed in an orphanage at some distance from their home, and the parish priest was arrested.[20] Liberals, whether Protestant or secular, were convinced that they were being cruel only to be kind: Catholics needed to be protected from those who were exploiting their credulity.

III. THE ERA OF RELIGIOUS INDIVIDUALISM

In the twentieth century, hostility to new religious movements has remained as strong as ever. Spontaneous violence has become less common, but harassment by central or local government or by others in positions of authority has remained very widespread, and ostracism by family-members, neighbours or workmates has of course been even more frequent. Probably no movement has suffered such widespread persecution as Jehovah's Witnesses, and while the worst examples have been encountered in totalitarian countries with governments that were often avowedly non-Christian, they also have suffered considerable harassment in countries that are both democratic and strongly Christian, such as the United States. For instance, in the year 1936 over a thousand Witnesses in that country were arrested for violating laws controlling the activities of travelling salesmen or restricting Sunday labour.[21] In Britain in recent years the Church of Scientology has been deemed such a threat

[20] David Blackbourn, *Marpingen: Visions of the Virgin Mary in Bismarckian Germany* (Oxford: Clarendon, 1993).
[21] James Beckford, *The Trumpet of Prophecy* (Oxford: Blackwell, 1975), pp. 34–5.

to national well-being that members of the movement have been barred from entering the country, and various universities have banned branches of the Central London Church of Christ from operating on their campus.[22]

Dislike of new religious movements may arise from resentment of their relentless evangelism, fear of their possibly disruptive effect on families, and sometimes perhaps a simple fear of the unknown, but seldom from strong denominational consciousness. This form of consciousness has been declining for a variety of reasons, including simple religious indifference, the diminishing importance of the issues which led to denominational divisions, and the diminishing importance of collective identities of all kinds.

One factor has certainly been the growing possibility of rejecting organized religion entirely. In most Western countries the proportion of the population declaring themselves without religion grew slowly from the late nineteenth century up to the 1960s. But since then there has been a much more rapid increase. In the Netherlands, for instance, one of the pace-makers, the proportion of the population without religion rose from 2% in 1899 to 18% in 1960; by 1986 the figure had shot up to 49%.[23] One result of this has been that the distinction between different Christian denominations has begun to seem less important than the distinction between Christian and non-Christian; indeed, the growth of total unbelief has even led to a greater willingness to take seriously the beliefs of adherents of non-Christian faiths. One reflection of the declining importance of denominational distinctions has been the formation of inter-confessional Christian Democratic Parties. In Germany, in the context of atheistic Nazism (and also of a strong and equally atheistic Marxist tradition) this happened as early as 1945. In the Netherlands, the land *par excellence* of confessional politics, Catholic and Protestant parties only came together in 1976. A similar situation can be seen in the United States, where since the later 1970s conservative Protestants have made (largely unsuccessful) attempts to form coalitions with conservative Catholics and Jews in order to fight what they regard as the hegemony of 'secular humanism'.[24]

Equally important, however, has been the fact that many of the doctrinal issues which provided the rationale for the existing patterns of denominational divisions were losing their significance, while new areas of difference were arising which tended to cause divisions within, rather than between denominations. For instance, it is hard to believe that many people now would regard differing doctrines of the Eucharist as a suf-

[22] Eileen Barker, *New Religious Movements* (London: HMSO, 1989), pp. 174, 188.
[23] Hans Knippenberg, *De Religieuze Kaart van Nederland* (Assen, 1992), p. 276.
[24] Steve Bruce, *The Rise and Fall of the New Christian Right* (Oxford: Clarendon, 1988), pp. 86, 126–8.

ficient ground for separating from their fellow-Christians, yet in the Reformation era this was one of the most bitterly contested issues, not only between Protestant and Catholic, but between Lutheran and Reformed. The most important development in the modern period has been the emergence of the critical approach to the Bible. In the late nineteenth and early twentieth centuries, this caused bitter disputes within most Protestant denominations, and it made the differences between established and dissenting denominations, or those of Lutheran or Reformed origin, seem relatively insignificant by comparison. Differences in approaches to the Bible continue to the present day to be a potent source of division between Christians, but denomination is a relatively poor predictor of how they will line up on this issue. In particular, national churches, such as the Church of England, Church of Scotland or Dutch Reformed Church, contain within them a complete range of approaches, from fundamentalist to ultra-liberal. Since the 1960s, four new sources of division have been the Charismatic Movement, Liberation Theology, the role of women in the church, and questions of sexuality (especially homosexuality). Again, sectarian differences are of relatively little relevance, although it is true that some denominations, notably the various branches of Pentecostalism, take a fairly consistently conservative line on most of these issues. On the other hand, those Catholics and Protestants who take a liberal approach to these issues would probably feel that they have more in common with one another than with the more conservative members of their own churches.

Since the 1960s active members of most churches have been strongly influenced by the ecumenical movement, and in particular joint services, discussion groups, pulpit exchanges, and so forth, have tended to bring them into close contact with active members of other denominations, with the result that a good many prejudices have been dispelled. The ironical result of this is that the strongest sectarian prejudices now tend to be found among inactive or even totally lapsed Protestants and Catholics. Those who have little involvement in church life may never have met a practising member of the 'rival' church, and they may retain a hostile stereotype of 'the enemy'. A good example of this phenomenon is Glasgow Rangers, the famous Protestant football club, which is regularly criticized by Protestant ministers, who see its unabashed sectarianism as an anachronism and a disgrace. Rangers fans, for their part, are often contemptuous of the Church of Scotland clergy, whom they see as traitors to Protestantism.[25]

[25] Graham Walker, '"There's not a team like the Glasgow Rangers": Football and Religious Identity in Scotland', in *Sermons and Battle Hymns*, eds. G. Walker and T. Gallagher (Edinburgh: Edinburgh University Press, 1990), pp. 149–50; Callum Brown, *The Social History of Religion in Scotland since 1730* (London: Methuen, 1987), pp. 242–7.

More generally, however, the decline in the strength of denominational ties seems to be part of the move towards a more fluid kind of society in which collective identities and fixed allegiances count for less and the individual claims the right to determine his or her life on a day to day basis, without too much reference to fixed codes of belief. In Britain, while church membership has dropped sharply during the last 35 years, membership of political parties has dropped even further, and some of the reasons may be the same. The kinds of community in which membership of a particular church or political party was once a badge of belonging – for instance the south Wales valleys or the dockland areas of Liverpool – are mostly in severe decline. Hereditary allegiances count for less in a world where teenagers have considerable freedom to go their own way, and parents have few sanctions. One manifestation of this situation is religious mobility. A study in the United States in 1984 found that a third of respondents now had a different religious or non-religious affiliation from the one they had in their childhood. (A similar survey in 1955 had produced the improbably low figure of 4% admitting to such switching.) While part of this increased mobility was caused by the growth in those refusing any religious label, most of it was caused by movement from one form of Christianity to another. The survey also showed a sharp drop since the 1940s and 1950s in the proportion of respondents admitting to prejudice against members of other denominations.[26] Another symptom is the weakening of the correlation between denomination and other beliefs and allegiances. When, for instance, religion tended to tie-up with a particular form of politics, the two kinds of commitment were mutually reinforcing; however, the recent trend towards political individualism has assisted the trend towards religious individualism, and vice versa. Furthermore a combination of greater tolerance and greater degrees of indifference, combined with an ethos of individual freedom and the weakening of parental influence, has led to an increase in the number of inter-confessional marriages so that more and more people are growing up with a foot in more than one confessional camp.[27]

The decline in the strength of sectarian consciousness and in the intensity of sectarian conflict may simply reflect the fact that the sites of religious conflict have moved elsewhere. In the period since Vatican II, while relations between Catholics and Protestants have improved enormously, there has also been a great increase in the level of conflict between Catholic and Catholic. And while most Protestants have adopted a friendlier attitude towards Catholics, attacks on the Roman

[26] Robert Wuthnow, *The Restructuring of American Religion* (Princeton: Princeton University Press, 1988), pp. 88–96.
[27] Figures for the USA are given in Wuthnow, *Restructuring*, pp. 90–1.

Catholic Church from a secular liberal viewpoint have become more frequent. Some sections of the British media have become accustomed to attacking Catholicism with a vigour and regularity worthy of Belfast's Martyrs' Memorial church – though the main theme of these attacks tends to be Catholic opposition to abortion, rather than idolatry and superstition.[28] And Islam (especially when deemed to be 'fundamentalist') has the capacity to unite liberal and conservative Christians, believers and secularists, in common fear and hostility. Once again, none of this can simply be dismissed as blind prejudice: deeply-held convictions and principles are usually involved, and many of the arguments advanced to justify intolerance are quite cogent ones. One of the most urgent problems of our times is that of how, in an increasingly pluralist world, people with strong but radically different convictions can live together in peace.

[28] A classic example of the genre was the 1994 Channel Four documentary on Mother Teresa, entitled 'Hell's Angel'.

I 2

A Postmodern Church? Some Preliminary Reflections on Ecclesiology and Social Theory[1]

RICHARD H. ROBERTS

DURING my latter years in the Department of Theology of the University of Durham I had the pleasure and privilege of working with Daniel Hardy, at that time Van Mildert Professor of Divinity. One of the words to which he then introduced me was 'societal'. I was puzzled: 'sociology' I thought I understood at least in part, likewise 'sociological'; but what was the *societal*? My subsequent experience has proven to me the wisdom of Dan Hardy's use of this term: it refers, it would seem to me, to the overall quality of a society which at its best has a supportive and enabling culture, a culture whose root paradigms are intact and capable of comprehending both differentiation into particularities and universals which hold the human together in the ancestral sense of a *religio*, a mutual binding informed by a gospel of grace and truth. So far as I am concerned, such a social reality does not by and large exist; but I believe that it should be evident in proleptic form in the church experienced as the foretaste of the Kingdom.

1. INTRODUCTION: THE CHURCH AND THE MARKET

My thoughts on the place of the church in a postmodern, market-led society were initially provoked by a report in *The Independent* on the 1991 General Assembly of the Church of Scotland. I was on the point of taking up the Chair of Divinity at the University of St Andrews and contemplating what my role might be in the context of Scotland. The writer of the article[2] noted the declining membership of the Church of

---

[1] This paper originated in contributions made to a conference of *The Gospel and Our Culture* project at Grange-over-Sands in Cumbria and in an Open College Lecture delivered in the University of St Andrews in December 1992.
[2] Diana Hinds, Religious Affairs Correspondent, 'Church's Gloom over its Dwindling Congregations', *The Independent*, 23 May 1991.

Scotland, but also the more serious fact that a poll in *Scotland on Sunday* had revealed 'an alarming lack of confidence among ministers and elders, portraying the church as an ailing institution whose days were numbered'.

I do not here propose to enter the dangerous area of demographic prediction on the basis of age profiles of church membership, or the specific question as to why certain age, gender or socio-economic class groups do or do not respond to the church,[3] but to address an underlying problem concerning the very configuration of culture and the societal structures and dynamics in the context of which the church must of necessity operate. At that time my thoughts began to turn to what the retiring Moderator, the Very Reverend Robert Davidson spoke of as 'an identity crisis centring around what we mean by claiming to be a national church' and the kind of relationship worshipping communities ought to have to the life of the community as a whole. Being myself at that time highly stimulated by postmodern 'Enterprise Culture'[4] and with a bumptiousness all too typical, I wrote to *The Independent* in the following terms:

> During the Thatcher era, and especially since the revolutionary events of late 1989 in Central Europe, we have gradually become more aware of the role of the market as an enabling means of energising and enabling human life, both individual and collective. However, the national churches of both Scotland and England display many of the sclerotic symptoms that mark nationalised industries: an all embracing rhetoric of monopoly and service to the whole nation disguises an actual failure to discern the market and to prepare goods and services required by the customer in, or outside the pew.
>
> Ministers and religious professionals (like academics) have much

---

[3] Michael Northcott (1993) provides a useful survey in his paper 'Identity and Decline in the Kirk', Edinburgh: Centre for Theology and Public Issues.

[4] As M. B. Reckitt Research Fellow in the Department of Religious Studies at Lancaster I was working in the context of interlocking postmodern networks legitimated by the motif of 'Enterprise Culture'. As indicated in my 'Religion and the "Enterprise Culture": The British Experience in the Thatcher Era (1979–1990)', *Social Compass* 39/1 (1992), pp. 15–33, this episode was, unfortunately, largely transitory. 'Enterprise Culture' has been aggregated into wider social changes in social stratification and the emergence of a new hegemony, best understood as the rise of managerial society. I shall return to this problematic in *Religion and the Resurgence of Capitalism* (London: Routledge [forthcoming]). For accounts of contemporary trends, see Willard F. Enteman, *Managerialism: The Emergence of a New Ideology* (Madison: University of Wisconsin Press, 1993); Peter F. Drucker, *Post-capitalist Society* (Oxford: Butterworth-Heinemann, 1993), esp. ch. 1; R. H. Roberts, ed., *Religion and the Transformations of Capitalism: Comparative Responses* (London: Routledge, 1995).

to learn from some experience of the active democracy of the marketplace. Theologians and their students will have to devise means of honouring ancestral traditions whilst at the same time thinking and enacting them through the dominant reality of our age, the market.

Here, like Abraham, the church and theologians will have to set out as risk-takers in covenantal faith on the path that leads to a truly enterprising religion. Moreover, we might do well not to forget that St Paul himself chose to launch Christianity in the marketplace of Athens (Acts 17.17).

Much water has passed under the bridge since the publication of this letter in May 1991; hard experience has caused me to repent some of the views expressed in this letter, both as regards the church and education. The market metaphor may be explored in order to understand the conditions for the emergence of an enterprising church which understands its place and the possible strategies open to it in the postmodern condition. What, however, the church (and education)[5] now face is the unconstrained triumph of the market metaphor and its comprehensive societal enactment resulting in massive attacks upon the integrity of many spheres of human life from which responsible autonomy has been removed. Later, in St Andrews as I experienced once more, at first hand, the important differences between the cultures and societies of Scotland and England, I became even more aware that my initial thoughts were inadequate in coming to terms with problems which affect the futures of the nations of Britain, besides that of British society as whole. Indeed, I would go so far as to say that Scotland and England require significantly different evangelistic strategies: the former would stress relative cultural homogeneity built up around a single shared (albeit layered) cultural identity; the latter would have come to terms with pluralism and develop a widely-based reflexivity grounded in a renewal of identities. Scotland is perhaps in a more superficially promising situation than England in this regard.[6] Indeed one might ask if a Scottish (relative) monoculture would be inherently more Christian, or more easily susceptible to re-christianization than an English pluriculture.

There are a range of ways in which the problem of the contemporary

---

[5] See R. H. Roberts, 'What is a University? – A Contextual Theology of Public Education', Christian Theology and Religious Education Conference, North of England Institute for Christian Education, University of Durham, 19 June–1 July 1994 (publication forthcoming).

[6] See R. H. Roberts, 'The Souls of Europe: Identity, Religion and Theology', Inaugural Lecture, University of St Andrews, *Informationes Theologiae Europae, Internationales Ökumenisches Jahrbuch für Theologie*, 1994, pp. 137–66.

church might be addressed. I have chosen for the present purposes to subsume the totality under the rubric of the modern/postmodern problematic. The latter is ramified and disputed, but it will allow us to outline a series of difficulties and possibilities in contemporary societal conditions. My approach to the problematic is conditioned by experience of church life and theological teaching in England and Scotland, besides participant observation in other contexts and research pursued simultaneously across a number of fields.[7]

In these brief reflections I intend to examine in a programmatic way how aspects of the modern/postmodern condition problematic must, it seems to me, be incorporated into the collective critical reflexivity of the people of God. In this setting we understand the church as lay and clergy, locally particular and globally universal, gendered and eschatologically one in Christ. My intention is to provoke, rather than foreclose reflection; the following are propositions associated with a *theologia viatorum*. Let us briefly survey the ground we are to cover.

The Christian church originated in *pre-modernity*; its energies have been sapped with a continuing and abortive struggle in and with *modernity*; it now exists in an era characterized as the '*postmodern condition*'. Whilst there is of course an extensive literature and considerable complexity attending these issues it is important to formulate a preliminary ideal typology in order to enable one to gain some purchase on the issues involved. Thus in *pre-modernity* religion and society enjoyed a state of relative harmony (albeit coercive). In *modernity* religion and instrumental reason exist in a state of deadly conflict as culture and society undergo secularization.[8] In *postmodernity*, religion is displaced, migrates and may become new religious movements (e.g. the Unification Church, Sokka Gakkai, the House Church, etc.), quasi-religion (Michael Jackson) or individualistic religiosity (New Age and Self Religions).

In the contemporary world, and in Britain, pre-modernity, modernity and postmodernity coexist uneasily in accordance with the distribution of economic and cultural capital in systems of national and social stratification (i.e. class). In an ever expanding market society and global order (driven forward by the rhetoric of 'choice' and the power of multinational capitalism), cultural capital is mediated through two main channels: the market (and the global media and information systems) and

---

[7] See, for example, as regards rhetoric and discourse theory R. H. Roberts and J. M. M. Good, eds., *The Recovery of Rhetoric: Persuasive Discourse and Disciplinarity in the Human Sciences* (Bristol: Bristol Classical Press / London: Duckworth and the University of Virginia Press, 1993).

[8] See the extensive literature on secularization. A useful bibliography can be found in Steve Bruce, ed., *Religion and Modernization: Sociologists and Historians Debate the Secularization Thesis* (Oxford: Clarendon Press, 1991).

education (understood in a broad sense so as to include residual tradition).

The market informs postmodernity: the needs and wants (real and artificial) of humanity as a whole are targeted with cultural artefacts (e.g. fashion and styles), cultural identities (cult personalities) and commodified sex and violence (in film, TV, video and now virtual reality) distributed in accordance with market research and the manipulation of desire. On the other hand, however, education systems (not least in Britain) are in the course of being redefined as the 'knowledge industry' operating in a largely closed and manipulated market dedicated to distributing 'packaged knowledge' and meeting centrally-defined production quotas of students in accordance with mandatory centrally-defined content (national curricula) and Taylorian systems of line-management controlling and enforcing 'total quality'. In such a context the established Christian churches stand between what Alasdair MacIntyre has called 'defeated tradition' and an increasingly alien human and social reality, which since the collapse of Marxism largely lacks the capacity for comprehensive and systematic critical and ethical evaluation.[9]

Yet the established churches have not yet been fully integrated into the new market order. How should they respond? What can they do? Can the Christian churches both preserve their theological identities and meet legitimate human needs?[10] Can they exploit the affinities between 'reflexive modernity' (and its need for heterogenization) and an unassuaged thirst for depth, meaning, myth, purposiveness – even ecstasy – characteristics of the postmodern condition?

II. THE ONSET OF POSTMODERNITY

A radical change has taken place in the last quarter century which is of profound importance for Christian theology, religious experience and the character of the human condition. This transformation is associated with what many sociologists, art historians and cultural interpreters have called the onset of the postmodern condition.[11]

In both the last century and the twentieth, much theology and church life has been dominated by two paradigms: the rise of historical-critical scholarship and secularization, respectively. As regards both scripture

[9] See my 'The Closed Circle: Marxism, Christianity and the "End of History"' in *The End of History*, eds. J. M. M. Good and I. Velody (forthcoming).
[10] For an excellent critique of cognate issues, see Philip D. Kennison, 'Selling (Out) the Church in the Marketplace of Desire', *Modern Theology* 9/4 (1993), pp. 318–48.
[11] For an introduction, see David Harvey, *The Condition of Postmodernity: An Enquiry into the Origins of Cultural Change* (Oxford: Blackwell, 1989).

and tradition, modernity was experienced primarily in the form of an attack upon the historicity and thus the authority of the origins and sources upon which contemporary church life was assumed to be based.

In society at large, modernity manifested itself through the onset of industrialization and the gradual disappearance of pre-industrial and pre-modern society. The latter transformation involved what Max Weber called the *Entzauberung* or demystification of the modern world. This was a complex process of secularization. Religion and theology were seemingly banished to the privacy of individual thought and feeling and to the margins of social reality. Correspondingly the centre seems to fall apart.

A Christian theologian like Dietrich Bonhoeffer could understand these processes as the progressive triumph of human autonomy, the kind of maturity the philosopher Immanuel Kant had called for in his 'Answer to the Question: "What is Enlightenment?"' of 1784: 'Have the courage to use your own understanding – *Sapere Aude!*'. Yet according to the *Letters and Papers from Prison*, Bonhoeffer tells his correspondent Eberhard Bethge that we must learn to live *before* God in a world *without* God.[12] Bonhoeffer's 'religionless Christianity' became a new paradigm for the post-war church, a view promoted by, for example, the distinguished Scottish theologian Ronald Gregor Smith, as a 'world come of age'.

Modernity understood as the juxtaposition of the attack upon sacred history and the secularization of culture and society have remained dominant motifs within theological reflection and ministerial training alike. Now, however, this consensus has been challenged on a number of fronts. Within the major world religions, Judaism, Islam, Christianity and Hinduism, fundamentalist movements have sprung up which have galvanized the world order. Outside such major religions, however, further phenomena occur which indicate that the secularization paradigm is deficient in other respects. The factors we referred to above, the emergence of new religious movements,[13] quasi-religious activities in popular culture (Michael Jackson in the Bucharest concert and the Scottish group Shaman) and other new forms of religiosity appear. These taken together indicate that whilst established religious traditions may believe that secularization involves a decline in formal religion as such, what has in fact happened is that the religious and the sacred would appear to have undergone displacement, migration and transformation. In postmodernity, religion and religiosity are very much alive, but by and large this life is outside churches which embraced 'religionless Christian-

---

[12] Dietrich Bonhoeffer, letters of 8, 30 June and 8, 16, 18 July 1944, in *Letters and Papers from Prison*, ed. E. Bethge (London: SPCK, 1944, rev. ed. 1967), pp. 324–9, 339–47, 357–63.
[13] See Eileen Barker, *New Religious Movements* (London: HMSO, 1989).

ity', thus taking the secularizing tendencies of the Reformation to their logical extreme.[14]

The Christian gospel originated in *pre-modernity*; it has been mediated to us through *modernity*; we now exist in a society in which *postmodernity* has made its appearance. The normal mediation of the gospel's encounter with modernity[15] as taught in many theology courses since the Second World War has been twofold: first by means of the Kantian critique of the possible knowledge of God; and second through the historical dimension, that is as relics of narrative grudgingly mediated through the historical-critical method. This double mediation is inadequate; it does not reflect the actual changes in society and culture that have attended the transition from pre-modernity to modernity, and from the latter to postmodernity. More important, it starves the church of its own resources, and prevents the reflective self-understanding that might come from a properly-informed human/social sciences approach to the continuing theological task.

III. A PRELIMINARY TYPOLOGY OF THE MODERNITY/POSTMODERNITY PROBLEMATIC

(a) Pre-modernity

Pre-modernity is that part of Western history prior to the rise of industrialism and is characterized (e.g.) by a visible, hereditary social hierarchy and static social order, organic communities, a biologically-determined division of sexual and familial labour, poor communications, low geographical mobility and a preponderance of rural over urban life. In European pre-modernity the role of religion and the Christian church was pervasive: the church was integral to the social order and sanctified

---

[14] It is important to note that the Reformation which sought reform actually involved secularization, a tendency noted not least by Karl Marx and Max Weber: the relatively light burden of an institutional external priesthood became a rigorous self-policing of the spirit.
[15] The literature is enormous, see for an introduction R. N. Bellah, 'Meaning and Modernization', in *Beyond Belief* (Berkeley: University of California Press, 1979), pp. 64–73; *idem*, 'New Religious Consciousness and the Crisis in Modernity', in *The New Religious Consciousness*, eds. C. Y. Glock and R. N. Bellah (Berkeley: The University of California Press, 1976); Peter L. Berger, *Facing up to Modernity: Excursions in Society, Politics, and Religion* (New York: Basic Books, 1977); Marshall Berman, *All That is Solid Melts into Air: The Experience of Modernity* (New York: Simon & Schuster, 1982); Anthony Giddens, *The Consequences of Modernity* (Cambridge: Polity, 1990); J. Habermas, *The Philosophical Discourse of Modernity: Twelve Lectures* (Cambridge: Polity, 1987); Max Horkheimer and T. W. Adorno, 'The Concept of Enlightenment', in *Dialect of Enlightenment* (London: Allen Lane, 1944, E.T. 1972), pp. 3–80; Agnes Heller, *Can Modernity Survive?* (Berkeley: University of California Press, 1990); Z. Bauman, *Modernity and the Holocaust* (Cambridge: Polity, 1989).

all aspects of a cohesive way of life. The idea of 'Christendom'[16] most aptly expresses this societal order: external threats (above all Islam) were excluded;[17] perceived internal dissent or subversion (heresy and the Jews) were suppressed and contained, respectively; there was relative unity, integrity and stability in the values-system.

(b) Modernity

Modernity as an intellectual phenomenon arose out of the triumph of dialectic over against medieval theological realism, the Renaissance 'measuring' of the human, the re-discovery of the agonistic self in the Reformation, and the Enlightenment 'turn to the subject'. Modernity as socio-economic reality stems from the rational organization of the division of labour undertaken in order to increase and transform 'natural' productive processes through the systematic application of practical intelligence linked to mechanical ingenuity and a system of contract law freed from ancestral constraints.

The 'modernity' mediating theology and reflected religious consciousness began increasingly to pertain to the private, individual and familial sphere (possibly focused in church life undertaken on an increasingly pastime and leisure basis). The 'modernity' experienced by the population at large was increasingly 'rational', socially-differentiated through the division of labour, and centred in commercial and state public demands and in an impersonal market. However, the two 'modernities' were, and largely remain, radically dissociated in Christian consciousness and its theologies: the disappearance of 'nature' went unnoticed; theology concentrated upon the tasks of *legitimation* and the enhancement of private piety; the greater crisis was devolved to Christian *social ethics*, but *theology* as such went on largely unaffected as a belief system taught to and by a clerisy[18] which itself underwent gradual attrition in the face of historical and positivist criticism.[19]

---

[16] A term used in mid-century Anglican social concern by, for example, the Christendom Group and Maurice B. Reckitt *et al.*; see for example, his edited collection, *Prospect for Christendom* (London: Faber, 1945). The idea of 'Christendom' has often been attacked for its intrinsic bias, see for example, A. Fierro, 'The Rejection of Christendom', in *The Militant Gospel: An Analysis of Contemporary Political Theologies* (London: SCM, 1977), ch. 2.

[17] See Edward Said, *Orientalism: Western Conceptions of the Orient* (Harmondsworth: Penguin, 1978²).

[18] T. S. Eliot, *The Idea of a Christian Society* (London: Faber, 1949), remains the locus classicus in this regard. Eliot focused explicit religious self-consciousness in an educated élite. It would be interesting and important to compare the socio-cultural strategies of the Anglo-American Eliot and his paradigmatic Scottish rival Hugh MacDiarmid (Christopher M. Grieve) and their efforts to create renewed metanarratives for their respective cultures in 'The Waste Land' and 'A Drunk Man looks at the Thistle', respectively.

[19] This criticism is acerbically expressed by John Kent, 'Christian Theology in the Eighteenth to the Twentieth Centuries', in *A History of Christian Doctrine*, ed. H. Cunliffe-Jones

(c) Postmodernity

'Postmodernity' (and the 'postmodern condition') is the form of consciousness and social life that has emerged in the context of the breakdown of classical high capitalism and its re-differentiation into 'late-' or
'advanced industrial society'. The sociologist James Beckford argues that
the latter refers to:

> the kind of social formation that was believed to be emerging in
> various parts of the already heavily industrialised world in the
> 1960s. It is characterised primarily by the growth in world markets
> in goods and services, the ascendency of service industries over
> manufacturing and agriculture, the growth in numbers and powers
> of multinational organisations, the separation of corporate manage-
> ment from share ownership, the levelling out of social class differen-
> tials and the crucial significance of theological knowledge and infor-
> mation technology.[20]

The 'postmodern condition' as such has been defined by Jean-François
Lyotard as:

> Incredulity towards metanarratives. This incredulity is undoubtedly
> a product of progress in the sciences: but that progress in turn
> presupposes it. To the obsolescence of the metanarrative apparatus
> of legitimation corresponds, most notably, the crisis of metaphysical
> philosophy and of the university institution which in the past relied
> on it. The narrative function is losing its functors, its great hero, its
> great dangers, its great voyages, its great goal. It is being dispersed in
> clouds of language narrative elements – narrative, but also denota-
> tive, prescriptive, descriptive, and so on. Conveyed within each
> cloud are pragmatic valencies specific to its kind. Each of us lives at
> the intersection of many of these. However, we do not necessarily

---

(Edinburgh: T. & T. Clark, 1978), pp. 459–601. For background on the relation of
theology to modernity, see Hans Küng, *Theology for the Third Millenium: An Ecumenical
View* (London: HarperCollins Academic, 1991), pp. 1–12, 257–84; R. H. Roberts, *A
Theology on Its Way? Essays on Karl Barth* (Edinburgh: T. & T. Clark, 1992), chs. 1 and
6; Rudolf Bultmann, 'The Idea of God and Modern Man', in *World Come of Age*, ed.
R. G. Smith (London: Collins, 1967); Julian N. Hartt, Ray L. Hart, and Robert P. Sharle-
mann, *The Critique of Modernity: Theological Reflections on Contemporary Culture*
(Charlottesville: University Press of Virginia, 1986); David J. Hawkin, *Christ and
Modernity: Christian Self-understanding in a Technological Age* (Waterloo, Ont.: Wilfred
Laurer University Press, 1985); Walter Kasper, *The God of Jesus Christ* (New York:
Crossroad, 1988), see references to 'modernity'.
[20] James Beckford, *Religion in Advanced Industrial Society* (London: Unwin Hyman,
1989), p. 3, reviews the terminological problem.

establish stable language combinations, and the properties of the ones we do establish are not necessarily communicable.[21]

More critically, David Harvey maintains that

> postmodernism, with its emphasis upon the ephemerality of *jouissance*, its insistence upon the impenetrability of the other, its concentration on the text rather than the work, its penchant for deconstruction bordering on nihilism, its preference for aesthetics over ethics, takes matters too far. It takes them beyond the point where any coherent politics are left, while that wing of it that seeks a shameless accommodation with the market puts it firmly in the tracks of an entrepreneurial culture that is the hallmark of reactionary neoconservatism. Postmodernist philosophers tell us not only to accept but even to revel in the fragmentations and the cacophony of voices through which the dilemmas of the modern world are understood. Obsessed with deconstructing and delegitimating every form of argument they encounter, they can end only in condemning their own validity claims to the point where nothing remains of any basis for reasoned action. Postmodernism has us accepting the reifications and partitionings, actually celebrating the activity of masking of cover-up, all the fetishisms of locality, place, or social grouping, while denying that kind of meta-theory which can grasp the political-economic processes (money flows, international divisions of labour, financial markets, and the like) that are becoming ever more universalizing in their depth, intensity, reach and power over daily life.[22]

The rejection and critique of traditional capitalism implied by the postmodern condition entails (amongst other things) a revaluation of the masculine, a 'masculinity' empowered in the military ideals of premodernity[23] and legitimated and realized in the predatory code of behaviour of high capitalism. The new dialectical cohabitation of premodernity and modernity, and the concomitant apparent superfluity of the traditional masculinities of earlier times, have led to a crisis in male identity which has yet properly to be addressed.

A distinctive feature of the 'modern' period is the marginalization and ghettoization of (originally pre-modern) theological discourse and insti-

---

[21] Jean-François Lyotard, *The Postmodern Condition: A Report on Knowledge* (Manchester: Manchester University Press, 1979), p. xxiv.
[22] Harvey, *The Condition of Postmodernity*, pp. 116–17.
[23] The moderate rehabilitation of the heroic virtue of *thumos* in capitalism is a central theme in Francis Fukuyama, *The End of History and the Last Man* (London: Hamish Hamilton, 1982).

tutionalized religion. 'Postmodernity' is characterized by a 'rebirth of religion' and an apparent re-legitimation of theologies. Both periodizations are, however, constructions which draw for their justification upon the interpretation of a wide range of heterogeneous material. Indeed, the relation of modernity to postmodernity is dialectical:

A work can become modern only if it is first postmodern. Postmodernism thus understood is not modernism at its end but in the nascent state, and this state is constant.[24]

Anyone who understands the implications of the latter observation will have some indication into the difficulties of enacting an *engaged* postmodern theology.[25]

IV. THEOLOGY AND POSTMODERNITY

From the theological standpoint postmodernity involves the following: pluralism, the collapse of grand narrative, a crisis of legitimation in received modernity, high levels of reflexivity, a rebirth of religion in New Age or fundamentalist forms, re-configuration and redefinition of social roles and cultural identities, fluidity, and, above all, an *individualistic ethos of self-development*. Postmodernity does not exist, however, as an epoch. In the era of advanced capitalism and the 'end of history' premodern, modern, and postmodern coexist within individual communities, within countries and dispersed in the global order.

The preaching/propagation of the gospel must take account of the context: how are we to respond? There are three obvious strategies that can be represented in terms of ideal types. The first is the traditional ancestral approach pursued as though nothing had happened: this is conservative stasis involving the defence of the remaining moral redoubts at the extreme periphery of human life. The second is the market approach, whether pursued in corporate and quasi-monopolistic terms (in the established Churches of Scotland and England), or as free-ranging entrepreneurial activity in a differentiated religious market. The third is a critical-affirmative and dialectical approach conducted through a human/ social science-informed theological hermeneutics which might exploit without bewitchment the possibilities of the postmodern condition. Un-

---

[24] Lyotard, *Postmodern Condition*, p. 79.
[25] As opposed to the catastrophic eschatologism of John Milbank, *Theology and Social Theory* (Oxford: Blackwell, 1991). See my review article of Dr Milbank's magnum opus in the *Scottish Journal of Theology*, 46/4 (1993), pp. 527–35.

fortunately, the first and the last strategies, straightforward pre-modern regression and postmodern refunctioning, may come so close together as to coalesce. The second, the market option, is the most obvious practical path for churches faced with financial problems, but this can easily damage living tradition by the latter's forced transmutation into the religious equivalent of 'heritage' and the basis of a strategy in which a sophisticated intellectual base is rationalized, denied its agency and absorbed into the managerial and training function.

What is important to note, however, is that the human appetite for 'religious' experience is far from dead. Established churches and denominations faced with dysfunctionality, and declining or age-restricted participation may believe that the very medium of their socio-cultural agency has in effect closed down, and that mythic narrative, ritual, corporate worship and ecstatic self-prostration take place, not least within the globalized pop culture industry. In the 'after-life of religion',[26] there are many unusual growths, some of which I have examined elsewhere.[27] Whereas 'New Age' phenomena may inhabit a variety of niches at the extremes of wealth and poverty in the socio-economic matrix,[28] there are fully globalized and extremely spectacular forms of quasi-religion which present the Christian church with an acute challenge.

Unfortunately it is not possible to present in visual form the example upon which we now draw.[29] Nevertheless, the cultural artefact in question is sufficiently well-known as to allow its use.

The singer and (now fallen) performer Michael Jackson's 'Dangerous' album and the remarkable Bucharest concert broadcast globally provided an extraordinary and very important example of an eclectic postmodern refunctioning of quasi-religion.[30] Jackson's concert contained at least the following: a) a redeemer myth (Heal the world); b) mysterious

---

[26] This term was coined by George Steiner, *In Bluebeard's Castle* (London: Faber, 1971), pp. 47ff.

[27] See my 'Power and Empowerment: New Age Managers and the Dialectics of Modernity/ Postmodern', *Religion Today*, 9/3 (1994), pp. 3–13.

[28] Thus New Agers may vary from management consultants earning thousands of pounds per diem to the much maligned 'New Age Travellers' whose existence is economically and legally marginal (and of course facing extinction with the creation of the new crime of 'aggravated trespass'). Any full account of New Age in contemporary Britain would have to take account of this wide dispersal. The work of Michael Northcott (New College, Edinburgh) on therapeutic New Age in Scotland, Marion Bowman (Bath College of Higher Education) on contemporary religion in the south-west of England, and Julia Iwerson (St Andrews/Marburg) on New Age and Celtic Christianity in Scotland is all relevant.

[29] In the Open College Lecture, edited video material drawn from the Michael Jackson 'Dangerous', Budapest concert was presented and than analysed.

[30] The difficulties that Michael Jackson began to experience in 1993 come as no great surprise to those who have read J. Randy Taraborrelli, *Michael Jackson: The Magic and the Madness* (New York: Birch Lane Press, 1991).

entry into the historical order (*Deus ex machina*); c) the quasi-miracle of 'walking on water' (the famous Moon Walk); d) repetition of collapse, death, resurrection, entombment/ascension; e) the presence of protective technological 'angels'; the *shekinah*-like presence depicted through light and dry ice vapour; f) aspects of a corporate quasi-religious act including mass local observance and a demonstrable corporate identity, fully globalized participation, and a carefully crafted ritual involving ecstasies and mass hysteria; g) an incarnational juxtaposition of the frail (yet extraordinary) flesh of the performer and 'divinity' provided technological universalization and 'transfiguration'. The impact of such a presentation and analysis of popular culture upon a Scottish audience was not inconsiderable.[31]

Such a ritual event is focused around a self-realizing globalized, quasi-religious artefact: the person and work of a Michael Jackson. It is important to note the self-modifications which turn what might well have been a mere entertainer limited to a niche in the culture industry into global cultural commodity. Thus Jackson (regardless of the pathos of his fall) combined: a) androgyny (in a gender-polarized world he appeals equally to both sexes); b) explicit sexuality, corresponding with what amounts to a new highest good and the celebration of the body in postmodernity; c) ambiguous racial/colour status, 'Black on White' and skin treatment for cross colour appeal; d) extraordinary virtuoso control of the body; e) personal identification with and embodiment of a quasi-salvific message; f) the ultimate in technology and thus the transgression of human bonds juxtaposed with a weakness all too literally now exposed.

Thus in economic terms Jackson exemplifies the total maximization of the person, personality and all physical and mental resources. In market terms the positive is expanded and the negative is modified or eliminated. The result is a form of quasi-religion (from a Christian standpoint of an undoubtedly pagan character), the extraordinary global success of which indicates that human needs are being tapped and indeed exploited. It is perhaps only Pope John Paul II at the height of his powers who could rival such a remarkable functionalization of affective mass religiosity within the ambit of Christianity.

V. THE DILEMMA OF ESTABLISHED CHURCHES

The dilemma is this: established churches in Western Europe often find

---

[31] Reaction varied from 'heretical blasphemy' to an acknowledgement that important questions were being posed.

themselves to be victims of their own conceptions of modernity with which they are locked in a fruitless struggle, and, correspondingly, they frequently believe that 'religion' is dying or dead. Yet, in reality, religion and forms of religiosity are very much alive and answering human needs in a global and local market place from which many established churches have explicitly or tacitly retreated.

Religious organizations like, for example, the state churches of Scotland or England tend to have the following features: a) an age structure which indicates that demographic processes will involve inevitable and increasingly spectacular decline; b) a social constituency which is not, generally speaking, representative of the population at large, from which, given present socio-political trends, it will be increasingly alienated; c) a progressive differentiation of culture away from literary or literate forms of mediation and reception compatible with an ancestral verbalized 'Word of God' mode of communication; d) general paralysis at the centre owing to fear of internal division and a tendency to resist the effort required to understand and respond to these factors; e) a cultural inheritance of militant 'presbyterian atheism' (Ian Bradley); f) a societal reaction against a tradition which involved forms of affective, cultural and sexual asceticism now out of touch and dissonant with contemporary mass culture which prioritizes feeling over the intellect;[32] g) an idea of culture as historical and dynastically transmitted tradition which prevents the emergence of the critical reflexivity essential to understanding and responding creatively to present circumstances.

There are a number of rather obvious consequences and ecclesial strategies which often emerge in such a situation. We note a few:

a) A traditionalist religious response which remains locked in a battle with a reluctant modernity in order to recover the past; this can sometimes verge upon theological necrophilia.

b) An almost complete loss of contact with the latent human and religious needs of the general population except on the level of rites of passage and a corresponding (and relatively cheap and easy to operate) displacement of the universality of the gospel onto the rhetorical level of 'serving the nation' largely through political intervention.

c) A complete refusal to engage in fundamental appraisal of a declining market, a problematic 'product' and a labour force largely trained in 'care and maintenance' of plant rather than in the dangerous and creative skills of religious enterprise.

---

[32] The recent and highly publicized debate on marriage and sexuality at the 1994 General Assembly opened up the abyss between parties in the Church of Scotland.

VI. POSTMODERNITY AND TRADITION: PRELUDE TO A RESPONSE

Earlier some indication was given of how displaced religious drives can manifest themselves in the 'postmodern condition'. In order, however, to understand better the dilemmas facing contemporary society and the established churches it is first necessary to explain more fully what is meant by *postmodernity*. To summarize, postmodernity does not just involve the death of, or incredulity towards metanarratives (i.e. the big stories of the human condition provided by Christianity and Marxism, for example) but an explosion in participation on a new level.

The new mediation is not through the transmission of cultural expertise across generations through education, but the thoroughgoing functionalization of virtually all cultural artefacts in a provider/receiver market. The expressive self can call upon such cultural artefacts and through a process of self-adornment *become* something new. In the Nietzschian world of postmodernity if we do not *become* through effort, performance and *exchange* then we cease to be; we are by implication dependent parasites. Reality *is* the mask we assume – there is nothing more, other than the will-to-power.

In the postmodern condition culture and human life is fragmented and temporally welded together by alliances that serve a purpose in the enhancement of the self and its performance. Religion(s), theology(ies), and forms of religiosity are but another form of cultural capital circulated in global and local markets. As Stewart Clegg has written:

> In the multi-dimensional pleasure dome of postmodern society, as the traditional spectacle of power retreats to the margins, the entire centre stage is increasingly occupied by the dispositional and the productive in a pleasure of new capacities, empowerments and pathways which are immune to any pretensions to 'painterly architectonics' that sovereign power might once have had. The canvas is not fixed; the palette is not given; the style is not dictated. Representations can be fixed anywhere, anyhow, anyway. This is the postmodern democratic freedom of the market. In such a world ... legitimations based on the fixity of hegemonic pathways cease to matter ... Perhaps this 'forgetting' of power may yet be the 'fate of our times'.[33]

Yet, we must ask, is such a 'forgetting' of power in the jouissance of self-indulgence to be our fate? I think not.

[33] Stewart Clegg, *Framework of Power* (London: Sage, 1991), p. 275.

VII. TRADITION, THE MARKET, AND 'ENTERPRISE FAITH': A POSTMODERN CHURCH?

The established churches are trapped between institutionalized tradition and the marketplace of human needs and wants. This is not, however, a neutral environment. As we have seen vast resources are poured into a world entertainment and publicity industry which refunctions anything and everything which can undergo profitable recapitulation up to and including religion and theological ideas and motifs. This flexibility is without precedent and without bounds; contemporary expectations are such that narrative structure is shattered repeatedly and a plethora of cultural artefacts and fragments of cultural identity can be juxtaposed with virtuoso intensity. A technological core, information transfer, virtual reality and what is called *hyperspace* (worlds which exist by virtue of electronic and cybernetic power) provide an immanent transcendence; omnipresence, bi-location, omniscience. Forms of omnipotence are practical possibilities which are limited only by the imagination of the empowered practitioner.

In such an era, any organization which purports to bear a message or reality of universal import cannot afford to ignore the marketization and commodification of the world order. Any such body that does so is by a sociological and cultural necessity locked into a social niche market, let us say retired people who still live with a sense of metanarrative – the Christian story, albeit heavily secularized. To go beyond strategic retreat (the equivalent of the gradual abandonment of manufacturing industry) to engage once more in the real world of religious need would require a theological revolution.

In the present Scottish context there is little sign perhaps of such global re-engagement with the societal marketplace. Much more tempting is the road into cultural national Christianity such as that proposed by William Storrar in his recent book on Scottish identity.[34] It would undoubtedly be possible to re-excite forms of religiosity in Scotland by exploiting a fusion of theology with nationalism. Indeed, one could perhaps imagine a new form of religious fundamentalism grounded in high technology, which might combine an eclectic refunctioning of Celtic spirituality with an atavistic appeal to chthonic identities.[35] This might prove to be a

---

[34] William Storrar, *Christian Identity: A Scottish Approach* (Edinburgh: Handsel Press, 1991). I am much in debt to William Storrar from whose eirenic and positive sense of national identity I hope I have learned much.

[35] That is, identities bound to the earth. I am conscious of taking liberties with Jane Harrison's account of the *Chthonioi*, see Jane Harrison, *Themis: A Study in the Social Origins of Greek Religion* (London: Merlin, 1911, reprint 1963), p. 292.

Balkan solution – which is perhaps no solution. Such a strategy might also, however, evade the kind of critical reflexivity which I believe to be essential if we are to confront forces which by their very transcendental power inform the immanence of the world system.

A responsible approach on the part of a postmodern church would involve a *principled eclectisicm*. In other words, it is impossible to conceive of established Christianity making any impression upon the national and global market of cultural capital and human identities unless it mobilizes *all* its resources. This means looking once more at the totality, and training potential professionals to look upon the total inheritance as a resource: the Tradition as a whole in its variety offers enormous resources, symbolic, mythic, narrative, ethical, theological. This new engagement with traditions (including both scripture and its diverse interpretations) will have to be undertaken within the context of a renewal of vision and goals. In the light of tradition and general policy the Christian or religious entrepreneur will have to scrutinize the human condition, the universal market, and seek for points of congruence.

If we neglect or fail in this task the world will not stand idly by. As we have seen, virtuoso figures like Michael Jackson (and even more problematically, Madonna) will proceed unchallenged to synthesize and synergize the cultural religious artefacts of the world. This exploitation may make the inheritance virtually irrecoverable.

At all events what I have tried to indicate in this brief paper is that postmodernity presents the Christian churches with an immense challenge which requires ruthless self-appraisal; a commitment to socio-cultural analysis which includes the church and religious bodies as agents implicated within this matrix; and a willingness to venture out in a newly defined enterprise of faith. This might be the way to the kind of meta-theory for which David Harvey had rightly called. Without it we shall be at the mercy of forces which we not only do not control, but would have wilfully failed to understand. We need to reconceive the societal – and reconfigure the theological task.[36]

---

[36] This I have attempted in my St Andrews Inaugural Lecture (see n. 6 above). It is a matter of the deepest sadness to me that it has not been possible for me to develop this line of reflection in Scotland.

13

On Anglican Polity

PETER SEDGWICK

Anglican polity is distinguished by its correlation of sacramental truth with a theological anthropology, which is designed to 'place' the Anglican church in its society. For the purpose of this essay I shall only consider the Church of England. The 'placing' of ecclesiology is not simply Erastian, nor is it to be reduced to the 'medieval vision of unitive society' wherein 'various configurations of coercive authority linked the spiritual and the temporal'.[1] Instead the normative role of ecclesiology within a general account of human society articulates a particular under-standing of 'the common good', which is both deeply theological and yet open to the vicissitudes of political life. The sacramental truth of Angli-can polity is not the same, either, as the presentation of the church as 'sacrament of the human race' characteristic of contemporary Roman Catholic ecclesiology.[2] First, the Anglican church is seen in far more Augustinian terms as a body that can and does err. A personalist model of the sacraments reflects a belief in the relationship of free, moral agents who nevertheless are called to mediate the saving activity of Christ through the ordained priesthood. The diffusion of doctrine into English civic life is through the liturgy, not simply as a teaching method but by the dynamics of praise.[3] The result of this is a penumbra of faith in English life brought about by the pastoral ministry and performance of the occasional offices by the local church 'placed' in its own context.

The particular theologians to be examined in this article are Hooker and Coleridge. Coleridge was deeply indebted to Hooker, while the influence of Coleridge was to pass through the Church of England, being found in such diverse writers as F. D. Maurice, T. S. Eliot, and (it need hardly be said) D. W. Hardy. This article is not a historical account of their influence, which has been provided by a number of authors and

---

[1] W. P. Haugaard, 'From the Reformation to the Eighteenth Century', in *The Study of Anglicanism*, eds. S. W. Sykes and J. Booty (London: SPCK, 1988), p. 15.
[2] A. Dulles, *Models of the Church* (Dublin: Gill & Macmillan, 1976).
[3] The best exposition is by W. A. Vanstone, 'Doctrine Diffused', in *Believing in the Church*, Doctrine Commission of Church of England (London: SPCK, 1981).

critical editions.[4] Instead I wish to draw attention to a particular feature of both their works. Implicit in the understanding of Anglican polity as a 'graced sociality' is the belief that church and people meet in a particular place, most memorably expressed by T. S. Eliot:

> Therefore, O God, we thank Thee
> Who has given such blessing to Canterbury
>
> So, while the light fails
> On a winter's afternoon, in a secluded chapel
> History is now and England
>
> Hence, the intersection of the timeless moment
> is England and nowhere. Never and always.[5]

When there is this intersection of church and people – a graced sociality which is the fundamental rationale for Anglican polity – a crucial question is the liberty and freedom with which this reciprocity happens. The structuring of this dynamic has long been the concern of D. W. Hardy, exploring both the complexity and the patterning of its organization. Coleridge has usually been presented as an exponent of the concept of the Idea, thus rendering Kantian epistemology more dynamic and less subjective than the phenomenal reason in Kant would allow, and as a counterbalance to the excessive individualism found in English anthropology. Colin Gunton's recent treatment of Coleridge, where Gunton takes up Hardy's understanding of sociality as transcendental and prefers to speak of it as a doctrine of the personal but not transcendental, since it is not constitutive of material existence, is an example of this articulation of a social vision.[6]

Coleridge, and Hooker before him, were however not simply exponents of a social philosophy. That confines Hooker to Book One of the Laws, and Coleridge's paradoxical relationship of the national church and the church of Christ is ignored. Both wrote to express how the social relationships of their day might be seen as expressing a fundamental liberty in human existence, which the Christian church could render explicit through its gospel of redemption. Consent to the activity of the church was therefore of paramount importance. Consent was given to an

---

[4] C. R. Sanders, *Coleridge and the Broad Church Tradition* (Durham, NC: Duke University Press, 1942); J. D. Boulger, *Coleridge as Religious Thinker* (New Haven: Yale University Press, 1961); W. L. Sachs, *The Transformation of Anglicanism* (Cambridge: CUP, 1993), pp. 38–43; J. S. Marshall, *Hooker and the Anglican Tradition* (London: Adam & Charles Black, 1963).
[5] *The Complete Poems and Plays of T. S. Eliot* (London: Faber, 1969), 'Murder in the Cathedral', p. 282; 'Little Gidding', pp. 192, 197.
[6] C. Gunton, *the One, the Three and The Many* (Cambridge: CUP, 1993), p. 223.

Anglican polity which restored sociality to its true freedom in that time and place. Neither writer was concerned with idealized conceptions of polity. The argument was directed at defending the status quo, which might then be perfected in ways which its current blemishes did not allow. Neither, however, were successful in their defence. Hooker's ecclesiastical polity became broken by civil war, while Coleridge's clerisy was eventually transformed by John Stuart Mill into a secularized utilitarianism, where pleasure was reconceived as ideals or values.[7]

The failure of their defence does not detract from the significance of their treatment of consent and liberty in considering a contemporary Anglican policy. The conclusion of this paper will examine in what way Anglican policy might take account of sociality and liberty in the pluralist society of the late twentieth century. In some ways, the task of the church is more difficult than ever. The Church of England has very little secular power, except in significant areas such as the formation of educational policy. The loss of power allows the Church of England to be seen as above party politics, which portray it as a well-meaning reconciler. This carries with it the danger of hubris, where it is confronted with issues which society cannot resolve, whether because they are not political issues (such as ageing or morality) or because they have defeated the conventional answers of politicians (such as the decline of the inner city).[8] Any answer which the church will give must at least respect the liberty and freedom to dissent of the inhabitants of that society.

What is meant by the concept of sociality which D. W. Hardy has developed? It is a 'necessary note of being', and so a transcendental, where being displays itself. The doctrine of creation shows the results of human thought, where the truth of sociality is explored. The higher possibilities for society are found through affirmation, while the critical negation of inadequate social categories denies the reductive tendencies found in society. This possibility for society is traced back to the divine ordering (logos) for society, where in many different forms society can become richer and more complex.

Sociality is formed by such factors as land area, the environment and the pressure of population on land use. Within society the conditions are those of social institutions (laws, customs, political organizations); economic arrangements; personal relationships; and culture. They are both the products and producers of a history which becomes ever more complex. Yet this is not just a general account of social theory, for these

---

[7] J. C. D. Clark, *English Society 1688–1832* (Cambridge: CUP, 1985), is an exposition of England as an ancient regime. For another modern treatment which highlights the role of religion, see L. Colley, *Britons: Forging the Nation 1707–1837* (London: Pimlico, 1992).

[8] B. Martin, 'Church and Culture', in *Say One For Me: The Church of England in the Next Decade*, ed. Wesley Carr (London: SPCK, 1992).

conditions can then be applied to empirical reality. It is a characteristic of Anglican polity that it was concerned with the application of its own reality to specific communities, in terms of a concern for all four of these categories.[9] It is not simply as though Anglican polity was concerned with the laws and customs of a society, and its culture (the first and fourth of these categories). There is a long involvement with economic philosophy, the generation of wealth, and its distribution, through such names as Malthus, Copleston and Whately, who wrote at the start of the nineteenth century on theology and political economy, and the only Archbishop of Canterbury to be once an economist, John Bird Sumner.[10] Personal relationships were also a matter for Anglican polity, in terms of the 'call to holiness', which repeatedly echoes through Anglican writing on spirituality, as the necessary requirement for political leadership. Laud, Wilberforce or the British Idealists would be examples of statesmen and theorists who expounded a theology which combined the demands of personal character with political life.

Anglican polity thus was about current practice, and the quality of current practice. The problem with Anglican polity is equally clear. The religious basis for national life gradually became elided into moral and social stratification where the English way of life was taken for granted as inevitable, but which depended on the particular class in which one was set. The strength of Anglican policy was its determination to affect the whole of life, in each particular town or village, paying attention to the precise particularity of that location. The sacramental understanding of true practice meant that a cleric such as George Herbert became the paradigm example of this ministry. Field workers 'would let their plough rest when Mr Herbert's Saints-Bell rung to Prayers, that they might also offer their devotions to God with him'.[11] John Habgood today speaks of the open church, which provides 'public access to the Christian faith' and caters 'for very different degrees of religious commitment'.[12] 'The breadth of vision and the wide tolerance' characteristic of the established church is not just a pastoral matter, but a contribution 'to the political life of the nation'. This is certainly characteristic of Anglican polity concerned with providing an 'effective symbol of the limits of nationalism'. A common language of hope and penitence is another aspect of such a polity.

[9] D. W. Hardy, 'Created and Redeemed Sociality', in *On Being the Church*, eds. C. E. Gunton and D. W. Hardy (Edinburgh: T. & T. Clark, 1989); *idem*, 'God and the Form of Society', in *The Weight of Glory*, eds. P. H. Sedgwick and D. W. Hardy (Edinburgh: T. & T. Clark, 1991); *idem*, 'Theology through Philosophy', in *The Modern Theologians*, Vol. 2, ed. D. F. Ford (Oxford: Blackwell, 1989).
[10] J. Atherton, *Christianity and the Market* (London: SPCK, 1992).
[11] O. C. Edwards, 'Anglican Pastoral Tradition', in *Study of Anglicanism*, pp. 338–51.
[12] John Habgood, *Making Sense* (London: SPCK, 1993).

Hooker wrote to defend the Church of England as a national church, and to defend its freedom to order its own external forms of worship and government. The church was, however, also a 'politic society' and in a Christian commonwealth there was but one society, made up of church and state. Parliament, therefore, represented the citizens both as members of a civil society and of the church.[13] However the local expression of the Christian commonwealth was through the incumbent of the village, as much as the lord of the manor; the visible church is identified with the whole body of the people, the *communio fidelium*, where lay power was exercised through powerful landowners, with the right of patronage and control over the incumbent.

Hooker is not an early advocate of the idea of the social contract.[14] The theory of consent is his concern, and not the reciprocal rights and duties of state citizens, which are the familiar discourse of political philosophy after Locke. Hooker wrote 'that strifes and troubles would be endless, except they gave their common consent all to be ordered by some whom they should agree upon: without which consent there were no reason that one man should take upon himself to be lord or judge'.[15] The exceptions are examples of divine intervention, such as the call of the prophets, or conquest in war by Divine Providence. However, the usual exercise of authority requires consent. The authority of parents is also unquestioned, but this does not extend beyond the family. All social authority and all social polity must rest on consent. Even if rulers display great virtue, 'for manifestation of their right, and men's more peaceable contentment on both sides, the assent of them who are to be governed seemeth necessary'.[16] The fallen nature of society makes government essential. Again the Augustinian emphasis is prevalent, as in Hooker's ecclesiology. Consent is given either by 'an order expressly or secretly agreed upon', 'by silent allowance famously notified through custom reaching beyond the memory of man'.[17]

Consent could therefore be given to the Royal Supremacy in the past, but still be valid today. What integrates Anglican polity with governmental and social custom is 'the general consent of all'. Law without consent is 'no more unto us than the counsels of physicians to the sick'. The cardinal factor is the 'consent of the whole church', without which there

---

[13] W. D. J. Cargill Thompson, 'The Philosopher of the "Politic Society": Richard Hooker as Political Thinker', in *Studies in Richard Hooker* (Cleveland: Case Western Reserve University Press, 1972).
[14] This contradicts the assertion of Gunnar Hillerdal, *Reason and Revelation in Richard Hooker* (Lund: CWK Gleerup, 1962).
[15] Richard Hooker, *Laws of Ecclesiastical Polity*, I.X.4 (Harvard: Harvard University Press, Folger Library, 1977–93).
[16] Hooker, *Laws*, I.X.4.
[17] Hooker, *Laws*, I.X.1.

could never be laws. Such consent binds 'each member of the church'. The practice of human community thus is guided by ethical principles of consent.[18]

Hooker thus combines the analysis of sociality with an understanding of ethical responsibility. Social community is analysed through his exposition of Laws in Book One. The laws of reason bind men even as men, whether they are in 'settled fellowship' or in 'solemn agreement'.[19] His concept of natural law is modelled on St Thomas; it is divine, universal, known through reason and the basis of all human law. How do we know what 'the dictates of right Reason' are? There are three answers. First, scripture provides confirmation for the precepts of the law of nature; secondly, there is the most sure and infallible, but hardest way, which is to go back to first principles; thirdly, there is the empirical method of discovering what has been held to be true universally. This is a sure sign that truth is to be found here.

> The general and perpetual voice of men is as the sentence of God himself. For that which all men have at all times learned, Nature herself must needs have taught; and God being the author of Nature, her voice is but his instrument.[20]

Hooker therefore sets up a dichotomy between two different aspects of the church. It is 'both a society and a society supernatural'. It is therefore governed by revealed, supernatural laws concerning worship, and by external laws which are left to the discretion of each individual church.[21] Such laws are positive, mutable and similar to the necessity of law in any other society. The authority of truth rests on consensus and the power of reason: 'That authority of men should prevail with men either against or above Reason, is no part of our belief'. Consensus does not resolve the argument, but it takes it in a new direction: 'That which all men's experience teacheth them may in no wise be denied'. Reason is a practical law: it teaches the control of the passions, the first kind of virtue, and the nature of justice. It is typical of Hooker's theology that he exalts religion to the highest of all virtues, beyond justice. Religion can be corrupted into superstition, the worship of false gods, or even into atheism: 'their evil disposition seriously goeth about therewith to apprehend God as being not God'.[22]

[18] Hooker, *Laws*, VIII.vi.11.
[19] Hooker, *Laws*, I.X.1.
[20] Hooker, *Laws*, I.VIII.3.
[21] Hooker, *Laws*, I.XV.3 and Book III.
[22] Hooker, *Laws*, V.iii.2.

Hooker's Anglican polity rests on a concern with the way in which human existence is structured through laws, human and divine, positive and natural. Although he was conservative in many aspects of his thoughts, reflecting the prejudices of his day, the theory of law which he provided enabled both social and ecclesiastical development. Stephen Sykes has recently argued this in an article on Hooker and the ordination of women.[23] His understanding of society and government relates the church to the whole of the created order. Within that relationship, the nature of human life is seen to have a purpose and direction, which participates in the life of Christ through the sacraments of baptism and Holy Communion. Theology involved the interpretation of God, the human community and the created order: 'God hath created nothing simply for itself, but each thing in all things, and of every thing each part in other have such interest, that in the whole world nothing is found whereunto any thing created can say "I need thee not"'. In that interpretation the sacraments are not 'naked signs' but 'means effectual' of 'grace available unto eternal life'.[24] Finally, Hooker makes the transition from sociality to ethical norms, but did not argue as Bonhoeffer did in rejecting sociality for ethical responsibility. For Hooker consent and liberty are the way in which society, and the conditions of that society, should function. Anglican polity is as much a polity of liberty as it is unitive or sacramental. The ethics of society are itself an expression of its laws; the law of reason is an ethical law: 'God hath not proved their hearts to think such things as he hath not enabled them to prove'.[25]

It was both the exposition of the fundamental principles of Anglican polity and the commitment to liberty which attracted Coleridge to Hooker. Coleridge became convinced for the defence of the Established church during the Catholic Emancipation crisis from 1825 to 1829. Coleridge began work in 1825 after the introduction of the 1825 Bill, and finally completed *On the Constitution of the Church and State, According to the Idea of Each* after the passing of the 1829 Act which repealed the Test Acts of 1673 and 1678. Coleridge went back to basic principles, sketching out his commitment to Ideas. Coleridge first admired Hooker twenty-five years before, but in 1825 he reread him. Just before his death in 1834 he referred again to Hooker. As Hooker hoped

---

[23] S. W. Sykes, 'Richard Hooker and the Ordination of Women to the Priesthood', in *After Eve*, ed. Janet Martin Soskice (London: SCM, 1990), pp. 119–37.
[24] Hillerdal, *Reason*, p. 133; Marshall, *Hooker*, pp. 137f.; W. R. Crockett, 'Holy Communion', in *Study of Anglicanism*, pp. 275.
[25] John E. Booty, 'Hooker and Anglicanism', in *Studies in Richard Hooker*, p. 216, on reason and scripture; Egil Grislis, 'The Hermeneutical Problem in Hooker', in *Studies in Richard Hooker*, p. 180, on universality of agreement. Peter Munz, *The Place of Hooker in the History of Thought* (London: RKP, 1952), discusses Hooker's relation to Plato and Aristotle.

to finish his *Laws of Ecclesiastical Polity*, so Coleridge hoped to finish his 'Philosophy' – the fundamental sketch of Anglican polity.[26]

Coleridge transforms Hooker's theology into his Idea of the state and the clerisy. An Idea for Coleridge is defined in *Church and State* as 'given by the knowledge of its ultimate aim'.[27] As Gunton says, it is 'neither a timeless Platonic abstraction nor the particular mental datum of empirical experience ... it is like the innate idea of the rationalist tradition', but it is dynamic, ontological and not simply regulative.[28] The national church is endowed by the state to promote education through its clerisy. The British Constitution is 'an idea arising out of the idea of a state'.[29] Again it was from Hooker that Coleridge defined the difference between ideas and conceptions. In a note on Hooker's works, Coleridge argued that a conception was a reflection of a thing, or a class of things, but 'an Idea is a Power (δυναμις νοερα) that constitutes its own reality – and is in order of Thought, necessarily antecedent to the Things, in which it is, more or less adequately, realized – while a Conception is as necessarily posterior'.[30]

The Constitution is an Idea which expresses balance, and this is worked out across the generations. There is a balance between permanence and progress. One is tied to those who are aristocratic, and have landed property. The other is linked to manufacture, commerce and the growth of science. The third estate is the *enclesia*, the national church which is 'an order of men chosen in and out of the realm ... the learned of all names'. Again the distinction between enclesia and ecclesia is worked out in a comment on Hooker's *Works*.[31] The ecclesia is 'the communion of such as are called out in the same body', even though their functions were distinct. The enclesia balances performance and progression, securing civilization. Its task is to

> guard the treasures of past civilization, and thus to bind the present with the past; to perfect and add to the same, and thus to connect the present with the future; especially to diffuse through the whole community, and to every native entitled to its laws and rights, that quantity and quality of knowledge which was indispensable both for

[26] Coleridge's debt to Hooker is found in K. Coburn, ed., *The Notebooks of S. T. Coleridge*, Vol. *1*, *1794–1804* (London: RKP, 1957), pp. 1052–3; E. L. Griggs, ed., *Collected Letters of S. T. Coleridge*, Vol. 2 (Oxford: OUP, 1956), p. 956; G. Whalley, ed., *S. T. Coleridge Collected Works* (London: RKP, 1984), 12 Marginalia 2; R. F. Bankley, ed., *Coleridge on the Seventeenth Century* (Durham, NC: Duke University Press, 1955).
[27] J. Colmer, ed., *Collected Works* 10 (London: RKP, 1976).
[28] Gunton, *The One, The Three and the Many*, p. 143.
[29] *Church and State*, p. 19.
[30] *Church and State*, p. 13 n. 1.
[31] *Church and State*, p. 45 n. 1.

the understanding of those rights, and for the performance of the duties correspondent.[32]

It is a classic statement of Anglican polity. The enclesia need not be Anglican, or indeed Christian, although Coleridge believed Christianity was the final revelation of God. The clerisy have those cultural experts who sustain the intellectual and moral life of the nation. They bind together all classes into national development. Theologians only form part of the national church, but 'the Science of Theology was the root and the trunk of the knowledges that civilized man, because it gave unity and the circulating sap of life to all other sciences, by virtue of which alone they could be contemplated as forming, collectively, the living tree of knowledge'.[33]

The essence of the clerisy, or enclesia's, task is education. Social progress and education would go hand-in-hand. But education was not enough. The goal must be civilization 'grounded in cultivation, in the harmonious development of those qualities and faculties that characterize our humanity – We must be men in order to be citizens'.[34] But the clerisy were not to be agents of social control, nor were the clergy simple political functionaries. Abandoning the traditional eighteenth-century exposition of the 'Anglican church-state' Coleridge defended the proper role of the clergy:

The fatal error into which the peculiar character of the English Reformation threw our church, has borne bitter fruit ever since – I mean that of its clinging to court and state, instead of cultivating the people. The church ought to be a mediator between the people and the government, between the poor and the rich. As it is, I fear the church has let the hearts of the common people be stolen from it.[35]

Coleridge had been critical of the Establishment as a young writer, but he came to distinguish between an established and a standing church. Both were national churches, but a standing church was established by government fiat. An established church had its own independence, materially and constitutionally, while being an essential part of the con-

---

[32] *Church and State*, p. 44. On Coleridge's political thought, John Colmer, *Coleridge, Critic of Society* (Oxford: OUP, 1959); John Morrow, *Coleridge's Political Thought* (London: Macmillan, 1990); David Calleo, *Coleridge and the Idea of the Modern State* (New Haven: Yale University Press, 1966); and the exchange between Peter Allen and John Morrow in *Journal of the History of Ideas* 46 (Jan.–March 1985); 47 (Oct.–Dec. 1986); 50 (July–Sept. 1989).

[33] *Church and State*, p. 47.

[34] *Church and State*, p. 89.

[35] Morrow, *Political Thought*, p. 146, citing *Table Talk*, 8 Sept. 1830, p. 109.

stitution. Coleridge wrote of the Concordat between Napoleon and the French Roman Catholic Church, and explained why he preferred the Church of England:

> Now this indeed is an establishment ... it has its own foundations, whereas the present Church of France has no foundation of its own – it is a House of Convenience built on the sands of a transient legislature – and no wise differs from a standing army.[36]

Coleridge, however, knew that Hooker's sacramental vision was also deeply rooted in participation in the grace of Christ. Hooker himself ended his ministry as a parish priest. Coleridge concludes his study of *Church and State* with an exposition of the ecclesia, the church of Christ. The latter 'is no state, kingdom or realm of this world', but rather is the 'befriending opposite' of the state. The church of Christ acts as a counter-force to whatever evils there are in a state. Equally the church of Christ radiates back whatever is a humanizing element in the aims of the state. This ecclesia is in tension with the enclesia. The enclesia rests on its material endowment, the Nationality. It is independent of Parliament, in that it cannot be dissolved by an act of Parliament, but it is a part of the idea of the British Constitution. The ecclesia is a visible, empirical community, which is not state supported, and asks only to be left alone. The enclesia gives hope and education to the nation: 'our Maker has distinguished man from the brute that perishes, by making hope first an instinct of his nature, and, secondly, an indispensable condition of his moral and intellectual progression'.[37] The task of Anglican polity is thus the combination of ecclesia and enclesia. The clerisy's work is 'to form and train up the people of the country to obedient, free, useful, organisable subjects, citizens and patriots'. Civility is defined as 'all the qualities essential to a citizen', so that 'the proper object and end of the National Church is civilisation with freedom'.[38]

As in Hooker, there is a strong emphasis on freedom. The juxtaposition of free and obedient echoes Hooker's earlier argument for consent. Yet Coleridge is not attempting a sophisticated form of social control. Alongside the Ideas of church and state is the Idea of liberty. Ideas 'correspond to substantial beings, to objects, whose actual subsistence is implied in their idea, though only by the idea revealable'. The idea of a person is known through the ideas of 'God, eternity, freedom'. So the 'aim and object' of the state is 'to secure to each the greatest sphere of

---

[36] Morrow, *Journal of the History of Ideas* 47 (1986), p. 646, citing Coleridge, *Collected Letters*, 2, p. 806.
[37] *Church and State*, p. 83.
[38] *Church and State*, p. 54. Calleo, *Coleridge*, pp. 117f., on the clerisy.

freedom compatible with the safety, the security and the unity of the whole ... by the restraint of all – to enlarge the outward spheres of the inly free, so as at the same time to increase the inward freedom of those, whose outward spheres it contracted'.[39] Within the task of the enclesia lies 'civilisation with freedom'. Historically the national church, or enclesia, created 'the substance of our liberty', by transforming the privileges attached to churches into asylum for fugitive vassals. Out of this came a class of freemen and the origins of towns. The history of the national church was a war against slavery and villeinage. The defence of liberty is a cardinal part of the idea of the state. In the poem reproduced in *Church and State* Coleridge wrote:

> Hence thro' many a fearless Age
> Has social freedom lov'd the land.

Nevertheless the ultimate freedom is the freedom of the church of Christ, 'the Church visible and militant under Christ'. It prizes liberty above all else. The social freedom of the citizens of a nation is taken up into the spiritual power of Christianity, where there are the ideas of freedom, goodness and truth. So, as in Hooker, Anglican polity is concerned with consent and liberty. Unlike Hooker, there is now a fundamental tension built into the life of society between permanence, progression and the balancing role of the national church. The national church does not unify and sanctify the polity in Coleridge, but holds the tension in balance, while educating and civilizing its members. A much more intractable tension is that between the liberty gained by the national church and the spiritual freedom of the church of Christ. Coleridge argued that the dichotomy must be maintained. Once again, it is a comment on Hooker's *Works* which reveals Coleridge's view of the church as Augustinian. Baxter's willingness to employ civil power reveals the often corrupt nature of ecclesiastical politics. It is 'pomp, pride, vanity and temporal tyranny' that destroy a church.[40] There was no retreat by Coleridge to a mystic, subjective concept of the church. However the church can be and often is prone to error. The relationship between the church of Christ and the national church is like that of an olive tree whose proximity to a vine improves the fruit. The olive tree perfects the vine, but the clerisy educates members of the church of Christ: it is a symbiotic relationship.[41] Once again, it is the particular English context that matters to Coleridge. As with Hooker and Eliot, the argument about polity is 'placed' in a particular location. It is the local

---

[39] *Church and State*, pp. 47, 116 n. 1.
[40] Morrow, *Political Thought*, p. 153.
[41] *Church and State*, p. 56; the reference to the olive tree is from Martin Luther.

church which is visible, concrete and the church of Christ: it is 'objective in its nature and purpose'. Equally the clerisy are found in local towns and villages, concerned with education and social development. The two combine in the one parish, encompassing the total social conditions (sociality) of one specific location.

What is the significance of this tradition of Anglican polity for our society today? England is a pluralist, secular, society in rapid change.[42] Even if the secularity is qualified by an awareness of the diverse beliefs which people do actually hold, churchgoing is a declining habit in Britain. The society is paradoxically distinguished by great conflict in such areas as race relations, the inner city and crime, and yet also by a high degree of social stability and consensus. How then might the Church of England respond to this complex situation in terms of the Anglican polity sketched above? I would characterize such a polity as being concerned with the whole of society, which is seen as 'graced', needing to be affirmed and criticized; and above all a polity which seeks to elicit a response which is based on consent and the liberty of the individual. The object of this polity is a full expression of freedom in society, which enables that society to form more satisfying and dynamic relationships.

One immediate comment must be to point to the immense care and attention which the Church of England has taken to understand what might be happening in society. Sociologists such as David and Bernice Martin, Robin Gill or Leslie Francis have painstakingly explored the nature of secularity. John Habgood's writings have been indebted to this tradition (*Church and Nation in a Secular Age*), as has Stephen Sykes in his consideration of the sociological context of liturgical change. The conflictual aspects of England have been known from the inside by Ken Leech (race relations, the inner city) and the Archbishop's Urban Theology Group which was set up after the report *Faith in the City*. The consensual element is also analysed in another report, *Changing Britain*. The consistently high standard of social research is affirmed by many writers from outside this country as a mark of contemporary Anglican polity.[43]

It is however not enough to know what is going on, important though that is. The task of Anglican polity is no longer to harmonize the pluralism into a greater whole. It seems another era, although it is only fifty years ago, that Archbishop Temple could refer to 'a civilisation on the way to becoming Christian'.[44] Anglican polity must accept the irreduci-

[42] Ninian Smart, 'Church, Party and State', in *Religion, State and Society in Modern Britain*, ed. Paul Badham (Lewiston: Edwin Mellon Press, 1989).
[43] A tribute is paid by Henry Clark, *The Church Under Thatcher* (London: SPCK, 1993). Clark is an American social ethicist.
[44] F. A. Iremonger, *William Temple* (Oxford: OUP, 1943), p. 544.

bly plural nature of society, without seeking to become concerned only with is own ecclesial identity. The task is therefore to address the pluralist, secular society in which the local and national church is set without pretending either that church and nation are a unitive whole (Hooker, and Temple) or that the clerisy can educate the nation (Coleridge and T. S. Eliot). Within the society, the church can seek to transform particular relationships, in such ways as other contributors to this volume (McFadyen, Selby) have discussed. In particular, the alleviation of destructive and damaging relationships is a clear priority arising from the Christian witness to reconciliation and healing. Despite Bernice Martin's thoughtful warning cited earlier in this article on the danger of hubris, the church has no option but to engage in such a task. At the same time, the church can also seek to nurture moral values by paying attention to the conditions in which moral development will take place. The strong emphasis in English ecclesiology in this century on *koinonia*, stemming from Thornton's work up through to the ARCIC report, enables a link to be made between the development of a community – in which moral values might be discerned – and the sacramental life of that community. Such a community would need to be open to its society and to seek to facilitate questioning and debate. It is therefore not a sign of weakness when the local and national church engage in open debate on an issue.

Stephen Sykes has pointed to the value of embracing 'ineradicable inter-religions and ideological conflict' with 'considerable intellectual and practical effort'.[45] 'The defence of the freedom of conscience' which he takes as central to Christianity is also the implication of this article. Anglican polity can seek to retain a central place in national life, despite the secularity of our society, if it is committed to a full engagement with the social change which constantly surrounds it. Unlike Hooker and Coleridge, there can be no assumption that the surrounding society is Christian. How the language of the Christian faith speaks to the language of secularized England is the question which confronts us. What is needed is a breadth of vision and wide tolerance which John Habgood points to as characteristic of Anglican polity in his recent collection of essays.[46] It is an emphasis Hooker and Coleridge would have affirmed as central to the nature of Anglican polity.

This means that the formulation of an Anglican polity in the late twentieth century for England is complex and subtle. We are given an Anglican tradition which affirms the presence of God in created sociality, and places a high value on freedom, or the liberty fundamental to living well. Hooker in the Eighth Book of the *Polity* uses Aristotle's *Politics*

---

[45] S. W. Sykes, 'Theology, Toleration and Conflict', in *Ideas and Politics in Modern Britain*, ed. J. C. D. Clark (London: Macmillan, 1990), p. 114.
[46] See n. 12.

(1328b) and Matt. 6.33 to argue that Christ's lordship is made effective when a polity enables citizens to live well, fulfilling their spiritual needs as the final end of polities. A. S. McGrade's recent edition of the *Polity* speaks of Hooker's 'remarkably republican conception of the Elizabethan settlement', where the community operates with a 'non-coercive definition of law' and the royal supremacy is restrained by Parliament.[47] Ordained ministry enables the commonwealth to function well for it reminds society that all forms of earthly welfare are good because they contribute to 'the exercise of virtue and the speculation of truth'.[48] Those who have prosperity but fail to see God's goodness in it put themselves under judgement. The famous rhetoric of Hooker's language in the Fifth Book on the power of ordained ministry ('the power of the Ministry of God translateth out of darkness into glory, it raiseth men from the earth and bringeth God himself down from heaven') is contextualized by the necessity of virtue and liberty for society to function well; the necessity of religion to enable virtue and liberty to flourish; and finally the necessity of ordained ministry for the continuance of religion. Paget, writing in 1899 in his commentary on Book Five, sums it up:

> The Ministry stands in the Commonwealth as God's ordinary provision for the regular maintenance and communication of that light and strength whereby men are enabled so to think and live as to receive from God, if it be for their good, the blessing of prosperity, and to use either prosperity or adversity in the right and fruitful way of happiness.[49]

It is no distance at all from Paget, writing on Hooker, to the Advisory Board of Ministry's report on *Ordination and the Church's Ministry*. We also find in this 1991 report Daniel Hardy (with Wesley Carr, Rowan Williams, Brian Russell, Gloria Rich and Nicholas Sagovsky) asking how the church might promote a pattern of common life in society. Here we find the primary task of Anglican polity today. In each village, suburb or town it is to be an institution that reflects the nature of divine action in the world beyond, but also including the visible church. There must be an interactive pattern of the local church and its cultural setting. The church is not to be identified totally with the Kingdom, yet it is an eschatological sign of it.[50]

In its most perceptive analysis, the report criticizes the way in which

---

[47] Richard Hooker, *Of the Laws of Ecclesiastical Polity*, ed. A. S. McGrade (Cambridge: CUP, 1989).
[48] *Laws*, V.lxxvi.3.
[49] F. Paget, *An Introduction to the Fifth Book of Hooker's Treatise of the Laws of Ecclesiastical Polity* (Oxford: Clarendon Press, 1899), p. 195.
[50] *Ordination and the Church's Ministry*, ABM Ministry Paper No. 1, 1991, pp. 8–12.

the church can be so easily viewed as a community. Instead the Church of England has rather been a network which 'crystallizes' in public worship and action. An over-stated view of ecclesial identity will preclude that engagement with society which this paper has shown is characteristic of Anglican polity. The church needs a distinctive language by which it interprets culture, without making that language inaccessible to public reference. Equally the organization and distribution of responsibilities ('polity') spells out the nature of authority and accountability in an institution. If ordained priesthood subsumes lay ministry under it, from a hierarchical model of trinitarian relationships, then the capacity to engender creative forms of participation in society is weakened and the characteristic Anglican stress on liberty is also lost.[51]

Such considerations mean that the current approval of ecclesial ethics stemming from the community in contemporary theology must be regarded with a certain caution. Timothy Sedgwick's own work on *Sacramental Ethics*, and his recent essay on economic life in the volume criticizing the moral teaching of the Episcopal Church (in the United States) present the most well-argued case for community formation, paschal identity and a graced identity.[52] Moral idealism is criticized since it is assumed that the 'ideas of individual dignity, universal community and human freedom complement each other and may be realized in history'. Further, 'All that is required is the transformation of the will ... Here, basically, is the liberalism of the American social gospel'. Sedgwick's quite proper criticism of this approach leads him to postulate the need for the church to be faithful to its own life rather than being an agent of social change.

But that, I believe, sells the pass. Anglican polity in England was never concerned solely with the church being faithful as a witnessing community. Even when Sedgwick pushes his concerns further in recognizing the need to encounter grace in the presence of the poor, the sick, the enemy and the alien, there is a prior requisite for the church to determine its identity over against the surrounding culture before it can engage in the critique of that society. He sees the church as enacting the story of Jesus through worship, before (it is a logical priority, not temporal) it contributes to the formulation of public policy.[53]

A different understanding of ecclesial identity and polity would see the institutional church touching social life at every point. The mission of the church enables the world to become more fully one, holy, and apostolic;

[51] *Ordination and the Church's Ministry*, pp. 20–3.
[52] T. Sedgwick, *Sacramental Ethics* (Philadelphia: Fortress, 1987); and T. Sedgwick and P. Turner, eds., *The Crisis in Moral Teaching in the Episcopal Church* (New York: Morehouse, 1992).
[53] T. Sedgwick, 'Graceless Poverty and the Poverty of Grace', in *Prophetic Visions and Economic Realities* (Grand Rapids: Eerdmans, 1989).

and as all the world realizes these, so catholicity is manifested. The task of the institutional church is not to realize the ideals of liberalism in a monolithic way, but to point to the expression of divine rule in what has been called 'the essential dynamics of human life'. Where the network of the church recognizes the hidden rule of God through the 'human need for peace and harmony, through the uses of power, law and order ... and through the motivation of an enlightened self-interest', there it will seek to work within these forms of social solidarity and prevent them falling into selfishness and sin.[54]

Such an ethic may well be premised on a communitarian self-identity. But it is also worth emphasizing that far more basic to Hooker and Coleridge is the Aristotelian understanding of the practice of the virtues in a political community.[55] It is not that either of these theologians deny the nature of Christian community, but that they saw beyond the Christian community a telos in which individual and corporate existence found a unity and ultimately an eschatological fulfilment. Even in the radically demarcated existence of contemporary modernity, where each self is divided into fragments and the hidden depths of each soul (or sexual being) are the primary referent of particular action, Anglican polity can witness to the need to live well in each particular locality.

The implications are, I think, fairly clear. First, the locality of the church's existence matters. What one says about social life, or how one lives as a Christian institution, must be in constant interaction with the local environment. Second, the importance of validating that which is good in the public realm (governed by the dynamics of survival where God creates by change and evolution) is of crucial significance. The public role of clergy is not simply to lead worship, teach, and enable the laity to lead Christian lives, but also to act as public representatives of the church in that secular, but graced world. Third, the church is an organization that is given its identity by God, and therefore can afford to have boundaries which are not distinct to the world. The task of the church is to illuminate the work of God in the world, and to call humanity to follow the action of Christ through the power of the Spirit in that world.

It must, finally, be conceded that the concern with the social expression of the virtues in a local community as the response to the dynamic of divine action could lead to a fragmentation that was very destructive of Anglican self-identity. It is, therefore, quite proper that the final word should lie with John Habgood, in defending the notion of catholicity.[56] Anglican polity can be held together both by the structuring of authority within itself and by the inheritance of doctrine. A community can renew

---

[54] Peter Baelz, in *Perspectives on Economics* (CIO, 1984).
[55] MacIntyre, *After Virtue* (London: Duckworth, 1981), p. 190.
[56] Habgood, *Making Sense*, 'Catholicity'.

itself by the dialogue between its original sources and the contemporary understanding of reality. Truth is built up by the historical process of community self-formation. That is the worth of a community ethic. In tension with it is the fundamental concern with virtue in a society which is so characteristic of Hooker, Coleridge – and, I suggest, D. W. Hardy. Anglican polity returns again and again to the unity under God of church and commonwealth. It is the most characteristic note of that polity, and with due attention to the complexity of our secular society, it can still be maintained today. It offers a far more rigorous engagement with polities than an evocation of liberation theology, and it also enables the self-structuring of Anglican church life to pay due attention to the realities of contemporary society. The parochial system, with sector ministers, is thus related to the society in which it is placed. In the church, God's love that is Christ takes form in the present and is mediated to humanity, but such formation is structured through the polity of the church. Therefore the nature of authority, and its location within the life of the church, is always to be seen as illuminating, and being illuminated by, the nature of the civil commonwealth. The one does not survive without the other: for Christ is present in both, calling people to freedom and service within the graced fellowship of the entire community that is the society wherein the church is set.

14

The Reform of Theological Education

BRIAN RUSSELL

THEOLOGICAL education has undergone a major period of development over the last ten years with a significant revision in the way in
which the future clergy are trained in the Church of England and in other
churches. The reconstruction of training programmes has been made in
the light of fundamental theological considerations. Dan Hardy has been
a central influence in this continuing process. He was Moderator of the
Board of Examiners of the Church of England and a member of its
Committee for Theological Education for seven years from 1982.

I. RE-FORMING THEOLOGICAL EDUCATION

The reconsideration of theological training took as its starting-point new
proposals contained in ACCM Paper No. 22, entitled *Education for the
Church's Ministry*, 1987. Dan Hardy chaired the Working Party which
produced this report in 1986 and, following its approval by the House of
Bishops of the Church of England, he chaired the Steering Group which
implemented the proposals.

The Report sought to address a situation in 1986 when there was no
longer a central core syllabus followed by all candidates in training for
ordained ministry. The curriculum was heavily overloaded and required
high quantities of written work which often hindered innovation by the
institutions and inhibited reflection and digestion of knowledge by the
students. At the same time there was growing expertise amongst the staff
of Colleges and Courses that could be given greater recognition and
standing, especially those staffs teaching for qualifications validated by a
University or other academic institution. There was no wish to create
institutions that could seal themselves off from the critical questions
facing the historical and contemporary study of the Christian faith and
its outworking. But this meant that the contribution made by University
Departments needed to be placed within an overall perspective of ministerial training. Students needed more than the acquisition of knowledge
and analytical skills. Importance had to be given to the development of
the whole person and the forming of a person to *be* a minister.

There was, in addition to these factors, an overtly theological concern.

The Church of England had relied, often very effectively, on its *implicit theologies*. This honoured a proper reverence for the mystery of divine truth and the provisionality of human attempts to grasp that truth. However, this lack of explicit theological standpoint increasingly found difficulties. Other churches found it difficult to relate to Anglicanism. The Church of England had a responsibility to its ecumenical partners to be more explicit, where possible, without reducing the profundity or breadth of what Anglicans believe.

Allied to this were mission considerations. It is increasingly the case that the church exits in a society which does not share or understand an implicit Christian ethos. There was a need to be clearer, and hence to allow people to take hold of a common faith which is in the church and which the church seeks to teach.

The recommendation of ACCM Paper No. 22 was that each College or Course training ordained ministers should look for a new coherence and to define an essential core for its syllabus. This renewed coherence was to be built creatively from the current circumstances and to reinforce the strengths that undoubtedly existed. Coherence was not to be found through reimposing a single syllabus. There was encouragement to be selective, since not every subject could be covered completely in every aspect. The importance of making connections between different elements of the curriculum was emphasized, but no one model for such connections was imposed. In making its response to ACCM Paper No. 22, each College and Course was asked to address three fundamental and interrelated questions. These three questions could be seen as a framework which has served as a means for working towards the renewed sense of coherence:

i) What Ordained Ministry Does the Church of England Require?

Responses were to take account of God's presence and action in the world and in the church, both as Creator and Saviour; and to give attention to the church's mission as well as its ministry; and in this context to explore the relation between ordained ministry and lay ministry. There was therefore to be a theological undergirding which provided aims for training for ordained ministry, i.e. statements about the purpose of ordained ministry in terms of knowing, doing and being.

ii) What is the Shape of the Educational Programme Best Suited for Equipping People to Exercise this Ministry?

Responses were asked to derive from their aims a set of objectives for training, meaning by objectives concrete ways of specifying what ordinands should be able to know or do or be, after having undertaken a particular part or course within the educational programme.

The educational programme was to include not only a curriculum of courses of study or syllabus, but also the structured elements of training in ministerial skills; the application and relating of practice and theology; pastoral formation; and personal and spiritual development and formation.

iii) What Are the Appropriate Means of Assessing Suitability for the Exercise of this Ministry?

Responses were asked to provide a plan for assessment which would gauge whether individual students had sufficiently met the objectives which had been outlined in response to the second question. There was encouragement to adopt a variety of means of assessment, provided that criteria were sufficiently defined so as to enable a measure of objectivity and confidence in the procedure.

It was significant that the Report did not advocate a unitary approach. The report itself outlined a discussion of each of the three questions in forms which were regarded as sample answers, containing many of the considerations necessary in making a response. Although Colleges and Courses found them a useful place to start, they were not used as controlling norms. The role of the Church of England through its central body was to consider each response to ACCM Paper No. 22, both for its substance and internal coherence, and to advise the Church of England accordingly on whether validation should be given for a five year period.

II. A THEOLOGICAL BASIS FOR RENEWED COHERENCE

The starting-point for a renewed coherence was to be the task and nature of the church, acknowledging that the ministry was the ministry of Christ in the church. The individual needs or preferences of particular students were to be interpreted in the light of their training being that of a preparation to exercise the ministry of the *church*. The Report emphasized that 'the church's task is to serve the mission of God in the World',[1] so encouraging a shift towards interpreting ministry and mission as interrelated notions and activities. The church responds to this universal presence of God, and in this sense the church and its ministers have a profoundly *public* part to play. The church should not only comment on social and public affairs, but rather the church and its ministers are integral to how creation itself can be brought towards the

---

[1] *Education for the Church's Ministry: The Report of the Working Party on Assessment*, ACCM Occasional Paper No. 22, 1987, paragraphs 26 and 27 on p. 7.

redeemed pattern that God wills for it. In the words of the Report: 'the central issue is how a new social order is re-established by God's activity within the damaged order of existence in the world, and how this is to be made possible in the present circumstances of the world'.[2]

It is undoubtedly significant that a great many responses from Colleges and Courses spoke of their theological basis in terms of understandings of God as Trinity.[3] Understandings of the Trinity can encourage ways in which the church's mission and ministry involve corporate life and work between the laity as well as between laity and clergy. However, the emphasis on the Trinity can also have limitations if this is allowed to reduce the sense of mystery of how the church shares in and understands God's activity and presence in the world. Building on suggestions made in the report,[4] it is possible to set out a model for how a theological basis can support the church's response to God's mission in the world:

DIAGRAM A

TRINITY AS COMMUNION
INTERDEPENDENCE OF PERSONS
↓
GOD'S MISSION IN THE WORLD
↓
CORPORATENESS IN THE CHURCH
↓
CHURCH'S MINISTERS PARTICIPATE IN GOD'S MISSION WITH DISTINCTIVE PURPOSES
↓
GOD'S KINGDOM

[2] *Education for the Church's Ministry*, paragraph 52 on p. 40. In an unpublished paper of 1990, Dan Hardy speaks about public theology as 'theology which draws to light the religious basis of public life, attempting to find the foundation of a true society in the presence and activity of God'. He believes that theology has a task in forming and promoting an understanding of 'the theological substratum of life in society'. The North American literature is also instructive. Edward Farley, *Theologia* (1983), argues the need for a new theological unity in theological education. Joseph C. Hough, Jr., and John B. Cobb, Jr., eds., *Christian Identity and Theological Education* (1985), and Charles M. Wood, *Vision and Discernment* (1987), both argue for different ways in which theological education could promote a new theological coherence. There is also a valuable discussion in David H. Kelsey, *To Understand God Truly, What's Theological About a Theological School?* (1992).
[3] *Ordination and the Church's Ministry*, an interim evaluation of College and Course responses to ACCM Paper No. 22, ABM Ministry Paper No. 1, 1991. The Advisory Board of Ministry of the Church of England established this Working Party to review all the College and Course responses to the first of the three quotations in ACCM Paper No. 22. The Working Party included Dan Hardy as a member under the Chairmanship of Rowan Williams.
[4] *Ordination and the Church's Ministry*, pp. 20–1.

The Trinity understood as communion provides the foundation. The picture is of patterns of relationship based on interdependence. Persons have individuality but that individuality is formed by *means* of relationship with other persons. There is a dynamic or interactive understanding of the eternal life of the Trinity, rather than a static view. Creation is seen as an outpouring of the divine life and an arena in which there is continuing interaction between God and all reality. In this way, the universe has freedom and yet is caught up in the redemptive purposes of God. The church itself is a created expression of the nature of God as communion. The church in its corporate life and worship can at best exemplify the corporateness and interdependence found in God's mission in the world. The church's ministers, as they participate in God's mission on behalf of the church, should also reflect the corporateness that is to be seen in the church. The ordained do not exhaustively contain or determine the identity and being of the church. There is no suggestion that the church is totally constitutive of God's Kingdom, nor that the church as it is presently found is totally separated or cut off from God's Kingdom promised through Christ and in the Spirit. The response currently made to God both indicates and draws the world towards becoming God's Kingdom.

Two different models may be uncovered in the responses from Colleges and Courses.

DIAGRAM B

TRINITY AS ONENESS
OR HIERARCHY
↓
CHRIST'S MINISTERS AS SERVANTS
↓
MINISTERS BUILD UP CHURCH FOR MISSION

In this model, the Trinity is understood more in terms of oneness than in terms of interdependence and communion. This might be read as a hierarchical understanding of the persons of the Trinity. The Son is conformed to the Father and the power of the Father is worked out through the Son by means of the Spirit. This can produce a notion of the church's ministers as obedient servants to whom is delegated authority and power. Thus a model which wants to emphasize humility can come to attribute dominance to the clergy. This model can reflect the assumption that God works primarily through the ministers to form the church, such that the understanding of the church is derived as a consequence of the understanding of ordained ministry.[5]

[5] *Ordination and the Church's Ministry*, p. 7.

This is a considerable contrast with Diagram A. Diagram A moves from the Trinity to God's mission in the world to the nature of the church and only then to discerning the distinctive part which the ordained play in this outworking. Versions of Diagram B could be read to suggest that it is the definition of the task given to the ordained which determines the ecclesiology. This could severely understate the way in which the church as a whole, through both laity and clergy, are caught up in participating in God's mission in the world.

There is also a third model:

DIAGRAM C

TRINITY FOUND IN MISSION IN THE WORLD
↓
MINISTERS AS PROPHETIC
↓
WORKING IN THE WORLD FOR THE KINGDOM

The model begins from a dynamic and interdependent notion of the Trinity and of the interrelation between the Trinity and creation. But, as in Diagram B, the link is then made directly from God's mission in the world to the tasks and responsibilities of the ordained. In Diagram C the emphasis is upon the minister as prophetic. The minister discerns God's mission in the world and points to the changes of structure, policy and attitude that will need to be made both by the church and the world. It is by such responsive work in the world that the world may be led towards God's Kingdom. In contrast to Diagram A, the minister could be seen as acting individualistically and the notion of the minister's role need not be closely related to an understanding of the church as either a corporate reality or an institution.[6] This is not to deny that the individual minister may have a prophetic task, but the prophetic task is shaped and nurtured by the church, even though at times there may be the need to challenge the structure and policy of the church. A further contrast between Diagram A and Diagram C is the lack of attention which Diagram C gives to the institutional church. It could be read to suggest that the coming of God's Kingdom is a gift set over and against the gift of the church. By contrast, Diagram A could suggest that it is partly in and through the church as a gift of God and as a means of the action of the Trinity that the world might be brought more nearly towards God's Kingdom.

The developments in theological education made under ACCM Paper No. 22 certainly show that greater emphasis is being put upon how the

---

[6] *Ordination and the Church's Ministry*, p. 14.

ordained can communicate their knowledge and understanding. There are a range of ways in which mission as part of ministry is understood in the responses. Two are offered for discussion.

The first is lettered 'A. Mission and Ministry', because it may fit fairly closely with Diagram A about the Trinity found above.

DIAGRAM D

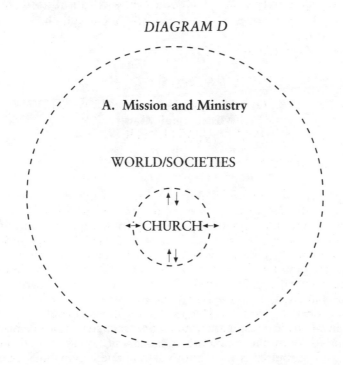

A. Mission and Ministry

WORLD/SOCIETIES

CHURCH

The diagram has soft edged borders for the world, for society and for the church. This is to suggest the element of development and the lack of clear boundaries. The church is part of the world and of the societies in which it is set and there is interaction between the church and society. This involves learning from all the diversity of different strands within that society. The church also offers something distinctive to that society, and through this interaction brings to awareness how response might be made to God's mission in the world.

Clergy are not to be concerned solely with churchgoers. Ordinands are to be helped to form an appreciation and understanding of the cultures found in Britain because these are contexts in which the communication of the Christian faith in action and word takes place. This includes understanding how the church in its ministry and mission is bound up integrally in local societies where there is disintegration and where for some personhood is denied. There needs to be help so that ordinands in their personal development can become part of a church which sustains its outgoing life when involved in the pain and suffering in contemporary society. Such situations may call for a patient or enduring spirituality and action if the church is to sustain its response to God's mission.

The diagram set out below offers some contrasts with Diagram D and might be seen to have some affinities with Diagram B set out above:

DIAGRAM E

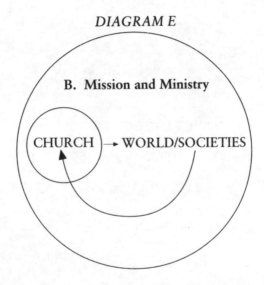

The immediate contrast is the clear delineation given to the world, its society and to the church. There is a clear sense of different identities and boundaries. The church is more of a self-contained reality with a much less complex pattern of different inter-relations. The church is seeking to take a theological understanding into the life of the world. The church is more clearly the agent, perhaps the sole agent, of such mission, and there is less of a sense of God's mission as already taking place and participating in the life of the world. When mission meets response, this may be part of a search to draw the world into the life of the church. This could be read to suggest that the understanding of the church is more of a sectarian or gathered entity, which seeks to gather the life of the world into the church so that through the church the world may grow into God's Kingdom. This diagram suggests that the church, and therefore the training of its clergy, should put less emphasis on understanding the local cultures of society in terms of their own internal coherence. Diagram D would suggest that the church's ministers have a distinctive responsibility in interpreting and evaluating culture.

III. Kinds of Integration

As part of its continuing review of the reform of theological education, the Advisory Board of Ministry asked a Working Party to look particularly at the College and Course responses to the second and third questions posed in ACCM No. 22, namely those regarding the educational programmes and forms for the assessment of ordinands during their time in training. This Working Party produced a Report entitled *Integration and Assessment* in 1992. The conclusion was that some of the central hopes which surrounded the implementation of ACCM Paper No. 22 had been realized.

One of the presenting difficulties in 1986 had been the *fragmentation* of the educational programmes in theological training. This had been highlighted by Peter Baelz in a paper entitled *An Integrating Theology* which had called for links to be made between academic disciplines in theology as well as between theology and experience. The curriculum might be constructed so that all the elements were closely interrelated with the effect that the curriculum could be seen as a whole and structured by a model of an *integrated code*.[7]

The word *integration* is itself open to a wide variety of interpretations. The procedures under ACCM Paper No. 22 have introduced a particular notion of integration, meaning by this the close co-ordination of objectives, educational programme and forms of assessment by reference to the central theological priorities and aims.[8] It is likely this concern for close interweaving will prove to be one of the most significant points of impact of ACCM Paper No. 22. There is evidence that this is being attempted in a serious way. Greater clarity about the aims of ordination training has helped Colleges and Courses to show how the parts of their curriculum, the teaching methods and the forms of assessment, are consistent with each other as a working out of the aims and objectives. For example, students can be helped to see particular ways in which they should develop so as to be able to be effective in working together as a team. The criteria by which students are assessed can give due weight to the development of ministerial skills and can help to guide students in their growth in prayer and their spiritual life. Skills can include the capacity to collaborate, or be agents of change and challenge. This has also helped to clarify ways in which the staff of Colleges and Courses can

---

[7] *Integration and Assessment*, pp. 25–6, referring to Peter Baelz, *An Integrating Theology*, ACCM Occasional Paper No. 15, 1983, and an article by Anthony Dyson entitled 'Collection Codes, and Integrated Codes', referred to in *Experience and Authority, Issues Underlying Doing Theology*, ACCM Occasional Paper No. 19, 1984.

[8] *Integration and Assessment*, pp. 11–12; *Education for the Church's Ministry*, paragraphs 56, 61–2, pp. 43 and 46.

be assisted in their own development as theological teachers and educators so that they can provide the forms of training now required.[9]

There has been renewed emphasis upon the fact that theological Colleges and Courses can only provide *initial* theological training. If theological education is to serve the task of God's mission, it will need to be conceived as a lifelong process of personal and corporate development. A training provided in Colleges and Courses can only serve as the initial stage in which the fundamental pattern is set. A system of profiling has been introduced to record the development of ordinands during their initial training so that there can be greater continuity between initial and continuing ministerial education. This should assist ordinands to bring together or integrate their experience and understanding before training with that which they gain during training and work this out reflectively during their participation in ministry.[10]

IV. ONE IN CHRIST: CHRISTIAN IDENTITY AND 'BLACK EXPERIENCE'

A number of the overall theological themes that have guided the reforming of theological education point directly towards the need to tackle the marginalization of black people in the British churches. There is a concern to take seriously God's universal presence and action as creator and redeemer, and how this is worked out in human and social affairs so that true society might be reconstructed as a response to God's mission in the world. This has implications for how the church can assist in addressing change in society so as to include 'black' people in ministry. The churches should not only participate in God's mission but reflect the best ordering possible in the light of that mission. The churches are to address this in terms of their structures and arrangements.

True society and true communion in the church must be based on a genuine diversity within an overall unity. Differences of race must therefore be an honoured part of diversity. This is no easy task. It might be said that there is a secret core in the life of British society, bound up with the history of an island and a fairly isolated culture, which is in some respect untouchable. It is as if this central core sustains itself by seeking to subsume or suck into itself any developments so that they are conformed to a single norm. It is such a concept of subsuming into a norm that helps to make sense of talk about *assimilation*, as a way of absorbing

---

[9] *Integration and Assessment*, pp. 13–14, 27, 35 and 64–8; see also *Staff Development in Theological Colleges and Courses*, ACCM Occasional Paper No. 34, 1990.
[10] *Education for the Church's Ministry*, paragraph 39 on p. 34; *Integration and Assessment*, p. 71.

racial differences into British society, and which in turn creates talk about *marginalization*, namely the pushing away to one side of that which cannot be subsumed. Such unconscious patterns of behaviour can lead participants in a society to view others as *outsiders* and to speak of British-born black people as 'immigrants'.

It is partly a question of considering what it means to 'be one in Christ'.[11] To be one in Christ is not to suppose that all are brought into a unity which is only *spiritual*, a unity deeper than or apart from matters of race or colour. Hopefully, being one in Christ is a spiritual unity that brings together different races; but oneness in Christ should include as a positive richness the differences in race that are to be found. These differences include approaches to worship, and ways of explaining and living out the Christian faith. Being one in Christ is not about being subsumed into a single or hidden norm.

If the aim is to expand and share the hidden norm or norms in British church life, one way to do this will be to place black clergy across the whole spread of the church so that this dimension of differences is given focus throughout the church. If black clergy are to be undertaking this pioneering work on behalf of the whole church, there will be a need for support networks to sustain them. This will be an exposed ministry. The Simon of Cyrene Theological Institute can now give particular help so that black people can own their own roots and identity.[12] In this way, they can become secure so as to be equipped to deal with the pressures of training and of ministry in a predominantly white situation. The Institute can also provide advice and support to Colleges and Courses in the training of white ordinands.

V. THEOLOGY ON REFLECTION

Faith in the City, published in 1985, made some far-reaching criticisms of

[11] Dan Hardy in an unpublished paper 'Why Special Training for Black Clergy?' speaks of the assumption that unity in British society is 'based on the commonness of traditional English culture and shared by black people only insofar as they are willing to be assimilated to it'. He raises as an issue how the church of Christ can 'incorporate racial and cultural variety, and so secure for diverse peoples the possibility of being themselves while one in Christ'. Dan Hardy was a foundation Governor of the Simon of Cyrene Theological Institute.
[12] The purposes of the Simon of Cyrene Theological Institute include the following: fostering lay vocations and equipping lay members of churches with black membership; fostering vocations to ordained ministry; providing courses of education and training for black ordination candidates prior to their ministerial training; providing training opportunities for white and black candidates who are undertaking ministerial training; providing in-service courses for white and black clergy; and undertaking study and research leading to publications concerning the theology and considered reflections of black Christians in a British context.

theological education in Britain. The report re-awakened awareness that the training of ordained ministers may not be equipping students sufficiently to see how to relate theology and practice across the wide range of circumstances in church and society. This raised anew the need for some inductive starting-points for theological understanding.

Theology must involve a complex range of interactions between experience and understanding.[13] People hold many assumptions and views – some personal and some shared with others in society, and these feed into experience. The use of experience, as a starting point for theology, has to reckon with the danger of replicating limited understandings, rather than letting experience challenge and be enlarged by an encounter with received theological ideas and practices. Reflection should ideally precede, accompany and follow action. Reflection should therefore involve analysis of action and constructive theological thinking.

Such reflection requires methods than can assist in analysing the implicit theologies which are met in experience. The use of a form of inferential reasoning can be a valuable tool. This involves asking in effect, 'what must these people be assuming unconsciously about the totality of reality as implicit beliefs, if the best possible sense is to be made of their life and actions?' The *best possible sense* is achieved by the most satisfying and comprehensive explanation that can be given. These explanations of the implicit beliefs that people have can only be described as inferences and not as strictly logical conclusions. An understanding of implicit beliefs is derived through experience, not in isolation from experience, but can only be an abstraction. People have genuine freedom to act, but in acting freely they express and convey the attitudes and implicit beliefs that they hold.

Implicit or local theologies will rarely be single, self-contained entities monolithic or uniform in all respects. Implicit beliefs can overlap, and different understandings can persist as strands or pockets within an amalgam or pluriformity of cultures in any society. Local theologies will be dynamic as well as persistent. A culture is both a precipitate of and a contributing factor towards, how the history of a locality has happened. The individuals and groups present both participate and modify their culture or local theology. But one of the strengths of this kind of approach is that individuals can be understood in terms of communal patterns of action and meaning.

The implicit theologies which will be found will need to be tested and challenged by reference to the corporate faith and living tradition of the church. But before this can happen, it is necessary to draw out from others the rarely expressed or articulated hopes and struggles that make

---

[13] See *Theology in Practice*, the proposals of the ACCM Working Party on Urban Studies Centres, ACCM Occasional Paper No. 29, May 1988.

up an implicit theology. Those who carry out this kind of interpreting need to have qualities similar to those of the poet or composer who can express for others what they cannot otherwise express. In this way the church's ministers can learn from what is found in mission.

PART FIVE: CHRISTIAN FORMATION

15

Paideia – What Can We Learn from the First Four Centuries?

FRANCES YOUNG

THE church grew up in a world fascinated by education, and adopted an educational model for itself. The more I explore the nature and activity of the church in Graeco-Roman society, the more sure I become that theology, liturgy and ethics were shaped by pedagogic ideals both comparable with, and challenging to, those of contemporary society. The church was a learning community, pursuing *paideia*, a word which implied a full and rounded educational process, the training of youth up to maturity physically, mentally and above all, morally. I am grateful for this opportunity to pull some of the threads together, and delighted to write in honour of my former colleague, Dan Hardy, whose career has been shaped by the conviction that today, in another society dominated by education, Christians have to appropriate and develop their very considerable intellectual heritage.

True, society then was very different from what we know – there was no presumption of equal opportunity, whether for women or workers. All the more remarkable, then, that a third-century Christian scholar[1] should argue for the superiority of Christianity to philosophy on the grounds that Christianity could educate even slaves and women to be good, whereas philosophy was élitist. When the Empire began to patronize rather than persecute Christians, the church was faced with the job of re-educating a whole society, and it produced a powerful 'totalizing discourse' into which all aspects of life and culture were embraced.[2] Too often, I suspect, focus has been on the 'initiation' process in the 'ritual' of baptism rather than the 'formation' process in the long period of preparatory catechesis; and the emphasis on static 'substance' categories and fixed dogma has too much obscured the presumption of personal growth and corporate pilgrimage in the moral and religious life

---

[1] Origen, *Contra Celsum*, VI.2; Greek text ed. P. Koetschau, *Die griechischen christlichen Schriftsteller der ersten drei Jahrhunderte* (Berlin, 1899); ET Henry Chadwick (Cambridge: CUP, 1953, 1965).

[2] See Averil Cameron's remarkable book, *Christianity and the Rhetoric of Empire. The Development of Christian Discourse* (Berkeley: University of California Press, 1991).

that pervades most patristic theological material.[3] The church was a lifelong, 'comprehensive', learning community. That is my thesis.

There will be three sections in this paper, each taking particular 'soundings' which contribute to the overall mapping of my theme. We will start with the clearest evidence for the thesis, and then trace back clues which confirm it.

I. FOURTH-CENTURY CATECHESIS AND THE NATURE OF DOCTRINE

By the fourth century it is evident that preparation for baptism consisted in attending a series of lectures through Lent in which the Creed was taught and explained and the sacraments were introduced. The aspiring Christian had already spent several years as a 'hearer', attending the Liturgy of the Word, or Mass of the Catechumens, though not of Eucharist which was reserved for the initiated. 'Catechumen' meant someone under instruction.

A natural starting-point, therefore, is the content of these lectures, and we have several examples that might be used. The classic set of lectures is that of Cyril of Jerusalem; but we also have material from Ambrose of Milan, together with advice for catechists from Gregory of Nyssa and Augustine. In this century, furthermore, the *Catechetical Homilies* of Theodore of Mopsuestia and the *Baptismal Catecheses* of John Chrysostom have come to light. This provides a wide geographical sample from approximately the same date: Palestine, Syria, Asia Minor, Italy, North Africa. We could, then, observe a range of particular, different approaches, often coloured by the individual instructor's characteristics, as well as a general pattern of Christian education, but for brevity's sake, we will concentrate on the lectures of Cyril of Jerusalem.[4]

Cyril's introductory talk (*Procatechesis*) and opening lectures are not

---

[3] See Frances M. Young, '*Paideia* and the Myth of Static Dogma', in *The Making and Remaking of Christian Doctrine*, Essays in Honour of Maurice Wiles, ed. Sarah Coakley and David Pailin (Oxford: Clarendon Press, 1993), pp. 265–83.

[4] Cyril of Jerusalem, *Procatechesis, The 18 Catecheses*, and *The Mystagogical Catecheses*, full Greek text only in Migne, *Patrologia Graeca*, vol. 33, 331–1180, though there are more recent editions of *The Mystagogical Catecheses* alone; ET of *Procatechesis* and *The 18 Catecheses* by E. H. Gifford, in *Nicene and Post-Nicene Fathers*, series 2, vol. VII, pp. 1–157. There are more recent translations of some or all of the material in e.g. *Library of Christian Classics*, vol. 4, by W. Telfer (London and Philadelphia, 1955), and *Fathers of the Church*, by L. P. McCauley and A. A. Stephenson, 2 vols., *Procatechesis and Catecheses 1–12* (Washington, 1968), and *Catecheses 13–18, Mystagogical Catecheses*, etc. (Washington, 1970).

concerned with 'doctrine' in our sense, but rather with the transformation of the whole person of the convert which is to take place through
baptism. This is a useful reminder that *doctrina* or *dogma* (depending
whether you were using Latin or Greek) simply meant 'teaching', and
implied the moral development involved in coming to maturity of mind
and will, as well as acquisition of knowledge and understanding, and the
training of the body through physical activity. The whole of education
took place in the *gymnasium* in the ancient world. Cyril assumes this
'whole person' training. In the third lecture, Cyril stresses that baptism is
concerned with both body and soul, the water for the body, the Spirit for
the soul. The body is important because it may become God's Temple
and is to be sanctified and resurrected (IV.23, 30), and so it needs discipline and training, an appropriate lifestyle, advice on food, clothing,
sexual abstinence within or without marriage (IV.24–29). But if only the
body is present and not the mind, it profits nothing; the new Christian
has to 'lift up the eye of the mind', and 'give the mind wholly to study'
(*Procat.* 1, 15, 16). For Cyril formation means fostering 'piety of soul
with a good conscience' (III.3).

There are other ways, too, in which Cyril's lectures betray the educational assumptions of the ancient world. All education was based on
classical literature. Once the three Rs were mastered, it was through the
reading and interpretation of literature that pupils learned grammar and
language, methods of interpreting words and figures of speech, the skills
needed for success in public speaking, and so on. But they also learned
through critical reading of literature to make moral judgements. Through
literature they acquired a culture and a view of the world and their own
place in it. In Cyril's lectures, the scriptures fulfil the same function, being
constantly quoted or alluded to in order to give authority to the points
being made, and to provide examples through its narratives. Cyril
expects his hearers to study when they are in church:

> Let the men when sitting have a useful book; and let one read and
> another listen ... And again let the party of young women sit
> together in same manner, either singing or reading quietly ... (*Pro-
> cat.* 14).

In a little section on the scriptures (IV.33) Cyril actually speaks of
'Christ's school', and tells the class to learn from the church which are
the proper books to read.

This last point also reminds us that education in the ancient world was
steeped in tradition. There was a tradition of classical literature, new
literature always being modelled on the canon of the ancient classics.
There were also traditional skills to be passed on. There were traditional
questions and traditional answers. Each philosophical school taught

according to its own tradition, which was believed to have been received from the master – Plato, or Epicurus, or Pythagoras, or whoever. Part of that process also involved the refutation of alternative views (*haereses* = 'options'[5]). It is hardly surprising then that Cyril's lectures are 'dogmatic' in teaching that 'this' is right, not 'that'. Nor that they are argumentative, offering proof of the 'correct opinion' (= *ortho-doxy*), refuting the views of Jews and Greeks and heretics and exploiting authoritative texts and logical reasoning to make his point firm. He, like other philosophical teachers, is offering a total world-view which derives from a tradition formed by the divine 'Logos' (Word/Reason) incarnate in the master, Jesus Christ.

From the perspective of a 'modern' critical approach to education, this might seem very constricting, suppressing inquiry and openness. However, we should exaggerate neither the 'freedom' of modern inquiry nor the dogmatism of ancient education. Modern education 'indoctrinates' with the 'facts' of scientific investigation, and most intellectual inquiry is within a framework limited by the 'commonsense of the culture'. Ancient culture may look remarkably homogeneous to us, but within it there was much debate about certain key questions. Freewill and fatalism, for example, was a major issue, on which each 'school' had its own position, and armed its adherents with the arguments that had been assembled over a long period of time to consolidate its position, as well as the means to refute alternative propositions. Even critical approaches generate traditions.

In fact, the questions concerning who we are, where we came from and where we are going to – in other words, questions about human nature, identity, purpose, lifestyle (= *ēthica*) – were central in ancient debate. Christian philosophy developed a distinctive theological answer to current philosophical concerns. Like other schools of philosophy, the church sought to develop and foster in its 'pupils' a whole understanding of and approach to life which was character-forming, bringing to birth in people the 'image of God' which had been aborted by sin. In other words, education was not just dogmatic but 'maieutic', an adjective which comes from the Greek word for midwifery.

This metaphor was first used for education in the context of Socrates trying by dialectic to show that pupils already know the truth and all the teacher has to do is to bring it to light by question and answer. Cyril, of course, is not practising dialectic in the Socratic sense. But as already noted, the opening lectures show that a great deal more is at stake than the rote-learning of credal propositions. Christian formation is about 'new birth'. So the first lecture is a call to cleansing and confession in

[5] See my article, 'Did Epiphanius Know What He Meant by Heresy?', *Studia Patristica* 18 (1983), pp. 199–205.

preparing for transformation or 'transplantation', and the second lecture concentrates on the nature of sin and the need for repentance. God's grace and the significance of baptism in effecting this salvation and sanctification forms the subject of the third. The summary of doctrines that follows in lecture IV is simply providing the overarching perspective or mind-set within which this new being and lifestyle makes sense. Cyril knows that this mind-set has to carry conviction, and the 'orthodox' answers to the questions about human existence have to be demonstrated, not only because he believes this to be the truth, but also because only right opinion about the way things are can ensure right living, true morals.

Cyril is anxious that vice mimics virtue; tares grow among the wheat; and there are wolves in sheep's clothing (IV.1). That is the motive for arming new Christians with weapons to confute the enemy. He sees Christianity as a 'method of godliness' which consists of two things, 'pious doctrines' and 'virtuous practice', and neither is acceptable without the other. After his introductory summary, the catechumens will be given the Creed. This is to be memorized (written on the heart), and the rest of the lectures (after a talk on faith in lecture V) consists of an exposition of it, clause by clause. The way that many of the clauses provide protection against false views is drawn out: there is only one God, not a God of good and a god of evil as heretics like the Gnostics and Mani have taught (lecture VI). Here is the typical teacher of the ancient world, asserting his 'option' is 'right', but also backing up the assertion from authoritative textual material. Each point is demonstrated from the scriptures.

Yet the Creed is not intended as a set of 'articles of belief'. Its purpose is closely related to the whole process of identity-formation already mentioned. Futhermore, Cyril is clear that it is not the whole of the faith. It is a starting-point for lifelong journeying, merely a summary of scripture which provides guidelines, a map for further explorations:[6]

> ... in learning the faith and in professing it, acquire and keep that only, which is now delivered to you by the Church, and which has been built up strongly out of all the Scriptures. For since all cannot read the scriptures, some being hindered as to the knowledge of them by want of learning, and others by want of leisure, in order that the soul may not perish from ignorance, we comprise the whole doctrine of the Faith in a few lines. (V.12)

It has long seemed to me striking how much Cyril expects of his

---

[6] This subject I explored in the so far unpublished F. D. Maurice Lectures at King's College, University of London.

catechumens. The contrast with the patronizing minimal expectations of most clergy in today's church is worrying, given both the universality and level of education common in our modern societies. Some of Cyril's audience were almost certainly illiterate. Some were probably not Greek-speaking – and it is likely his lectures were translated into Syriac as he went along. Yet living in a society which treated books with reverence, which expected learned people to communicate their learning, and which counted on wise people to advise on how best to live life, Cyril takes on this demanding educational task, which both conforms to and challenges the assumptions of his culture.

It is often said that we only see the ancient world from an élitist perspective, because we rely on élitist literary remains. But the Christian church had no élitist barriers to membership. It gave opportunity to those excluded from high culture to participate in a particular version of it – though the real élite had scorned its barbarian origin and its unsophisticated literature in barbarous translationese (in the post-Constantinian era, classical forms increasingly shaped Christian content).[7] Cyril's lectures bear out the interpretation of the church in the ancient world as fundamentally an educational institution. Nor should we imagine it was confined to the initial state, the training of converts. The formal instruction of catechumens was both prepared for and reinforced by the weekly or daily homily expounding scripture within the liturgy, an ongoing, lifelong process of *paideia*.[8]

II. THE BIBLE AND ITS INTERPRETATION

There is little dispute among scholars about the fact that exegesis of scripture was deeply influenced by contemporary methods of literary interpretation. Less widely recognized are the implications of this, not to mention the significance of the fact that scriptural texts were so central to the church's activity. As we have already seen, literature lay at the heart of education, and so the role of scripture in the life of the church is central to our thesis that the church was an educational institution. What the church did was to substitute one body of literature for another.

The period of early Christian development which might be termed the Age of Scholarship began in the third century, and here we can observe quite clearly the development of a full programme of scriptural interpretation analogous to the activity of the Hellenistic scholars of Homer and

---

[7] I explored a particular example of this in 'Panegyric and the Bible', *Studia Patristica* 25 (1993), pp. 194–208.
[8] See Young, '*Paideia* and the Myth'.

the Classics. The greatest Christian scholar and educator of that time was, of course, Origen.[9] The precise level of his educational activity has been a subject of some discussion, for although tradition tells us he was once appointed by his bishop to instruct catechumens, the account of his education programme which has come down to us from the pen of his pupil, Gregory Thaumaturgus, suggests a form of Christian University following the full conventional classical curriculum, including mathematics and musical theory, in preparation for the higher learning of the doctrines of Christian philosophy. For our immediate purpose, it is most important to note that his principal activity was the interpretation of scripture, in both commentaries and sequences of homilies (or sermons) which followed through whole books of the Bible. Furthermore, he compiled a work known as the *Hexapla*, which set out the Hebrew and several different Greek versions side by side in columns, enabling the practice of textual criticism according to the professional canons of ancient scholarship.

At one level, then, we apparently have a Christian philosophical school, taking on the full professional disciplines conventionally required, apparently existing alongside the normal activities of the church. This picture may be regarded as having both positive and negative implications: it shows Christianity as a serious intellectual pursuit, but also sets that apart from normal church activity, the realm of the élite or the specialist. At another level, the catechetical and homiletic activity suggests an understanding of the church itself as a kind of comprehensive education system within which people with different capacities and opportunities could develop to their own level. Indeed, recent scholarship[10] has challenged the long-standing interpretation of Origen as élitist, classifying people according to their capacity to read scripture literally, morally or spiritually. Rather his three levels of meaning are to be understood as three stages in an educational process potentially open to everyone. It has been noted that his homilies offer material for his varied audience at many different levels, for the stage of purification, for knowledge of the Logos, and for union with God.

Furthermore, the various levels of meaning are not exclusive alternatives. In the past much has been made of Origen's allegorism. It is true that later exegetes of the so-called Antiochene School attacked Origen for excessive allegorization, and apparently countered with methods of in-

---

[9] For studies of Origen supporting this summary, see Joseph Wilson Trigg, *Origen: The Bible and Philosophy in the Third Century Church* (London: SCM, 1985 (first published, Atlanta: John Knox Press, 1983)); H. Crouzel, *Origen*, ET A. S. Worrall (Edinburgh: T. & T. Clark, 1989 (French ed. 1985)); Karen Jo Torjesen, *Hemeneutical Procedure and Theological Method in Origen's Exegesis* (Berlin: de Gruyter, 1985).

[10] See books in previous note, and also Karen Jo Torjesen, ' "Body", "Soul", and "Spirit" in Origen's Theory of Exegesis', *Anglican Theological Review* 67/1 (1985), pp. 17–30.

terpretation more nearly akin to the interpretative techniques of the grammar and rhetorical schools.[11] But Origen himself initiated the use of such methods, and one can see that both commentaries and homilies are indebted to the oral practice of school-teachers commenting on grammar and content.[12]

When the technology of the age was restricted to manuscript copies, no two copies would be entirely identical. Deciding between different 'readings' (*diorthōsis*) would therefore first occupy the class. The *Hexapla* is evidence of Origen's attention to 'the letter' of the text at this level. In fact, it was his view, adopted from Jewish tradition, that not a jot or tittle was insignificant. Often, it is true, he decided between the alternatives on the basis of their potential to offer deeper meanings, but his exploitation of the material is itself evidence of his interest in standard 'school' questions.

Next the school class would be concerned with making sense of the 'signs' written on the paper (*anagnōsis*). Ancient manuscripts had no punctuation or word-division, so sometimes there were considerable problems in construing sentences, and there might be more than one way of 'reading' the material. Grammatical analysis was therefore important, as was discussion of vocabulary, with many of the classical texts being ancient and using archaic language. Etymology fascinated ancient linguists, and was understood to be a key to meaning, as was the identification of figures of speech, like metaphor or irony. In the schools, noting stylistic devices was particularly important since literature was to provide models for future composition. All this comment on the 'letter' and style of the text was known as the *methodikē*. Origen's exegetical works abound in discussions of this kind. True his motivation is usually different – he is not training budding rhetoricians but potential 'sons of God'. So, often, it is analysis of the 'letter' that provides the key to the deeper (allegorical) meaning; for it is the identification of figures of speech, such as metaphor or symbol, or the use of etymology, or the consistently idiosyncratic usage or symbolism of a term in scripture, which provides the key. School methods furnished Origen with his exegetical procedures.

Real erudition, however, was displayed in the schools in identifying what the text might be alluding to. Background points had to be clarified; context expounded; gods and heroes identified; stories, myths, legends, histories, and so on, narrated, in order to ascertain fully what comparisons were implied or what esoteric sense was built into the text

---

[11] See Frances Young, 'The Rhetorical Schools and Their Influence on Patristic Exegesis', in *The Making of Orthodoxy. Essays in Honour of Henry Chadwick*, ed. Rowan Williams (Cambridge: CUP, 1989).
[12] I have developed this argument in the, as yet unpublished, Speaker's Lectures delivered in Oxford, 1992 and 1993. See also Bernhard Neuschäfer, *Origenes als Philologe*, 2 vols. (Basel: Friedrich Reinhardt, 1978).

by the author in order to be discerned only by those who knew enough to recognize what was going on. Through such commentary on texts (known as the *historikē*), pupils were assimilated into their cultural heritage. Such material also figures large in Origen's exegetical works, often showing off his learning, as when he tells the reader everything he knows about the production of pearls (*Commentary on Matthew* X.7). But such material also provided a vehicle for broadening the reader's knowledge of the great library of scriptural texts, drawing connections across the whole scope of the canon and creating a unitive vision of the truth revealed by inspiration of the Spirit. Here is an important clue to the process of substituting a different literary canon, not so well known to Gentile converts, but increasingly the basis of a new *paideia*, modelled on current school practice.

For Origen, the very creation of the world was motivated by the divine intent to educate fallen spirits back to perfection, and the principal conception of Christ's work of salvation is that of enlightening minds with revelation of truth through the incarnation of the Logos, which he conceived as God's accommodation to the human level of discourse, like parents or teachers using 'baby-language' for the sake of educating the immature. Perhaps then his adoption of school methods is scarcely surprising. But I would argue that it has its roots in already existing assumptions that the church is a learning community with scripture as its literary basis. My evidence lies in second-century material.

The Apologists of the second century had many charges against Christianity with which to deal, not least of which was their abandonment of Greek culture, including the traditional myths and legends which undergirded religious customs and were enshrined in the classical literature which provided the basis of education. It was assumed that nothing could be new and true. To meet this, they took over the argument of some contemporary scholars that the Greeks had copied many things from barbarians, who had priority in the development of astronomy, geometry and writing, astrology, magic and divination – indeed the original, universal wisdom was to be found among the Brahmans, Jews, Magi and Egyptians.[13]

So the Apologists argued that Greek philosophy was derived from Moses, who pre-dated Plato. They showed that the Jewish writings provided an account of origins superior to that of Hesiod: Theophilus of Antioch summarizes Genesis to give a programmatic history of culture including the origins of language, hunting, herding and agriculture, city-building, music, metalwork, warfare, priesthood, and many other con-

[13] As shown by Arthur J. Droge, *Homer or Moses?*, Hermeneutische Untersuchungen zur Theologie 26 (Tübingen: J. C. B. Mohr (Paul Siebeck), 1989), to which work I am indebted for the details in this and subsequent paragraphs.

temporary discussion topics. Moses was claimed as a more antique classic than Homer, since he pre-dated the Trojan War and gave the Egyptians their culture. Thus the Bible was ranged against Homer, Hesiod, Orpheus and the Sibyl, the ancient literature and prophetic oracles of Graeco-Roman tradition.

Jewish apologists like Josephus had anticipated much of this, but Gentile Christians had to go further, justifying their rejection of their own culture in preference for this barbarian body of literature. The argument that, because Christ had fulfilled the prophecies, the scriptures were proved true was not just directed at Jews; it also vindicated this cultural takeover, the substitution of a Logos enshrined in foreign books for the traditional rationality found in the classical canon.

The Jewish scriptures were at the centre of Christian debate in the second century, not only externally with Greeks and Jews, but also internally: Marcion wanted to replace both classic canons with exclusively Christian literature. What was going on was a battle of literatures. Why? Because, for Jews as well as Gentiles, literature was understood to be the source of wisdom about life, and so the basis of all training and education, whether in the practical skills of reading, writing and speaking, or in such fundamentals of lifestyle as ethical advice, moral examples, and philosophical truths. Origen's assumption that the church is a learning community, educating according to God's *paideia*, on the basis of the scriptures, had its roots in the tradition he inherited.

III. What Kind of Social Entity was the New Testament Church?

Some years ago I hazarded the suggestion that 'from a very early date the homily was the bishop's lecture on the literature that really mattered, namely the scriptures. Everyone studied week by week with the Christian "grammaticus"'.[14] The question is how far back can such a claim be made?

In important articles heralding the 'sociological approach' to the New Testament, E. A. Judge argued that the church of St Paul was to be understood less as a religious group, more as 'scholastic community'.[15] He designated Paul a 'sophist', a term justified by Paul's travelling and

[14] In Young, 'The Rhetorical Schools'.
[15] E. A. Judge, 'The Early Christians as a Scholastic Community', *Journal of Religious History* 1 (1960–1), pp. 1–8, 124–37; and 'St. Paul and Classical Society', *Jahrbuch für Antike und Christentum* 15 (1972), pp. 19–36. For the following paragraphs, see my fuller discussion in *The Theology of the Pastoral Epistles* (Cambridge: CUP, 1994).

preaching behaviour. He notes that Paul was sponsored by about forty patrons, and another forty or so persons can be identified among his professional following. He 'is always anxious about the transmission of the *logos* and the acquisition of *gnōsis* ... The Christian faith, therefore, as Paul expounds it, belongs with the doctrines of the philosophical schools rather than with the esoteric rituals of the mystery religions.' The parallels between Paul and travelling preachers of the Cynic type have been further explored by Abraham Malherbe.[16]

The sociological parallel to the early church most commonly accepted and most widely explored, however, is the household. Does this undermine the case? Judge thinks not. Ancient society was not made up of classes (high, middle, working, etc.), but competing vertical hierarchies: most people were in some sense dependants or 'hangers-on' – the clients, employees, tenants, servants, slaves, ex-slaves and kinsfolk beholden to a head of household. In such a society, Judge suggests, philosophical ideas did not circulate widely through 'the formal tradition of the great classical schools', or even through street-preachers, but through the talk that took place in household communities. This is confirmed by the fact that the role of the head of household in the education and instruction of those belonging to his little empire is a standard *topos* in ancient ethical texts.[17] To fulfil their teaching obligation, heads of households might employ a kind of philosopher-chaplain. This is where Paul and his patrons fit in so well.

But there is one other feature of the early church that also has to be drawn in, that is its analogies with the Jewish synagogue.[18] In the Diaspora, gatherings would take place, often in a household, for prayer and study of Torah, an activity which replaced the sacrificial rituals of the Temple for those remote from it. According to the 'new Schürer', 'the main object of these Sabbath meetings was not religious worship in the narrower sense, but religious teaching, i.e., instruction in the Torah'; so Philo is 'not far wrong when he calls the synagogues schools (*didaskaleia*)', describing them as places 'where "the ancestral philosophy" was cultivated and every kind of virtue taught'.[19] There is good evidence that Jewish schools and synagogues were influenced by the surrounding Hel-

---

[16] Abraham J. Malherbe, *Paul and the Popular Philosophers* (Minneapolis: Augsburg Fortress, 1989), reprints his important articles on this subject.

[17] David C. Verner, *The Household of God: The Social World of the Pastoral Epistles*, SBL Dissertation Series 71 (Chico: Scholars Press, 1983).

[18] See James Tunstead Burtchaell, *From Synagogue to Church. Public Services and Offices in the Earliest Christian Communities* (Cambridge: CUP, 1992), as well as my *Theology of the Pastorals*, chapters 4 and 5.

[19] The new Schürer, *The History of the Jewish People in the Age of Jesus Christ*, vol. 2, revised and edited by Geza Vermes, Fergus Millar and Matthew Black (Edinburgh: T. & T. Clark, 1979), pp. 424–5.

lenistic culture in which education had a high status – they simply substituted their own literature, the Torah and the Prophets, for the classics of Graeco-Roman culture. Like the philosophers, they sought in ancient texts true words of wisdom and the right way of life.

The earliest Christians were regarded as atheists because they did not practise recognizable religious rites. Rather they taught a way of life on the basis of a textbook received from the divine *Paidagogus*. That the earliest church was a learning community is borne out by subsequent development. True, more usual religious features crept in as analogies were drawn between Christian activities and mystery-religions, between sacrifice and the Christian Eucharist, and so on. But the aim of the church remained spiritual *paideia*.

16

Christian Education in a Capitalist Society: Money and God

JOHN M. HULL

INVITING theology to engage with the forms of society, Daniel Hardy says that this should be done not simply in symbolic terms but through analysis of particular social structures. It is not enough to offer merely transcendent symbols which suggest meanings; one must give a more practical shape to our life with God by relating these to our social structures: '... there is an inevitable interaction between concepts of social structure and those of God'.[1] Perhaps because theology has tended to emphasize the absoluteness of God, Hardy continues, whereas social theorists have generally emphasized the relativity of social structures, it has not been easy to establish such connections. Moreover, theology should seek to engage with the most universal aspects of social form, since if examples of limited applicability are taken, there will be a tendency to descend into 'sectionalised identity and ultimately to self-isolation'.[2]

This approach has important implications for the religious education of adults, which will be developed in relation to money. Not only is money one of the most universal of social structures, but it occupies a central place in that form of society which, originating in Europe and in North America, has established its influence if not its domination in all parts of the human world: capitalism. In a word, you can have money without capitalism, but you cannot have capitalism without money. There are close cognitive and affective links between concepts of money and concepts of God, which together constitute a climate of spiritual formation so powerful and so ubiquitous as to be almost invisible. A much neglected but nonetheless central task of adult education within the Christian traditions lies in unravelling these connections and exposing them to the challenge of Christian discipleship. Some of what will be said here is also relevant to Jewish adults, and the theme is highly significant

---

[1] Daniel W. Hardy, 'God and the Form of Society', in *The Weight of Glory: A Vision and Practice for Christian Faith: The Future of Liberal Theology. Essays for Peter Baelz*, eds. D. W. Hardy and P. H. Sedgwick (Edinburgh: T. & T. Clark, 1991), p. 132.
[2] Hardy, 'God and the Form of Society', p. 133.

for the self-understanding of all the great traditions of faith, many of which have developed their own distinctive response to money.[3]

I. THE NATURE OF MONEY

Various materials, both natural and artificial, have been used to facilitate exchange or as a medium of payment. These materials have included animal hides, cowrie shells, whisky and precious metals. Although some of these materials (whisky and animal hides) retain their use-value even when used primarily for exchange purposes, others (cowrie shells, silver and gold) have little use-value apart from ornamentation or ceremony, and may become mainly devoted to exchange values. In all such cases, these materials retain their concrete character. The whisky is measured and remains whisky; the gold is weighed to make sure that the right amount is being exchanged for the goods offered; even the cowrie shells are examined for their number and quality.

The move from the concrete to the abstract took place with the creation of coins in the Greek cities of the eastern Aegean in the seventh century BCE. The essential features of the coin are stamped upon it: a numerical equivalent and an issuing authority. The latter may have been a temple, a city or a state. The first feature meant that the coin represents quantitative value expressed in abstract terms; the quality and the concrete attributes of the coin are irrelevant.

It took centuries to realize fully that the reality of the coin lay in this abstract relationship rather than in its physical properties. Gradually it became apparent that the number-value and the source of authority did not have to be printed upon a precious metal or upon any metal whatever, but could equally be printed upon paper or written in a ledger or preserved electronically. Although in principle the coin was from its beginning abstract, the process of realizing this can be called 'the spiritualization of money'.[4]

Money became unique amongst the commodities. Indeed, it became

---

[3] Thomas Crump, *The Phenomenon of Money* (London: Routledge & Kegan Paul, 1981), pp. 283–9. Crump distinguishes between pre-literary religions where the link between money and the sacred is maintained and the literary religions where money is generally regarded as being part of the profane world. Within the literary religions, Crump distinguishes the western traditions (Judaism, Christianity and Islam) from the oriental traditions (Hinduism and Buddhism). The separation of religion from money is sharper in the Western religions although throughout both Europe and Asia money has long been established as autonomous and the various institutions of money bear little stamp of their indigenous religious culture.

[4] Georg Simmel, *The Philosophy of Money*, ed. David Frisby (London: Routledge, 1978, second edition 1990), p. 198.

the commodity which represented the mutual relationships or the social values attributed to all other commodities.[5] Having no intrinsic properties of any use, money became the most generally useful of all objects. Having no value (you can't eat or drink a coin, wear it for warmth or make love to it) money became supremely valuable as the representative of all other values. Because money is the means to all ends, it quickly becomes an end in itself.[6] Those who first found money convenient because it facilitated 'selling in order to buy' soon discovered that money was even more convenient because it made possible 'buying in order to sell'.[7] As the most purely general and most fluid expression of human will and desire, money quickly established its autonomy, an autonomy which was the very incarnation or the very spiritualization (depending upon whether you emphasize the concrete nature of the symbol or its universal meaning) of the autonomy of the human will and reason.

It was in the presence of coins that people first encountered things made in space and time, which transcended both space and time.[8] Although the wine might go sour and the iron become rusty, the coin had much the same value here as there, tomorrow as today. Its essence seemed to lie beneath its qualities. Although it could certainly be hoarded in a treasure-trove, it did not reach its full flexibility as money until it was circulated, in and out of the commodities which represented it. Money gave an immense impetus to the scope of the merchant classes, and merchant capital began its long career.

Human beings have now lived with money for more than two and a half millennia. Philosophers from Aristotle to Kant and beyond have explored the meaning of money, but its influence upon habits of thought and social relations goes beyond the overt philosophical interest which money has attracted.[9] The impact of money in moulding human life including perception and cognition can only be compared to that of language. Language and money are the two great institutions, created by human beings, which, having attained a significant degree of autonomy, now recreate us in their own likeness. Each institution offers a subtle interplay between the internal life of the individual and the wider life of

[5] Simmel, *Philosophy*, p. 120, etc.

[6] Simmel, *Philosophy*, p. 232, describes money as 'a completely engrossing final purpose'.

[7] George Thompson, *The First Philosophers*, Studies in Ancient Greek Society 2 (London: Lawrence & Wishart, 1961² (first edition 1955)), p. 195.

[8] Alfred Sohn-Rethel, *Intellectual and Manual Labour: A Critique of Epistemology* (London: Macmillan, 1978), p. 56.

[9] Marc Shell, *Money, Language and Thought* (Berkeley: University of California Press, 1982), especially the essay on 'Dialectic and Monetary Form in Kant and Hegel', pp. 131ff.; and Sohn-Rethel, *Intellectual and Manual Labour*. Sohn-Rethel attempts a transcendental reduction of the concept of money modelled upon Kant's transcendental reduction of cognition.

society, between the subjective and the objective.[10] Each thus occupies what Donald Winnicott would have called 'intermediate space'[11] and is thus a fruitful ground both for human development into increased adaptability and maturity, and also for the play of fantasy, regression and self-deception.

Money tends to inflate the sense of personal freedom. Because we are the speakers, we do not notice very much the language which speaks through us. Because we are the buyers and sellers, we do not notice very much the structure of money which envelops us. Nothing appears to be so much my own as what I say and spend. The truth is, however, that just as there is no private language so there is no private money. It is as social selves bound together in solidarity that language and money create us. The institutions which made social intercourse in both ideas and materials so human have become the source of division and domination. In this capacity, however, language and money conceal themselves. They actively resist clarification and disclosure.

II. THE CONCEPT OF MONEY AND THE CONCEPT OF GOD

Matthew and Luke report that Jesus said it is impossible to serve God and Mammon (Matt. 6.24; Lk. 16.13). 'In reality, money in its psychological form, as the absolute means and thus as the unifying point of innumerable sequences of purposes, possesses a significant relationship to the notion of God – a relationship that only psychology, which has the privilege of being unable to commit blasphemy, may disclose'.[12] In money, all commodities meet for purposes of comparison. All their various qualities disappear and they are reduced to a single standard. Money is thus the meeting point of innumerable particularities, the concrete in which all other concretes are related, the point at which the one and the many coincide, the little which encompasses the big, since each coin is related to the entire coinage and thus to the entire world of things.

Referring to Nicholas de Cusa, Simmel remarks that God is indeed the coincidence of opposites, the one who is like money in that as the ground, representative and equivalent of all things, God is the most general and at the same time the most specific of things, both in time and yet timeless, in space yet not confined anywhere. There is no doubt, Simmel suggests,

[10] Simmel, *Philosophy*, p. 120, compares coins with words; see also p. 470.
[11] Donald W. Winnicott, *Playing and Reality* (New York: Tavistock, 1971); cf. Simmel, *Philosophy*, pp. 68, 80.
[12] Simmel, *Philosophy*, p. 236.

that the feelings which money arouses 'possess a psychological similarity to those aroused by the idea of God in the believer ... Money provides an elevated position above the particular and a confidence in its omnipotence ...'.[13] Being thus engrossed in the nature of money gives one a view from above upon the nature of life, rather similar to the point of view which the believer can adopt. Just as one struggles restlessly until one obtains the supreme satisfaction of the ultimate resting place in God, so also the struggle and the agonized quest for money reaches its sense of 'blissful peace' and achievement when the money is won. In both cases, consciousness attains the blissful awareness of standing at the 'focal point of existence'.

> The frequent animosity of the religious and clerical mentality towards money matters may perhaps be traced to its instinct for the similarity in psychological form between the highest economic and the highest cosmic unity and to its awareness of the danger of competition between monetary and religious interests – a danger that has been shown to exist not only where the substance of life is economic but also where it is religious.[14]

So striking are these parallels that something beyond mere parallelism is at stake. The links between the concept of money and that of God are found not only at the subjective level, in the sense of ultimate concern as a psychological phenomenon, but objectively as well in the structure of the concept. 'Money is the symbol in the empirical world of the inconceivable unity of being, out of which the world, in all its breadth, diversity, energy and reality flows'.[15] The concept of money is thus akin to that of being itself. Free from all particularities, it can sometimes be rightly described as liquid money, taking the shape of all things, flowing into the form of all interests, uniting all subjectivities, relating all things and yet being free from the particular characteristics of anything. It is the closest analogue we have to the power of being itself, since money offers no resistance to any intention but supports the positive value of every entity. Money is 'a measure of things without being measured itself, a purpose that can be realised fully only by an endless development'.[16] Money represents the perfect flux and balance of absolute universal lawfulness. God, by the same token, is the unmoved mover,[17] the One whose universal availability corresponds to his omnipresence. The same

---

[13] Simmel, *Philosophy*, p. 237.
[14] Simmel, *Philosophy*, p. 237.
[15] Simmel, *Philosophy*, p. 497.
[16] Simmel, *Philosophy*, p. 511.
[17] Sohn-Rethel, *Intellectual and Manual Labour*, p. 53f., 'Abstract Movement'.

Lord is Lord of all and bestows his riches upon all who call upon him (Rom. 10.12).

Going beyond the analysis offered by Simmel, Sohn-Rethel and Thompson, a biblical theology for adult education must distinguish between God as a universal and God as having a preference for the poor. Similarly, one may emphasize the formal universality of money and its undifferentiated power to impose a pattern upon all values, and (on the other hand) what we might call the preferential power of money. It is noteworthy that Simmel pays very little attention to this latter aspect.[18] Simmel does refer to the tendency of money to cluster together, thus giving an advantage to the person who already possesses a great deal of it.

> Through the process of centralisation that is inherent in money, the preliminary stage of accumulation in the hands of scattered individuals has been surmounted. The centralisation of monetary transactions on the stock exchanges counteracted the superior power that individuals could wield by monetary means.[19]

Simmel's analysis at this point, however, is purely formal. Instead of the wealthy individuals being scattered, their monetary resources are concentrated and unified in the stock exchange, which does indeed centralize and thus balance out the transactions of those who participate in it. It never seems to occur to Simmel that if money has a tendency to concentrate in the hands of a few people, who may furthermore institutionalize their monetary interests in a solid phalanx, there must be others, perhaps many others, perhaps most others, who discover that money is sucked away by this very same centripetal force.

It is significant that Simmel distinguished between the character of religion, spirituality and the law on the one hand and that of money on the other, remarking that while money offers its services equally to every purpose within its sphere of influence, religion, spirituality, law and metaphysics tend to become partisan, ultimately allying themselves with one interest or another. Thus money 'does not exist in an antagonistic relationship to other things as do the other forces as soon as they transform their general meaning into a particular one'.[20] Simmel thinks that money preserves its completely indifferent and impartial quality even

---

[18] Simmel was, of course, aware of the misery of poverty (e.g. p. 120) but his emphasis is almost always upon the universality of money rather than money as an instrument of oppression. Vilar reminds his readers that 'this so-called egalitarian quality is one of money's main enigmas', indeed, it is one of the 'deceptive' aspects of money: Pierre Vilar, *A History of Gold and Money* (London: NLB, 1976), p. 9.
[19] Simmel, *Philosophy*, p. 504.
[20] Simmel, *Philosophy*, p. 469.

when it is negotiating between people, which is why most disputes can be solved through money. Simmel does not sufficiently emphasize the power of money to influence the law and that religion can be the expression of the power of the wealthy.

If money adapts itself to every human intention, it is available for the intentions of those who would exploit and oppress others. To say that it is equally available to the poor and oppressed would mean but little since most money is concentrated in the hands of the oppressors. The truth is that Simmel's book is about the philosophy of money, not about the politics of poverty. It is typical of his approach that when he writes about the links between spirituality and money, he emphasizes the power of money to create 'an abstract existence', 'an island of subjectivity, a secret, closed-off sphere of privacy'.[21] Simmel sees spirituality mainly in aesthetic terms, rather than as an ethical or political quality.

Just as we may ask whether money is not only universal but also has a preference for the rich, so we may ask whether God, who is universal, also expresses a preference for the poor. When the universality is emphasized, God may be interpreted as the superstructure of financial consciousness.

This is the emphasis which we find in Marxist authors such as Thompson and Sohn-Rethel. The remarkable book by the latter takes not so much money itself but the moment of commodity exchange as being the base from which the superstructure of financial consciousness arises. While Kant was correct in arguing that the presuppositions of the knowing mind lie beyond the mind itself, he was mistaken in locating these structures in the transcendental *a priori*. The so-called *a priori* elements arise from differences in the outlook of the mental and the manual labourer. They may be discovered in an analysis of the exchange relationship in which the nature of money reaches its most abstract form. The social origin of its philosophical *a priori* is not recognized by the European bourgeois mind. That illustrates the fetish-like quality of these conceptions and the false consciousness which they generate.[22] It is because of this abstract quality that there is an affinity between exchange relations and spirituality, while the separation of thought from intention in the exchange transaction[23] tends to internalize the spirituality. Thus we reach the notion of internal spirituality as a falsifying projection of exchange relationships. Likewise, God is abstract, spiritual, unified, transcendent, mysterious and so on.

[21] Simmel, *Philosophy*, p. 469.
[22] Sohn-Rethel, *Intellectual and Manual Labour*, pp. 27, 72, 'The Phenomenon of the Exchange Abstraction'.
[23] Sohn-Rethel, *Intellectual and Manual Labour*, p. 26, comments on the emergence of the private imagination.

When the distinction between the rich and the poor is emphasized, then the preferential nature of money and the preferential bias of God towards the poor will emerge. For all of its power in unmasking the identity of the concept of the universal and abstract God as the fetish-like projection of money in the exchange relationship, Marxist theory finds it difficult to account for those cases where the concept of God is that of one who has a preference for the poor. A striking example of this is found in the otherwise excellent book by Thompson previously referred to. 'In the Hebrew prophets', Thompson observes, 'for the first time in history, the dispossessed peasantry found a voice – a voice preserved in writing and treasured from that day to this by generations of European peasants struggling against the same wrongs and inspired with the same hopes'.[24] As in other ancient oriental monarchies, Thompson suggests, the idea of the king was imposed upon the people by the ruling class as a means of consolidating its power, and had the Hebrew kingdom remained united and strong no doubt the eighth-century prophets would have been suppressed. As for the vision of God in these prophets, 'its moral nobility springs from its historical origin as a vision of the classless society that had passed away and was to come again'.[25]

This brief account is quite unsatisfactory. Why did not a similar voice of protest break through when monarchical institutions were temporarily weakened in other ancient oriental states? Thompson makes no reference to the Exodus tradition and does not appear to realize that the prophets of the eighth century already stood in a stream of social and political protest. In that sense Thompson is much inferior to his Marxist contemporary Ernst Bloch, whose *Das Prinzip Hoffnung* was published in German in 1979, between the first and second editions of Thompson's own book. In his earlier discussion of totemism, Thompson had remarked that 'the ideological superstructure has developed to the point of reacting on the social organisation out of which it has grown'.[26] If, however, in the God of the Bible we already find a creative superstructure capable of transforming the social relations of society, then there is a possibility that theology itself could become an educational force and even a revolutionary power.

This is hinted at but not overtly acknowledged towards the end of Thompson's argument. Discussing conditions in the late Republican period, he notes the growing gulf between the rich and the poor, and that while the wealthy lived in appalling luxury, the philosophers had not a word to say on behalf of the poor. They themselves were almost without exception aristocrats living comfortable lives. They had little or no con-

[24] Thompson, *The First Philosophers*, p. 100.
[25] Thompson, *The First Philosophers*, p. 101.
[26] Thompson, *The First Philosophers*, p. 55.

tact with the labouring people, who still had a healthy view of the world because of the praxis imposed upon them by their labour. At this point, and without explanation, Thompson quotes in full the *Magnificat*:[27] 'He has filled the hungry with good things, and the rich he has sent empty away' (Lk. 1.53). Thompson regards Christianity as the heir to both the false consciousness of Greek philosophy and the prophetic protest of the Hebrew tradition. These two aspects of the Christian tradition have jostled each other ever since, and this is the point at which the educational task of the church with its adults must commence.

III. ADULT CHRISTIAN EDUCATION AND MONEY

Much Christian adult education concerning money is confined to the use of money by the individual Christian, often in terms of Christian stewardship or the practice of charitable giving. The biblical teaching on tithing or St Paul's collection of Christian aid for the Jerusalem church may be used as models. This approach is inadequate because:

1. It is confined to one aspect of money – money as individual gift – and says nothing about the other functions of money such as its exchange function and its pricing function.

2. It does not deal with money as a social institution and thus fails to empower Christian adults for the lay apostolate within the secular world.

3. In its treatment of the Bible as a resource for educating about money, this approach seldom refers to the socio-economic conditions in the ancient Near East nor in the Graeco-Roman world during the early Christian period. Biblical interpretation is thus narrowed to the ethical issues seen in the light of a theology of individual responsibility. The significance of the teaching of Jesus regarding the Great Reversal of the relationship between the rich and the poor can only be fully understood in the light of the economic situation of Palestine during his lifetime.[28]

4. Although the teaching of Jesus regarding money and wealth is of central importance for Christian education on this subject, one cannot understand or apply the sayings of Jesus if two thousand years in the

[27] Thompson, *The First Philosophers*, p. 333.
[28] Justo L. Gonzalez, *Faith and Wealth: A History of Early Christian Ideas on the Origin, Significance and Use of Money* (San Francisco: Harper & Row, 1990); and Pedrito V. Maynard-Reid, *Poverty and Wealth in James* (Maryknoll: Orbis Books, 1987).

evolution of money are ignored. In the study of Christian medical ethics, it is taken for granted that advances in medical technology must be understood if the ethical situations arising from them are to be dealt with responsibly. It is no less true that the changes in money which have taken place in the last ten or twenty years must be tackled if there is to be any responsible education.[29]

The difficulties in undertaking such a programme of education are implicit in the body of this essay. Money, like language, is so much a part of our daily lives that it hardly attracts attention as a subject demanding analysis. One is immersed in it, and the educational process which requires a detachment from it will encounter resistance. People with sight do not know that they have sight; they are not aware of the extent to which their thought patterns, personalities and intercourse with the world are patterned by their eyesight. The same is true of our participation in money.

The resistance which such an educational programme will encounter is, however, more deep-rooted. It is the nature of money to be secretive. Not only is there a strong social taboo against talking about money and against disclosing one's personal income and one's family budget, but financial institutions are shrouded in mystery.[30] The force which resists demystification is undoubtedly fear, springing from the realization that changes in lifestyle may be demanded.

This fear will be greatest amongst those who have most to lose, and these constitute a certain class or category of possessors and users of money. Individual interest will thus be collated into social class interest, and the well known techniques of resistance will come into play.[31] In the case of Christian adults, many of these techniques will be of a theological nature.[32] Jesus said that his kingdom was not of this world, so why are we studying money? The unravelling of these theological expressions of personal and social class interest will be a major task in the educational programme.[33]

The following points could usefully be borne in mind.

1. The study of money should be multi-disciplinary. Philosophy, soci-

---

[29] Howard M. Wachtel, *The Money Mandarins: The Making of a Supranational Economic Order* (London: Pluto, 1990).

[30] 'Bankers ... are notoriously secretive, are reluctant to grant interviews, and have no tradition as memoirists ...', Watchtel, *Money Mandarins*, p. xvii.

[31] Anna Freud, *The Ego and the Mechanisms of Defence* (London: Hogarth, 1968 (first published 1936)).

[32] Social and Community Planning Research, *The Gospel, The Churches and The Poor* (London: Christian Aid, June 1994), ch. 6 'Coping with Emotional Reactions'.

[33] I have discussed this problem in *What Prevents Christian Adults from Learning?* (Philadelphia: TPI, 1991), but not in connection with money.

ology, history, anthropology, economics, literature and theology; all have a part to play. Since the tendency of resistance is to compartmentalize one's assumptions about money, the educational programme must insist upon connections.[34]

2. Adults are best educated when they are enabled to move freely in and out of theory. Theory and practice should alternate. First, one has a session on the theory of banking, including various categories of banks and the various functions of banks. Next, one makes contact with the public relations department of a bank and arranges for an educational visit. Or again, one organizes group discussions around the question as to whether people experience money differently at different stages of their own lives and whether there are characteristic attitudes towards money on the part of children, adults in middle life and retired people. Next, one introduces the James Fowler theory of faith development, opening up the possibility that this might interpret the previously reported materials.

3. In order to overcome the misleading and superficial familiarity of money, an education concerning money should deal with problems. This subject lends itself to a workship approach in which teams of men and women undertake to collect and report on various issues such as the history and present policies of the International Monetary Fund and the World Bank, the nature and causes of third world debt, and the present situation and prospects of the gold mining industry. The technique is to confront mystification head on. Vagueness is a defence mechanism. When a study group finds that it is becoming vague, it should be trained to respond by resisting the vagueness.

4. Poverty is the other face of money. The life of St Francis of Assisi should be considered as a protest against the birth of the commodity culture.[35] Attitudes to poverty are created by attitudes to wealth. The examples of adult education offered by William B. Kennedy and his colleagues in *Pedagogies for the Non Poor*[36] deserve close study. In the report recently published by Christian Aid[37] attitudes to poverty are related to a number of modes of church allegiance, each of which has a characteristic theological stance. This report offers interesting educational material for the local church. To what extent does my local church conform to one of the theological types illustrated in the report? Are attitudes to poverty consistent with this mode of allegiance, as the Christian Aid report would lead us to expect?

5. The theological education of adult Christians concerning money

---

[34] For a vivid and entertaining book suitable for adult study see Michael Kidron and Ronald Segal, *The Book of Business, Money and Power* (London: Pan Books, 1987).
[35] Leonardo Boff, *St Francis: A Model for Human Liberation* (London: SCM, 1985).
[36] Alice Fraser Evans, Robert A. Evans and William B. Kennedy, *Pedagogies for the Non Poor* (Maryknoll: Orbis Books, 1987).
[37] Christian Aid, *The Gospel, The Churches and The Poor*.

should focus upon two things. First, the structural affinity between money and God should be explored. What are the God-like qualities of money? What are the money-like qualities of God? Consider the implications of the financial metaphors used in theology, e.g. Christ paying the price of our sins, or the use of money in the parables of Jesus. Secondly, the differential option for the poor should always be emphasized. This becomes a question of one's fundamental theological perspective. Education concerning money is part of the programme for the evangelization of the bourgeois church.[38] The character of such an educational programme would differ considerably when conducted amongst people who were on the poverty line themselves. The gospel is not good news for the rich. The rich young ruler went away sorrowful. What is the cost of discipleship for Christians from the wealthy world today? Education concerning money must always be illuminated by a passion for social justice.

6. In using the Bible, the broad context should always be kept in mind. Money is the most general of things, and the various attitudes in the Bible towards things should be studied as the context for understanding money. Collect fifty or one hundred sayings or references in the Bible about things. Study these more or less at random in relationship to the viewing of TV advertisements on video. Similarly, although the teaching of Jesus about money is very important, this should be seen as part of his more general approach to social status.

CONCLUSION

It is not the task of the church to manage the world's money. It is the task of the church to proclaim good news to the poor. In this connection, it is necessary for the church to attack the mismanagement of money (and the church itself is not exempt) and to enable church affiliated men and women to distinguish between money as a means of exploiting the poor and money as a means of creating social justice. Such an education is an essential part of the engagement of the church in contemporary life, which must bring the church to a critical relationship towards capitalism. Christian education cannot solve all these problems but, at its best, it can make resistance more difficult, and can bring Christian adults nearer to the challenges of discipleship.

---

[38] J. B. Metz, *The Emergent Church: The Future of Christianity in a Post-Bourgeois World* (London: SCM, 1981).

17

Intellectual Inquiry and Spiritual Formation

DIOGENES ALLEN

THERE is a noticeable gap between academic theology and the practice of Christian devotion. Consider, for example, the following statement of the agenda for theologians by James McClendon that opened his review of Geoffrey Wainwright's *Doxology*, an approach to systematic theology from the standpoint of the praise of God:

> The major problems facing Christian theology in the Western world at the present time – problems neither new or transient but persistent since the Enlightenment or earlier – may be summarized under the headings of RELEVANCE (the gap between modes of thought available to theology and those prevailing in the wider society), PLURALISM (the conscious plurality of the world religions, but also the ongoing plurality within Christianity itself), and (inclusive of these two) TRUTH or TRUTHFULNESS (the question, whether any existing theology may be judged true by the standards of truth acceptable in general, or even in the Christian community) ... Theology has ... proved to be a frustrating discipline to many intelligent Christians, who perceive its standing problems and deplore its lack of headway despite its many changes of method and angles of approach.[1]

Although McClendon himself does not approach theology as he has described it, he has described the approach that is typical of a large part of academic theology today. For example, in the widely used textbook, *Christian Theology*, edited by Peter Hodgson and Robert H. King, each chapter summarizes traditional Christian doctrines around one of the classical *loci*, examines the challenges posed to the traditional doctrines in modern times, and then gives a constructive response in terms set by the Enlightenment challenges. It is this last feature – a reconstruction in terms set by the Enlightenment challenges – to which I object. It is to approach theology from issues that are primarily *extrinsic* to the nature

[1] James McClendon, *Faith and Philosophy* 3/2 (1986), pp. 222–3.

of God, and not from issues that arise *in the first instance* from the nature of God and ourselves in relation to God. The latter problems are primarily *intrinsic* to theology, and for that reason arise in every age and culture. They do not have to be characterized by such qualifications as 'the Western world' and 'since the Enlightenment'.

I do not mean to imply that extrinsic issues are irrelevant to theology. Quite the contrary, they are integral to the theological task of relating all things to God. But when theologians have not worked through problems intrinsic to theology for themselves, they miss the spiritual formation that can result from this engagement, with the result that extrinsic problems lead them to regard theology as a 'frustrating discipline' and to 'deplore its lack of headway'. The treatment of extrinsic problems while neglecting those that are intrinsic also greatly contributes to the gap between intellectual inquiry and devotion.

I. THE ROLE OF SPIRITUAL FORMATION IN INTELLECTUAL INQUIRY

Intrinsic to theology is the nature of the reality to be known and our human capacity to know that reality. God's essence far surpasses the power of our senses and intellect to know it. This is suggested by the absence of any representation of God in the Holy of Holies in the Temple of ancient Israel. It underlies Thomas Aquinas' claim that God is not a member of any genus, and the stress in neo-orthodoxy that God is not a being among beings, but wholly other. The only way God can be known is by God revealing Godself. God has done so in many ways, but God has most clearly revealed God's intentions to the people of ancient Israel and above all in Jesus Christ. In addition to our inability fully to comprehend God intellectually, even with God's revelation, our hearts and minds have been perverted by disobedience or sin. The reception of God's revelation requires repentance; an increase in our understanding of God's revelation requires continuing spiritual growth. As it is expressed by Wittgenstein,

> In religion every level of devoutness must have its appropriate form of expression which has no sense at a lower level. This doctrine, which means something at a higher level, is null and void for someone who is still at the lower level; he *can* only understand it *wrongly* and so these words are *not* valid for such a person.[2]

[2] Ludwig Wittgenstein, *Culture and Value*, trans. Peter Winch (Oxford: Blackwell, 1980, 2nd ed.), p. 32e.

An increase in our understanding of God leads in turn to an increase in our love for God and our love for neighbour.

The difficulty of knowing God because of God's nature and our condition clearly implies that in theology intellectual inquiry cannot properly be detached inquiry. For example, Juliana of Norwich compares knowledge of God to wounds. She specifies three wounds: the wound of contrition (repentance and continuing repentance for one's disobedience); the wound of compassion (love of neighbour); and the wound of longing (love for God).[3]

People can of course be taught theology and, given intelligence and diligence, even perform well as theologians, but this may be no more than a knowledge *about* God. Richard of St Victor stresses that it is useless for us to know about God unless we have a longing for God:

> ... it is vain that we grow in riches of divine knowledge unless by them the fire of love is increased in us. For love arising from knowledge and knowledge coming from love must always grow in us, each ministering to the increase of the other by mutual growth, and love and knowledge developing in turn.[4]

Both Juliana and Richard understand the Christian life as involving an ascent toward God or becoming closer to God. This understanding is common to all Christian spirituality. A divorce between intellectual inquiry and spiritual formation occurs when intellectual inquiry is not concerned with ascent toward God. This happens quite easily because spiritual ascent is not required for discussing doctrines. Doctrines themselves do not include our response, whereas our response is the focus of devotion. The crucial question for ascent to God is how may we find God, or be present to God, who is beyond the capacity of our senses and intellect? As we have said, only by God's self-revelation. But in order for us to know God not only must God reveal Godself, we must also respond by receiving God's self-revelation. It is only by spiritual formation that we can respond, and thus begin our journey into God. Our lives must increasingly be formed by God. We rise to God through an increase in knowledge and love of God, and the goal of our ascent is to culminate in some form of union with God. There is no detached knowing of God any more than there is a detached love of neighbour or a detached attitude toward one's failure to obey God.

Where there is academic inquiry concerning what people with a commitment to God have said, thought, and done, we have the study of

---

[3] Juliana of Norwich, *Showings*, trans. Edmund Colledge and James Walsh (New York: Paulist Press, 1978), p. 127.
[4] Richard of St Victor, *Selections from Contemplation*, trans. Clare Kirchberger (London: Faber & Faber, 1957), p. 161.

religion, not theology. The Bible and theology are approached historically, sociologically, psychologically, and politically. Now that the study
of religion has become normative in most academic centres, intellectual
inquiry has increasingly become identified with these approaches. Theologians find themselves required to justify their work in terms of extrinsic
standards, such as McClendon mentions. This is not wholly illegitimate,
and it can be valuable. But a preoccupation with extrinsic issues has
caused many theologians to neglect the intellectual inquiry that is intrinsic to theology, inquiry which requires personal involvement and an
aspiration to know and love God.

For most of Christian history, intellectual inquiry and spiritual aspiration toward God went hand-in-hand. For example, Anselm in his *Proslogion* begins, as he always does when he engages in intellectual inquiry,
with meditations intended to awaken the mind from its torpor:

> Come now, little man,
> turn aside for a while from your daily employment,
> escape for a moment from the tumult of your thoughts.
> Put aside your weighty cares,
> let your burdensome distractions wait,
> free yourself awhile for God
> and rest awhile in him.
> Enter the inner chamber of your soul,
> shut out everything except God
> and that which can help you in seeking him,
> and when you have shut the door, seek him.
> Now, my whole heart, say to God,
> 'I seek your face,
> Lord, it is your face I seek'.[5]

Anselm believes that to increase our knowledge of God through intellectual inquiry we must on *each occasion* of inquiry begin by seeking to
free ourselves from all distractions so that we may desire God with our
whole heart. Rather than having our mind and heart filled with a multi-
tude of desires, pulling us in different directions, we must focus on God,
whom we do not see, but whom we hope to come to know face to face by
increasing our understanding of God. The mind is to be aroused from its
torpor 'to the contemplation of God' (p. 239) by being reminded that
God is not a member of the created order, but dwells 'in light inaccessible' (p. 240). Accordingly Anselm confesses, 'I cannot seek you unless
you show me how, and I will never find you unless you show yourself to
me' (p. 243). These remarks, as well as lamentation over the effects of

---

[5] *The Prayers and Meditations of Saint Anselm with the Proslogion*, trans. Benedicta Ward
(Harmondsworth: Penguin, 1973), p. 239.

our disobedience which hinders our search, and a fervent expression of hope because of our redemption by Christ, fill about nine times as much space as the above quoted passage. Anselm concludes this meditation with the remark that in our intellectual inquiry we are not to expect fully to understand God:

> I am not trying to make my way to your height, for my understand-ing is in no way equal to that, but I do desire to understand a little of your truth which my heart already believes and loves. (p. 244)

This heartfelt meditation occurs *before* Anselm presents his ontologi-cal proof. In this reflection on God's existence, Anselm comes to under-stand that God's existence is not like the existence of all else that does exist or might exist. God's existence is a necessary existence. Through this intellectual inquiry, Anselm has come to understand something he had not understood before, but which he had believed and loved. He has found a precise way to distinguish God and the world, and thereby to prevent the mind from confusing God with what is not God.[6] With this understanding, he has now drawn closer to God whom he has been seeking.

Robert Sokolowski has argued convincingly in *The God of Faith and Reason* that Anselm's preparation for intellectual inquiry is intrinsic to the inquiry itself and, more generally, that without spiritual formation there is no discernment of God in theological inquiry.[7] We cannot here reproduce Sokolowski's argument, but it is clear that Anselm's inquiry is motivated by a love for God, and that he believes that his inquiry has resulted in an increased understanding of God. His intellectual inquiry is concerned with matters that are intrinsic to theology, namely the nature of God and our human condition. They are transcultural matters. They should be present, affecting any theological inquiry in any culture and at any period of time, because God's nature does not change and all human beings are limited in their capacity to know God and suffer from the effects of sin.

Anselm is convinced that theological inquiry is possible only for someone who has become converted to a spiritual perspective. His inquiry, like that of his master, Augustine, is based on belief. He writes, 'I do not seek to understand so that I may believe, but I believe so that I may understand; and what is more, I believe that unless I do believe I shall not understand' (p. 244).

Anselm does not seek to *arrive* at belief by a study of the world and the views of the world prevalent in the various fields of inquiry. Nor does he

---

[6] We will see how useful this is to Bonaventure.
[7] Robert Sokolowski, *The God of Faith and Reason* (Notre Dame: University of Notre Dame Press, 1982).

think that he has to solve various problems extrinsic to theology *before* he can believe and, that unless he does so, he cannot engage in theological inquiry. Rather, Anselm, as a practising Christian, has been engaged with the reality of God and, because of that engagement, he believes and loves, and seeks *more* understanding in order to know and love God better. His frustrations spring from God's hiddenness, our human limitations, and our disobedience.

I submit that one who has wrestled with these intrinsic matters, as has Anselm, regards the problems extrinsic to theology differently from those who have not been shaped or formed by wrestling with the problems intrinsic to theology. One does not think that one must deal with various extrinsic problems, such as McClendon has described, *before* one can engage in theological inquiry. Above all, one does not think that one may somehow *arrive* at a spiritual perspective by approaching theological inquiry from a naturalistic perspective. It should be no surprise that theologians who neglect the study of questions that are intrinsic to theology, and who do not become formed by this study, should find theology a frustrating discipline and deplore lack of progress with solving problems extrinsic to theology.

If one has spent, as I have, most of one's academic life wrestling with problems extrinsic to theology, such as those posed by Logical Positivism, and by the modes of thought prevalent since the Enlightenment, and by the recent concern with pluralism, one is indeed pleased and even relieved when one believes one has found a way to deal with these and other extrinsic problems. But one's engagement with them is not marked with the kind of anxiety which fears that; unless one finds a way to deal with them, theology and the faith upon which theology is based cannot be held with intellectual integrity. If one's need for redemption and one's aspirations are operative, and if one has wrestled with the spiritual ascent toward God found in all major theologians prior to the Enlightenment, and in some of them since, one's concern with extrinsic matters is serious but not decisive for one's theological inquiry. This is one of the great benefits of studying those theologians who wrestle with questions intrinsic to theology for those whose task is also to be primarily concerned with intellectual inquiry. To be unengaged and to be spiritually unformed or even malformed does indeed open a theologian of today to the frustrations and despondency that McClendon so frankly states.

II. THE ROLE OF INTELLECTUAL INQUIRY IN SPIRITUAL FORMATION

Not all forms of spiritual formation are concerned with intellectual inquiry. For example, Bernard of Clairvaux focuses much of his attention on the earthly life of Jesus, especially on his crucifixion, and seeks to be emotionally affected by gazing on them lovingly. By virtue of an increasingly purified love, he hopes to achieve a closer and closer unity with God. Bernard is not concerned with intellectual inquiry, as were the academic theologians of the universities. He is quite content with the doctrinal orthodoxy he inherited.

Ignatius Loyola owes a great deal to the affective spirituality of Bernard. In his *Spiritual Exercises* he relies heavily on the use of the imagination. We are to bring before our mind's eye various events of the life of Jesus as vividly as possible, so that we may be affected by them. As we increasingly commit ourselves to Christ's kingdom, we are to seek to discern God's intention for us that we might do God's will. Thus Loyola's use of contemplation differs from the use of contemplation in speculative spirituality. There contemplation is to increase our understanding and love of God until it culminates in knowledge of God face to face. Loyola's spirituality is explicitly a *practical* spirituality. Contemplation is used to form one so that one is better able to discern and to do God's will in daily life.

Not all speculative spirituality is concerned with intellectual inquiry. For example, Evagrius of Pontus, who is so important for the ascetic theology of the Eastern church and, through John Cassian, a major influence on the Western church, focused almost exclusively on pure prayer as the means to knowledge of created beings and to a knowledge of God face to face. Continuing intellectual inquiry into the meaning of Christian doctrines by him or others seemed to have no role in his understanding of our spiritual ascent.

There are, however, some types of speculative spirituality in which intellectual inquiry is integral to the spirituality. We can see this clearly in Bonaventure. In *Disputed Questions on the Mystery of the Trinity*, Bonaventure is engaged in intellectual inquiry concerning the movement within the divine life of the Trinity. He subsequently uses what he has learned from this intellectual inquiry in his spiritual classic, *The Soul's Journey into God*. What he has learned from his intellectual inquiry forms the rungs of a ladder, so to speak, for our ascent into the life of God. Bonaventure's inquiry into the movement in the inner life of God is guided by what God has revealed Godself to be, Father, Son, and Holy Spirit. From what God has revealed Godself to be, Bonaventure seeks to understand the reasons or the principles of the divine movement in God. Although Bonaventure is deeply influenced by Augustine in other works, his reflections on the Trinity are based on an analysis of goodness, not human cognitive experience as in Augustine. He fuses important elements from Denis the Areopagite, Anselm, and Aristotle into an original synthesis.

According to Denis and Plotinus, good is by its nature self-diffusive. By this principle, God is necessarily self-communicative. But this neoplatonic principle of the self-diffusion of the good is not sufficient for Bonaventure. God is not only diffusive by nature but also by will. In addition, he argues, following Anselm, that God is such that none greater can be conceived. Accordingly, the goodness of God is such that none greater can be conceived, and the highest good must be the most self-diffusive:

the greatest self-diffusion cannot exist unless it is
actual and intrinsic,
substantial and hypostatic,
natural and voluntary,
free and necessary,
lacking nothing and perfect.[8]

The created universe is not sufficient to be considered the self-diffusion of God's substance and nature. The only possible self-diffusion of God is God. So the primary diffusion of goodness is the Son and the Spirit. God's diffusion of Godself by nature is the Son who, as the perfect diffusion of the Father, is himself God. God's diffusion of Godself by will is God the Holy Spirit who, as the perfect diffusion of God the Father and Son, is itself God. Since one diffusion is by nature and the other by will, the Son and the Spirit are distinct.

Bonaventure argues that there are and can be only two such diffusions of God. According to Aristotle, the only ways something can happen are by accident, by nature, or by will. God does not act by accident. God acts by nature, and since this act is perfect, there can be only one Son; God acts freely, and since this act is perfect, there can be only one Holy Spirit. God can thus be seen to be three and only three persons. Although Bonaventure has much more to say about the interrelations in the life of God, this is all we need for our purposes. For we can see that, by using the principles that good is self-diffusive, that God is perfect, and that God acts by nature and by will, Bonaventure has made the movement of the Trinity accessible to thought, and thereby to devotion. Even though he relies on Denis' principle that goodness is self-diffusive and, as in Denis, the ascent of the soul culminates in ecstasy, in this part of his work Bonaventure does not use the *via negativa*, which is so associated with Denis' account of the ascent. In Bonaventure it is what can be put before the mind that is vital for the ascent.

In the *The Soul's Journey into God*, Bonaventure seeks to specify various features of nature, human nature, and God for the mind to

---

[8] *The Soul's Journey into God*, trans. Ewert Cousins (New York: Paulist Press, 1978), p. 103.

contemplate. In the 'Prologue' he stresses, as do Juliana, Richard, and Anselm, that one needs to be involved with God in order to know God. Although Bonaventure is writing for believing and practising Christians, he emphasizes that the readers must prepare themselves with an earnest intent of ascending into the life of God. Otherwise, the knowledge he imparts will be useless.

The organization of *The Soul's Journey into God* is modelled on the vision of the six-winged seraph that appeared to St Francis. Two parts of the book direct one to contemplate the vestiges of God in the universe; two parts focus on the image of God in human nature, especially as restored by Jesus; and two parts direct us to contemplate the Trinity. The mind is thus to look outward, inward, and upward in its journey into God. In the fifth and sixth meditations the mind is instructed to look upward by reflecting on two names of God, being and goodness, respectively. The name of God as 'being' enables Bonaventure to understand the unity of God, and the name of 'goodness' enables him to understand the movement in God's life. Our concern is with the movement in God's life.

In meditation six, Bonaventure draws on his earlier work, *Disputed Questions on the Mystery of the Trinity*, in order to provide rungs for our ascent. In other words, he tells us which things to think about as we contemplate God's inner life as Father, Son, and Spirit and how, by thinking about them, to move more fully into the life of God. Inquiry into the Trinity, which is often an occasion for bafflement for many Christians, and sometimes even an embarrassment, in Bonaventure's hands becomes a part of our spiritual formation. His intellectual work on the Trinity, presented in meditative form, gives a conceptual structure to God's love for God. This conceptual structure is such that it enables us to see, on the one hand, the inadequacy of the universe as the highest or best reality, because it is not great enough or good enough to be the perfect diffusion of God's goodness. On the other hand, it enables us to recognize God's generosity in creating a glorious universe when God did not need to make a universe at all, since God is already fully and perfectly self-expressive in God's own inner life as Trinity. This generosity includes God's intent for human beings to share as fully as possible in the divine life which, because of our sin, is achievable only through the Holy Spirit bringing us into full unity with the crucified-incarnate Son. By tracing (or 'reducing', as he would say) the biblical account of creation and redemption into the movement in the divine life itself, Bonaventure has immensely heightened our understanding of God's transcendence and generosity. Contemplating what Bonaventure's intellectual work has made accessible to us should ignite an ardour for God. By contemplating God's life, which Bonaventure has made accessible to our understanding, one may have one's love for God so purified and heightened that one may, even in this life, experience in a moment of ecstasy the presence of God face to face. At first sight intellectual inquiry into the movement in God's life may seem a most unpromising place to look for anything significant for our spiritual formation, but in the *The Soul's Journey into God* Bonaventure shows just the opposite.

It is worth noting that Bonaventure's inquiry into the movement in the divine life shows the inadequacy of the work of Plotinus, Hegel, and Process theologians. Good is indeed self-diffusive in Plotinus, but the diffusions are not perfect or full, and all the diffusions are necessary, including those that give us the universe, since the One or the Good is impersonal, without will. Hegel's divine movement is the movement of the universe itself. As we saw in Bonaventure, the universe is too small and not good enough to be God's self-diffusion. It is in no way coequal to that than which none greater or better can be conceived. The panentheism of Process theology is distinct from Hegel's pantheism, but it has similar inadequacies. In Process, not only does God need a universe in order to increase in value, God is a being among others. In all three views it is not possible to characterize a divine generosity that is comparable to the immense generosity Bonaventure is able to characterize through his understanding of the movement in the divine life. He enables one to see the immense importance of the notion commonly expressed in theology and spirituality, which at first sight seems peculiar and even repulsive, that God can love only God. That is, nothing can be as full a diffusion of God as the movement of God in the divine life itself.

III. QUESTIONS EXTRINSIC TO THEOLOGY

Anselm and Bonaventure considered questions extrinsic to theology, as have theologians before and after them. This is because the consideration of questions which are extrinsic to theology, nonetheless is integral to the task of theology. We can compare its task to that of a flashlight or torch: it casts light enabling us to see. In theology we seek to see all things in the light of God, but if we have not wrestled with questions intrinsic to God's nature and our condition in relation to God, then our batteries will be weak and the bulb will cast only a weak light.[9]

But it has been difficult for some theologians in the modern period, as they wrestle with extrinsic problems, to cast light on them. At various times in the modern period the prospects for theology, because of developments in science and philosophy, have looked dire. This certainly was

[9] This is fully argued in my article, D. Allen, 'Manifestations of the Supernatural According to Simone Weil', in *Cahiers Simone Weil* (September 1994). A German translation will appear in a forthcoming *Festschrift* in honour of Gerhard Sauter.

the case when I was a student in the 1950s. But today the situation in both areas has been transformed, as an atheistic point of view, even if dominant, is no longer considered to be indisputably normative. But whether the situation is favourable or unfavourable at any particular time, Christian thinkers, who are rooted in the examination of questions intrinsic to theology and whose intellectual work is integral to their spiritual formation, do not take their bearings solely, or even predominately, from the state of the discussion of extrinsic problems. Such thinkers can live with temporary frustrations and lack of headway because they have wrestled with questions intrinsic to God's nature and our condition, and they have found both illumination and nourishment.

Presently, the issue of foundational versus anti-foundationalism, which underlies much of McClendon's characterization of the intellectual situation, has created such a dust storm that theologians have trouble getting their bearings. But let us recall that extrinsic questions, even though they challenge a theologian's vocation, do not define that vocation. A theologian's vocation is to so understand the self-manifestations of God that it casts light on all areas of thought and life, including those matters which challenge the vocation itself. Let me illustrate this with the issue of foundationalism.

Foundationalism in philosophy was an attempt to find foundations for our claims to knowledge. Although particular truths are discovered at different times and are rooted in various historical and cultural circumstances, it was once believed that, if our claims could be shown to be necessary or incorrigible, they had universal validity. Descartes thought the mind had the power to find incorrigible principles to serve as the foundations of knowledge. Locke tried to find foundations in sense-experiences that are incorrigible. Kant based necessity and universality on the synthetic activity of reason. The overthrow of all these attempts, and the claim that there are no foundations, make it appear as if there is nothing upon which to rest our truth-claims. They are all a matter of historical and cultural circumstances, and therefore lack universal validity. All claims, including theological ones, are social constructions.

It is widely assumed today that foundationalism and anti-foundationalism are the only alternatives. Perhaps an analogy may help loosen the grip of the assumption and enable us to see that there is another alternative. Some people were once troubled about what the earth rests on. Things fall unless they rest on the earth, but what does the earth rest on? What keeps it from falling down? John Locke mentions the Indian story that the earth rests on the back of a giant elephant. But that is only a temporary expedient, since we must now find out what the elephant rests on. As he pointed out, to say it rests on the back of a giant turtle does not get us out of the difficulty. The turtle must rest on something or it will fall.

So too it seems with truth-claims. Without a foundation for our claims that transcends our culture or subculture, we are left with relativism. It seems that the only thing to stop our free-fall from relativism into nihilism is some sort of legitimate or warranted social consensus. In America the best known attempts to provide such a consensus are Richard Rorty's work in philosophy and George Lindbeck's in theology. But both eschew universal claims and provide no warrant for universal truth-claims or claims that transcend a culture or subculture.

But Christian teachings concerning our knowledge of God transform the situation. The entire framework of foundationalism and anti-foundationalism is transcended by the conviction that God must manifest God-self and that we must become spiritually formed in order to respond to God's manifestations. Such a view did not arise because of a lack of confidence in our ability to gain knowledge as such. Nor did it arise because of the failure of attempts to know God. It arose after our reception of God's self-manifestation. From God's self-manifestation, theological reflection led to the realization that we can know God only in so far as God makes Godself known. This was learned from wrestling with questions intrinsic to God's nature and our condition. The transcultural status of theological claims that arise from questions intrinsic to theology is not based on the possibility of an incorrigible foundation, nor is it threatened by the absence of such a foundation.

Warrant for Christian claims can be found because all claims about God are *suspended*, so to speak, from that which is not a member of the universe. Just as the earth without anything to rest on is not in danger of falling, because it is suspended in space by forces between various bodies, so too are theologians able to practise their vocation without an incorrigible foundation on which to rest their inquiries, and without fear that the lack of such a foundation renders their claims mere social constructions. God's self-revelation provides the light by which theologians practise their calling to seek to understand God and all things in relation to God. Of course such understanding as theologians are able to gain is deeply affected culturally. But because God, who is related to history and society, also transcends all history and culture, what is understood is not necessarily culture bound. A theologian who has wrestled with questions intrinsic to theology, questions that are not culture bound, knows this, and should not be intimidated by the extrinsic claim that because there are no foundations to knowledge to give our claims universality, all claims must be culture bound.[10]

Probably most of a theologian's work in the Western world today will be directed toward extrinsic matters because there are so many new intellectual, technical, and cultural developments which need to be

[10] See n. 9.

understood in the light of God. But that work is likely to be more intellectually fruitful, and will be more relevant to spiritual formation, if it is deeply informed by questions that are transcultural, not in the sense of developing a 'global theology', but in the sense of a theology that is suspended from God who is not a member of the universe.

18

The Indispensability of Theological Understanding: Theology in the University

COLIN GUNTON

DANIEL Hardy's observation that theology is part of public discourse in Britain in a way it is not in the United States of America was well illustrated in the British daily press during the 1993 Christmas season. Not only did *The Times* publish, as a leading article, a positive and sophisticated articulation of the truth of the incarnation, but the correspondence columns of *The Independent* contained, in response to a continued attack by the scientist, Richard Dawkins, on the propriety of theology's place in the university, two letters whose differences are significant. It was the professor of theology whose contribution was defensive. Too strong a religious commitment, he claimed, is a problem in face of the main thrust of a degree in theology, which is the critical examination of texts. The abandonment, implicit in that contention, of theology's claims for a place in the university as a distinctive discipline, in favour of the supposedly objective study of texts or of history, is, I shall argue, fundamentally mistaken, because it represents a quest for respectability by means of an evasion of that in which true respectability lies. It was a Member of Parliament – significantly, himself a scientist – who affirmed in the second of the letters that the study of theology requires a basis in religious truth. That was a welcome voice, and in this paper an attempt will be made to build upon it.

It is as well to profess at the outset that I shall be concerned in this paper with Christian doctrinal or systematic theology, that is to say, with the exposition and articulation of Christian claims to truth, both theoretical and ethical. That is not to exclude from all consideration the other disciplines that make up the world of academic theology today, but to face the problem at its most intractable. It is possible to justify biblical studies as a branch of history, literary criticism or classical studies; to find a place for ecclesiastical history as pursuing the objective study of Christian thought and institutions; for the philosophy of religion as pursuing the disinterested evaluation of religious claims to truth. But with Christian doctrine and ethics, the same cannot

266

be done, unless they are to be treated purely historically. They must be justified for themselves, as disciplines in their own right, or they lose their *ratio essendi*.

To the discussion of the propriety of such studies, another prefatory remark must be made. It is that in so far as there is self-conscious thought in the public realm about the place of theology, it takes the form of two apparently contradictory beliefs: that theology is inappropriate in an institution devoted to free inquiry and that theology has abandoned its right to a place because theologians spend more time undermining than defending the faith that they are believed to hold. This very fact, along with findings that a majority of the population confess to some form of Christian belief, indicates that there is no simple thesis about secularization that can bear directly upon our topic. Accordingly, to obtain as clear a picture of the situation as is possible, I shall treat the discussion under a number of heads, concluding with the more systematic considerations.

I. HISTORICAL AND SOCIAL DIMENSIONS

Any approach to historical considerations will be influenced by assumptions about the character of Western culture. Different theories of history produce, in general, two positions. First, what can be called the discontinuity view holds that there is a breach or rupture in the development of our culture so radical that the modern university is required to be something different in kind from its predecessor, whose domination by theological considerations is precisely what had to be broken in order for freedom of thought and inquiry to emerge. Before that time, the argument might go, all inquiry was contaminated by alien interests; now only those disciplines which pursue value-free inquiry may be allowed. The argument has some plausibility, but it holds only on an 'all or nothing' view of cultural development, and on the view that there is today an infamy to be expunged. Some aspects of this must be considered later, but the thought that theologians at modern universities are the enemies of free inquiry is little, if at all, short of ludicrous. University theologians are far more free to dissent from the orthodoxies of the day than are natural scientists.

Second, on the increasingly plausible view that, whatever discontinuities there have been, there is also a continuity of culture, stretching through the monastic institutions which kept learning alive during the 'Dark Ages', to the first universities where the sciences began to develop, and then to those of today, there is little objection to theology continuing to play a part in the, albeit immeasurably expanded, range of respectable disciplines. Theology, it might be argued, played a part in bringing things to where they are today, and it would be a gross act of ingratitude to perform an act of euthanasia on a body which, despite some signs of decadence – and there it is not alone – shows every evidence of attracting students and staff, and producing literature of sufficient quality to be published by leading university presses. Notice that this is not a merely conservative argument of the kind that theology has the right to be taught in the modern university because, as a matter of fact, the university was the creation of the church, and that because theology has always been there, there is reason to hold that it should not be expelled. It is an argument from the dynamics of culture, that theology has played, and can continue to play, a positive, perhaps indispensable, part in the movement of thought that is central to human culture.

Such a consideration leads us into more general social considerations. One could add an argument with contemporary appeal, based on the fact that the universities began as places to train clerks to run church and state. They were, that is to say, centres of vocational training. The fact that the modern state requires the development of a far greater range of skills to man the complex institutions of today need not alter the fact that the church, whether or not established, remains one of them. Might it not be claimed that just as lawyers, teachers and physicians are trained at universities, so there is a place for Christian vocational training? There is much to be said for this view, particularly in the light of government insistence that children in British schools should be taught about the Christian faith. But it will not do as it stands, for the defence of a subject requires more than an appeal to current government policy, which may change rapidly enough to endanger any defence built upon it.

To put an opposing secular argument more strongly, it might be said that the state needs teachers, lawyers and the medical profession in a way that, even as containing an established church, it does not need exponents of the Christian faith. That is true: theologians are not as universally needed in the same practical sense as are members of other professions. Theology's defence requires a different appeal to social utility, and it might go something like this. A healthy society, particularly in an era of highly centralized bureaucratic government, needs a range of institutions that are not under direct state control. Accordingly, only the most totalitarian vision would hold that a university, whether or not subsidized from public funds, should be allowed to train personnel only for institutions approved or run by the state itself. It has been argued, for example by the philosopher of science, Michael Polanyi, that the health of any society depends upon the flourishing of a range of institutions, particularly voluntary ones.[1] Similarly, the Chief Rabbi has argued for

[1] Michael Polanyi, *Personal Knowledge: Towards a Post-Critical Philosophy* (London: Routledge, 1962, 2nd edition).

the importance of communities intermediate between society as a whole and the families that make it up.[2] Except on a view that the existence of churches is so harmful that they must be actively discouraged by law – and we have recent examples of the failure of states that held such views, and acted accordingly[3] – there is an unanswerable case that these voluntary communities have a claim on institutions of learning for the education of their personnel.

But the allusion to the voluntary nature of modern religious communities reminds us that there is running through modern Western culture a deep strain of paranoia about religious institutions, particularly Christian ones. It takes a number of forms, and is illustrated by the lament sometimes heard that one may satirize and attack Christianity in modern media of communication, but not the other 'minority' religions present in our society. Whatever the truth of that, it does bring to the surface the ideologically loaded character of modern secular social theory. A recent article on the controversy about Salman Rushdie's *Satanic Verses*, by the sociologist David Martin, reinforces the point. Professor Martin observed that his colleagues, by virtue of their captivity to secular ideology, were unable to come to grips intellectually with the complexities of the situation.[4] When a case such as this reveals what he calls the paradoxes of liberalism and secular ideology's sheer impotence, the argument is strengthened for the social necessity of scholars able to bring to bear on contemporary questions other intellectual perspectives and traditions than the fashionable. Moreover, as the example shows, many of the questions that trouble our modern culture are theological in character and cannot be understood adequately without some of the tools of systematic theological inquiry.

II. INTELLECTUAL: (1) THEOLOGY'S HERMENEUTICAL INDISPENSABILITY

But such pragmatic considerations are not enough, so that we must turn to the intellectual case against the discipline, and in particular to an examination of the kind of consideration underlying the case of Richard Dawkins, that intellectual history has simply made the subject imposs-

---

[2] Jonathan Sacks, *The Persistence of Faith: Religion, Morality and Society in a Secular Age* (London: Weidenfeld & Nicolson, 1991).

[3] It is significant that Romania, to take one example, is concerned to develop faculties of theology in its universities because of a felt need to contribute to the spiritual dimensions of society after an era in which materialism reigned.

[4] David Martin, 'On Calling Islam "Medieval" ', *King's Theological Review* 13 (1990), pp. 11–13.

ible. Such a case requires a particular view of the development of modern culture, namely that science has replaced theology as the sole source of truth, and that the latter should therefore retire or be retired from the scene. One rejoinder to that is that it relies on a view of the relations between theology and science that recent historiography has rendered obsolete. John Hedley Brooke, in what is likely to become a standard history of the relation of science and religion in recent centuries, has shown that the development of science reveals a whole range of ways, few of them entirely negative, in which theology and science have come into intellectual relation.[5] Over against the hoary myths about Galileo and Darwin, distorted by their use in secularizing propaganda and now much subject to revision, one could cite the cases of the heroes of modern science, Newton, Faraday and Clerk Maxwell, for example, whose science was deeply and positively influenced by their theology.

More interesting is the fact that in more recent times scientists have begun to indulge in all kinds of theological speculation. It has indeed been said that there is speculation, wild speculation and cosmology, but the impact of the famous theological dictum at the end of *A Brief History of Time* indicates a serious interest in the theological dimensions of the debates of scientists.[6] Have the theologians no place in assessing and advancing the discussion of *The Tao of Physics*[7] and *The Mind of God*? Clearly they have, for theologians are among those cited by Paul Davies in the latter work, even if, revealingly, T. F. Torrance is described as a philosopher.[8] Here we can advance a strong argument in favour of theology's indispensability, that without trained theologians we shall simply not understand many strands of contemporary intellectual debate.

This, moreover, is a matter which takes us well beyond the theological speculations of cosmologists. The intellectual history of our culture is inextricably bound up with theology in other ways also. One example is to be found in Hans Blumenberg's influential *The Legitimacy of the Modern Age*. While Blumenberg's is an argument which charts with approval the displacement of God from the modern world, his argument is in part advanced with the help of theological categories. For example he understands the development of modern science as a second overcoming of gnosticism, a claim which is simply unintelligible without some measure of systematic theological understanding.[9] That is to say, modern intellectual culture would be immeasurably the poorer without

[5] John Hedley Brooke, *Science and Religion: Some Historical Perspectives* (Cambridge: CUP, 1991).
[6] Stephen Hawking, *A Brief History of Time* (London: Bantam Press, 1988), p. 175.
[7] Fritjof Capra, *The Tao of Physics* (London: Fontana, 1983, 1st edition 1975).
[8] Paul Davies, *The Mind of God* (Harmondsworth: Penguin, 1993), p. 167.
[9] Hans Blumenberg, *The Legitimacy of the Modern Age*, trans. R. M. Wallace (Cambridge, MA, and London: MIT Press, 1983).

theology as a partner in some of the many dialogues taking place in our attempt to understand why things are as they are today. At the very least it has an indispensable hermeneutical function in enabling our increasingly perplexed modern culture simply to understand itself.

III. Intellectual: (2) Considerations of Content

A further set of arguments in defence of the indispensability of Christian theology have much to do with its capacity to contribute to the richness of our culture, and particularly its thought. The arguments can be articulated under the following three heads: plurality; universality; unity and plurality.

1. Plurality. Christian theology, particularly in the light of considerations advanced in the previous paragraphs, is needed in the interests of a genuinely plural culture, where truth is given the opportunity to emerge by the encouragement of a plurality of claims for truth.[10] Over against this, the permission only of a biblical or religious studies assimilated to the norms of other disciplines represents a form of homogenization which is hostile to a genuine plurality of voices. May the distinctively Christian voice be the only one not to be heard? The representation of other *intellectual* communities in the university than those directly justified by the immediate needs of the state is a bulwark of intellectual freedom and diversity, not a threat to it, so long, that is, as other desiderata are fulfilled. Two are as follows.

The first is that other communities are not precluded from requesting a similar claim to consideration. In a culture historically formed by Christian theology, it has the right to claim a prominence in certain respects, though not in others. It certainly may not do it by asserting the legal power of establishment, and one must concede that the paranoia mentioned above has been fed by such behaviour as that referred to by Stephen Sykes in connection with the founding of the University of London.[11] We shall consider the matter of toleration below. But, so far as the main point is concerned, it should be noted that Jewish studies already have an established place in some university institutions, and are

---

[10] Here the need for a plurality of voices in a rich culture is to be distinguished from a dogmatic pluralism which serves as a cover for claims that really everything – for example, every religion – is really the same.

[11] Stephen W. Sykes, 'Theological Study: The Nineteenth Century and After', in *The Philosophical Frontiers of Christian Theology*, eds. B. Hebblethwaite and S. R. Sutherland (Cambridge: CUP, 1982), pp. 95–118 (p. 109).

the main exception to what appears to be the general rule, that non-Christian religions are still normally represented by Western scholars who are not members of them.

The second desideratum is that the communities represented should be genuinely intellectual in character. Here we reach the fine line, which is indeed a line of demarcation, between the properly passionate and rhetorical advocacy of a position and improper proselytization. However that be drawn, it brings us to what is perhaps the most central question of all in the intellectual case for the continuing presence in the university of this discipline. At the outset, it cannot be emphasized too strongly that pretensions to presupposition-free and entirely dispassionate inquiry are a sham. All genuine intellectuals wish to advocate their positions, as witness the debates between modern cosmologists. The alternatives are self-delusion and boredom. The heart of the matter is how they do it, and here all I am doing is advocating the oldest of all instruments of intellectual advance, the public articulation and discussion of difference.

At this stage, however, a number of careful qualifications are needed. First, the argument must not be seen as recommending some supposedly 'postmodern' position according to which everything goes, with the result that academia comes to be seen as an unregulated marketplace. On the face of the matter, such recent developments bring certain advantages to an unfashionable discipline. What might be called the left-wing form of the argument is that if all is intellectual flux, and each discipline must live by its own intellectual (or anti-intellectual?) lights, then none has the right to exclude another from intellectual respectability. The right-wing form of the argument is from the market. If there is a market for theological studies, then who is to deny them the right to continue? In a marketplace in which one institution has announced the development of a degree in bird-watching, what has theology to fear?[12] More moderately, one might argue that just as departments of English literature and music serve those with interests in those activities, so departments of theology serve those with an interest in religion.

There is something to be said for both forms of the postmodern argument, for they do indicate that in an era when a culture's most cherished intellectual assumptions are under question it is difficult to exclude anything with a *prima facie* claim to be respectable (if that is the word in such a situation). But, though enticing, they are inadequate, for they effectively concede the case against an intellectual discipline by defending it on other than intellectual grounds. By conceding the right of everything, such contentions prove too much, and so, too little. Do they justify, to use a hackneyed example, astrology? The day may not be far off when an attempt is made to develop such a degree, but on what

[12] 'Everything' is probably the answer.

grounds? That a certain significant percentage of the population takes it seriously? We are here launching out on to the open sea without compass or rudder, and must begin to exercise control by a more ordered appeal to intellectual considerations.

A beginning can be made by referring again to the increasingly and widely accepted philosophical claim that there is no thought without presupposition. All disciplines represent some form of faith commitment, in the general sense of that word as implying confidence in the rationality, coherence and worthwhile character of the object of study. Science is a case in point. Without confidence in the reliability and inherent meaningfulness of the material world, there would be no science. It is only a combination of ideological factors dominant in modernity and the cultural and technological success of science that makes such matters invisible.[13] Theology has come into question as a result of the obverse: ideological opposition and its apparent cultural failure. We are then faced with the question of criteria. What kind of presuppositions are acceptable? What is it to be respectable, in the sense of being able to command the respect of or similar respect to other disciplines? One suggestion for the rights of a discipline in an era when foundationalist claims have been shown to be untenable is that to secure respect the claims made must be 'contestable'. That is to say, the basis and assumptions on which a discipline is founded must be subject to public articulation and debate. Here we come again to a comparison with astrology. There is a *prima facie* case for saying that the claims of astrologers are so slippery as to be incontestable: that its predictions are not predictions, because they cannot finally be falsified.

But is the same not true of Christian theology? On one level, Christian theological claims are contestable, because they are contested. Indeed, one of the reasons for theology's rejection by rationalists is that its assumptions are so contestable as to be meaningless. There comes a time when contestability is so unanimous that the place of a discipline in a culture becomes indefensible. But we have certainly not reached that stage, and are not likely to reach it in view of the fact that the clay feet of liberal and secular thought are becoming manifest in this very respect. Indeed, the argument can be reversed, so that it can be argued that theological questioning is an urgent need if the strengths and weaknesses of modernist thought are to receive the testing they manifestly require.

To the criterion of contestability must therefore be added a second: a proven and living tradition of serious thought. There needs to be no serious denial of the former. Whether or not they are today widely

---

[13] We should be quite clear about this. On certain extreme postmodern views of intellectual life, even science ceases to have a basis in universal reality and becomes no more than an epiphenomenon of the Western mind-set.

accepted, theology has made contributions to thought about, among other things, the nature and status of the human being, and in particular to ethics. In an age when it is widely felt that morality is in disarray, and there are fears, justified or not, of the breakdown of social order, even contributions from the past are to be welcomed. As to the latter, whether theology still has a living contribution, something will be said below.

The second qualification concerns the complicated question of the relation between intellectual integrity and toleration. One could not justify the presence in an institution dedicated to processes of intellectual debate disciplines whose fundamental intolerance made its pursuit impossible. Here we need to be aware of both the meaning and the origins of the modern notion of toleration. Toleration implies disagreement, even disapproval, because one does not need to tolerate what one likes or agrees with. What toleration, as a way of approaching personal differences, requires is a refusal to allow differences to be decided other than by argument and by the appeal to evidence, however intractable is the matter of deciding what counts as evidence in a dispute about fundamental matters. In our context, this means that the life of the university, however acrimonious its debates, *presupposes* the encouragement of difference. One cannot imagine that under modern conditions this will be in the slightest endangered by influence exerted by theological arguments.

It must, however, at this stage be conceded that there have been occasions, albeit ones whose significance has been distorted by secularizing interests, when ecclesiastical bodies have improperly interfered in due intellectual process. But such occasions pale into insignificance in view both of more than counterbalancing contributions to intellectual life and of the gross and murderous behaviour of the avowedly atheist regimes that have dominated the history of the twentieth century. Recent history suggests that regimes founded on purely rational principles, for example those of Marx, have been the most savagely repressive of all. If the university can tolerate, indeed encourage by promotion, Marxist literary critics and sociologists, need it be afraid of a discipline some of whose modern representatives have been at the forefront of the propagation of toleration?

Supporters of the secular case will be surprised, if not outraged, at such a suggestion. Is not religion the source of intolerance? Whatever is often assumed in arguments such as that, tolerance is not a natural human quality, nor one justified merely by reason. That may be a dogma of the modern Enlightenment tradition, but it is false. It was John Locke, who has some claim to be regarded as an Anglican theologian as much as an Enlightenment philosopher, whose writings on toleration have so shaped the modern view. But Locke was not the first, and it must be recalled that he was a member of a college whose Cromwellian head anticipated his work. In *Of Toleration*, John Owen argued for its necessity theologically, Christologically in particular.[14] The roots of the modern conceptions of toleration, however much they also owe to Athens, are to be found in part in a theology, a concept of God, which, however repressed during long centuries of 'the total Christian society', provides a more adequate underpinning of the life of the university than its alternatives. Once again, therefore, we find our discussion inextricably bound up with theological considerations.

2. Universality. There is a case for saying that just as without theology university life would be the poorer, and particularly in great danger of succumbing to the homogenizing pressures that so threaten the modern world, so also it has important things to contribute to debates about universality. Here we can be briefer, because the matter has been much written on in the modern world, by writers as different as Newman and Pannenberg.[15] One would be hard put, and for several reasons, to claim that all of today's universities require theology if they are to be genuinely universal. That kind of universality is not attainable in any one institution. It can be argued, however, that the intellectual life represented by the university system requires theology by virtue of the fact that a discipline concerned with the existence and nature of God is of its very nature interested in questions about the meaning of the whole.[16]

But what kind of universality are we seeking? Not that of Christendom, in which the queen of the sciences appeared to be able to override the autonomy of the others. Pannenberg's recent bid for an understanding of theology as a constitutional monarch is in part based on the idealist categories of the whole and the part. Any partial claim for knowledge implies questions about its context, and finally about the whole of the history in which it is set. That final question is the question of God, a concept which therefore serves to underwrite the unity of the whole, and accordingly of the many partial intellectual endeavours which make up the modern intellectual world.[17]

There is much to be said for an argument that the parts are incomplete without the whole, just as there is for the argument of the former

---

[14] John Owen, *Of Toleration, Works*, ed. J. H. Goold (Edinburgh: T. & T. Clark, 1862), volume 8, pp. 163–206. And, showing that this is not just the product of Dissenting demands for toleration, but derives from a deep, if sometimes buried, Christian tradition, he cites Tertullian: 'nec religionis est cogere religionem, quae sponte suscipi debeat, non vi' (It is not the function of religion to compel religion, which should be adopted freely, not imposed by force).

[15] J. H. Newman, *The Idea of a University* (Notre Dame: University of Notre Dame Press, 1982); on Pannenberg, see n. 17.

[16] The argument becomes the stronger in view of the effective renunciation by philosophy of most of its pretensions to universality, as well as by the sheer diversification of the sciences.

[17] Wolfhart Pannenberg, *Theology and the Philosophy of Science*, trans. F. McDonagh (London: Darton, Longman & Todd, 1976).

Secretary of State for Education that education is incomplete without knowledge of both science and God.[18] But there is also much to be said for the fact that the contingency and relative autonomy of the sciences throw doubt on the validity of an argument from their alleged incompleteness to the necessity of a single unifying factor or from an argument that sets divine unity over against cultural plurality. Rather, it is preferable to offer a theologically derived principle of unity that provides an ontological basis for the genuine unity in diversity of the created world. What is needed, accordingly, is a conception of theology which offers to our fragmented world a theological vision of unity grounded in a God who gives both reality, interdependence and (a relative) independence to the things that have been made, because he is himself unity in relation.

3. Unity and plurality. The specifically Christian theological contribution to modern intellectual life is thus to be found in its doctrine of God who by virtue of a pluriformity in his relations to the world generates the articulation of a wide range of insights about the world and life within it. For example, the doctrine of the incarnation of the eternal Son of God in human flesh itself ramifies into a series of questions about the nature of the human, involving considerations outside the scope of biological and evolutionary discoveries, which without it are in danger of becoming reductionist and depersonalizing. Closely linked to this are inquiries about the nature of the person and of life in community.[19] Similarly, attention to the doctrine of the Holy Spirit enables the articulation of considerations about the nature of human and artistic perfection, as well as contributions to modern debates about ecology without which all would be the weaker.

That claim brings to the centre a most important point about the nature of human culture which also has a bearing on the general case. Only on the assumption that we can find out anything we want on the basis of our autonomous reason or inquiry; that is to say, only on the foundationalist assumption that there is one and only one approach to truth – the sceptical-secular-rationalist or empiricist – can it be denied that a particular discipline like Christian theology has anything otherwise unobtainable to offer. Theology's justification in the intellectual firmament will thus derive above all from the contribution it can make by virtue of its attention to the question of God. It cannot, in a modern public institution, compel even its practitioners to affirm belief in God, but it can live, unashamed, by the intellectual contribution made by the thought of those who do so affirm. The discipline thus, finally, lives by its

[18] John Patten, 'Must Think Harder', *The Spectator*, 2 October 1993, 14–15.
[19] There is a strong argument that the very concept of the person is derived from Christian thought about the being of God. See John D. Zizioulas, *Being as Communion: Studies in Personhood and the Church* (London: Darton, Longman & Todd, 1985).

ability to contribute from Christian sources things that would not otherwise be said. (That is a justification also for the presence of 'other religious traditions'.)

To return to historical considerations, we can again appeal to the unique contributions to thought which have been made in the past. The fact is that, for all its historical failures, Christian theology has produced a series of intellectuals, often towering minds, who have made contributions to culture well beyond the Christian significance of what they have written. It is of the nature of the Christian faith to generate intellectuals, even though it has also its fair share in producing anti-intellectualism, particularly perhaps in England. (Daniel Hardy has himself, in an important paper, traced some of the reasons for this.[20]) Is that tradition played out? Before leaving the University of Birmingham for the rather more ecclesiastically connected Durham, Daniel Hardy remarked that he valued his many years in the former as a secular institution in which theology must stand not on inherited establishment privileges, but on the integrity of its intellectual achievement. The same must be said in defence of appointments in Christian theology. It is in this respect – if not in all – that theology must be justified by its fruits in the modern world, and the foregoing arguments will convince only if there is genuine and continuing intellectual achievement that has something worth saying outside as well as inside both church and academy.

[20] Daniel W. Hardy, 'The English Tradition of Interpretation and the Reception of Schleiermacher and Barth in England', in *Barth and Schleiermacher: Beyond the Impasse*, eds. J. Duke and R. Streetman (Minneapolis: Augsburg Fortress, 1988), pp. 138–62.

PART SIX: HOPE

19

Community of Hope

ESTHER D. REED

I. HOPE IN CONTEXT: 'IN THE TWILIGHT OF THE GODS'

A NYONE who has seen the paintings and drawings by Peter Howson
will have found him/herself facing the questions: Why is it increasingly difficult in our culture to speak of hope? Who in this modern world has time to think of hope? Peter Howson is an artist whose expressionism is raw and mostly disturbing. Canvases painted throughout the 1980s and 1990s bear grim titles:

> *Just Another Bloody Saturday* (1987)
> *Death of Innocence* (1989)
> *A Bridge to Nowhere* (1991)
> *Blind Leading the Blind* (1991)
> *Age of Apathy* (1992)

His palette is dark. Human skin looks reptile-like. Muscles are wasted. Male figures are trussed and strung up. In *Cerberus* (1992), a woman rides a savage fighting-dog in red stiletto shoes. In the cycle of *The Blind Leading the Blind*, religious imagery is found amongst the violence and squalor. A lone man clutches a prayer book; crosses hang around necks as decoration and are trampled underfoot; abandoned chapels teeter at the edges of cliffs, near the sewage outlets. In the words of one commentator:

> Not an optimistic world. The institutions that served as lamps in the past are not here – a chapel becomes a false beacon; a signpost is hooded like a Christ-less cross; lust sits on a hero's pedestal.[1]

There is little if any sense of community. The blindness of jingoism, feigned personal independence, bigoted patriotism, social rectitude and political correctness, have led to despair. Yet Howson's work is not completely without hope. David Kiehl describes a gritty Glaswegian vitality; a spirit that encourages us to take on the problems that face us –

---

[1] David Kiehl in *Peter Howson: Blind Leading the Blind* (London: Flowers East Gallery, 1991), pp. 24–6.

'head on and fists up'. There can still be heroes if they strive towards the light.

II. HOPE IN CONTEXT: A NEW STOICISM

Another artist of our times is David Hockney. A recent collection, 'Some Very New Paintings', was completed after working on the sets for two operas, *Turandot* and *Die Frau ohne Schatten*. Described as the painting of sound, the collection is full of tangled forms that mean different things on different levels.[2] At a deep level they are about creativity. Big and unifying designs are suggestive of maternity and fertility. Using the form of a river, Hockney paints movement and space in colours that flow around the canvas. The life-force is represented by a river in a landscape that is internal not external. A sense of life is the deepest thing; movement is life. Deliberately untitled, Hockney wants the viewer to find music in each design, to sense the pleasure principle in art that is open to the future and finds beauty in life. In his own words:

> [t]he future is unborn, the future is also that life force that I interpreted making the golden river become the tree of life, sperm, a force that is bigger than us, greater than us and that we acknowledge ...

However bad our struggles in life are, Hockney believes it to be the duty of an artist to alleviate the sterility of despair.[3] His sense of life on a deep level gives him cause for hope. Hockney himself has a Christian background, but the sense in which he allows the pleasure principle in art to mirror something of the natural life-force moves him closer to a new stoicism of inwardness together with consciousness of the cosmos.

III. TWO CLEAR TENDENCIES: THE APOCALYPTIC AND THE STOIC

Howson and Hockney illustrate two clear tendencies in contemporary Western art and culture. One is apocalyptic in its disclosure of what is often concealed to sight, dealing with the tragic human predicament in the spiritual vacuity created by the expulsion of God from the streets. The other is neo-stoic, not in its suppression of the passions, but in its searching for and finding of happiness through correspondence with the life-force. One tendency, the apocalyptic, confronts and fights against

---

[2] 'A Conversation between David Hockney and William Hardy' in *David Hockney: Some Very New Paintings* (Glasgow: William Hardy Gallery, 1993).
[3] See also *David Hockney: That's the Way I See It* (London: Thames & Hudson, 1993).

present experience, destruction and the darkness, 'with gloves on and kicking'.[4] The other, the neo-stoic, lets go, sinks back into the dynamic substance that is nature and seeks transformation through correspondence with it. It is wrong to ossify the work of either artist, in its variety and subtlety, under generic and controversial categories; neither Howson nor Hockney is doctrinaire or a closet philosopher. Their differences, however, which include form and technique, use of the medium and interpretation, warrant a general contrast. Howson is an apocalyptic painter in so far as 'apocalyptic' is an adjective that applies to the critique of popular culture that rises above mediocrity to glimpse the background of catastrophe.[5] The apocalyptic painter weeps over the city that seems oblivious to impending disaster. Hockney, by contrast, sees through the suffering to potential transformation through correspondence with nature. It is important for him that the viewer finds music, life and movement in the design. All expresses the fact of continual change that is part of the cosmic condition of being alive. Human life is directed not towards what is revelatory and critical, but towards an increasingly enhanced harmony with the existent God-nature.

IV. THEOLOGICAL RESPONSIBILITY

Theological statements cannot be uninformed by their contemporary context. Much of Dan Hardy's work calls for awareness of the complex contextuality (interwovenness) of social interaction.[6] A basis in creation and redemption, not solely in confession of the risen Jesus, requires that our ecclesiology is neither pre-trinitarian nor isolated from the complexity of the world in which we live. The hermeneutic compass of contemporary ecclesiology must include multiple social and individualist forms of dissociation and expression if the task is not to be distorted by reduction. It is Dan Hardy's firm conviction that theology is God, community and world involving:[7]

> The scope of the Spirit's work is as wide as the cosmos and is concerned for every aspect of history, institutional as well as individual. For every area there is a message of hope. It is not simply to be identified with the great hope in Jesus Christ, but, before him, it

[4] Kiehl in *Peter Howson*, p. 26.
[5] I am partially indebted for this definition to Umberto Eco, *apocalypse postponed*, ed. Robert Lumley (London: BFI Publishing, 1994), ch. 1.
[6] See D. W. Hardy, 'The Spirit of God in Creation and Reconciliation', in *Christ and Context*, ed. H. Regan and A. J. Torrance (Edinburgh: T. & T. Clark, 1993), pp. 237ff.
[7] D. W. Hardy, 'The Future of Theology in a Complex World', in *Christ and Context*, p. 21.

embraces innumerable lesser hopes inside and outside the Christian church. The Spirit brings the taste of a better future and creates a thirst for more.[8]

If, as Christians confess, the inner pattern of Christian hope, as well as truth, is trinitarian, 'active everywhere, working to bring all things, including our understanding and actions, into its movement',[9] then the possibility of hope in *all things* lies in God. But the question that Dan Hardy poses to contemporary theology is the following: 'What are the *marks* of the activity of the Trinitarian God in the contextuality of the world?'[10] Given that the Christian hope has a trinitarian structure, how are the origin, direction and finality of hope in God to be discerned? With this in mind, the remainder of this essay is an exercise in the foundational theology of Christian community that seeks to expound the doctrine of the Holy Trinity as having intensely practical import. It is basically the question raised by the agency of God in the world; the scope of hope in Christ that is quickened and effected by the Holy Spirit.

V. Two Potential Dangers

There are at least two potential dangers: (1) a materialized eschatology, derived from utopian thinking; the possible claim that Christian hope can be translated into historical terms, which risks tying it to the frame-work of history, and turning resurrection hope into dreams and specu-lations not based on the promise of divine fulfilment; (2) a naturalized eschatology, derived from a form of cosmolatry; the claim that antici-pated amelioration in the human sphere is through increasingly improved harmony with the existing God-nature that is the world.

(1) Both these dangers, in different ways, locate the basis of hope solely in natural, historical and material processes. A materialized eschatology is a jargonized way of describing the tension that arises between present experience and future hope when the anticipation of justice, liberation and well-being is linked to social and political systems. While the mean-ing of Christian hope can never wholly be extricated from given socio-cultural situations, neither can it be emptied into contingent historical processes. This is a familiar problem, or a bad 'dialectic' of unresolved contradiction, that still plagues and troubles our time. Recently, it has received a fresh twist as apocalypticism has become commonplace in the media and popular imagination. The Western world has become so

---

[8] D. W. Hardy and D. F. Ford, *Praising and Knowing God* (Philadelphia: Westminster, 1985), p. 145.
[9] Hardy, 'The Spirit of God in Creation', p. 240.
[10] Hardy, 'The Spirit of God in Creation', p. 252.

accustomed to the prospect of history unfolding before us as an apocalypse that Umberto Eco can remark that apocalyptic is a communication phenomenon typical of our time.[11] He makes 'apocalyptic' into an adjective which applies to the critique of popular culture that complements a familiar tendency merely to absorb such messages, process and transmit them. Images of the apocalypse, whether ecological or nuclear, are evoked in observations on what Eco calls 'mass culture'. Less than this, however, lone individuals who critique the mass culture, which is, he says, the most striking phenomenon of our age, mark the irretrievable loss of those solitary figures who rise above banal mediocrity. In other words, his definition of apocalyptic applies not only to end-time visions brought about catastrophically, but also to the lesser loss of the culture of 'supermen' who shun the vulgarity of the crowd.

It was Nietzsche who wrote that there would come a time when one will wisely refrain from all constructions of the history of humankind, a time when one no longer considers the masses at all but only the individuals who constitute the wild stream of becoming: 'No the *goal of humanity* cannot lie at the end but only *in its highest specimens*'.[12] But if, in Nietzsche's words, the nobles and the highest have no effect on the masses, then all must wither up and die. The vision of culture, as well as of individual old age, against which Nietzsche battles and that informs Nietzschean attitudes and Eco's treatment of them, is fearful:

> 'The last scene of all
> That ends this strange eventful history,
> Is second childishness and mere oblivion,
> Sans teeth, sans eyes, sans taste, sans everything'.[13]

The discovery of a sense of history was advantageous if, and only if, it quickened life and action. Otherwise historical knowledge and anticipation of the future were a luxury to be detested because of its degenerating effect on human energy.

Today we may not tremble at the choices offered by developments in historical consciousness during the nineteenth century. Nietzsche is as culturally contextualized as the rest of us. Who among us, however, is not apprehensive at the task of living in an age where history is increasingly 'a record of self-production' and refined egoism?[14] Who would

---

[11] Eco, *apocalypse*, ch. 3.
[12] Friedrich Nietzsche, *On the Advantage and Disadvantage of History for Life*, trans. Peter Preuss (Indiana: Hackett Publishing Co., 1980), p. 53.
[13] Nietzsche, *On the Advantage*, p. 57. The quote is from W. Shakespeare, *As You Like It*, Act II, Scene VII.
[14] This phrase is lifted from Peter Preuss' introduction to Nietzsche, *On the Advantage*, p. 1.

deny all justification for Eco's designation of the 'integrated' individual as the consumer of mass culture, silent in the face of the supposed end of history; banal, and sustained only by a total lack of faith in the possibility to transform the state of things?[15] The more we are concerned, however, the greater is our responsibility to understand Eco's lamentable condemnation of today's 'supermen' as undeniably inadequate. (Peter Jenkins describes *Nijinsky*, a figure painted by Howson, as deprived of all but proud inadequacy.[16]) The more we weep, the weightier is the theological responsibility to explicate a Christian ontology of hope. Even if we broaden the paradox with Jean Baudrillard to admit, 'it is likewise always better to be made happy, or unhappy, by someone else rather than by oneself',[17] the theological responsibility merely increases. If we can see the reasons why Andy Warhol's paintings screamed out, 'I want to be a machine', the theological responsibility for learning afresh about hopes is not less but greater. Thus, whether we hold that Christian hope is a *spes docta* (learned hope),[18] an 'appetitive movement' that arises out of love of God,[19] or the saving knowledge that 'God has entered into our world',[20] the theological task is to be accountable to and for that hope in every situation.

(2) The second potential danger is that of a naturalized eschatology that absorbs hope within the infinite creativity of nature. It is particularly acute in our day as the tendency to see nature as dynamic substance and, potentially, the provider of supreme community, becomes more pronounced. Take, for example, the ecofeminist work of Rosemary Radford Ruether. She seeks a cosmological spirituality for paradigmatic communities that are dedicated to the renovation of the cosmos and to living in accord with nature. Bemoaning the religious purism of Christianity, she advocates a syncretizing process that could combine Hebrew, Oriental, Asian, Graeco-Roman, Middle Platonic and Stoic cosmologies. Where, she asks, are the cosmogonic stories and pictures that combine Christian with Platonic and Stoic concepts of the Logos, that Logos 'which stoics saw as the immanent life-power of all beings'?[21] How are classic tensions between Greek and Christian thought patterns to be resolved? For Ruether, the Christian character of hope lies in the effort to unify cosmo-

[15] See Eco, *apocalypse*, p. 19.
[16] Jenkins in *Peter Howson*, p. 18.
[17] Jean Baudrillard, *The Transparency of Evil: Essays on Extreme Phenomena*, trans. James Benedict (London and New York: Verso, 1993), p. 168.
[18] Michael J. Scanlon, OSA, 'Hope' in *The New Dictionary of Theology* (Dublin: Gill & Macmillan, 1990).
[19] Thomas Aquinas, *Summa Theologiae* XXXIII, 2a2ae, 17, 8 (London: Blackfriars, Eyre & Spottiswoode).
[20] Karl Barth, *The Epistle to the Romans* (Oxford: OUP, ET 1933), p. 314.
[21] Rosemary Radford Ruether, *Gaia and God: An Ecofeminist Theology of Earth Healing* (New York: HarperCollins, 1992), p. 231.

gony and eschatology under the divine promise in 1 Cor. 15.25–28 that 'God may be all in all'. This requires consciousness of human existence as the self-awareness of nature, along 'a continuum of organised life-energy'.[22] It has an affinity, she admits, with the pagan naturalism in which hope wells up from the matrix of life that is in the heart of matter.[23]

Quid novi? Communal life for the Stoics, especially the late Stoic utopianism of Seneca, Epictetus and Marcus Aurelius, was not confined to the human sphere but was backed up by the cosmic sphere, of which it formed a part.[24] Ernst Bloch, whose own refunctioning programme of utopian visions promoted basic stoic insights,[25] described the utopianism of ancient stoicism as directed not towards what is explosive in history but rather 'towards what is an increasingly improved harmony with the existing God-nature that is the world'.[26] For Seneca, the happy person was the one who is content with the present lot; reconciled with his/her circumstances.[27] For Seneca, however, hopes (*spei*) and fears (*timori*), especially about the future, disturbed the tranquillity of the mind. Hope and fear were the bane of human life because they lowered the authority of the highest good that was life in accordance with nature (*Vit. Beat.* XV:5). Classified as a passion, *spes* (not *elpis*) was regarded as an obstacle to rational, virtuous and happy living.

It is certainly not only an ancient idea that nature is more than dead matter, that it is dynamic substance and provider of hope for spiritual and social transformation. Similar ideas are evident today. Alice Walker wrote in 1992, in the preface to the Tenth Anniversary Edition of *The Color Purple*, of the book's intent:

> to explore the difficult path of someone who ... breaks free into the realization that she, like Nature, itself, is a radiant expression of the heretofore perceived as quite distant divine.[28]

Everyone, she writes, has the possibility of a conscious connection to

[22] Ruether, *Gaia and God*, p. 250. Cf. David E. Hahm, *The Origins of Stoic Cosmology* (Ohio: Ohio State Univ. Press, 1977).
[23] The implications to this effect in *Gaia and God* were made explicit at the 1994 Summer conference for the British and Irish School of Feminist Theology (BISFT). Tapes of Rosemary Radford Ruether's lectures are available from BISFT.
[24] On Stoic utopianism see Ernst Bloch, *The Principle of Hope*, Vol. 11 (Oxford: Blackwell, 1983), pp. 494f.
[25] On this see R. H. Roberts, *Hope and Its Hieroglyph: A Critical Decipherment of Ernst Bloch's Principle of Hope* (Atlanta: Scholars Press, 1990), pp. 156ff., 204.
[26] See Roberts, *Hope*, p. 156.
[27] Seneca, *De Brevitate Vitae* I:1 and VI:1f. in *Moral Essays* 11, trans. J. W. Basore, Loeb Classical Library (London: Heinemann, 1970).
[28] Alice Walker, *The Color Purple* (London: Women's Press, 1992), p. 1.

'All That Is'. The book is about rebirth into feelings of 'Oneness' with the Great Mystery that is recognizable by the worshipper of Nature. Similarly, Margaret Atwood writes:

> Ask the spider
> what is the name of god, she will tell you: God is a spider.
> Let other moons pray to the moon. O Goddess of Mercy,
> you who are not the moon, or anything we can see clearly,
> we need to know each other's names and what we are asking.
> Do not be anything. Be the light we see by.[29]

Nature is conceived as operating in the manner of divinity. Impersonal, like an intelligent light, nature's deity and active cause are corporeal. As for ancient Stoics, nature is a living being, ensouled with the power of sensation. Each life owes its existence to that of all others. It is evident in Margaret Atwood's work especially, that there is no future life other than the total integration with the physical and biological life of the cosmos. She knows no hope outside this same process in which nature is the womb and tomb of all:

> There is no future,
> really there is none
> and no salvation
> To know this is salvation[30]

Hope, for Atwood, rests in the attempt to synthesize, harmonize and unify human ideals and relationships with the matrix of life that surrounds us. Poetry, and possibly theology, becomes a form of cosmobiology. Ruether also, in effect, redefines and consequently empties resurrection hope into the natural recycling of physical substance: 'we can encounter the matrix of energy of the universe that sustains the dissolution and recomposition of matter as also a heart that know us even as we are known ... the ongoing creative Matrix of the whole'.[31] There is no hope outside the natural process, and that is careless of the single life.

[29] Margaret Atwood, *Poems 1976–1986* (London: Virago Poems, 1992), p. 147.
[30] Atwood, *Poems*, p. 141.
[31] Ruether, *Gaia and God*, p. 252.

VI. THE TRINITARIAN STRUCTURE OF CHRISTIAN HOPE

What, then, is the task that confronts us? Bearing in mind that the context in which we speak of God is not a container but the 'braiding' or 'connecting' of what we should otherwise see as divided,[32] how is the hope of the Christian community to be depicted in a distinctive and recognizable way? How is it recognizable as distinct from any tendencies towards a materialized apocalypticism or pagan naturalism? How are the above tendencies overcome, not in a negative way or 'dialectically', or in a manner that is merely theoretical, but in a positive, passionate way that reflects the inner pattern of Christian hope?

Too narrow an approach leads to a restrictive answer. It is not enough simply to look at what is visible and present; what one might call a 'phenomenology' of the spacio-temporally locatable church. To attempt to identify and explicate hope as an essential characteristic of Christian community from what is historically knowable, geographically locatable, or sociologically analysable, is insufficient and can lead only to distortion. No empirically visible manifestation of Christian community can embody that to which the Apostles' Creed refers in the phrase: 'I believe in the ... Church'. No ecclesial community can manifest Christian hope other than in a partial, limited way. This has been true from the beginning. No New Testament writer knew of a perfect Christian community. This is especially true when speaking of hope. Everywhere there is a sense of contrast between the present as it is experienced and the future as it is anticipated, between the church as God wills it to be, and the church as it is. Martin Luther's comment in 1531 remains apt, 'There is no greater sinner than the Christian Church'.[33] Its outward determination of living hope (1 Pet. 1.3) calls for μετάνοια, literally, transformation by the Spirit. Although the Christian community is, of course, empirically visible, theological knowledge of hope looks more to things that are unseen than to things that are seen (2 Cor. 4.18). The Christian community is contextualized culturally, with historically conditioned features of existence. Its state of being, however, also has a theandric subsistence, pertaining to both God and humankind. In so far as it is grounded in God, the church has two aspects, the divine and the human, that permeate each other. The writer of the letter to the Ephesians in 3.9–11 describes his mission:

to make all people see what is the plan (ὀικονομία = also fellow-

---

[32] Hardy, 'The Future of Theology', p. 22.
[33] Martin Luther, W.A. 34/1.276.7f.

ship) of the mystery hidden for ages in God who created all things; that through the church (ἐκκλησία) the manifold wisdom (σοφία) of God might now be made known to the principalities and powers in the heavenly places.

The church is made a witness by God to the essence of all things being derived from future fulfilment and anticipation of the complete penetration of the whole world by the Holy Spirit of God. The Holy Spirit makes of the church a community of hope. Thus, only a sophialogy, or doctrine of the Holy Spirit, that reconsiders the evangelical witness of the Holy Spirit to the mysteries of God is adequate to the discerning of our culture's needs and the responsibilities of the church in being the community of hope for the world.

Doctrinally speaking, as Vladimir Lossky puts it, 'The Church is an image of the Holy Trinity'.[34] In the church the Father, Son and Holy Spirit may be glorified as the Holy Spirit grants to each person the possibility of fulfilling the likeness of God in the common nature. In the church, Pentecost was/is the sequel and result of the likeness of God entering the historical process in person.[35] An early authority, the anonymous sermon commonly called *Clement's Second Letter to the Corinthians* affirms:

> Guard the flesh so that you may share in the spirit ... This flesh is able to share in so great a life and immortality, because the Holy Spirit cleaves to it.[36]

The Holy Spirit is the guarantee of the certain expectation of future glory that is the product of divine grace and Christ's prevenient merit. The Holy Spirit does not add hope to the church but makes it of its very essence, qualifying the very being of the church as the body of Christ in the world. In the midst of present needs, this involves deep changes in our way of thinking in order to be open at all times to what Gabriel Marcel, a Christian existentialist, calls 'the supernatural connection between a return (νόστος) and something completely new (καινόν τί)'.[37] Piercing through time, the prophetic character of hope throws us into a dynamic in which future and past subsist in the moment now. But how are these connections to be asked and dealt with? This is where biblical exposition

[34] Vladimir Lossky, *The Mystical Theology of the Eastern Church* (London: James Clarke, ET 1957), p. 176.
[35] Lossky, *Mystical Theology*, p. 159.
[36] *The Library of Christian Classics*, Vol. 1, *Early Church Fathers*, trans. & ed. C. C. Richardson (London: SCM, 1953), pp. 193–202.
[37] Gabriel Marcel, 'A Metaphysic of Hope', in *Homo Viator* (London: Victor Gollanz, 1951), p. 67.

comes into play, as we pick up strands that weave a way of thinking about the 'why', 'what' and 'how' of Christian hope that penetrate into the inmost depths of reality and the communal life of the church.

VII. THE LOGOS OF CHRISTIAN HOPE[38]

(a) The 'logos of contrast' compares present experience to future hope. The believer, says Paul, hopes not for what can be seen but for what cannot be seen. What can be seen is temporary, but what cannot be seen is eternal (2 Cor. 4.16 – 5.10). Experience and hope stand at variance. In the passage as a whole, Paul sets out a series of contrasts in which the present life is compared to the eternal ages of glory:

things present	things to come
things momentary	things eternal
things light	things weighty
affliction	glory

The 'logos of contrast' compares the present life to the eternal ages of glory that are to come. In hope we are saved, says Paul (Rom. 8.24), but we do not see that for which we hope. We wait for it with patience. The whole creation groans as if in labour. It can do nothing but wait and hope for liberation from bondage to corruption. (Cf. Rom. 16.15; 1 Cor. 15.20ff.; Col. 1.15ff.)[39]

(b) The 'logos of confidence' is that in which hope is a synthesis, and a reconciliation of what is seen and what cannot be seen. Throughout scripture, hope is a word of certainty. Its dominant meaning is found in the relation of faith to the faithfulness of God (Ps. 42.5–6; Ezek. 29.16; Mic. 7.7; Phil. 3.4; 2 Thess. 3.4). To hope in God is almost identical to having absolute trust in him. This brings us to a very big difference between hope in popular thought and hope in the Christian tradition. In popular thought, hope is characterized by uncertainty and ideas of possibility. It is the separation between the ideal and the real.[40] In scripture, hope is about being sure and steadfast in what God has done, is doing, and will do, and it is this certainty that opens up possibility. What is visible, says Paul, makes little or no difference to the content of Christian

[38] Space limitation prevents engagement with questions of how the biblical passages quoted are also contextualized. It is assumed, however, that scripture still impresses upon us an appropriate frame of reference for our understanding of Christian hope.
[39] The logic of contrast and contradiction is stressed in the Introduction to Jürgen Moltmann, *Theology of Hope* (London: SCM, ET 1967).
[40] See Paul Hessert, *Christ and the End of Meaning* (Massachusetts: Element, 1993), pp. 226f.

hope that relates not to external things but to the things of faith (2 Cor. 4.18). Christian hope rests on the divine act of salvation in Christ and carries an element of sure confidence because this act has been accomplished (Phil. 1.20; Heb. 3.6; 1 Pet. 1.21). Anticipation of the eschaton is not blind optimism that all will turn out for the best but the presence of eschata[41] in the here and now.

(c) The 'logos of commonality' is not a system of reasoning but the transmuting power that connects the 'why', 'what' and 'how' of Christian hope. If the 'why' of Christian hope is the contrast between present experience and future hope; if the 'what' is our confidence in Christ that God will reconcile all things to himself (Col. 1.20); then the 'how' is the church's mode of existence as inhabited by hope because of its proclamation in the Spirit of Jesus as Lord. By linking 'how' with 'why' and 'what', we learn something new. We learn that we cannot dismiss the 'how' and say that it is only subsequent to the 'what' and 'why', because that is to separate the common action of the Trinity. It is to bring the Holy Spirit into the discussion only after the structure of the church's hope is in place Christologically. The 'logic of commonality' is about the hope of the Christian community and its very existence being constituted Christologically and Sophialogically from the very beginning (Isa. 42.1–9; Ezek. 11.19, 18.30; Matt. 3.16; Jn. 3.5–6; Rom. 8.11; Gal. 3.3). 'Why', 'what' and 'how' cannot be divorced and we must keep asking and dealing with their connection if the content of Christian hope is learned and lived.

(d) The 'logos of compassion' concerns precisely this question of how Christian hope is learned among the urgent needs of the day. It is about giving content to the 'how' of Christian living: the creation of space to breathe at the heart of the most impossible. One of the most significant words of the Gospels to describe Jesus' ministry is compassion (Matt. 15.32, 20.34; Mk. 5.19, 8:2; Lk. 7.13). We read about Jesus' suffering with those who were hungry, blind, disturbed and grieving. This is no theoretical matter but an everyday re-discovery of God's truth that shines through its life in the world. It is a work in which there is no such thing as failure, only the vocation to participate in the likeness of Christ. Kierkegaard named hope 'the missionary of heaven' – that which is sent out or forth to produce a particular effect.[42] In a poetic image of hope down on all fours creeping into the cave that he was inhabiting at the time, Kierkegaard writes that hope was one of few visitors in that particular dark place. Like Kierkegaard's visitor, the church is called to be hope that becomes so vividly visible in history that humankind can touch it.

---

[41] John Zizioulas uses the term *eschata* to refer to the foretaste of eternal life given in the Eucharist in *Being as Communion* (New York: St. Vladimir's Seminary Press, 1985), pp. 114ff.

[42] Søren Kierkegaard, *Either/Or*, Part 1, trans. H. V. Hong and E. H. Hong (Princeton: Princeton Univ. Press, 1987), p. 483.

(e) Finally, the 'logos of consummation' is about the place of the church within the promise of God that all things should flourish without corruption.[43] Words of George Herbert come to mind:

> I gave to Hope a watch of mine: but he
>   An anchor gave to me.
> Then an old prayer-book I did present:
>   And he an optick sent.
> With that I gave a viall full of tears:
>   But he a few green ears:
> Ah Loyterer! I'le no more, no more I'le bring:
>   I did expect a ring.[44]

The imagery opens up fresh ways of looking and suggestion. The symbol of an anchor is, of course, an ancient Christian depiction of confidence in Christ. The homilies of St John Chrysostom contain the example of steersmen who, when the sea is raging and the clouds are rushing together, lay hold of the sacred anchor and find therein the hope in God that remains unshaken and unmoved.[45] It is the imagery of the ring given by the bridegroom, however, that speaks most directly of the ultimate hope of the Christian community to be joined in union with Christ in the age to come (Joel 2.26; Song 1.1–2.2; Jn. 3.29; Eph. 5.27; Rev. 21.2–9, 22.17).

It is increasingly difficult in our culture to speak of the nuptial union as a 'showing' (epiphany) to humankind of the order of the last days. Some feminist disenchantment with marriage causes many to question whether biblically sanctioned patriarchal structures render marriage inherently patriarchal, and thus incapable of symbolizing the most intimate encounter between God and humankind. This calls for far deeper reflection than is possible here. For the moment, however, let us accept that what the Book of Common Prayer calls 'the Mystical Union that is betwixt Christ and his Church' is the ultimate and glorious hope of the Christian community that has been promised through the resurrection of Christ. This is what Karl Barth calls the real *future*, distinguished from the mere futurity of the church.[46] It is the promise of rejuvenation and renewal such that

---

[43] Irenaeus, *Against Heresies*, Book V, 'Redemption and the World to Come', in *Early Christian Fathers*, Vol. 1 (London: SCM, 1953), pp. 385ff.
[44] George Herbert, 'Hope', in *The English Poems of George Herbert*, ed. C. A. Patrides (London: Dent, 1974, reprinted 1991):
  optick: telescope; also, eye glass.
  ring: i.e., of Christ the Bridegroom.
[45] Homily XVI in *The Homilies of S. John of Chrysostom*, A Library of Fathers of the Holy Catholic Church (Oxford: John Henry Parker, 1842), pp. 264ff.
[46] Karl Barth, *Credo* (London: Hodder & Stoughton, ET 1936), p. 119.

God not only sustains and sanctifies the church but brings it to ultimate glory in union with his son. The 'logos of consummation', however, is not confined to the church. The church is not divorced from the world nor suddenly separated from the final destiny of the cosmos as a whole. Creation too, writes Paul, awaits the revealing of the children of God (Rom. 8.19).

VIII. SEE I MAKE ALL THINGS NEW . . .

John on Patmos heard the words:

> See, the home of God is among mortals.
> He will dwell with them as their God, and they shall be his people, and God himself will be with them. (Rev. 21.3)

That's the way John sees it – the vocation of all things is to participate in the fullness of divine life in free harmony with the will of God. So also for Irenaeus: 'God is rich in all things, and all things are his'.[47] All things are renewed in Christ, and in him the promise of incorruption is given to the created order as well as to the church. Note, however, that in envisioning this perfect unity John conceives no need for either church or temple. There will be a new heaven and a new earth without any church as previously known.[48] What clearer confirmation can there be that God's purposes of blessing reach beyond the church to all things? The Christian community is a provisional rather than ultimate entity because God's dealings with the whole cosmos mean that it lives in anticipation of the fulfilment of creation's purpose. The church cannot exist for itself but is in service to the coming of God's reign. As Lossky writes: 'The entire universe is called to enter within the Church ... that it may be transformed after the consummation of the ages, into the kingdom of God'.[49]

CONCLUSION

Thus, the hope of the Christian community is no less real or relevant for

[47] Irenaeus, *Against Heresies*, p. 391.
[48] On the relevant distinction here between church and kingdom of God, see W. Pannenberg, *Theology and the Kingdom of God*, ed. R. J. Neuhaus (Philadelphia: Westminster, 1969), pp. 72ff.
[49] Lossky, *Mystical Theology*, p. 113.

city life than that of any materialized eschatology. It is no less pervasive, immanent or beautiful than any neo-stoic hopes for harmony with nature. The 'logos of consummation' is based, like every aspect of the hope of the Christian community, upon a right understanding of the common action of the Trinity to draw all being, immaterial and physical, toward the good.[50] It is difficult to know why, in its histories, the Christian community has shown so little sign of hope. At its heart, however, is the hope of an outpouring of divine energies and the transformation of the whole created universe. There is nothing to say that these purposes of God cannot be frustrated by refusal to follow in the way of Christ. However, the very breadth and inclusiveness of the eschatological hope mean that, from the vantage point of faith, all human time and space is enveloped in eternal love and waits on God alone.[51]

[50] Lossky, *Mystical Theology*, pp. 100ff.
[51] My thanks are due to Dr Chris Southgate and the Revd Jeremy Law for their comments on an early draft of this piece.

20

On Tearing the Darkness to Tatters: Hope for this World?

ANN LOADES

Of recent attempts to commend hope perhaps the most provocative is that of John Kekes' *Facing Evil*.[1] It is not the purpose of this essay to engage with all the intricacies of his argument, but sufficient must be said to force upon us the issue of why we might not simply rest with what he says, but find resources for hope which can embrace his but go beyond them. Briefly, Kekes agrees that Christianity is correct in its view of our weakness (which he re-describes), but argues that it is incorrect in its hope of supernatural help. The Enlightenment, its intended successor, then, is correct in its view that we can depend only on ourselves, but incorrect in reposing hope in human reason and decency.

Kekes holds out to us 'a reasonable and modest hope' of his own careful and critical fashioning, the key to which is 'to increase the limited control we have over our lives by developing the appropriate institutions in our society and the reflective temper in ourselves' (pp. 236–7). His crucial starting-point is his invitation to learn the lesson that we ourselves are agents of 'the contingency, indifference and destructiveness that jeopardize the human aspiration to live good lives' (p. 5). Human beings find satisfaction in the exercise of their talents in appropriate conditions but are vulnerable to multiple handicaps, the contingencies of life. Being at the mercy of natural forces, coming to undeserved harm are matters serious enough to perplex us, but our plight is most profoundly threatened by our own sheer destructiveness, shown in the ways in which we are ripe and ready for 'malevolence, rage, fanaticism, cruelty and selfishness', all of them 'active and regular performers in the repertoire of human motivation' (p. 25). Assuming the tripartite characterization of things in the world to be properly evaluated by contingency, indifference and destructiveness, and ourselves simply to be part of the world, we are as it were bound to embody its general features. Adversity then is intrinsic to our lives in ways we may not recognize despite our experience of the tensions between our aspirations and what we do, as self-saboteurs.

We may think then of evil (undeserved harm) as moral, that is, chosen

---

[1] John Kekes, *Facing Evil* (Princeton: Princeton University Press, 1990), referred to by page number in the text.

and caused by human beings; as nonmoral, that is, caused by non-human agency; and unchosen, yet caused by human agency. It is his remarks on this third category and on 'insufficiency' which help to focus our attention on an account of how it is that people may not have chosen to become the dogmatic, insensitive or weak beings they are, but how they may nevertheless be the sort of persons who are extremely likely to cause, and keep on causing, serious evil. The evil that they do is characteristic and predictable, though unchosen (p. 75). The point is not to isolate those who exhibit insufficiency (he analyses expediency and malevolence too) from the rest of humankind, but to indicate how lack of control results from our not having the cognitive, emotive or volitional capacities to exercise it. 'True hope', then, is thus deemed to be intimately connected with the possibility of extending within ourselves the area we can control, though that very possibility itself is 'tainted' by the contingency, indifference and destructiveness which are among our most fundamental human characteristics.

In the course of his critique of the extent to which choice, action, improvement and responsibility matter 'insofar as they are signs of the deeper, more fundamental consideration of character, moral agency, achievement, and desert' (p. 99) Kekes focuses on the example of two children murdered by someone himself brutalized in childhood (pp. 97–8). Writers on the problem of evil, theological or not, are familiar enough with examples of children who suffer undeserved harm. Our version of the problem, and Kekes', is exacerbated if we take the example of a child dying at the hands of other children. 'He had never encountered anything like it, and hoped he never would again.'[2] But why should a police officer in charge of an investigation thus express his own sense of shock at a child's dying, and in so doing, express a particular social mood? For the journalist learning all he could, and presenting it judiciously and fairly ('Everything in this book is true to the best of my knowledge' ... no imagining, invention or embellishment of what happened) gives us a picture of insufficiency, of a world in which it is indeed the case that children not yet in their 'teens will have to endure the knowledge of their own embodiment of that insufficiency'. They will have to come to some understanding of what they did when in law, at least, a consideration of the facts of the matter would begin with the presumption that they were unable to understand the seriousness of their actions. Growing up for them will involve a more or less precarious attempt to establish a self with sufficient control over the contingency, indifference and destructiveness which resulted in the killing. The mood of shock, we might say, is because their disastrous actions which brought irretrievable harm to another, younger child, simply and unendurably force our own insuffi-

[2] David J. Smith, *The Sleep of Reason* (London: Century, 1994), p. 1.

ciencies on our attention. Being children, they had to face a prosecution which had to rebut the presumption that they were unable to understand the seriousness of their actions in order to obtain a conviction. Suppose them not to have even that initial privilege of childhood, but to be ourselves, having to endure a self-understanding which however tentative and approximate or (preferably) thorough-going and adequate, will encourage in us Kekes' 'reflective temper'; and thereafter develop in us some shreds of true hope in order to engage in social and political reform as best we may, without over-reaching ourselves.

To proceed with Kekes so far is to follow him in his attempt to shift 'Western sensibility' in interesting ways. We are not good and gone to the bad, but thoroughly 'mixed', though if anything, blacker than we have been accustomed to paint ourselves. For it is not that we have at our disposal trans-empirical resources of freedom, rationality and morality which can foster 'our primary potential for goodness' in competition with 'natural causes', since freedom, rationality and morality are simply among the natural causes we can identify (pp. 140–1). In particular, for all that can be said about enlarging our capacity for control over what we are, it does not follow that thereby we are inevitably bound to foster our good potentialities: hope itself can exhibit bad character, malicious desire.[3] Things can go in any direction, so to speak, but whatever the case, we cannot count on 'outside' help. For Kekes, as we have indicated, true hope depends on cultivating better understanding of the conditions of our lives, doing what we can to mitigate the worst in the favour of the better, and realizing that we may fail. We have to live without a Kant-style belief that we are aligning ourselves with 'cosmic justice', and above all, we have to learn to live without the expectation of salvation:

> The enlarged understanding I am recommending permits true hope because it saves those who possess it from the futility of hounding the unresponsive heavens to relieve their misfortune and because it prepares the people who have grown to develop it to pick up the damaged pieces, if they can be picked up, and go on. True hope does not come from there being a guarantee that good projects reasonably conducted will succeed. It comes from the confidence that we have done what is in our power to make them succeed and that if they fail despite our merits and efforts, we need not be destroyed as a result. Thus, the possession of an enlarged understanding does not promise good lives; it promises to make lives as free from evil as the essential conditions permit. (p. 189)

Thus far, we might say that we have a re-interpretation of what the

[3] Louis P. Pojman, *Religious Belief and the Will* (London: Routledge & Kegan Paul, 1986), p. 222.

Christian tradition has said of our mortal weakness – indeed a re-interpretation which reinforces it. Kekes has also tidied away 'Enlightenment' hope in human reason and decency in so far as such hope depended on the supposition that these run on a distinguishable and parallel track with 'natural causes' but from which they may be clearly distinguished. He has helped to demolish our confidence that our rational and moral choices (and we might add, even our hopes) align us with a transcendent moral order. Such a moral order as there is will be one which we can modestly but with determination strive to bring about.

Understandably, Kekes wants to avoid as much as he can of 'the minefield of Kantian exegesis' (p. 136), but much though we may share his wish, there are aspects of Kant's thinking which take us closer than Kekes can to some at least fingernail hold on what the Christian tradition may have to offer in relation to the experience of profound failure and indeed destruction, the aspects of human living where the pieces cannot be picked up and where human lives are destroyed. Kekes learns from tragedy about the essential conditions of life, but sheers away from the hopelessness that responding to tragedy may provoke in us. (His examples are *Oedipus the King*, *King Lear* and *The Heart of Darkness*). At one level, Kekes' enlarged understanding and reflective temper are of a piece with the Socratic-Kantian habit of self-questioning and of questioning by others. Kant's preoccupation with truthfulness, however, as being at the very core of such relationship to God as may be possible, precipitates in him transformation from elation inspired by respect for another or by the spectacle of the heavens (for him an indication of divine infinity and grandeur) to a humility associated with his way of signifying deity. Thus God is deemed to be for us (in Kant's ultimately apophatic theology) holy lawgiver (and creator), good governor (and preserver) and just judge. This profoundly juridical sense he has of God takes shape because he fosters a particular mode of self-appraisal in himself, evident in the last part of his third *Critique* and in late essays on the failure of all attempted philosophical theodicies and on eschatology. The dissolution of all pretence, self-indulgence and the sheer opacity of human beings to themselves as to one another, yet without possibility of mistake (divine judgement) is yielded to him by the very language he uses to make his moral experience clear to himself, cluttered as he knows he is by circumstance and the confusions of self-interest.

Michalson's treatment of Kant's *Religion Within the Limits of Reason Alone* reminds us, as Kekes' position does, that we could be anything, good or above all, bad (radical evil).[4] Unabsolved of our obligation to

---

[4] Gordon E. Michalson, *Fallen Freedom: Kant on Radical Evil and Moral Regeneration* (Cambridge: CUP, 1990), referred to by page number in the text; I. Kant, *Religion Within the Limits of Reason Alone*, trans. T. M. Greene and H. H. Hudson (New York: Harper, 1960), referred to in the text by *Religion* and the page number.

make ourselves not merely better than we are, but good, yields dividends about the pathos of a struggle we will all lose in our efforts to re-order what is naturally given to us. (One important difference between Kekes and Kant is that whilst both may agree that evil arises in ways we may not finally be able to conceptualize, Kekes displays no Kantian unease that reason must cohabit with sensuousness.) In addition to the pressure point which provokes words about God as just judge, there is another in which Kant invokes the Johannine metaphor of 'rebirth'. In this intellectual limitation marked by appeal to scripture when struggling with the nature of moral regeneration (*Religion*, pp. 43, 184), Kant is unclear about how to make sense of attributing identity to a moral agent as a free being, with motivations bearing on present decisions clarified in connected and explicable ways; and further, Kant's talk of 'regeneration' is also connected to reference to divine aid as an object of rational hope. How indeed do I hope for divine assistance without allowing my trust in its delivery to undermine me morally, except as a means of keeping me morally stimulated and encouraged? There are acute difficulties here in Kant's understanding of how a divine judge may view both revolutionary dispositional change and gradual reform of our sensuousness. It may have a use if the divine view could somehow be related to the way in which we infer that we had or have a change of heart from our gradual self-reform, with the 'how' of the process, whatever its degree of achievement, opaque to us.

An even more interesting and severe pressure point is Kant's attempt to come to terms with what Michalson calls 'Autonomy and Atonement' which is what will edge us from Kant to attempt a specifically Christian perspective in relation to Kekes' criticism of Christianity. On the one hand, Kant's view is that there can be no unpaid moral debts in the progress towards renewal, curious though it is that there seems to be more continuity of self yielded by the accumulation of wicked than of virtuous acts, with punishment of wickedness occurring temporally during the process of change. Punishment is understood in terms of the struggle for renewal, and indeed of a kind of Christlikeness, astonishingly, since the 'new self' endures such suffering for the 'other' one. Important here is less 'morally legislative reason' manifest in the Teacher of the Gospels, but more Kant's belief that the moral outcome of his combat is to break the power of evil, so that evil can no longer hold, against their will, those to whom a moral dominion, an 'asylum' is now offered (*Religion*, p. 77). In other words, as Michalson puts it, there is something distinctive about Jesus, for although without his historical appearance we would not (for Kant) be less rational or less moral in potential, we might be less able to act morally (p. 121). Kant is unable to make much sense of 'God so loved the world' but gets on better with 'Which of you convinceth me of sin?' in so far as that can mean that

Jesus' living and dying is somehow required to free us to make good our essential moral capacities (*Religion*, p. 59, on Jn. 8.46).

Much though Kant fears 'a grace dreamed of in slothful trust' (*Religion*, p. 182), of which even prayer for 'change of heart, the putting on of the new man, called rebirth' could presumably in itself be an instance, it is again in his remarks on prayer that we find yet another of his interesting limit points. Predictably prayer must be undertaken firmly to establish the intention to further moral goodness in ourselves, 'and repeatedly to awaken the disposition of goodness in the heart' (*Religion*, p. 181). At one level he discusses even the Lord's Prayer in terms which make it virtually redundant: 'One finds in it nothing but the resolution to good life-conduct which, taken with the consciousness of our frailty, carries with it the persistent desire to be a worthy member in the kingdom of God', a wish which, if genuine, of itself achieves its object (*Religion*, p. 183). We can note here that whilst Kekes too has a place for mercy, forgiveness, generosity, and the justifiable overruling of moral requirements (p. 160), for him prayer even in Kant's sense finds no place in developing enlarged understanding and reflective temper in ourselves. We may perhaps push Kant over the limits which he occasionally approaches, given that he uses the Johannine text in his own way, for instance, when considering 'the personified idea of the good principle' as the one who assumes sorrows 'in fullest measure in order to further the world's good', who takes upon himself every affliction, 'up to the most ignominious death, for the good of the world and even for his enemies', and is yet victorious in the face of the fiercest onslaughts (*Religion*, pp. 55ff.). It may be that because the juridical emphasis of the Johannine text comes in for an extended series of reflections (*Religion*, pp. 136–7) that Kant's own struggle with the 'Spirit of Truth' and with scriptural exegesis brings him back at least at one point from supposing all forms of prayer to be dispensable (*Religion*, p. 103 on Jn. 6.13 and 5.39).

If, with Aquinas, we may suppose Kant to hold that 'prayer is the interpreter of desire'[5] we can notice that in attempting to interpret the doctrine of God as Father, Son and Spirit, Kant does not recommend that we 'invoke' God in terms of 'this multiform personality', but that 'we can call upon Him in the name of that object loved of Him, which He Himself esteems above all else, with which to enter into moral union is [our] desire and also [our] duty' (*Religion*, p. 137). It could well be that what lies behind Kant's text at this point is the Johannine discourse of chapter sixteen, followed by the great prayer of chapter seventeen with Jesus' approaching death. And at this stage we may turn to those two chapters directly, rather than filtered through Kant as it were, to find some way of thinking hopefully in relation to the utter despair which

---

[5] Aquinas, *Summa Theologiae*, 2a 2ae 9 ad 2.

may confront us in tragedy, hope which we need not suppose to be false although it may both embrace and yet go well beyond Kekes' proposals, as I think Kant does when he too faces our final 'limit'.

There are many ways of reading this Gospel, but one way is to appreciate the double focus of the text. One focus is on the Jesus the disciples first met and knew, who baffled and bewildered them, and the second is on the Jesus known to the community for whom this Gospel was written, thinking about the relationship between Jesus and his disciples and themselves, living on the other side of Jesus being raised from death by the God he calls Father, a Father holy and righteous to whom he prays, and who has not abandoned him. We could say that the Johannine motif of 'ascent' to God receives one of its expressions in the great prayer of aspiration attributed to the Son, who prays for his and his Father's own, not that they should be taken out of the world but that his Father should keep them from evil. At the point where Jesus comes to plain speaking, the disciples grasp the meaning of the horrors ahead, said in the simplest possible way: 'I came forth from the Father, and am come into the world; again, I leave the world, and go to the Father'. As God remains with Jesus, his disciples are meant to learn that God through him remains also with them, and it takes some persuading, because they are under threat. 'You shall be scattered', though he promises them peace and exhorts them to courage, because 'I have overcome the world', a world in which despair, remorse, isolation and bitter defeat have their place.

Rather than Kekes' examples, we might turn to H. F. M. Prescott's *The Man on a Donkey*,[6] cast in the form of a chronicle of the sixteenth-century Pilgrimage of Grace, which would illustrate what Kekes says about contingency, indifference and destructiveness and the part these may play in our lives. Here is one historical episode, transfused with a 'Johannine' understanding of continued divine presence, in response to which we may find courage. The horror here is the discovery of the extent of Henrician mercy for Aske, about to die a traitor's death, a 'mercy' gained for him by July's plea that he 'be full dead before he be dismembered'. To this the royal response is, 'Tell him that surely he shall hang till he be full dead' (p. 673). Aske, the Great Captain of the Pilgrims, is put in chains and pushed out from the top of the tower of the great Keep at York. A week later:

By this time that which dangled from the top of the Keep at York, moving only as the wind swung it, knew neither day nor night, nor that it had been Robert Aske, not even that it had been a man.

Even now, however, it was not quite insentient. Drowning yet never

---

[6] H. F. M. Prescott, *The Man on a Donkey: A Chronicle* (London: Eyre & Spottiswoode, 1953), referred to in the text by page number.

drowned, far below the levels of daylight consciousness, it suffered. There was darkness and noise, noise intolerably vast or unendurably near, drilling inward as a screw bites and turns, and the screw was pain. Sometimes noise, pain, darkness and that blind thing that dangled were separate; sometimes they ran together and became one. (p. 688)

It is half-crazed Malle who somehow knows of God 'moving nigh-hand' in the darkness, 'beyond the furthest edge of hope' (p. 689). And Aske himself is supposed to have reached the point where he is 'aware of One – vanquished God, Saviour who could as little save others as Himself. But now, beside Him and beyond was nothing, and He was silence and light' (p. 690). And Malle is the one who whispers 'No darkness, no darkness, for God hath come so nigh in the darkness that it tore all to tatters, and now is quite done away' (p. 693), and sees among the remnants of a meal in the deserted Frater of a Priory fragments of fish and of honeycomb.

I have suggested in this essay that there is much to be learned from Kekes' treatment of evil, in order to see what 'hope' might amount to when we face our own insufficiencies. In practical terms, some greater control over ourselves may indeed be hoped for as we instil within ourselves a sense of what we are, and alert ourselves both to our potential for choosing and causing harm and to our potential for doing better, as particular persons who constitute certain societies. To learn about these possibilities is to learn also about hope. I have also suggested that Kant, the Enlightenment representative from whom Kekes wishes to distance himself most clearly, helps to nudge us in the direction of a reconsideration of Christian hope in relation to ultimate futility, the occasions on which people are indeed destroyed in their efforts to engage with evil, especially when social and political stakes are high. Sometimes we are engaged in good and worthwhile projects which can be reasonably and modestly conducted, but sometimes some of us have to engage unavoidably with situations of great complexity and importance, the stuff of at least some political and social tragedies. The choice might well then be between the hopelessness past which Kekes wants to negotiate us, whilst learning from tragedy the extent to which we are indeed too often the authors of our own misfortunes, and the kind of hope which is akin to courage. This needs to be subject to a 'divine' scrutiny of the kind Kant seems driven to indicate, a possible safeguard against malevolence and destructiveness beyond Kekes' 'enlarged understanding', though it is far from irrelevant also to thinking of ordinary human weaknesses and insincerity.

Kant hoped for moral 'rebirth', and in his writing this is connected, despite himself we may think, with thinking about the particular historical person of Jesus whose dying seems to make us freer to live morally. Taking clues from some of Kant's own biblical references, I have suggested that as Kant goes beyond Kekes, so he is at a number of points brought up against his own limits, and seems to be on the verge of seeing that he must go beyond them as we may be driven to do to rediscover the possibility of hope and its relation to salvation, which *cannot* be interpreted to mean salvation from death. Just as we gain clues about what hope means from the very devising of our very limited projects, so we may learn a little about salvation from our successes. And when the stakes are higher than those involved in our manageable range of projects, hope and salvation may have a place even in relation to what may seem to be complete disaster. This is to turn to the possibility that there is something other than either hopelessness or resignation which is needed in response to the apparent utter failure of the supposed good.

After juxtaposing Kekes and Kant, and then Kant and texts from the Fourth Gospel, I then in effect lay side by side part of that Gospel and a historical reconstruction of Robert Aske's challenge to his king in the Pilgrimage of Grace, and since it is written in the form of a novel, the complexity of motive, human insufficiency and aspiration can be explored to disaster point. Only fish and honeycomb in the leftover chaos of a hurried meal are seen by Malle as signs of the presence of one who was 'still the last dear love of a vanquished and tortured man' (p. 688). And it is Malle who says, 'So men may have courage' (p. 689). In the form of a novel exploring a historical crisis, one of many such possible crises in a world in which the worst has its place, for reasons Kekes shows us, we may begin to suppose that we might hope in a different way.

This need not be construed as a 'false hope', if by that we mean what may save us from disaster, but a hope which might sustain at least some in appalling extremity, dying with, if not dying for, a 'Father'. This may be a hope that we do not want to have to have, but one which may in the end sustain our more modest expectations for this world, and preserve them from mediocrity, rather than our modest hopes being the only 'true hope' there can be.

PART SEVEN: A RESPONSE TO CONTRIBUTORS

A Magnificent Complexity: Letting God be God in Church, Society and Creation

Daniel W. Hardy

Introduction

WHEN it was first suggested, I was – to say the least – hugely surprised by the prospect of a volume of essays dedicated to me by a number of my friends. And I am still awed and humbled by this outpouring on my behalf, the more so because its main instigator is my close long-time colleague, David Ford, with whom I have shared so much theological thought and activity.

At the same time, I am pleased and relieved by the way in which it has been constructed, not as focused on me but on the dimensions and tasks of theology in our day with which I have been concerned as I have followed my vocation in theology. And it is to the contributions which the essays make to theology that I address myself in what follows. My purpose is to engage with them, seek to understand the significance of the response they make to some larger issues confronting theology, and press forward with these questions.

Let me say at the outset that I am delighted by them, and the serious-ness with which they address these major issues. I am also grateful for the opportunity they provide to consolidate my purposes and concerns in theological work. As I move from one phase of my life to another, the opportunity to respond to them has enabled me to develop the lines of my further work in theology, when I hope for the right circumstances in which to continue with it.[1] In that sense, the essays contributed by these fine colleagues and the response I now make to them are the gift and sign of my own future work.

The overarching issues of the book, as I now understand them, have to do with the integrity of theology within itself and its coherence with the wider issues raised by human life in the world today. To be sure, the topics discussed are not the only ones involved, but they do represent

[1] This was written on the day on which I submitted my resignation as Director of the Center of Theological Inquiry.

major dimensions in the question of the inner integrity and external coherence of theology.[2]

I. MEDIATIONS: OPENING THEOLOGY

Theology, it seems to me, suffers impoverishment through the self-limitation of its resources. It is a matter of fascination and interest to me, as I think it should be with others, how many characteristics of the world in which we live reflect, possibly in refracted ways, the work and purposes of God. It is not that I would wish to suggest that these bear a correspondence to God, whether direct or analogical, for that would suggest a relationship which may be much less rich and complex than the one which actually pertains; accordingly we should not treat them as forms of 'evidence' for God, or 'vestiges' of his presence. Even so, there is no reason why we should not expect a relationship which is much more multifold than the ones normally explored in theology, which are centred for example on those of rationality, word and (less successfully in recent years) sacrament.

It has proved a strong temptation for theology through the ages to concentrate its energies on responding to the master-disciplines most influential in forming human opinion. Through much of Western human history, these have been those of philosophy and its variants. Perhaps this is understandable, given the enormous task of responding to the issues raised in order to show the credibility of the Christian *paideia*. But it has resulted in a loss of attention for the issues raised elsewhere. And this has become more and more problematic in modern times, not only because of the range of legitimate and fruitful avenues to human understanding and practice which have appeared but also because the master-disciplines by which they were once co-ordinated have lost their capacity for synthesis. The danger is that theology will increasingly lose touch with the richness and problems of modern life and understanding, and become increasingly abstract.

Approaching theology through the many fruitful avenues of modern understanding is not necessarily easy, for the developing complexity of understanding and practice resists overarching unifying insights and methods, whether those of philosophical or scientific discussion, or – still more, because of their tendency to abstractness – by the imposition of 'theological' conclusions. But the danger of not doing so is that theology

---

[2] One of my own major concerns, not represented here, is with how the sciences assist in understanding the conditions of life in the world, and therefore intersect with theological understanding.

will become an increasingly 'academic' pursuit, 'academic' in the wrong sense.[3]

Why should these many avenues to human understanding and practice not be treated as *loci* for understanding the abundance of God and of God's purposes and work? Each may then be capable of concentrating new insight into the conditions through which they come to be as they are, are nourished and corrected, and ultimately brought to their completion – all of these as formed by God. Such an approach may not lead in so many unrelated directions as might first appear, but to the realization that they are integrated at a more profound level.

These issues form a *leitmotif* of the present book. How many and rich are the ways by which the purposes of God can be traced! And how much do they enrich our life in the world with God, and even our awareness of the very being of God! And how convergent do they become when they are seen to manifest the work of God! It is not that the issues raised are simply traced, and in the book we find how rich and difficult is the process of tracing them.

Jeremy Begbie's essay shows the richness which emerges when one theologizes *through* music, through facing the dynamics of music itself. In focusing on the relation between divine eternity and created time, he addresses one of the most intractable issues in current theological discussion, where so few have been prepared to face the convergence of the two which is implied in considering the nature of the God who – in Christian understanding – is deeply implicated in history.

In retrospect it now seems that we have lived with a certain kind of compromise for some centuries, one which has now dissolved. Where there was an identifiable teleological pattern in world-history, it could be seen to correspond to the timeless purposes of God. Perhaps this was in evidence in the directional pattern of music in the Western world as Jeremy Begbie describes it.[4] But with the widespread resistance to teleology which has marked modern times, and the resultant dislocation of the correspondence of God's purposes with the world, evident in the difficulty with which people speak of providence today, how can musical form suggest the convergence of eternity and time in God's work?

As Jeremy Begbie analyses it, John Tavener's music provides one response, 'constructing self-contained units of internally coherent material with often only the loosest connections between them', as if we were moving from icon to icon. There is no teleology in evidence here, not

---

[3] There is an important distinction to be made between disciplines which are – because implicitly rooted in common understanding and practice – *prepared* for their relation to the complexities of the world as it exists, and those which are not. While both may be intensive and disciplined, the sense in which they are 'academic' differs widely.

[4] Such a pattern is found, for example, in Bach's music, not only in its tonalities but in the symmetrical arrangement of his Passions.

even compressed teleologies.[5] Instead, these units are seen as 'musical decompression' – the opening of an aural space of freedom – more like places for mystical unity with the Eternal. Perhaps, in a manner which befits icons, it is the suffusion of such music by prayer that opens them, not to sheer vacuity, but to what Tavener takes to be the eternity of God, the negation of created time. But as Begbie points out, this seems to advocate developing an 'immunity' to the opportunities and threats which appear in time, which (together with the implied view of Christ as 'a divine timeless presence inserted into time, rather than of a transformative within created time') is less helpful in dealing with the time which permeates our existence in the world.

The alternative which he offers is potentially much more helpful, music as continuity in temporal succession as the healing of the temporal distension which is evident in the fragmentation of the meaning of human life through temporal discontinuity. By such healing, our fragmentation is healed, and our attention directed to the divine unity.[6] Such a continuity is interwoven with the physical; as Zuckerkandl suggests, it may grant a 'peculiarly profound experience of time ... as a function of the interrelationship between physical realities, and thus as an intrinsic aspect of created being'. By such means, human beings may participate in the relation of physical entities in such a way as to bring the possibility of peaceful life and interaction with the time granted by God to creation. As I see it, music – simultaneously external to us and internal to us – has the capacity to shape our life through the presentation of an ordering in and of time whose possibility God has conferred. Of course, how – and whether – music functions in such a way is a question which would have to be answered for particular instances, not only particular pieces but also particular performances.

Does such a view of the healing in which we can be immersed through music deal adequately with the understanding of time as it has developed recently? Certainly it gets us beyond the 'container' view of time, and presents music as time-involving in its healing for those who are time-involved. Perhaps it does not make so clear how dependent this is on the construction of the music itself, as it intersects with the actual patterns of our lives. If we recall the scientific view that time is affected by what occurs in it, the shaping of particular music alters the configuration of time itself, a view which suggests that music is still more time-involving in its impact upon us – who are also more time-involving than we

---

[5] These have been one major modern response to the difficulties of finding a pattern in history. Kant's compression of the conditions of intelligibility comes to mind.

[6] A practical version of this view may be found in the PhD thesis of Mary Butterworth. The beneficial effects of music therapy for autistic students were studied musically, psychologically and theologically (University of Birmingham, 1990).

recognize! The issue here is one of the complexity and contingency of the historical process itself. While it is, as Begbie suggests, plausible to see music as a physical process capable of healing the *distentio* of our past, present and future, the manner in which it does so may be much more complex.

It is attractive to follow Karl Barth in linking the redemptive value of music to the dynamic interrelatedness of the triunity of God, as Begbie suggests, and illuminating to see musical phenomena as examples for the enfolding of created time in eternity. These integrate music into the task of conceiving the way in which the history of the temporality of redemption in Jesus Christ is received (perichoretically) into the co-inherence of members of the Trinity in 'pure duration', thereby precluding any conflict between the 'times' of life, beginning, succession and end. One great virtue of the approach is that it shows something of the complexity of the means by which created time is enfolded in eternity – which is far beyond the barren analogical correspondences often found between salvation-history and the life of the eternal God. But how helpful this will be will depend very much on the development of these approaches, and especially whether they take account of the endless possibilities for order and energy which arise in the contingencies of history, and their generation, sustenance and completion in God. There is no small risk that the patterns found in history, and the self-involvement of the dynamism of the divine life with history, will be underrated through our wish to find regular, repetitive patterns.

> The nerve-threads are strings
> on a violin, out of the heart
> winds the ribbon of melody.
>
> Round and round the potter's lathe,
> life lurches in a spinning wheel,
> the giddy ghost of the trinity.
>
> Let me dance, let me dance,
> give me madness for the waltz,
> three great beats of eternity.[7]

There is an abundance in God and in the lifting of human life to God, as well as in hints of these which are found in ordinary life, which outstrips the formalisms of so much theology (and the music which it leads people to admire). That is why the heart-beat of Christian faith in

[7] Micheal O'Siadhail, 'Invocation', in *Hail! Madam Jazz* (Newcastle: Bloodaxe Books, 1992), p. 60.

worship needs theological attention as never before, and particularly where it intersects with the theory and practice of Christians.

There is an enduring problem which permeates conventional theology, which is that forms of practice – ecclesial, liturgical and ethical, for example – are seen as derivative from belief and theology, 'disciplines of application' which are brought into play only after these last are settled. But, properly speaking, the issue of an active relation to God – which, God being *God*, means praise of God – permeates all the rest: there is a direct involvement for this active relation in ecclesial, liturgical and ethical practice; and the disciplines of ecclesiology, liturgiology and ethics are 'architectonic' ones, concerned with the proper shaping of this involvement.[8]

The course which *Stanley Hauerwas* describes deeply mixes profound issues of the God we worship with characteristics of liturgical practice. Likewise, it challenges students to associate issues of goodness (ethics) with those of polity (politics); the discovery of truth about our lives is as much communal as individual. And none can be separated from active worship as the discovery of truth about creatures.

Such an insight has implications for the traditionedness of theology and virtues. Amongst those who stress their importance, traditions are often seen as genetic-human accounts or contexts for belief and virtue. But their source and nourishment is in coming to know God in worship. Ultimately, therefore, it is not traditions in themselves which defend us from the 'ahistorical accounts of truth and rationality so characteristic of modernity', but their nourishment in the worship of God. Likewise, it is not their connection with tradition which authenticates particular kinds of moral behaviour, but the fact that they are drawn to be what they are by the elevating holiness of God which we find in worship.

At the same time, as Stanley Hauerwas suggests, the continuing of this tradition is in being gathered from world, homes and families to constitute a community capable of praising God – which therefore serves as a 'foretaste of the unity of the communion of saints'. Hence the inseparable connection of ethics and ecclesiology.

I suspect that I differ from Hauerwas in my view of the relation of the church to the world, however. True, as he says, we are gathered through our worship, because worship puts all that we do before God; and that establishes a contrast with the world by which it knows that it is the world. But it is also true that the first thing that one discovers in worship is that we are human beings *in* the world, and – even while being drawn

---

[8] This is a stronger view of ethics than Stanley Hauerwas suggests when he says that 'insofar as ethics has a task peculiar to itself it is to assemble reminders from the training we receive in worship that enable us rightly to see the world as well as how we continue to be possessed by the world'.

to the holiness of God – not in ourselves holy. The very activity by which those who gather in worship are a community in contrast to the world also identifies them with the world, those who are not so gathered. In their common worship they are constituted as ethically responsible before God, but ethically responsible in and for the world. Their 'segregation' (to use Hauerwas' word) is also a responsibility. But of course he is right to say that 'we cannot presume that those to whom we witness already have learned what we have learned by the necessity of our being gathered' – that is the ethical responsibility which is derived from the praise of God.

The proper content of worship, of community and of ethics is established by the One who is worshipped, who is remembered through the tradition and anticipated in our midst. The urgent question, therefore, is the identity of this One who is called by the name God. That is not found by invoking external criteria of truth or by the use of forms of ahistorical, neutralized 'rationality' and 'values', however, but by allowing these to be transformed through worship itself, by which they are lifted to their own true content – not instantaneously, but through practice in the community. That is what produces the historical dynamic in which people are *found* by truth and goodness in the practices of thinking and doing. Of course, this is not smooth sailing, as if 'every day in every way I grow better and better'. It is instead one which requires the inspiration and redemption of God realized in the community of those who worship by the practices of adoration, confession and forgiveness, thanksgiving, intercession and petition in the ongoing history of the community.

While I agree with almost all of what Stanley Hauerwas goes on to say about Word and sacraments, there is more that needs to be said about them. He is right to insist on the ethic of preaching as preacher and congregation standing under the Word, but it is important to recall the placing of this, like all ethics, in the dynamic of worship as the practice by which a community proceeds with its history with God. And the calling to ordained ministry is that of focusing the many ministries of the laity in the worship of the community.

Likewise, baptism is, I believe, the sacrament of life itself, whereby the direction of life is called out from us by God and confirmed within the community of Christians – 'the necessary presupposition for the very existence of the church'. It is this, as Hauerwas rightly states, that makes the wilful ending of life unacceptable for Christians, not some arbitrary set of rules. But I think more needs to be said about how marriage or singleness contribute to the life of the church, for I believe that dedication, the learning of mutual dedication after the pattern of God's self-dedication to us, is the fundamental virtue of the community.

The Eucharist, however, is the sacrament of the fulfilment or completion of life, by which we are incorporated into the 'economy' of God's salvation. To understand it requires that we appreciate how God deals with human beings in their history, redeeming them in and through their ongoingness. It is this which, in the final analysis, must shape our understanding of Christ's accomplishment, his place in the fullness of God's work, and the manner in which we should live life in the responsibility which arises in worship – with all the implications that has for 'ownership', the societal practice of alienating people in punishment (prisons) and death (capital punishment). It is when ethics – and for that matter theology and ecclesiology – are treated in the way Stanley Hauerwas outlines that we find its full implications!

It is remarkable that the richness and depth of connection which Begbie and Hauerwas trace between eternity and time in music and between praise and community and practice is as much present in language itself, as *Micheal O'Siadhail* shows so well. His essay also provokes fascinating thoughts – part reminder, more redemption – of years of research in the use of language in theology in the wasteland left in Oxford by positivistic influences.

For years, I thought language to be too shifty to be as effective as ideas themselves in theology and its relation to other forms of life and understanding; certainly they were two different mediums, and I found great difficulty in expressing ideas in writing. Hence, I can well understand that language 'stops' the world by writing it, and thereby concretizes the universal as Edward Farley suggests. At the same time, I think it only a half-truth to suggest (as he does) that relation to the sacred 'can only take place in the experience that preserves the absence'; what is mediated in language is mystery which is both 'shining' and dark – or in Barth's terms 'unveiling' and 'veiling'.

But language is not only to be seen in its relation to mystery. It is also a matter of connecting the manifold which confronts us from beyond and within ourselves. And much as I value the ways in which this has been done, in the Psalms for example, or in the poetry of Shakespeare or Coleridge, the complexity thus to be expressed must also be addressed in the terms of today. And this, or at least attempts to do so which take account of the theoretical accounts of the world which permeate our thoughts today, is rare.

> Sax and rhythm. The brightness of a reed,
> winding tube and crook are working on
> another hue of the tune that moves
> into its own discourse: *Bud Freeman,*
> *Johnny Hodges, Charlie Parker.* 'All right?'
> he drawls, then scats a little as we clap
> a tradition of subversions. But he's off again.
> I watch swarms of dust in the spotlight,

swirls of galaxies, and imagine he's blowing
a huge balloon of space that's opening
our world of order. In a waft of creation
his being becomes a music's happening.
A red-shirted pianist now leans to seize
a gene of the song which seems to veer
and improvise, somehow catching a moment's
shifts and humours. Hail! Madam Jazz.[9]

I admire the attempt, shown in this poem, to 'stand in the crosslight, to stand where all we can grasp of the world around us, scientifically, sociologically, culturally, can still be spoken of with wonder and compassion'.

The precondition of that, in fields of knowledge now far too extensive to be grasped by a single encyclopaedic mind,[10] is a dedication to others which includes the readiness – as well as the capacity – to respect and hear sensitively what they have to bring from the storehouse with which they are acquainted. Such readiness is based on a wonder and compassion which are themselves intimations of the congruence between people which it is the purpose of communities and societies to establish – another form of expression of the inmost structure of Christian faith.[11]

What is dazzling to the likes of me is the 'hope that revelling in the marvel of language and poetry may reflect something of that ultimate fullness'. They may concentrate the fullness of nature and thought, faithful to nature but concentrating it by the combination of concept and metaphor artfully used,[12] by the combination of awareness (conscious or subconscious) of layers of rules, images and developments – the *anamnesis* of an individual or community – with deviation and reconfiguration, combining in 'a tongue at large in an endlessness of sentences unsaid'.[13] What the poet does thereby is not only to elaborate upon the past but anticipate the fuller, future meaning which is embedded in past and present. It is a marvellous liturgy of meaning which can result.

It is that which makes me slightly suspicious of the way in which Richard Wilbur traces the disposition of the poetic mind to assert that all

---

[9] Micheal O'Siadhail, 'Cosmos', in *Hail! Madam Jazz*, p. 148.
[10] It is notable, however, how frequently this aspiration still survives in academic study in the humanities. Certainly it does in theology.
[11] Cf. Daniel W. Hardy, 'The Future of Theology in a Complex World' in *Christ and Context*, ed. H. Regan and A. J. Torrance (Edinburgh: T. & T. Clark, 1993), pp. 36–42.
[12] With Wordsworth, Coleridge thought that 'accidents of light and shade' such as twilight and moonlight offered the possibility of combining 'faithful adherence to the truth of nature' with the 'modifying colours of the imagination'. Cf. Samuel T. Coleridge, *Biographia Literaria* (London: Routledge & Kegan Paul, 1983), Vol. II, pp. 5–7; and *Aids to Reflection* (Princeton: Princeton University Press, 1993), p. 393 and note 34.
[13] Micheal O'Siadhail, 'Freedom', in *Hail! Madam Jazz*, p. 111.

things are comparable to 'the ground of comparison [which] is likely to be divine'. Yes, perhaps, but it depends on the way in which the comparison is drawn, and what is the ground of comparison to which this points. As Micheal O'Siadhail says, language in its richness and complexity glimpses the fullness and diversities of our cosmos and culture, the one abundance – in the hands of a seer, narrator, praiser in the crosslight, a lover – refracting the other, some 'irrepressible richness' 'running through it all':

> Abundance of joy bubbling some underground jazz.
> A voice whispers: Be with me tonight in paradise.[14]

It is not simply the comparability of things and the ground of comparison which allows poetry to point to the divine; after all, that could be quite misleading.[15] Instead, it is the poet's capacity to trace things in their particularity, and to find in their *historical* diversity and 'leaps to greater intricacy' that 'irrepressible richness' as 'time thickens' into the knots of history in which the divine is known.[16]

II. SUBSTANCE: THE INNER COHERENCE OF THEOLOGY

A short while ago, I mentioned the community of wonder and com-

---

[14] Micheal O'Siadhail, 'Invitation', in *A Fragile City* (Newcastle upon Tyne: Bloodaxe Books, 1995) p. 69.

[15] The comparability of things (or people) might be based in a ground of comparison which is far from the divine. For example, gazing at the opposite sex, comparing one to another, might be based in a universalization of pulchritude (an aesthetic universal of a special sort), and thereby lead to the misuse of a particular person and postulating an inadequate universal. That would not point to the divine, only to some generic quasi-divinity.

[16] Acorns of memories, berries of dreams.
Does every pilgrim's tale sleep in one moment?
Some inbred
whole uncodes in a tree's limbs,
spreads in slow workings of the environment.
Soil, air, water and sun quicken
a word in the seed.
Time thickens.

'Disclosure' in Micheal O'Siadhail, *Hail! Madam Jazz*, p. 121.

passion on which 'standing in the crosslight' must rest, and its roots in the inmost structure of Christian faith. What is this inmost structure, and how is it evident in the most direct response which Christians make to (or in) it, in their believing? *Stephen Pickard* takes up the issue at a crucial point, seeking to recover the triune character of God as inherent in believing, statements of belief and the community of believers. This is a particularly important set of issues in a time when there is such disagreement about the nature and importance of right belief, and when so few see belief as giving 'expression to a fundamental bond in the Spirit with the God of Jesus Christ'.

It is unfortunately typical of Christianity – in the USA at least – for belief to be polarized between the two options which Pickard identifies, 'hard objectivism' (although this is now said to avoid the propositionalism with which he identifies it) and that which arises from human religious subjectivity (we should recognize that this now may, at its extreme, include dispensing with any real referent for religious language or spirituality, so that they become important in their own terms). Quite apart from the resemblance which I think these bear to prevalent modern conceptions of the basis of human knowledge, empiricism and idealism, neither allows that the very act of believing, its formulation and sharing, are *loci* for the dynamic realization of the work of the triune God.

If believing is to be the means by which, through the Spirit, Christians are to be united with God through Jesus Christ, it will require, however – as Stephen Pickard suggests – that it is of the nature of the *triune God* to be implicated in the *believing of human beings* as the *church*. For the unity of Christians in believing with God through Jesus Christ through the Spirit depends on the co-operative agency of all three (God, Christ, the Spirit) as humans believe together as the church. The three need to be taken together and not (as is usually the case) separately. And all need to be taken more seriously, and seen in more dynamic terms, than is often the case. One such linking of the issues in dynamic terms is Stephen Pickard's assertion that 'God is present in the believing [or the believer's interpretative response to the gospel] such that belief is Spirited along in a manner which honours the God of Jesus Christ', as Spirited response to the gift of God in Jesus Christ.

I say 'one such linking' to suggest that there may be others less closely wedded to the Western view of the Trinity (in which the prime role of the Spirit is to incorporate believers into Jesus Christ and thus into God) and to the emphasis on the moving of the human being (by the Spirit to be one with Christ) to respond through a free act of believing. Such views have overtones of trinitarian belief as that to which the human being responds, that is as 'external' to the believer until responded-to. It is at least as helpful to regard the dynamic of the Trinitarian God as antecedently present in the movement of response, and then additionally 'blessed' – or activated – when the believer assents, much as William Law did when he suggested, 'Believing within this trinitarian dynamic drew the believer deeper into the divine reality'.

This is an important issue, since it has to do with the character of the divine-human relation, and whether there is a fixed boundary between the two – each being itself by contradistinction from the other. I am inclined to think that, if we are to talk of boundaries at all, the 'boundary' is much more fluid, altering with both divine and human initiatives, much as the 'shifting' which Micheal O'Siadhail indicates in the love of two human beings:

> Nothing can explain this adventure – let's say a quirk
> of fortune steered us together – we made our covenants,
> began this odyssey of ours, by hunch and guesswork,
> a blind date where foolish love consented in advance.
> No my beloved, neither knew what lay beyond the frontiers.
> You told me once you hesitated: *A needle can waver,*
> *then fix on its pole;* I am still after many years
> baffled that the needle's gift dipped in my favour.
> Should I dare to be so lucky? Is this a dream?
> Suddenly in the commonplace that first amazement seizes
> me all over again – a freak twist to the theme,
> subtle jazz of the new familiar, trip of surprises.
> Gratuitous, beyond our fathom, both binding and freeing,
> this love re-invades us, shifts the boundaries of our being.[17]

If there are 'boundaries', therefore, they 'shift' with the 're-invasion' of love from each side. In such a case, the 'otherness' of each is not so much fixed as it is conferred ongoingly by the other.

When we think of this in trinitarian terms, it suggests a God whose perfection is perfected (or 'expanded') in the original and ongoing act of conferring the freedom of otherness on human beings, and is fulfilled in so far as it is ongoingly responded to by human beings through their conferral of an otherness upon God which has the character of trust. Indeed, there is gratuitous freeing on both sides, based on dedication and trust (the 'binding' to which the poem refers) through which the freeing is never arbitrary. The same is the basis for the community of human beings.

How then are we to *think* the theocentric, trinitarian dynamic which

---

[17] Micheal O'Siadhail, 'Out of the Blue', in *Hail! Madam Jazz*, p. 118.

appears thus? When this dynamic operates through the conferral of otherness by God and by human beings in dedication and trust, it would be problematic to locate it in ways which might distance it – as an 'in-itself' or 'principles' – from us, as axioms or fundamentals, for example. Thinking it is more likely to take the form of an ongoing dialectic between 'highly concentrated' statements of belief and 'extended forms' of the same, the latter arising from the freedom which has been conferred – a freedom through which we can explore – and the former from the use of this freedom in dedication and trust. The same combination, I suppose, would be reflected in the 'trip of surprises' and the 'gratuitousness' in the relationships of human beings, and would generate the complexity of expression between them which is summarized in the 'communicative patterns of belief' of which Stephen Pickard speaks. Within the mutual conferral of freedom, trust and dedication whereby a community is formed, the same dynamic of freedom and dedication amongst the members will embody the trinitarian dynamic.

In tracing the appearance of this dynamic, I am of course utilizing the 'grading in Christian belief' to which Stephen Pickard calls our attention, whereby we sift the rich forms of God's interaction with creation to arrive at the 'essential unity of Christianity'. I think it is important, however, to recognize that these rich forms are not found only in the Judaeo-Christian tradition understood in its own terms. That which we call this 'tradition' is itself a concentration of a wider historical diversity. The concentration was not arrived at by excluding this diversity, but by engaging with it to find its deeper meaning in a deepening of Christian faith. It seems to me that, throughout the history of the Christian tradition, this 'external' diversity has always been woven into deeper expressions of Christian faith, which in turn found expression in a new simplicity. When confronted with new circumstances, this in turn was 'extended', folding other diversities into a 'new simplicity' later. What we see here is how the grading of Christian belief takes the form not only of a logical but also a historical hierarchy. In the ongoing dynamic of history, 'simplicities' result from the enfolding of wide diversities, and fund still more.

The way in which all this happens is not only, or even primarily, with singular human beings. For God is concerned with the common humanity of human beings; and the trinitarian agency which is implicit in believing is also operative in the constitution of 'a new communion of persons in society and the wider creation'. The co-inherent agency of the Triune God found in believing is also operative in the determination of the body of the believers. So the church is neither only 'context' for belief nor only 'guardian'; in so far as it is – and remains – the church, it is the social *form* of the truth of the gospel of God, and ordered by it. At this point in Stephen Pickard's argument, I am inclined to appeal less to 'governing doctrines'[18] than to the polity of the church as the means intrinsic to the church by which it is (or should be, since it rarely is) ordered as the social form of the truth of the gospel of God. The supposition that there are 'governing doctrines' which stand over the community to guide it is more characteristic of those churches whose basis is confessional or magisterial (whose polity is secondary and derived from doctrine). In my view, the truth of the gospel of God should be directly translatable as the social form – the polity – of the church. In this respect, the polity of the church is comparable to the believing of the community of Christians as the work of the Triune God.

A remarkably pertinent and interesting test-case for the Trinitarianism which is implicit in the believing of the church is found in *Stephen Sykes'* essay ' "Orthodoxy" and "Liberalism" '. It is a matter of special concern for the current debate amongst Christians, who so frequently identify themselves by finding or constituting an alternative from which they wish to differ.

The two terms, I think, are too readily co-opted by parties which wish to stress, respectively, what we might call 'purity' and 'engagement', and adopt strategies appropriate to their convictions.[19] In fact, as Stephen Sykes makes clear, 'orthodoxy' and 'liberalism' are not inherently antithetical. To state the point positively, as he does not, they are probably necessarily complementary – as are the 'concentration' and 'extension' discussed above – as 'moments' in the dynamics of the believing of the church. Where they become problematic is when either, or both together, fall into that which undermines them, 'heresy'.

If one does not agree with Walter Bauer's view that orthodoxy is the construct of a dominant party in the church,[20] an alternative theory of orthodoxy is necessary. An undeservedly neglected view is provided in the work of the distinguished Durham Professor H. E. W. Turner which Sykes presents. In this account, the history of the belief of the early church manifests fluidity and variety, geographical as well as historical. The fixity derives from three aspects, 'the religious facts themselves', the biblical revelation, and the Creed and Rule of Faith. The first of these suggests a primary grasp – seen in worship and pattern of life – of the

---

[18] William Christian's argument for governing doctrines is interestingly similar to the view of doctrine as cultural-linguistic rules found in his fellow Yale scholar George Lindbeck's *The Nature of Doctrine* (Philadelphia: Westminster, 1984).

[19] This was a matter which I tried to analyse in 'The Strategy of Liberalism', in *The Weight of Glory*, eds. D. W. Hardy and P. H. Sedgwick (Edinburgh: T. & T. Clark, 1991), pp. 299–304.

[20] While not posed as an issue of orthodoxy, a similar claim is implicit in Maurice Wiles' view that the forms of Greek philosophy overcame the theology of the early church. See Maurice Wiles, *The Making of Christian Doctrine* (Cambridge: CUP, 1967), and *The Remaking of Christian Doctrine* (London: SCM, 1974).

Trinity, and comprises 'a relatively full and fixed experimental grasp of what was involved religiously in being a Christian'. The second traces these 'religious facts' into the use of certain characteristic forms of theological argument in the Bible.[21] And the third argues for a stability in the pattern of teaching in the Apostolic Church. While all of these allow for considerable variety, they provide the continuity against which the fluidity of doctrine and practice is to be measured.

By comparison with the account of Trinitarianism in believing which Stephen Pickard offers, and with which I find myself largely in agreement, Turner's is more cautious, appealing to observational fixities through which the identity of Christianity is maintained in all the fluidity occasioned by different circumstances. Pickard's gives primacy to the involvement of the Trinity in the 'being a Christian', where Turner seems to emphasize the human-experimental grasp of the Trinity which is traceable both in scripture and the patterns of belief.

For both, however, liberalism serves as an important test. For both, legitimate variation is found *within* Christian belief. But neither seems fully to address the issue to which liberalism points – the position vis-à-vis Christian belief of forms of life and thought less immediately connected with scripture, tradition and reason. Are they 'external' as enemies, or linked (however tenuously) to Christian faith? How are they to be met?[22]

Liberalism – along with its insistence on making Christianity justifiable to those influenced by modern expectations about the world, rationality, and human responsibility – raises the most difficult questions for believing. How are the undeniable achievements of modernity to be addressed within the dynamic of believing? The attempt to circumscribe the possibilities of human thought and life, by setting limits which will appear authoritarian if not totalitarian to those committed to modern ways, will not do. This was Newman's strategy in equating liberalism with a 'false liberty of thought' which extends itself to matters beyond human reach (first principles, including the truths of revelation). Recog-

---

[21] This argument foreshadows in some respects the conclusions of the canon-criticism of Brevard Childs, which argues for the stability of certain thematic emphases in the Bible, and that the agreement of a canon freed the early church for new forms of doctrinal expression appropriate to the new situations in which it found itself. See Brevard Childs, *Introduction to the Old Testament as Scripture* (Philadelphia: Fortress, 1979), and *Biblical Theologies of the Old and New Testaments* (Minneapolis: Fortress, 1993).

[22] The issue recalls St Paul's discussion of Abraham as 'double ancestor' in Romans 4. Abraham was not only 'father of many nations', 'the ancestor of all who believe without being circumcised'. He was also 'ancestor of the circumcised who are not only circumcised but who also follow the example of the faith that our ancestor Abraham had before he was circumcised'. Those 'who believe in him who raised Jesus our Lord from the dead ... for our justification' participate in the same heritage; their faith too is reckoned to them as righteousness.

nizing the deficiency of this strategy does not mean accepting what is often considered the alternative, stigmatizing all efforts to find the direction of life and thought, and thereby declaring oneself free of all standards.

What seems to be the root of the problem is the question of the status of the world, human understanding and life before God and in the economy of salvation. Are they rightfully independent, giving their otherness and freedom by God, and thus made free to fulfil (or reject) their place in the dynamic of God's work? Or is their independence limited by being contained within a pre-existing conformity to God from which they escape only at their peril? What then is the 'true' condition of the world, human understanding and life? The phrase 'image of God' is often applied to human beings, but what does it mean – that human beings are in (analogical) correspondence to God, or that they are given their otherness (covenantally) with the expectation, but not a contractual requirement, to trust the One who gives it?

Interestingly, it is the second, covenantal, option which suggests that liberalism (and the various manifestations of it which Stephen Sykes mentions, biblical criticism, feminism and the Johannine basis for the authority of the church) should not be treated as homogeneous. The use of the techniques which have emerged with the rise of liberalism leads to results which must be weighed one by one. But weighed by what standard? The answer, I think, is that they must be judged by whether they lead to the use of the otherness granted by God in free response to the graciousness by which God confers it.

But how is it possible for this free response to occur, particularly when there are so many, and such deep, obstacles to it? The issues are both complex and difficult. And when analysed as carefully and perceptively as *Alistair McFadyen* does, they are seen in sharp relief in child sexual abuse, although by no means limited to that.

It is a welcome move to advance beyond the well-entrenched habit of treating damage and healing as loss and retrieval. The supposition that there is a 'given' order of perfection by which to measure damage and restoration rests, I think, on the uncritical acceptance of an analogical correspondence (mentioned above) of 'original perfection' and Creator to which we ought to be returned through healing, a pre-existing conformity which must be restored. The effect is to postulate a perfection which may never be in evidence (as with Arthur, Frances Young's son), and to disallow the positive value of all that has happened in the history of life as it is actually lived. In effect, it reduces all the meaning of life to the logical question of how near or far we are from that pre-existing conformity.

To treat the history of life in terms of the dynamics of relationality – of human beings and of their interaction with the dynamic relationality of

God – offers the possibility of a much more convincing account of human life with God. What McFadyen succeeds in showing is how the convoluted patterns of relationship which occur in sexual abuse, incapable of being healed by 'normal' therapeutic means (because of the deficiency of notions of the good employed in therapy), may nonetheless be healed through the activity of the Triune God who 'acts on, in and towards the world in ways which make available new energies for trans- formation ... precisely at the points of most damage'. Such a release of energy is seen primarily in the resurrection of Jesus.

This is a convincing account of how distortion occurs in relationality through the interdiction (by the command of secrecy) of the passage of information from the immediate context of abuse to other rational struc- tures and resources both in the child and the child's situation, thereby binding his or her faculties and horizons to the abuse – in effect re- centring the child's world upon the abuse. There is an important issue here about what constitutes health, not the totalitarian dynamic of abuse but a dynamic distribution within the child and between the child and his or her situation; this deserves more discussion.

It is particularly helpful, I think, to see abuse as 'a highly energised information event' which cannot be transformed through exchange, and which therefore requires a massive effort to re-establish a structural equilibrium – a new, rigid and closed structure of identity which cuts the child off from the disequilibrial dynamics characteristic of fuller life.[23] The effect may be even more drastic than McFadyen suggests, however, because such an effort – without access to the energy mediated in the surrounding society – either draws on the energy of the abuse or con- sumes all the child's energies. Any 'resolution' of the dynamic of abuse would be achieved through a spiralling downwards into lassitude.

He offers a convincing redescription of damage in such terms, seeing 'damage [as] a blocking of the energies of dynamic relationality commu- nicated to us in God's creative and saving presence and action, through the Trinitarian dynamic of transcendence and immanence'. Correlatively, healing is seen not as restoration of a pre-existing, fixed, static order which corresponds to a divine being also (and necessarily still more) fixed. It is instead being 'called into a future development of, an increase in, dynamic order through relation to that of others, to self and to God'. Healing is increase of freedom, made possible 'through the creative activity and ordering presence of the Triune God ... available to human beings through "natural" forms of sociality', but also by God acting to make available new energies of transformation, as seen in the resurrec-

---

[23] For a helpful discussion of the issues involved in equilibrium and disequilibrium, see Walter Buckley, *Sociology and Modern Systems Theory* (Englewood Cliffs: Prentice-Hall, 1967), ch. 3.

tion of Jesus and 'the re-concentration and focusing of the energies of community which followed' and are mediated by the worshipping Christian community.

This line of thought opens a convincing way of explicating the conditions of the dynamics of human relationships as deriving from the creative and redemptive activity of the dynamic Triune God. The heart of the matter is not, as it has so often been in theology, the establishment of a correspondence with God, but the tracing of the impact of the ordered energy of the Triune God within human relationships as 'natural' (created), damaged and redeemed. The one issue which is not addressed, however, is how 'the world is caught up in the *dialectic of transcendence and immanence* which is characteristic of God's reality'.[24] Here, as mentioned before, the key issue is how God gives otherness to humans in such a way that they respond in freedom. To speak, as Al McFadyen does, of God as source and call (to dynamic order), and thereby increasing freedom, does not yet speak of how human beings learn to respond to each other and to God.

Al McFadyen presents child abuse as an information event with certain relational dynamics which are so harmful to the abused as to be beyond the reach of the good offered by therapy, and which require healing by being opened to a new kind of disequilibrial intensity through the salvation of God. The information event in this case is one-to-one, closing off the wider contacts through which the information can be processed, and the necessary healing opens the abused to a wider and more dynamic world. As we move to *Peter Selby*'s contribution, we find ourselves in a different kind of 'information event', the economic relationships of people in a city. And the question is how, in this case, there may be love?

Modern cities are economically-driven, compressed societies upon which – like it or not – humanity today depends, which focus human strengths and achievements, as well as the concomitant social pressures. Can love be incarnate there, or is it bound to other worlds ('religion' or 'romance' or, it might be added, simpler local units of the sort often advocated today[25])? The theological move which Peter Selby suggests is to 'build time into love', as something presupposed or contained in love, both for God and for human beings. Then we may see that the pre-existent Christ is the constant orientation of the creating and redeeming love of God towards the historical flux and ambiguity of the social life of human beings. And we also see that lovers whose love endures and is fulfilled in a shared history, reflect the dynamic of God's relationship with the elect.

---

[24] The italics are mine.
[25] See, for example, Wendell Berry, *Sex, Economy, Freedom & Community: Eight Essays* (New York: Pantheon Books, 1993).

In both cases, we see that the character of love is to 'provide an environment of security in which the unknown future of society can be faced', even in the face of radical disappointment. The 'specifically divine history' is the foundation for societal love, and offers space for an unknown future – neither self-aggrandizing nor defensive, but carrying forward the love revealed in the past dealings of God with God's people, knowing only that this has proved trustworthy. This would free the church for an eschatological faith which could serve as the basis for an appeal for the nation to act justly and compassionately.

In many ways, Peter Selby's strategy is strikingly similar to the emphases we have seen in Pickard and McFadyen, but transposed from ontological and information-theoretic to social-historical-eschatological terms, and there to argue for an opening of historical and social limitations to provide 'space' for human life. In accordance with the economic determination of cities as such (how often they are seen simply as situations in which economic transactions take place!), the focus of attention here is economic – debt, supposedly the index to decline and health, despair and confidence.

The issue is both microcosmic and macrocosmic. As Peter Selby's analysis shows, the positive attitude towards consumer debt belies the cause for much debt: straightforward need, or 'voluntary' credit transactions. In historical-social terms, the major problem is that rising indebtedness exchanges future freedom of action for external controls, whether at the hands of banks or governments. Such involuntary indebtedness manifests a dynamic of power seen in biblical times as itself requiring stringent control if exploitation was not to follow.

Far from a sign of health, escalating debt severely diminishes the freedom of all sectors, whether those intent on protecting (or, we may say, enhancing) what they have, or those already indebted beyond their ability to repay. Both are so much in bondage to economic necessity as to be incapable of concern for the well-being of society. They are in thrall to a complex form of idolatry (which, like all idolatries, is then turned into magical means of control by those able to do so), and thereby closed to the social transcendental which results from the constant orientation of the creating and redeeming love of God towards the historical flux and ambiguity of social life. By contrast, God offers in Christ a love which opens history to the future and redeems those now enslaved so that their only obligation is 'to love one another'.

What Peter Selby offers is a comprehensive account of the hope formed in Christ by which the economic realities which now bind people may give way to space for, and the actuality of, mutual love. The church itself must pave the way for this, however, and in more thoroughgoing terms than Peter Selby attempts to discuss. It is far from even recognizing the theological significance of its own economic realities, much less the theological implications of the economics which prevail amongst those who 'getting and spending, lay waste our powers'.[26] Although Selby is right in the general lines of his proposals, I think, and in calling for orientation to the eschatological reality of 'treasure beyond price', how the church can enable a dynamic growth to mutual love and hope is a question which needs a good deal more attention. Although mutuality and equality are *minima*, radical trust, love and hope conferred by each on others will be hard-won, and require drawing directly on the redemption of Jesus Christ. And that, in turn, requires a different dimension of historicality than Peter Selby discusses here, one which contemplates the pivotal historical importance of Jesus Christ as the event by which God opens societies for love, and finds the difference which it makes for the economic freedom of those now bound by debt.

It is too easy to discuss the dynamics of God's work and its correlates in the understanding of human beings in the world at a level of generality unconnected to, and in some cases unprepared even to be connected to, the dynamics observable in the world. The great merit of the essays we have just been considering is that, despite the care for theory which they show, they show the convergence of theology with crucial practical situations in the world today. In my experience, the integration of theology at such a high level of theory with practical issues is unfortunately rare.

As strategies which offer new perspectives on the substance of Christian theology, however, they may be culpable for another kind of generalization. They speak in such universal terms about the economy of God's salvation that they may lose touch with the pivotal points in history through which this economy came to be and is as it is. The risk is that their arguments, valuable as they are for the insight they bring to practical situations, consist of general ontological, information-theoretic or social-historical accounts, and lose the contingencies, particularities and 'knottedness' of history.

> Like pegs, our forearms held the skein's coil.
> Arcs of the knitter's hand unloop
> and ball by turn. Sweep and detail.
> A feeling of beginning in childhood's windup
> I keep on recalling. Somehow I'm between
> a yarn uncoiling to a tight ball of destiny,
> a ball unravelling back the promise of a skein.
> Plain stitch and design, point and infinity.
> Who changes the world? Oh, this and that,
> strands as they happen to fall, tiny ligatures,
> particular here-and-nows, vast loopings

---

[26] William Wordsworth, 'The World is Too Much With Us' (1807).

of pattern, the ties and let-gos of a knot,
small X-shapes of history; our spoor and signature
a gauze of junctures, a nettedness of things.[27]

III. Sources: The Coherence of Theology with Scripture

These issues come to the surface when we turn our attention to the question of the place of the Bible in the theological-historical heritage of the church.

The various kinds of study of the New Testament (NT) which have prevailed in recent times can be regarded as attempts to revivify the position of Jesus in the church and the world. But, as *James D. G. Dunn* indicates, this presupposes a mutuality of interdependence between the NT and the church which needs to be considered. He focuses on three aspects of the role the Bible plays in the church, information, definition and inspiration.

Dunn suggests that the Bible provides the church with *information*, not with statements of timeless truths or codes of practice but with a series of stories. Here, the negative point is more helpful than the positive. Perhaps the range of genres presented is more complex than 'stories', and likewise the kinds of reading, meaning and ascription of truth which are appropriate to them; some issues can be sharpened, or diffused, and in more different ways, than a single genre will allow.

Along with such 'stories', however, goes the supposition of their historicality, the occurrence of what is narrated at particular points, and with these the conviction that God is acting and revealing himself in them as encountered by people themselves living historically. They and their telling are highly contingent and context-specific, both in themselves and in their expression. All such (public) matters are rightly open to (public) historical investigation, together with the ideologies with which such procedures are imbued, just as the faith of the church is also vulnerable to historical investigation. The correct conclusion is that 'all formulations and practices are integrally contingent' – not unconditioned absolutes – and that this reflects the action of 'a God who has made his self-revelation so vulnerable to ... historical processes and ... the need for historical scrutiny'.

Here the issue is at its most difficult. While professionals are necessary to guide such inquiries and communicate their fruits, as Dunn claims, in practice this may lead to an inattention to the character of the dynamics

---

[27] Micheal O'Siadhail, 'Perspectives', first stanza, in *Hail! Madam Jazz*, p. 126.

of God's activity in the particularities of history as such. The matters to be negotiated are so wide-ranging, and so closely coupled with modern presuppositions about the autonomy of the scholar, that they are likely to facilitate practical neglect for a matter as difficult as the discernment of God's activity in history. In other words, the data and procedures are so complex as in practice to favour an inductive method which has little theological outcome. There can be historical scrutiny but little, if any, of the theology of history which is needed.

The Bible, Dunn suggests, gains its *defining* role from its reference to Jesus who is *himself* 'the distinguishing feature of Christianity'. The church is wholly dependent on the Bible to tell us who he was; and *'all subsequent statements are dependent on and derivative from the NT accounts'*. While I find Dunn's other arguments helpful and convincing, about the canon as limitation of diversity, the necessity of reference to the Old Testament (OT) and the determination by tradition or traditions of authoritative weight for different portions of the Bible, I am troubled by the narrowness of his reference to Jesus and the primacy of *derivation* as the means for arriving at other statements of faith.

Why am I troubled by reference to Jesus as *'the* distinguishing feature of Christianity'? Within the centrality of the historicality of Jesus for Christian faith, it seems to me that there is not less, but a great deal more, involved in reference to Jesus than is suggested here. Yes, this can be enlarged by recognizing its connection to the Old Testament (OT) and with the justification brought about in Jesus. But it still seems to me that there is a *density of reference* which is not singled out even then, but which is conveyed in such expressions as 'my Son, whom I love; with you I am well-pleased' (Lk. 3.22) through which Jesus' mysteriously close relationship to God appears.

Placing the Bible within a 'developing trajectory' of the truth of God mitigates the problem, but how then do the subsequent statements 'draw on biblical assertions, themes and precedents'? That the Bible is one (internally complex) term in a complex interaction with later statements is true, of course. But I am constantly struck by how attainment in discerning the meaning and truth of biblical material goes hand-in-hand with deepened awareness of the dynamics of God's action through all of history. That in turn raises the question of what constitutes 'tradition', and whether that can be localized in authoritative documents and institutions. The answer is, I think, 'it all depends'; it depends on whether they function within the dynamic of all human life with God which is centred on the holiness or worship which is God's.

The *inspirational* role of the Bible arises from its importance in worship; the Bible consists primarily of the 'materials of worship' and has always functioned within worship. This means that the proper place of the interaction between the Bible and the *traditio* of the church is within worship. Hence, we might say, the 'moment' between the readings of the Bible and the recitation of the Creed in liturgical worship is highly significant. The saturation of the Bible with worship, and its use in worship, are why it continues to function as word of God, means of grace, power of conversion and source of liberation now, and why it permeates European tradition by what it *means*. But I would continue to insist that this testifies more to the worship of God which is intrinsic to scripture itself, and draws worship from those who read it, than to scripture *per se* or the appropriate skills of researching and reading it.

As one might expect from a collection of writings which perpetuate the traditions which identify the religious life of not only Jews but Christians, the Bible is polymorphous in concern, presentation and effect. One might say that it perpetuates a tradition for life by the varied means characteristic of life itself. Exactly that this is newly reopened by biblical scholars themselves and by the burgeoning discussions of hermeneutics not only does, but should, make one cautious about oversimple explanations about how the Bible is or should be employed in theology and the life of the church.

When we approach the subject of biblical theology, however, we find tendencies to find the unity of the Bible in the development of moral and religious ideas contained in it. *Dennis Stamps*, however, opens the possibility of a biblical theology which – so far as the church is concerned – sees the Bible as an entextualization of 'the contingent dynamic process of postulating transcendentals which expand, inform and critique the empirical practice or praxis of social realities'. Putting this slightly differently, we might say that the Bible is itself a hermeneutic for the constitution of social reality which is then taken up in the subsequent hermeneutics for such a task. This view will, he says, get us past the usual difficulty with biblical theology: 'as the Christian church, in all its diversity, reads and interprets its sacred text ... and searches for ways to let the text speak and inform its life and praxis ... biblical theology becomes problematic because it entails interpretation coupled with application within the context of a specific human situation'.

Focusing his concern on the church, Dennis Stamps suggests that reading Paul's epistles shows how context-specific – and therefore contingent – is Paul's view of the church; there were specific issues between writer and recipient in each case, from which (when taken together) one can derive a theology of the church. That is to say, his ecclesiology is polymorphic, as regards the church unit in each place, the structure of leadership and other roles and the place of the particular church in a wider church community, the worship and practice of the churches, and other issues such as law, freedom, worldliness, the gift of life, eschatology, and so forth. Amongst these, in addition to the ecclesiology being discovered, is a desire for stability and security for the communities which leads Paul not to face some ideological and cultural issues (e.g., the place of slaves and women).

What Dennis Stamps focuses on is the governing presence of a particular set of circumstances, which is present not only in Paul's ecclesiology but even in his use of metaphor – as in the tension between narrow and wide reference. 'The church Paul worked with was a church very much in process and full of problems.'

How does this help biblical theology? Dennis Stamps wants, I think, to see a way in which Paul's multifold-but-synthetic conception of the churches in their contexts can be used generatively in the contingent pragmatics of Christian communities today; both share in the task of 'opening up richer possibilities of social order to meet the contingencies to which human beings are subject'. In doing so, he makes use of the conception of 'transcendental sociality' which I have advanced, seeing Paul's articulation of church life as one capable – by the use of an appropriate hermeneutics – of informing Christian communities today. This would serve as one field in which the problems arising from the restrictive use of biblical theology, to which he pointed at the outset, were met. Taking this as one instance, biblical theology itself would then be seen differently, as 'entering into the ongoing critical project of human discovery involved in the fundamental operation of human thought and life'.

The great virtue of Dennis Stamps' argument, I think, is that it moves us beyond two conventional ways of relating Bible to theology, the overgeneralized and the overspecific, those which rest in generalities about the importance of Bible to church and those which overdefine the means by which the Bible is translated into theological terms. Both are highly questionable in today's discussion. Typically, these paths are monolithic, by-passing the actual multi-levelled relation of the two in favour of pious statements or the authoritative imposition of biblical modes of thought, frequently unified as 'the' ways of the Bible, on the theology and practice of later (and contingent) thought and life, or vice versa. In some ways, the difference between his proposal and the conventional ones is parallel to the difference between parallel and serial interfaces in computer technology; whereas the former provides a 'waterfall' of unrestricted communication between two parties, the latter sharply restricts communication between the two to a narrow channel.

Yet there are unanswered problems, chiefly those of the presence of God's action in this 'transmission'. How is it that this can be adequately identified in Paul's theology of the church and its implications for later times? The problem is one of practice, not principle, since Dennis Stamps' proposal has no in-built restriction for the transmission.

Robert Morgan's essay confronts exactly this issue as the substantial question of how Christian orthodoxy is maintained in the community of the Church. Given the mythicizing – and relativizing – of specifically Christian belief to which many have been attracted in recent years, it is an important issue.[28]

In that debate, and its counterparts now, it is as if history has been reversed. When the early Greeks set aside the mythological world for philosophy, in order to consider the world, human social order and God by philosophical means, religious issues were unavoidably at the heart of their discussions. In effect, those who now insist that claims to the uniqueness of Christ are mythological are making just such a move, suggesting that these claims are vestiges of the mythological in religion and need to be supplanted by a philosophically credible version. Their argument proceeds, however, more by assertion than philosophical defence. And why stop short with claims about Christ? The thrust of the argument is to submit all religious belief, all philosophy and all means of communal agreement to re-examination. That result would not be the targeting of certain portions of Christian belief as 'mythological', 'relative', or 'metaphorical', but to raise far more fundamental questions about the entire basis of the world, human life and society, whether scientific, philosophical or religious.

Robert Morgan sets out to show how, even while these issues abound in current theological discussion, Christians can intelligently maintain that the 'givenness of the revelation of God in Christ implies a substantial continuity through all true formulations', and that the very attempts to define what counts as substantial continuity helps to sustain Christian community. His argument advocates a view of Christian belief in Jesus as 'practical truth' which functions as a rule-like means of preserving orthodoxy.

Locating the issue as one of the incarnation,[29] Morgan differentiates several levels of consideration: mystery (the event acknowledged by faith), myth (narrative about gods), theological reflection on faith (variable through time) and doctrine (a sedimentation through generations which is more stable). For those like myself who differentiate between *historical* reflection and the *theological development* of an architecture for the tradition of faith in the present day, his levels are problematic. I must constantly substitute 'historical reflection' for each use he makes of

---

[28] The 'mythicizing' in Birmingham (a discussion from which I was excluded) and Oxford, where Bob Morgan was an 'interested observer', was a strategy intended to disprivilege Christian belief by philosophical and historical arguments. Both kinds of argument were used to show that Christian belief in the Incarnation was a form of special pleading which should be dispensed with in favour of universal theism.

[29] It needs to be recognized that this term has a special place in English theological debate, as inclusive of 'revelation' in the more specifically Reformed tradition and 'the Christ' (as in the question of how the historical Jesus is seen as Christ) in other, more historically-focused, forms of discussion.

'theology', and reserve 'theology' for the endeavour of ordering the tradition of faith for the present – what Morgan is himself doing. It is another matter whether we agree on the strategy for doing so.

In his discussion of doctrines and their normative importance, Morgan wishes to focus on the faith which is to be believed by Christians: 'In knowing and relating to the crucified and risen Jesus through the Spirit we know and are in relationship with God'. It is this which serves as the criterion of orthodoxy, preserving faith from distorted alternatives.

The way it does so is as the *'practical truth* of the incarnation' or the 'implicit faith' which is simply accepted – in an appropriately 'low-key' way – by church believers. This is what is affirmed and preserved in the *doctrine* of the Incarnation. The 'what' (we are told) which epitomizes the NT witness is a general assent to 'the One who is trusted, obeyed and worshipped ... as the way, the truth and the life'. This is to be distinguished both from the 'how' question and from its own implications. So this 'practical truth' stands for a mystery not fully understood, which may lead to disagreement about ways in which it is elaborated, while also leading to agreement that some ways are to be rejected.[30]

This 'identity', not established through metaphysical 'essentialism', is a referring to the One who is believed as the 'saving revelation of God'. Morgan says that not even questions of truth apply to this, because for these to arise it must be 'fleshed out in some theology', but here he is using a very restricted notion of truth. Conformity to this One is in itself a lived assertion of truth in the more basic sense of 'straightness' or conformity to the truth.

His argument, it seems to me, is governed by the primary relation of believers to the One, which is – like the noumenal realm in Kant – distinct from the ways in which it may be known or practised. The identity established through this primary relation is therefore (unlike Kant) maintained through a variety of practices – sharing scriptures, tradition, creeds, sacraments, and so forth – which also engender diversity.[31] Amongst these, the task of doctrine is to secure orthodoxy against intrusions; and dogmatic definitions, as 'the post-reflective summary of the institution's teaching', protect against unacceptable diversity. In effect, they say 'these, and not these', with regard (presumably) not only to beliefs but also to practices. Since the 'identity' correlates notions of humanity and God, they exclude some Christologies and notions of God – while allowing issues less directly involved to remain amorphous.

---

[30] Whether it is the 'practical faith' or the *doctrine* which serves as the criterion is sometimes not clear in Morgan's argument.

[31] Why these do not have internal criteria for limiting the range of acceptable diversity is not clear. It seems to me that they do, as the existence of canon and lectionaries, ecclesial polities, ecumenical councils and liturgical norms testify. Doctrine is not the only, or even the primary, means of controlling diversity.

Bob Morgan is committed to the doctrine of the incarnation as the most suitable 'post-reflective summary' of the 'practical truth' of the identity of Christianity. But as he expounds it, the doctrine is treated more as a *transcendental rule for belief* (cf. 'what Christians say about God and what they say about Jesus condition one another'), which holds the 'practical truth' in place while itself saying little about God and Jesus. His reasons for preferring the doctrine, which speak mostly of its power adequately to correlate the issues involved, seem to confirm this. As if to show how close it remains to the 'practical truth' espoused by Christians, he shows how it – that this Jesus was *vere homo* and *vere Deus* – was assumed by the NT writers.

One question which needs to be raised is whether the combination of 'practical truth' and doctrinal rule is the only or best way of preserving orthodoxy. Others who wish to speak of narrative and theology intend by doing so to approximate as nearly as possible to that bond which is established between human beings and God in Jesus Christ. Are they to be excluded in principle to the far side of the impassable gulf between practical truth and theology?

The other issue appears in the contrast which Morgan wants to draw between this 'practical truth' and its protective doctrine of the incarnation, on the one side, and mythology and theology on the other. Morgan holds that the incarnation when understood as doctrine is the 'golden thread' of continuity in orthodoxy by which one can distinguish Christianity from the mythologies and theologies with which it is so frequently confused. By contrast, mythologies are 'pre-reflective', while theologies are 'reflections' upon the 'practical truth'; and both need to be controlled by the doctrine of the incarnation as 'post-reflective' summary. Neither mythologies nor theologies are in themselves problematic so long as recognized as such. And of course, they are regularly employed in the service of the presentation of the incarnation, in the NT and beyond, as Morgan shows in his analysis of John and the Gospels.

But is this set of tools for discriminating between mythologies and theologies, or between either one and the legitimacy of the 'practical truth' protected in the incarnation, very helpful? It is quite possible for truth to be pictured in mythological terms, or in theological ones for that matter. Therefore, while Bob Morgan's argument is convincing in its own terms, it does not altogether succeed, not least because it shares the Kantian influence which permeates the mythicizers of Christianity. In their terms, the *doctrine* of the incarnation is 'a construction built on the variegated evidence to be found [in scripture]',[32] and therefore like (or the same as) myth, not the doctrinal form of the 'practical truth' which

---

[32] Maurice Wiles, 'Christianity without Incarnation', in *The Myth of God Incarnate*, ed. John Hick (London: SCM, 1977), p. 3.

Morgan wants it to be. In the end, I am convinced that the incarnation must be seen as the concentrated historical occurrence of the dynamic relation between the mystery and revelation of God and humanity which pervades all history. That requires a theology of history. Arguing about the levels of rationality, and what can be assigned to what level, will not get us far. But the notion of practical truth does, and in one particular (that is non-universal) way, provide a *minimal standard* of orthodoxy. And in that sense, it is very useful.

IV. CONTEXTS: THE INTERWEAVING OF THEOLOGY

Concentrating on the issues of the tradition seen in its own terms ignores the complex relations of the diverse forms of the tradition as such, and thus with what is often called their context. But it is misleading to treat these forms as units neatly demarcated from each other, or from their context. Their relation is one of complex overlappings and interweavings and shifting boundaries. It is these which come to the forefront in *Hugh McLeod*'s engrossing account of forms of the Christian tradition in the modern West.

A fine example of social history, McLeod's account orders religious events and movements by their complex social interaction. If anything, I think, this underestimates the depth of the factors which united and divided them, which were even more closely interwoven with their identities as the people they were, the ecclesial bodies in which they were joined and the situations – national, governmental and other – in which they found themselves. For these 'identity' issues go remarkably deep, and suggest how divisions bred conflict.

And these issues were undoubtedly intermingled with their very 'godliness', although I hesitate to use the term in such a polyvalent way. In that, they were affected by issues which go to the heart of what Christianity is. When this nexus of practices, societies, identities, situations and religious convictions is taken seriously, the interactions which McLeod traces make the arena of religious differences appear more as titanic struggles – far from the more idealized views of the era adopted by people today, in a situation in which religious differences are contained within an environment neutralized by factors external to religion, for example law and the acceptance of tolerance. Perhaps the violence seen in Belfast, Bosnia and Rwanda are examples of the depth of the factors involved in religious differences, and not only instances of social conflict in the name of religion.

When these deeper matters are considered in the account which McLeod offers of the fluctuations of scale, intensity, significance and forms which have marked sectarian conflict since the Reformation, some issues will not appear the same. How accurate, for example, is it to use the title 'sectarian conflict' when what is at issue are often *churches*? In what McLeod calls the confessional era, the state was itself so closely allied to the church as to be only relatively distinguishable from it, and therefore did not so much 'impose a particular form of Christianity' as manifest its own religious *alter ego* amongst the people. This would only be seen as 'confessional' or the 'privileging of one denomination' by those who supposed religious neutrality on the part of the state – a much more recent idea, probably traceable to John Locke's view that states should not act in matters which could only be settled by *persuasion*, which found its way only gradually into general acceptance. McLeod seems to me to overlook the integration of religious views with the formative institutions of society.

Why did so many of these syntheses of religious views with public institutions (for the issue was not simply one of 'cultures') emphasize 'the alien character of those belonging to other confessions'? One major answer was that they were likely to be seditious, thanks to a religious allegiance by which they were united to a foreign power, or in other cases to their individual conscience. But there were also *theological* issues within the dominant positions, as witness the sharp cleavage of elect from reprobate which characterized Calvinism (more than Calvin, thanks to the adoption of the Ramist logic of dichotomies) and that between the universal church catholic and the rebellious sects. These issues tended to produce alienation of bloc from bloc, to which national differences were secondary.

When it came, toleration came slowly, precisely because these issues were so much intermingled, politics with principle and principle with profound religious issues – as can be seen in relation to Catholic Emancipation in Ireland. While popular movements and attitudes were important, toleration was not only a mood amongst the 'élite'; it was given legal force, and (in a fashion appropriate to social-structural change) gradually changed the scene. And the practices of the churches followed.

The story continues a complex one to the fluid society (but marked by neither fluid governmental structure nor religious institutions) of the present day. I pick this era for comment only as illustration of my wish to extend Hugh McLeod's analysis by giving greater prominence to the interweaving of national, political and legal issues with those of religious conviction and identity. And I consider it important to explore the roots and dynamics of religious identity and opposition in the habits, personal and psychological as well as intellectual and moral, of those involved. As he suggests, 'none of this can simply be dismissed as blind prejudice'. The present issue is how, in an increasingly plural world (whether it is *pluralist* is another matter), 'people with strong but radically different convictions, can live together in peace'.

How indeed? The issue is an exceedingly difficult one. A large part of the difficulty derives from the multidimensional character of the issues involved. How the religions and denominations are historically interwoven, how they yet differentiate themselves through the interpretation of their history, their preferred languages and conceptualities, their conceptions of tradition, their view of the place of human reason and practice – all of these suffused with their perceptions of the being and presence of God, the determinative events of history and the norms for faith and life; these are the central issues in a complex and multidimensional dialogue which has barely begun. Until the issues which constitute other traditions as themselves are reconciled with the content of particular religious traditions, and differences accounted for within each, difficulties and conflicts will remain. For Christians, that will mean accounting for the 'otherness' of others not as cause for religious alienation, but as an aspect of the provenance of the dynamic activity of the Triune God which calls all not only to difference but to love. And that will demand the facing of a theological task which few envisage as yet.

If Hugh McLeod faces us with interreligious alienation – as understood through social history – as a practical 'contextual' task, *Richard Roberts*' essay faces us with a range of issues equally, if not more, serious. It comes like the starburst of a firework rocket, illuminating all that is beneath. It requires – and asks for – a total reconfiguration of religion and theology to meet the present situation of religion.

It does need to be noticed that it is the *religious* situation, broadly speaking, with which Roberts' essay deals, and a *religious* response for which he asks. His supposition, it seems to me, is that religion is a kind of meaning-system or culture. While that is no doubt correct, it must not be supposed that it is only, or even primarily, that.[33] A major issue is the position of theology, not as reflection on faith and its meaning-system, but as the endeavour to develop a dynamic form for the tradition of faith – including cultural and other elements – in the present day. That issue is not addressed where the emphasis is on the development of religious forms which will maintain their meaning in the present day.

Roberts is right, of course, to point to sociality as indicative of 'a society which at its best has a supportive and enabling culture, a culture whose root paradigms are intact and capable of comprehending both differentiation into particularities and universals which hold the human

---

[33] Designating it as such prejudges a variety of issues. See Daniel W. Hardy, 'Theology and the Cultural Reduction of Religion', in *Christian Theology and Religious Education: Connections and Contradictions*, ed. J. Astley (London: SPCK, 1996).

together in the ancestral form of a *religio*, a mutual binding informed by a Gospel of grace and truth'. He is equally right in his supposition that, while it 'does not now by and large exist ... it should be evident in proleptic form in the church experienced as the foretaste of the King-dom'.³⁴ It is that foretaste with which we should be concerned.

But my view is that theology itself – that is God and God's dynamic activity in the world – translates into the sociality of the church, and with that into the sociality of society at large. Hence, I am always concerned when that linkage is displaced or the series of links is severed, as it may be when, on the one hand, we attend directly to cultural forms, and lose their specifically religious character, and on the other hand divorce them from theology and sociality at large.

Nonetheless, Roberts' penetrating analysis of the religious situation is exactly to the mark. The reason it is so devastating in its implications is that it applies equally well to all the meaning-systems by which sociality is maintained, and therefore must be met if religion is to connect with them. In effect, he is saying 'this is the world in which we exist, like it or not, and therefore the world in which traditional religion must speak if it is not to fade away'. Despite the fruitless controversies with which it has been preoccupied, there are religious impulses amongst the people with which it can reconnect if it will only recognize and face its task.

The fruitless controversies derive from the fact that Christianity orig-inated in *pre-modernity* and – still caught there – continues to fight unsuccessfully with *modernity*,³⁵ and does not yet recognize how seriously it is displaced in *postmodernity*. It is clear, however, that these three phases coexist in the social structure of the contemporary world. There the Christian churches are, I think, paralysed by their inability to conceive what is best for them to do. So they return to habitual tasks and preoccupations.

Given this paralysis, the combination of postmodernity and its accom-panying religious practices are the unavoidable context for the forward movement of religion. The churches may be tempted to pretend that nothing has happened (and thereby be forced to the periphery of human life), or reconstitute themselves 'as free-ranging entrepreneurial activity

---

³⁴ After my regular lectures in Durham on the church, I was often asked, 'But where does this church exist?' My response was that it does, but only in glimpses and fragments here and there.
³⁵ It should be recognized that these remarks apply to some of the essays in the present book, perhaps especially those which try to solve the problems associated with the sources of Christian faith. Roberts identifies the underlying difficulty as a failure to employ a 'properly-informed human/social sciences approach to the continuing theological task'; the result is that the church is starved of its own resources. In effect, we might say, these approaches fail to answer Dietrich Bonhoeffer's probing question, 'Who is Jesus Christ for us today?'

in a differentiated religious market' (and thereby risk damaging the living tradition by rationalizing it, denying its agency and absorbing it into forms of management),[36] or combine the two as indeed they do today. But the only satisfactory option is of another kind! 'a critical-affirmative and dialectical approach conducted through a human/social science-informed theological hermeneutics which might employ without bewitchment the possibilities of the postmodern condition'.

I agree. But it needs to be a *theological* and *ecclesial* hermeneutics, which reaches amongst the economic-cultural-quasi-religious constructs (like the phenomenon of Michael Jackson which Roberts discusses) and which respond to – and construct – current religiosity. Such a hermeneutics would construct forms of sociality which mediate the being and activity of God in church life in such a way as to meet 'the latent human and religious needs of the general population'. In that, I think the task of theology is not only to be 'another form of cultural capital' (in Clegg's phrase) but to uncover the Godly basis for human sociality – even in the unprecedented fluidity of the present situation. That would involve a principled use of this fluidity,[37] not an 'eclecticism' which would abandon the need to establish priorities within the 'total inheritance' of the tradition. In these respects, I differ somewhat from Richard Roberts' proposals.

So far as the Church of England is concerned, the issue is how – through the redevelopment of its special character – it will respond. That is *Peter Sedgwick*'s concern. And there are refined issues involved in his understanding of the Church of England,[38] which go beyond the cultural ones which predominate in Richard Roberts' analysis, particularly those of ecclesial polity. But it is as illuminating an appreciation of the Church of England as Roberts' is of the religious situation today.

Little understood even by those loyal to it, Anglican ecclesial polity is a sophisticated dynamic of interconnections, one which spells out a theo-

---

[36] An example might be those movements which identify God as the source of 'spiritual power' which is channelled through those who learn to follow God.

[37] The way in which I have sometimes spoken of this is in terms of complexity, that is, the co-inherence of order and chaos.

[38] Like Peter Sedgwick, I shall use 'Anglican' as an adjectival form of 'Church of England'. But, particularly as one who is binational in involvement, I am aware of the problems of substituting 'Anglican' for 'Church of England' where the discussion is of England. The term 'Anglican' is often used not in this neutral adjectival sense, but to suggest that the Church of England is but one church in England, and therefore a sect. Many – including many of its own people – may want it to be, and may point to the fact that it is only one church in the world scene; this inclination obviously figures in current debates, either (as in those following from the ordination of women to the priesthood) where the status of the Church is linked by some to its standing with the Roman Catholic Church, or where there is increased awareness of the reduction in its standing in the national life. Nonetheless, it remains the established Church of – not simply in – England, a position which should not be taken to imply that it is *privileged* as such, only that it is *responsible* as such.

logical-ecclesiological contribution to the emergence of civil society. It claims neither completeness nor infallibility, but – in the provenance of God – the capacity to bring free, moral agents together by their common consent in a fashion which mediates the character of God and God's saving grace in human society. The visible means by which it achieves these purposes are not so much theoretical as liturgical and practical-political. These are the ways by which the purposes of God are enfolded into the human community in the created order, and thereby unfolded into human society at large. While the theoretical concentration of Sedgwick's essay is very valuable, more attention needs therefore to be given to the practices of liturgy and polity in the church for these reasons.

The embodiment of 'graced sociality' which is thus sought is, as Sedgwick suggests, the fundamental rationale for Anglican polity. Of course, it is crucial that it both beget and further the freedom of reciprocity between people who, in a sense, give each other otherness in mutual trust, and sustain it through ongoing, self-correcting forms of social life.[39] What is the source of such benefits? Not power (and I fear that Peter Sedgwick is preoccupied at times with the Church's loss of power), but the display of the being of God in a true sociality – which is discovered within the worship of the Triune God. Of course, that involves deep exploration of the conditions in creation and the being and activity of God through which sociality may respond to the self-giving of the Triune God.[40] And it requires the translation of these possibilities, and the practices of worship which mediate them, to the different conditions involved in local situations, communities and issues today – those which Sedgwick identifies so helpfully.[41]

The hallmark of Anglican polity has been its 'determination to affect the whole of life' through the particular congerie of features characteristic of the 'local' situation – local, it must be remembered, at a number of different levels. The church is not therefore 'private', but the correlate of the state in one society in maintaining *religio*, the fundamental bond by which human beings are joined together in a world where 'nothing is found whereunto any thing created can say "I need thee not"'. What the church mediates – through the mutual consent of its people – is the being and purposes of God, not in some vaguely personal or spiritual way but through its very institutions.

---

[39] That is, as *ecclesia semper reformanda*.

[40] This is the sense in which the 'social transcendental' was intended in 'Created and Redeemed Sociality', in *On Being the Church*, eds. C. E. Gunton and D. W. Hardy (Edinburgh: T. & T. Clark, 1989).

[41] 'Local' here should not be understood in a geographical sense. In the contemporary situation, it must be taken to mean 'viable social unit for particular purposes', which of course will vary according to the purposes involved. In that sense, 'specific communities' will vary by social, economic and political considerations.

These, of course, are a slightly glossed version of the views of Hooker and Coleridge which Sedgwick expounds so well. Where Coleridge is discussed, however, there is a more serious issue which appears. In Coleridge's view, the position of the Constitution in England, not to be confused with the written form favoured by the more text-centred Americans (perhaps because of their Puritan inheritance), is that of an Idea expressing balance between stability ('permanence') and progress. Within this, there is an *'enclesia'* ('an order ... chosen *in and of* the realm, and constituting an estate of the realm') whose task is to 'balance' permanence and progression – 'to bind the present with the past; to perfect and add to the same, and thus to connect the present with the future' and to prepare its citizenry.[42] As distinct from these 'lateral' functions, there is also the *ecclesia*, comprised of those 'called out of the World ... in reference to the especial ends of that communion', that is of the church of Christ as a public and visible community. Coleridge distinguishes between 'the church as an institution of Christ and as a Constituent Estate of the State', '*Ecc*lesia one with but separate from *En*clesia'. So there is what we might call a double mediation through which the purposes of God are present in society, through the *Ecc*lesia present in the *En*clesia present in the nation.

As always, however, it is easier to identify the functions of the latter than the former. The latter is concerned with cultivating the people (but note Coleridge's sad statement, 'I fear the church has let the hearts of the common people be stolen from it.'). The former, as the 'befriending opposite' of the state, however, concentrates on the ground of humanity which is found for Coleridge in the Reason, 'the organ of the supersensuous', and on that 'Faith which is "the substance of the things hoped for", the living stem that will expand into the flower, which it now foreshews'.[43] There is a direct expansion of the Idea of the Constitution implicit here, a Faith and Hope specific to the church of Christ, yet one with the broader purposes of the *en*clesia. These are the counterparts of the permanence and progression which are the rightful concern of the *en*clesia, and derive from the understanding of God's salvation which it is the purpose of theology to plumb.

The major issues for the church today are not dissimilar. While I agree with so much of what Sedgwick suggests is needed, I fear that in the end his suggestions confine the church to concern with the gracing of a free and moral society in particular situations, without drawing upon the other side of Hooker's and Coleridge's concerns. The question of how

---

[42] Interestingly, this is an early statement of disequilibrium. See the earlier essays by Pickard and McFadyen.
[43] Samuel T. Coleridge, *On the Constitution of Church and State*, ed. John Colmer (London: Routledge & Kegan Paul, 1976), p. 175.

the being and purposes of the Triune God can be fashioned for the people in the liturgy and polity of the church, and thereby cultivate a civil society and its polity, remains an urgent one.

All of the three issues with which we have just been concerned – the alienation of Christians from each other, the religious situation today, and the situation of the Church of England – converge upon the extraordinarily difficult issue of the ministry of the church and the ordained ministry in particular. Why? Perhaps it is because the issues as regards God, church and world are so complex today that Christians tend to personalize them through concentrating on the one-to-one relation of the individual Christian to the personal God. Where the church is concerned, it is easy to displace this relation onto a power figure, the cleric. This is the special importance of the issues which *Brian Russell* takes up in his essay.

At (of all things) a garden party at Buckingham Palace after the approval of ACCM Paper 22, *Education for the Church's Ministry*, I was approached by an old friend, now a bishop, who said, with an amused chuckle, 'You've put a bomb in the middle of the Church of England!' I took it that he recognized the Paper as a far-reaching and constructive move forward for theological education in the church, which it has proved to be. For, as Brian Russell notes, it was intended to capitalize on the strength and diversity found in the theological colleges and courses of the Church of England, and to build these as well as build on them. Not only, as Brian Russell says, did they manifest the church's 'proper reverence for the mystery of divine truth and the provisionality of human attempts to grasp that' but also (as he only implies) a balanced diversity of embodied responses to these.

The new arrangements were to allow each college to develop for itself a well-thought conception of the ordained ministry which the Church of England requires, and to manifest that in educational objectives and a well-formed educational programme. That was not necessarily to suggest a 'core', for these arrangements were not designed to require each college to produce its own version of what was then to be discarded, the old and increasingly unworkable GME Syllabus and GME Examinations. What was sought was a balanced set of objectives and a programme which would provide basic formation for ordinands in the range of resources and skills necessary for the church's ministry today. Finally, colleges were to develop means of assessing how far their students had met the objectives, by methods actually suitable to the varied objectives and elements of the educational programme set out; since the goals were not only cognitive, other means of assessment might be more appropriate than the written examinations and essays used heretofore.

The responses to the questions about ministry, educational programme and methods of assessment were then to be reviewed by the Courses and

Examinations Subcommittee of ACCM, and if satisfactory approved for a period of five years, after which the process would need to be repeated. Instead of central examinations, there would be college or course assessment, with the participation of an external examiner approved by ACCM.

What the arrangements provided was a version of the *ecclesia semper reformanda* suitable to theological education, stimulated and shaped by a set of crucial questions having to do with the internal and external dynamics of the church. It was hoped that they would elicit a conception of the Church of England as manifesting the work of the Triune God in the church of Christ in the special circumstances of England, and they implicitly acknowledged that ordinands were to be prepared to work with lay people to make the church an embodiment of the church of Christ for the society of the nation – thereby 'to serve the mission of God in the world', relating ministry to mission in the public sphere.

As much as they disliked the old centrally-imposed theological education, the colleges and courses as a group were suspicious and fearful of the new process, which expected them to operate in responsible freedom in serving the interests of the church. Their responses, which Brian Russell analyses, provide fascinating insight into the conceptions of God, church and ministry which prevail in the church. They vary from monarchial conceptions of each (implying strong views about the one God and a chain of command through the ordained ministry in the church to the world) to a dynamic conception of each (emphasizing the economic Trinity in the world joined to strong views about the responsibility of the ordained ministry to focus and build up the work of the church). They are strikingly different in their conception of the dynamics of the church, the one emphasizing linear movement from God through priest to church to world, and the other seeing a recursive dynamic from God in the world through a prophetic ministry which forms the church to work in the world. Despite their differences (which seem to stem from transcendent and immanent conceptions of God, and conceptions of God as Father and as salvific, respectively), it is noticeable how crucial they make the role of the ordained (as priest-in-obedience-to-God and prophet-in-the-world), and how relatively underdeveloped are the notions of lay ministry, the church and its mission.

It is particularly interesting how closely these coincide with the problems identified in previous essays in this book. To mention only three of the issues, it seems that the question of how the Triune God acts through the believing of Christians in the church (Pickard) has not been widely considered. It seems that the effects of God's work in non-religious situations (as seen in McFadyen's and Selby's essays) are not clearly seen, which tends to produce a centripetal notion of the church. And it appears that neither the distinguishing features of Anglicanism (Sedgwick) nor what are the urgencies of the religious situation today (Roberts) feature large in the priorities of educating the ordained. These questions, all of them urgent for the understanding of the church and its ministry in the world, need to be taken into Brian Russell's largely structural analysis of the issues now outstanding for the church's theological education.

V. FORMATION: THE COHERENCE OF THEOLOGY WITH EDUCATION

In all the foregoing essays, as well as those which follow, it has been implicit that an educated intelligence is crucial to theology, church and the establishment of their coherence with issues of life in the world. That is not necessarily a popular view in a time when, both in theory and practice, many divorce both theology and religious practices from the activity of the mind. It is noticeable, for example, how often today theology is equated with abstract fixities of belief, and religion is placed completely in the affective domain.[44]

But what is it for theology and church to be learned and intelligent? How are they structured and practised as learned and wise, and how do they form themselves in theory and practice? How far are the means of being intelligently formed to be found in their very object, the God known in creation, redemption and fulfilment? How far are they found in educational institutions, their theory and practice, and all the disciplines found there? And how are the two mutually coherent? These are some of the greatest difficulties confronting faith, theology and the church today, as responsible to the God who creates and sustains and fulfils, directly or indirectly, all the other domains of life through the study of which human intelligence is formed. The essays by Frances Young, John Hull, Diogenes Allen and Colin Gunton approach different aspects of the issue.

Frances Young's contribution focuses directly on how from the start 'the church was a lifelong, "comprehensive", learning community', at first because of the demonstrable superiority of Christianity to philosophy in teaching the good, and later because it was faced with the task of incorporating a whole society through its involvement with education. Let me try to explore with her some of the questions involved.

---

[44] This was one of the original causes for my concern for the health of Christianity and the church, as in the 1950s I saw more and more attention being given to 'experience' – non-rational involvement in things religious. It turned me toward directly theological study, and – to my surprise – altered the course of my life.

The issues, of course, have to do with the *what* and *how* of church education. The further issue is how these intersect with the what and how of education outside of purely Christian situations. In her examination of Cyril of Jerusalem, a fascinating picture emerges.

On the one hand, education might be for specifically Christian purposes. For example, in Cyril of Jerusalem, education prepares for the transformation of the whole person in the impending baptism, and is orientated to this 'new birth'. It therefore concentrates on issues such as the cleansing and confession which were necessary to new birth, God's grace in baptism as effecting salvation and sanctification, and the framework of theological truth in which all these are grounded.[45] The fact that these were regarded as a 'method of godliness' in which pious doctrines and virtuous practices are interconnected indicates, I think, how closely they intersected with the philosophy and educational practices prevailing elsewhere in the Greek world.

For in the Greek world, *doctrina* or *dogma* were the developing of the total person for mature understanding and practice of truth and goodness, the training of the body, and the inculcation of the duties of citizenship in the society, together with the skills necessary to such pursuits, language, grammar, reading, judgement, persuasion. These were not taught, one might say, as abstract skills with no agreed body of understanding, no canon of literature and no accepted skills, but within traditions which established these things, and for their perpetuation.

The close integration of Christian purposes and the practices of a 'total education' was not accidental or contrived. Given a broad conception of the divinely ordered Logos present in the Incarnate Jesus Christ but operative wherever truth and goodness were sought, education could be a primary means of conformity with the Logos. Hence Christianity offered a supervening and pervading order for education which gave it its orientation, and made it a comprehensive, lifelong process. At least in principle, this also opened education to all, treating all (in a term from Calvin) as 'teachable'. These characteristics seem to have demonstrated the intrinsic superiority of Christianity as *paideia*. Interestingly, this was because the 'internal' characteristics of Christianity proved capable of orientating, ordering and integrating the practices of education which were 'external' to Christianity.

Did Christian convictions and practice inhibit the breadth of education? As Frances Young presents it, it seems to have been a capacious form of learning, which accommodated within it much dispute, issues on which there was no agreement, and so forth. That is to say, it provided

---

[45] It seems to me to prejudge the value of these to label them a 'mind-set' which must carry conviction, or 'orthodox' answers which have to be demonstrated. They were, I think, seen to participate in the truth, and not only as matters of personal or ecclesial belief.

'space' for variation, difference and dialectical probing, and was not therefore as confining as those with modern liberal educational values might suppose.

But its position could not be guaranteed; the direction of contribution could be reversed. That was what appears to have happened when 'in the post-Constantinian era, classical forms increasingly shaped Christian content'. I wonder if it was because the vitality of the belief in the Logos of God present in Jesus Christ had diminished, and if so, whether it was because classical *practices* had overtaken the *orientation* offered in the Logos – their 'extensiveness' overwhelming the 'intensiveness' of the Logos? Such an account would parallel what has occurred in modern times.

The textual counterpart of the Logos was seen in the role of scripture in the church as educational institution. While, as with Origen, there might be the wide variety of studies found in a classical curriculum, they were centred in the interpretation of the Bible. In that two characteristics were combined, the church as comprehensive in its intellectual reach while still orienting these by focusing on biblical interpretation. As Frances Young indicates, this involved an educational process (leading from literal to moral to spiritual reading) which also required close reading (to identify variants), judgement (decision between variants), discussion of vocabulary, identifying the use of words and figures of speech, construing sentences, discovery of allusions, establishing the kind of text (myth, philosophy, history, etc.). What is extraordinary is the degree of educational concentration and sophistication in evidence here. They would form a well-developed counterweight to the variety of studies in the classical curriculum, while also integrating their skills into the study of *this* text – which corresponded to the supposition (by Origen) of the necessity of enlightenment to appreciate the Logos as God's accommodation to human discourse.

These cases provide fascinating insight into the co-ordination of general education (*paideia*) with God's *paideia*, whether – as we might interpret it – by rooting their theory in the Logos of God in Jesus Christ or by co-ordinating classical educational practices with the deepening study of the scriptures. By these means, furthermore, the constitutive principles and practices of sociality for the Greeks were made coherent with those of the church. Frances Young's study is full of rich implications for the establishment of a theoretical and practical coherence between learning as generally understood and the bases for it in Christian theology and life. And it is fairly clear that this coherence was not achieved through the domination of general educational practices by narrow, authoritatively-imposed Christian ones. Can such a coherence be re-established today? The perception of Christian faith as a coherent form of wisdom and practice may depend on it.

345

Suppose, however, we concentrate on what is perhaps the most directly formative influence in modern society, one which now outreaches both education and theology in its effect – money. How can they be brought to bear on that? That is the significance of *John Hull*'s contribution.

His discussion is at first concerned with the extraordinary character of money, how a piece of money becomes an *abstract reality* which possesses universal value as 'the means to all ends' and therefore attracts attention to itself as 'an end in itself', while also serving as an expression of the comparative value of particular commodities, as a *concrete universal*. As 'the most purely general and most fluid expression of human will and desire', it becomes autonomous in its power and therefore capable of moulding what lies outside of itself.[46] So far as human beings are concerned, it may (like language) recreate us in its own image, displacing our human self into an ideal money-formed self. Whether it binds us together in solidarity, as John Hull suggests, I am more doubtful. It seems to me that money may draw us into itself, but as an abstract reality which blurs distinctions, and is as such neither individual nor social. It is only in so far as we retain a sense of separate identity 'holding' the money, as 'mine' or 'ours', that we give money the capacity to divide or unite.

The coincidence of most general and most specific can be seen in this conception of money (as the medium of economic unity) or in the corresponding conception of God (as the medium of cosmic unity), which may explain the problematic relation between money and religion, either being translatable into the other. But such conceptions are more problematic than John Hull seems to allow, since they make money into a principle of material unity, and God into a principle of cosmic unity. Neither conception is true to what is involved. Hence, the educational discussion of the conception and use of money, and of theological norms must begin with the critique of the conceptions. Is it the case that money is an abstract but concrete universal? Or is it in fact always positive and partial (that is, non-neutral) and manifest in the particular values which particular things have? Is the same not also true of God?

While, therefore, money may be an instrument for the exchange of goods whose value is determined in the exchange, at another level the value of money is set in exchange for other money. The idea of money as abstract/concrete universal may in fact serve as a *false universal*, obscuring the fact that money is always partial and particular, its value always established in exchange. Where it is used as the means of establishing the value of concrete things, people and processes, it establishes values in ways different from other, possibly more particular and humane (not to say Godly) ways of doing so. That would explain how money seems to

---

[46] This is what happens when things are treated only as their comparative monetary value.

cling to some and not others, who may use it to perpetuate and increase their money – even in an apparently equal exchange.

Seeing money in these terms brings us much closer to theological norms of the sort to which John Hull appeals. It is not that God is sometimes partial (as in 'preference for the poor'), but always so – 'sharp as a two-edged sword' (Heb. 4.12). Hence, it would seem, the coherence between money and theology must be found not in universals, but in partiality, the partiality of God testing the partiality of money.

As society is drawn increasingly into money-exchange-based valuations, forming people in the intelligent search for the coherence of conceptions and use of money with theological conceptions and norms is an exceedingly important task. In order to do so, it is necessary to probe the comparability of money and God as universals and the 'partiality' of each. The key issue is which partiality is good, and by what standard.

Where we face the question of how education and theology converge in seeking the good, we are in the field of issues taken up by *Diogenes Allen*. As he approaches them, the questions are similar to those which were discussed in Frances Young's contribution. How can the standards and procedures of inquiry today – as set in most educational institutions, whether 'theological' or not – be made coherent with the ascent of human beings to God which is at the heart of Christian faith? It is an extremely fundamental question, tantamount to asking how all the 'ordinary' pursuits of human life are related to the soul's quest for God.

Part of the difficulty of the issue is establishing what it is that makes the usual ways of pursuing intelligent inquiry problematic, and what is the origin – historical and conceptual – of the problem. Diogenes Allen suggests that it is issues which are 'extrinsic' to theology which are the problem, as distinct from those which are 'intrinsic' to it, those which 'arise from the nature of God and our human condition ... and arise in every age and culture'. But I think he means 'extrinsic' and 'intrinsic' to *spiritual theology* of the sort with which he is specially concerned. For, even apart from those concerned with extrinsic questions, there are many who concentrate on the issues which are intrinsic to theology as a discipline, remaining within what I have sometimes called 'monological' theology, the tradition interpreting itself, who still miss the spiritual formation which is at the heart of theology. I think Allen's concern is with the positive question of what is proper to spiritual theology, and separating this from what may distract from it. That is genuinely difficult to specify.

As far as I am concerned, it is a matter of what it is which serves to incorporate inquiry into the theocentric dynamic in which the knowing of God consists. Ultimately, this is only answerable by reference to the holy and abundant 'I am' of God, and how God – by the affirmation 'I will be there with you'[47] – so turns towards us as to make our inquiries appropriate to the knowing of God, despite our limitation and sin. By what means do we stand within this theocentric dynamic, and what aids and hinders it? Here is where we can learn much from the great spiritual writers with which Diogenes Allen acquaints us, and the multiple issues with which they were perennially concerned: the goal, path, motivation, hindrances, aids, criteria and fruits of the spiritual life.

But these are subtle issues and difficult to correlate with the problems of 'academic theology today'. Is the fact that the Bible and theology are approached 'historically, sociologically, psychologically, and politically' itself injurious, or is it only that they are so often used idolatrously (as valuable in their own right and therefore substitutes for the knowing of God through them) and magically (to provide human beings with control over them), and hence not incorporated into the theocentric dynamic?

It is, as Diogenes Allen suggests, very much a matter of attending to God and the human condition through intelligent inquiry. But these are even wider-ranging issues than he suggests, at least in this essay. For attending to God through inquiry is also moving to more profound ways of knowing God, much as did Anselm, Aquinas, Bonaventure or Loyola in their days, or Calvin and Luther in theirs. The very attempt to do so needs to incorporate other and more recent ways of knowing the human condition – individual and social, the condition of the world in which they are embodied, and the definitive acts by which God formed and redeemed us and our world. As Allen has often said elsewhere, the Book of Nature and the Book of the Word meet in the knowing of God. The principal issue is how in our day these may indeed meet, and not – through the fragmentation of ways of treating them which abounds today – distract us from the knowing of God with which, as embodied human beings in the world, we are to be concerned. There is no way of prescribing in advance how this may occur. But it is clear that it will integrate inquiry into the divine life in relation to worldly being and events, and thus integrate theological with other forms of inquiry, *unfolding* the former into the latter and *enfolding* the latter into the former. As yet, we are only at the brink of this task.[48]

Allen's treatment of these matters is rich and helpful, above all because it confidently reasserts the dynamic which is central to Christian faith and life, the ascent to the knowing of God, and thereby establishes the limits of what one could call 'professional' theology and religion, and of those who accumulate and manipulate knowledge and skills 'having to do with' God. In the skilful distillation of the great tradition of spiritu-

---

[47] Exodus 3.1–12.
[48] My response to this problem was given in the Director's Report in the *Annual Report for 1993* (Princeton: Center of Theological Inquiry, 1994).

ality which Allen provides, what is normative for theology is the way of ascent to God which occurs through God's awakening us, freeing us from distractions, focusing our minds and hearts on God – all of these through God showing Godself as distinct from the world and showing us how to ascend to the knowing of God. As thus seen, theological inquiry presupposes the following of a spiritual trajectory which occurs through conversion and spiritual formation.

Given current standards, which give priority to 'extrinsic' questions addressed to theology, whether from beyond or within its tradition, the argument for following this movement may appear at first to be a form of special pleading. But actually it is not, because its location is (as Allen says) within universal questions of the human condition, 'issues that arise from the nature of God and our human condition ... [which] arise in every age and culture', 'the nature of the reality to be known and our human capacity to know that reality'. Hence the ascent toward God is not only 'common to all Christian spirituality', but also the rightful companion to intellectual inquiry. It was for that reason that 'for most of Christian history, intellectual inquiry and spiritual aspiration went hand-in-hand'. The problem is that this companionship has been displaced by the power of academic approaches whose standards are extrinsic to theology.

It seems to me to be profoundly important to develop possibilities for incorporating into theology forms of inquiry which follow the dynamic of worship of God. I am less sure that there is a single tradition regarding the right relation between human beings and God, which can be distilled and followed. The form in which Allen puts this is potentially problematic: as God reveals Godself to them, so they are to ascend to God, the goal being 'some form of union with God'; and if we detach ourselves from this knowing of God, we are fundamentally untrue to it. Such a 'tradition' threatens to oversimplify legitimate differences about the relation between human beings and God (whether, for example, it is covenantal, analogical, etc.), correlative differences about the means and goal of theology and the spiritual life, and even fundamental issues about the nature of the trinitarian activity of God. The spiritual path into which rational theological inquiry needs to be drawn must be specified in the capacious way which always seems to have accompanied holiness.

In modern times, the issues addressed by Frances Young, John Hull and Diogenes Allen are found in their most acute form in the public provision made for education, that is in universities. There society itself may find its way to the true sociality which was discussed earlier. What kind of education needs to occur there, and how does theology figure in it? A striking feature of universities today is their tendency to lose direction, particularly by substituting narrowly 'efficient' liberalism for a fuller kind of liberality more in accord with 'the gracious liberality of God'. That is what has forced theologians in England to fight a rearguard battle, to justify the place of theology in a university as well as to pursue theology. The battle has been lost in the USA, where the 'troops' fight on another 'battlefield'.

The issues come to a focus in the discussion of the place of religion and theology (and the relation between them) in education as a whole. The level at which they are addressed here is universities, but the issues are the same elsewhere.[49] The power of education – which in some respects resembles that of money – makes this discussion very volatile and important. *Colin Gunton*'s contribution directly confronts the remarkable range of issues involved.

Whatever the successes of the early Christians, how coherent is theology with the purposes and disciplines of a modern university? Setting aside the claims occasionally made, that theology is inconsistent with the free inquiry normative to a university and that theologians have become 'antitheologians' and therefore incapable of sustaining their subject, Colin Gunton concentrates on central issues. He provides responses to each identifiable issue, accumulating a case that theology is justified by its 'fruits' in academic life: *how* it performs its task will show *why* it is needed. Theology is at least 'functional' in this respect.

The range of issues is remarkable; they are both social and intellectual. In a 'value-free' society, theology is justified by its critical power. In the dynamics of culture, theology has had, and does have, an important role. Where universities are seen as centres of vocational training, church vocations should be among them. Where people need to be prepared for a present and developing variety of social cultures and institutions, they confront many issues for which the tools of theological understanding are necessary.

In the more specifically intellectual domain, theology has both a hermeneutic and a substantial function. In the first case, theology has 'an indispensable function in the culture's attempts to understand itself, by whatever means are chosen, whether scientific, historical or cultural'. In the second case, theology closely matches the underlying values of the modern university, in which a tolerant plurality of cultures, communities and truth-claims is considered necessary (theology is one, alongside other religions); in which different – and again tolerant – forms of advocacy are important (theology is one); in which different forms of study are rooted in faith-commitment (theology knows how to deal with these); where issues are contested (religion is experienced in handling contestation); where tolerance-in-difference is needed (theology seeks to defend toleration);

---

[49] That remains the case despite the fact that, for a variety of reasons, education in schools is taken to be 'religious education' and that in universities is largely 'religion' or 'theology'. The presupposition of the former is induction into religion as 'culture', while that of the latter is education into the intelligent grasp of religion or theology. The implications are discussed in Hardy, 'Theology and the Cultural Reduction of Religion'.

where homogeneity is avoided (theology contributes to debates about the nature of universality); where there is pluriformity (the Christian doctrine of God is generative of a range of insights); and where truth is threatened by monolithic approaches (attention to God undermines these). In other words, Christian theology makes a strong theoretical and practical contribution to the cultural and intellectual pursuits of a university.

Given the functional conception of universities today, it is natural for Colin Gunton to cast his argument in those terms. In effect, it says, 'here is what you do; this is how what we do contributes to that'. Of course, he would be the first to admit that all will depend on how theology actually performs in these functions.

What is particularly interesting is that it implies that a university is a collection of needed disciplines in a loose functional relationship. Given that, the best answer that we can now hope to find to our question ('How closely do the intelligence and learning which are formative for theology and church cohere with education?') may be that theology stands within a loose collection of disciplines, justifying itself by the recognized contribution which it makes – which is always being assessed by its actual performance.

Is a stronger relationship possible? An argument from the comparability and contribution of theology to other forms of study might not uncover it. Perhaps the quality of its contribution derives from its special character as the positive study of that which is pivotal for all the rest. To make and sustain its character as such – in addition to its functional value for other discussions – would not necessarily end in claiming 'queenship' for theology, which is compatible neither with the substance or limitations of the discipline.

As may appear from my comments about these four contributions, I also search for the co-inherence of the theory and practice of education, as formative of intelligent human life, with the dynamic activity of God. For this, more attention needs to be given to the ontology of human life, identifiably the same and yet developing, and how that co-inheres with the ordering of energy which occurs from God because it is in God. Such a task cannot be undertaken by itself, without also seeking to develop ways in which theology may 'raise' other forms of inquiry. The two tasks are interdependent, the one a 'concentration' of the 'extension' in which the other consists. That also tells us why they must be pursued by people dedicated to *theology*, but who are knit together in *collegial relationships* with those whose expertise lies elsewhere in the broad span of inquiries. In so far as that does not occur in universities (or seminaries in the USA), whether because excluded in principle or practice, it must be attempted elsewhere.[50]

[50] This is the reason for the programme of interdisciplinary consultations held at the Center of Theological Inquiry in Princeton, N.J.

VI. HOPE: THE COHERENCE OF FAITH WITH POSSIBILITY

As the essays in this book presume an educated intelligence in faith and its practice, so they also presuppose the possibility of a good end – to which these lead. Often, little is said about this, however, or the means by which it comes. But the actuality of this outcome – not simply its possibility – is on trial amongst those who are unsure of the viability of Christian faith. What good does come of it?

How one asks and answers the question is the subject with which Esther Reed and Ann Loades are concerned. In their essays, two different – although not entirely separable – ways of addressing the issue are seen, one primarily about what kind of future for human community may be hoped for, and the other primarily about the human contribution. On the way to making positive proposals, they also confront some of the deep convictions which today obscure Christian hope.

Esther Reed sets out to free Christian hope from confusion with the substitutes now used, unscrambling it first from apocalyptic struggles with the spiritual vacuity of the present, and then from 'neo-stoic' quests for transformation through harmony with a nature seen in divine terms. These remain as dangers, as they 'locate the basis of hope in natural, historical and material processes' – whether by translating Christian hope into purely historical terms, or confusing it with a form of cosmolatry in which we assimilate ourselves to the patterns of a living quasi-divine nature. Far from notional possibilities, the analysis shows how much present they are in various forms of art, literature and philosophy today.

The major issue to be confronted is how, in contradistinction from these options, hopes for *Christian community* are to be seen in the 'positive, passionate way that reflects the inner pattern of Christian hope'. Such a possibility will have to be sought beyond the present, empirical, culturally-contextualized and historically-conditioned reality of the church, as *transformed* by the Spirit. That does not mean that when found it will be discontinuous from the church we know, because the being of the church – in so far as it is grounded in God – is 'theandric', with divine and human aspects permeating each other (a good example of the interweaving which characterizes true contextuality!). It is grounded as such through the activity of the witness of the Holy Spirit to the mysteries of God, and this makes the church responsive to cultural needs and the community of hope, 'a dynamic in which future and past subsist in the moment now'.

Despite the helpful way in which she specifies this double contextuality of the church as arising from the Spirit of God witnessing to the mysteries of God, there is possibly a problem in the basis to which Esther Reed points. Since the emphasis is so much on the Holy Spirit as 'qualifying the very being of the church as the body of Christ in the world', *how* the Church *hopes to be* the *body of Christ* is never fully clear. Is this answered by her multidimensional appreciation of 'the logos of Christian hope'? She describes it as contrastive (the present contrasted to eternity to come), synthesizing (of what is seen and what cannot be seen), communal (a mode of existence 'inhabited' by hope, 'constituted Christologically and Sophialogically' from the beginning), compassionate (the everyday participation in the likeness of Christ) and consummating (the hope of the Christian community to be joined with Christ). The question *may* be answered *if* the *relation* in each case is seen as *of Christ*. In other words, the issue is how the logos of hope which is operative in each of these dimensions is Christ, with the Holy Spirit energizing the ways in which Christ does so.

Perhaps the crucial issue has to do with the 'logos of commonality'. *How* does the inhabiting of hope which derives from 'its proclamation in the Spirit of Jesus as Lord' constitute the hope of Christian *community*? Formally, of course, Esther Reed is right to suggest that the Spirit is not to be introduced *after* the Christian community is constituted Christologically. But how does the prophetic witness of the *Spirit of Christ* form the dynamic by which the church will be? Even the logos of compassion and that of consummation do not quite answer this question. Doesn't the future hope of the church as community rest on its response to the covenantal trust and dedication through which God constitutes mutuality in difference, a response which is ever-new in the Spirit? And that would have to be given institutional form in a fashion adequate to the Christian hope.

With *Ann Loades*' essay, we look at the issues in a different way, as a question about how *human beings* in a problem-ridden, evil and tragic world *can* hope. In a fashion appropriate to an age saturated by convictions and anxieties about human autonomy, the discussion here turns around the issue of human potentiality. Carefully engaging with two major treatments of autonomy, John Kekes and Immanuel Kant, Ann Loades centres on the hope of *the human being* in *God*: what is the scope of possibility for the human being and what are the resources? As such, it focuses more on anthropological issues than temporal or eschatological ones.

In a world properly understood (according to Kekes) as a domain of contingency, indifference and destructiveness, whether in 'nature' or in us, human beings had better recognize their capacities and limitations. They are saboteurs and also aspire to better. In this, so Kekes thinks, Christian understanding is helpful, but fundamentally flawed because of its insistence on the necessity of 'supernatural' help (that is, 'trans-empirical resources of freedom, rationality and morality which can foster "our primary potential for goodness" in competition with "natural causes"').

Overall, his strategy is to help human beings understand their situation better, and, by framing their expectations better, to increase their capacity, that is, their hope.

Of course, the crucial issue is the existence of evil, the focus of Kekes' book. But here also, he suggests that human beings need to understand their situation. As Ann Loades expounds the portions of his argument with which she wishes to deal, there is non-moral evil, that which is caused by non-human agency; that which is chosen and caused by human agency; and that which is unchosen and caused by human beings. Hope consists of extending the area we can control 'to mitigate the worst in favour of the better, realizing that we may fail' – increasing the sphere of our autonomy – not in seeking help elsewhere; and hope comes from confidence that we have done what is in our power. In other words, as I see it, hope is the reflection that 'we have done what we can' within the restricted limits of our responsibility.

Even in its own terms, it seems to me that this argument is not as strong as it first appears. For example, it overlooks the fact that we cannot know what are the limits of our responsibility ('what we can') or know our own powers ('we have done') in the ways that Kekes suggests. And it is in those areas that the theological discussion continues today, not simply presenting a 'supernatural supplement' of the kind which Kekes supposes, but seeking to understand how the domain of human responsibility and agency – radically affected in themselves by sin and evil – is permeated by the action of the Triune God.

That 'overlapping' of the fundamentally human and the godly is the area with which Ann Loades is concerned. So far as 'human' potential is concerned, she agrees with Kekes' efforts to alert us to it, and thereby learn about (human) hope. She focuses, however, on a side of human potential which is underestimated by Kekes, its 'down side', the futility of our attempts to be morally responsible even in modest circumstances. This, she suggests, implies the need for a kind of 'divine scrutiny' of the sort which Kant proposes, which induces human autonomy to self-scrutiny, and renders it capable of transformation. 'Kant's preoccupation with truthfulness as lying at the core of such relationship to God as may be possible', together with the conception of God as holy, good and just in creation, preservation and judgement, brings about the humble self-appraisal required of human beings when they reach their limits. Such awareness, she says, sharpens 'the pathos of a struggle we will all lose in our efforts to re-order what is naturally given to us', and may also help with the 'how' of our self-reform and in breaking the power of evil in the will itself.

The focus through which 'rebirth' – of the kind needed where there are greater expectations and failures – takes place is contemplation by which we enter moral union with the one whom God esteems above all else,

Jesus (cf. John 16–17), and thereby become freer to live morally. At that point, the clues about hope and salvation which we learn from our own limited projects and successes give way, when there is tragedy, failure and futility, to something else, not hopelessness or resignation but a different kind of hope and salvation. It is in confronting tragedy that we meet God.

For all its promise, I find myself wanting to question the premises of this line of argument, whether in Kekes' version or Ann Loades'. The argument supposes, I think, that human beings are differentiated from the divine by the power to act. The consequence is that enlarging human power reduces the field of divine activity. The divine need only be appealed to, if at all, where human power reaches its limits. And that is either avoided by redefining its limits, calling human power within these limits 'hope' (Kekes), or established by finding limits and calling what arises beyond them hope (Loades).

These strategies seem to exclude the divine from the ordinary exercise of human power, and that is what I find problematic. Let me outline an alternative which may move us beyond such difficulties.

Suppose that the divine is *itself* in *granting otherness* – the otherness appropriate to a human – to the human being, in the expectation that the human being will know that goodness consists in granting the appropriate otherness to the divine (that is, in the worship). Then a human being may enlarge the field of his or her activity indefinitely; indeed, by doing so, the human confirms the action of the divine. The problem arises in so far as the human being fails to grant appropriate 'otherness' to the divine, preferring other directions of activity instead. In this view, hope arises in the gift of otherness by the divine, and is fulfilled in the return gift of otherness by the human to the divine. In other words, when the human being can extend his or her freedom to say 'let God be God', there hope is fulfilled.

In conclusion, let us recognize how the issue of promise is present in all the dimensions which have been explored during the course of this book. The ways in which theology may be opened to new possibilities and yet find the nature of the dynamism of the Triune God operative in them for the salvation of humanity, how in doing so it continues to engage with its own heritage, how to recover the dynamic of Christian life in the religious and ecclesial life of people today, and how these converge with the educational practices which are formative for human society: all of these need to be placed within the dynamic whereby we reach toward the future of humanity with God.

One of the most serious inhibitions to such hopeful action in the company of God is the sense of futility which is so common today. Dark predictions of the future highlight present tendencies and add a sense of urgency about human life in the world, but just as often they paralyse human behaviour. Add to this the vast complexities of understanding and life today, and the damage to confidence and hope which so many have suffered.[51] The consequence is that people feel both cut off from the future and overwhelmed by the present, to such a degree that they are 'on overload' and incapable of movement.

But the very complexity which today marks the world as human beings now understand it, as well as their life and institutions, is itself a *sign of the future*. That, and the order which arises from it, only to yield more complexity, are the creation as now understood; and they are also the future ahead of us. The exact outworking of this ordering and reordering of energy (that is the temporal aspect of complexity) is, of course, a mystery, but not in all respects. It is for that reason that this mystery does not simply dumbfound us, rendering us agnostic about the future; many of its main features can be anticipated. The ordering and reordering of energy, whether in nature or human society through history, is an instance of what we can anticipate.

Furthermore, we should expect to be able to trace the active agency of God in the course which the future will take. The discovery of the agency of the Triune God – and the God of such a magnificently complex creation could only be thus – may lead us to understand what may be made of the future which we can anticipate. Of course, the exact character of the operation of this agency will, in a way related to the outworking of the ordering and reordering of the energy of the created order, be mysterious; that we might call the mystery of the *being* of God. But the *activity* of this God can be anticipated, in such a way that we can act accordingly. It must be remembered that the agency of God in creation is such as to constitute the otherness of the world, animate and human nature, in responsibility; and this covenant is not abrogated in the future. The ordering of the energy of nature and society by God are therefore contingent upon the human response to God. It will be through this response that the activity of God is fully realized in the future.

The future of the created order can be anticipated in some respects. The agency of the Triune God can likewise be anticipated, but, in some respects at least, it is contingent upon right human response. The character of the future is therefore dependent upon the human response of faithful and loving dedication, trust and loyalty to God's agency. That is what will make the future hopeful.

---

[51] These are traceable, I think, to the diminished possibilities of dedication and trust which have followed from (and also produce) the collapse of human societies. They are the human foundations of confidence and hope.

Bibliography: Daniel W. Hardy

PUBLISHED ARTICLES AND BOOKS

'What Framework for Theology?', *Regina* (Birmingham: The Queen's College, 1967).

'What Does It Mean to Love?', *Theology* 73 (1970), pp. 257–64.

'Teaching Religion: A Theological Critique', *Learning for Living* 15/1 (1975), pp. 10–16.

'The Implications of Pluralism for Religious Education', *Learning for Living* 17/2 (1977), pp. 55–62.

'Man the Creature', *Scottish Journal of Theology* 30/2 (1977), pp. 111–36.

'Truth in Religious Education: Further Reflections on the Implications of Pluralism', *British Journal of Religious Education* 1/3 (1978), pp. 102–7; republished in John Hull, ed., *New Directions in Religious Education* (Lewes: The Falmer Press, 1982).

'Guidelines in Current Theology', *The Bishopric* [Church House, Birmingham] 1/3 (1979), pp. 4–8.

'Christian Affirmation and the Structure of Personal Life', in Thomas F. Torrance, ed., *Belief in Science and Christian Life: The Relevance of Michael Polanyi's Thought for Christian Faith and Life* (Edinburgh: The Handsel Press, 1980), pp. 71–90.

'Natural Science and Christian Theology', *King's College Review* [King's College, London] 3/2 (1980), pp. 41–9.

'Christ and Creation', in Thomas F. Torrance, ed., *The Incarnation: Ecumenical Studies in the Nicene-Constantinopolitan Creed A.D. 381* (Edinburgh: The Handsel Press, 1981), pp. 88–110.

'Today's Word for Today: Gerhard Ebeling', *The Expository Times* 93/3 (1981), pp. 68–72.

With David F. Ford, *Jubilate: Theology in Praise* (London: Darton, Longman & Todd, 1984); published in the USA as *Praising and Knowing God* (Philadelphia: Westminster, 1985).

'Religious Education: Truth Claims or Meaning-Giving?', in Marius Felderhof, ed., *Religious Education in a Pluralistic Society* (London: Hodder & Stoughton, 1985), pp. 101–15.

'The Nineteenth Century in Britain: Coleridge, the Agnostics and the

Idealists', in *Papers of the Nineteenth Century Theology Working Group*, Vol. 13, American Academy of Religion, 1985.

'Thanksgiving (USA)', in J. G. Davies, ed., *A New Dictionary of Liturgy and Worship* (London: SCM / Philadelphia: Westminster, 1986), pp. 504–5.

'The Repossession of the Church in Birmingham', *The Bishopric* [Church House, Birmingham] 8/2 (1986), pp. 9–19.

'Coleridge on the Trinity', *Anglican Theological Review* 69 (April, 1987), pp. 145–55.

'The English Tradition of Interpretation and the Reception of Schleiermacher and Barth in England', in James O. Duke and Robert F. Streetman, eds., *Barth and Schleiermacher: Beyond the Impasse?* (Philadelphia: Fortress, 1988), pp. 138–62.

'Rationality, the Sciences and Theology', in Geoffrey Wainwright, ed., *Keeping the Faith: Essays to Mark the Centenary of Lux Mundi* (Philadelphia: Fortress / London: SPCK, 1988), pp. 274–309.

'Thomas F. Torrance', in David F. Ford, ed., *The Modern Theologians: An Introduction*, Vol. 1 (Oxford: Blackwell, 1989), pp. 71–91.

'British Theologians: Theology through Philosophy', in David F. Ford, ed., *The Modern Theologians: An Introduction*, Vol. 2 (Oxford: Blackwell, 1989), pp. 30–71.

'Created and Redeemed Sociality', in Colin E. Gunton and Daniel W. Hardy, eds., *On Being the Church: Essays on the Christian Community* (Edinburgh: T. & T. Clark, 1989), pp. 21–47.

'The Doctrine of Creation in 19th Century Theology: A Preface to Discussion', in *Papers of the Nineteenth Century Theology Group*, Vol. 16, American Academy of Religion, 1990.

'Systematic Theology', in J. L. Houlden, ed., *Dictionary of Biblical Interpretation* (London: SCM / Philadelphia: TPI, 1990), pp. 665–7.

'God and the Form of Society', in Daniel W. Hardy and Peter H. Sedgwick, eds., *The Weight of Glory: A Vision and Practice for Christian Theology. The Future of Liberal Theology: Essays for Peter Baelz* (Edinburgh: T. & T. Clark, 1991), pp. 131–44.

'Epilogue: The Strategy of Liberalism', in Daniel W. Hardy and Peter H. Sedgwick, eds., *The Weight of Glory: A Vision and Practice for Christian Theology. The Future of Liberal Theology: Essays for Peter Baelz* (Edinburgh: T. & T. Clark, 1991), pp. 299–306.

'Sociality, Rationality and Culture: Faith Embedded in the Particularities of History', in *Papers of the Nineteenth Century Theology Working Group*, Vol. 18, American Academy of Religion, 1992.

'Worship as the Orientation of Life to God', *Ex Auditu* 8 (1992), pp. 55–71.

'The Future of Theology in a Complex World', in Hilary D. Regan and Alan J. Torrance, eds., *Christ and Context: The Confrontation be-*

tween *Gospel and Culture* (Edinburgh: T. & T. Clark, 1993), pp. 21–42.

'The Spirit of God in Creation and Reconciliation', in Hilary D. Regan and Alan J. Torrance, eds., *Christ and Context: The Confrontation between Gospel and Culture* (Edinburgh: T. & T. Clark, 1993), pp. 237–58.

'Covenant', 'Creation', and 'Worship', in Paul A. B. Clarke and Andrew Linzey, eds., *The Dictionary of Theology and Society* (London: Routledge & Kegan Paul, forthcoming 1995).

'Creation and Eschatology', in Colin E. Gunton, ed., *The Doctrine of Creation* (London: SPCK, forthcoming 1996).

'God in the Ordinary: The Work of J. G. Davies (1919–1990)', *Theology* (forthcoming 1996).

'Theology and the Cultural Reduction of Religion', in J. Astley, ed., *Christian Theology and Religious Education: Connections and Contradictions* (London: SPCK, forthcoming 1996).

DOCUMENTS

'The Church in Change' in *Structures for Ministry* (Birmingham: Church House, 1974).

With Alan Bryman and J. G. Davies, *In-Service Training for Clergy* (Birmingham: Institute of Worship and Architecture, 1975).

Education for the Church's Ministry (London: Advisory Council for the Church's Ministry, 1985).

The Future of the Center of Theological Inquiry (Princeton: Center of Theological Inquiry, 1991).

Planning for the Future of the Center (Princeton: Center of Theological Inquiry, 1991).

The Center's Identity and Future Program: The Director's Report for 1991 (Princeton: Center of Theological Inquiry, 1992).

An Unfolding Strategy: The Director's Report for 1992 (Princeton: Center of Theological Inquiry, 1993).

The Nature of Theological Inquiry: The Director's Report for 1993 (Princeton: Center of Theological Inquiry, 1994).

The Logic of Interdisciplinary Studies and the Coherence of Theology: The Director's Report for 1994 (Princeton: Center of Theological Inquiry, 1995).

UNPUBLISHED PAPERS AND ADDRESSES

'The Doctrine of Sin: An Investigation of the Theories of Karl Barth and

F. R. Tennant' (Thesis, General Théological Seminary, New York, 1963).

'Anglican Theology' ('La Théologie Anglicane', Université de Lyons, 1966).

'The Method of Duality in Theology' (Birmingham University, 1967).

'Language and Theology' (Thesis, Oxford University, 1968).

'Anxiety in Theological Perspective' (Institute of Religion and Medicine, Birmingham, 1969).

'A Taxonomy of Theologies' (Birmingham University, 1971).

'The Study of Theology' (Birmingham University, 1972).

'Reality and Its Realization in Theology' (Birmingham University, 1972).

'The Methods of Knowledge in 17th and 18th Century Theology' (Birmingham University, 1972).

'Christian Theology as Realism' (Birmingham University, 1973).

'The Ordination of Women to the Priesthood' (Birmingham Diocesan Synod, 1973).

'The Ideal of Integration in 17th and 18th Century Theology' (Birmingham University, 1974).

'Theology and the Effect of the European Enlightenment' (Birmingham University, 1974).

'Completeness and Change in Christian Doctrine' (Birmingham University, 1974).

'Unity and Duality as Theological Ideals' (Birmingham University, 1975).

'The Use of Information-Theory in Theology' (American Academy of Religion, 1975).

'Theology and the Academic World' (Birmingham University, 1977).

'Coleridge and Hegel' (Birmingham University, 1978).

'Coleridge's Hunger for Eternity' (American Academy of Religion, 1978).

'Christianity as the Foundation of Moral Life' (Birmingham University, 1979).

'The Training of Lay Readers' (Diocese of Birmingham, 1979).

'The Black Manifesto' (Birmingham University, 1980).

Interfaculty Lectures: 'Realization Theory', 'Relativism', 'Operationalism' and 'Subjectivism' in Theology, and 'Openness to the World and to God' (University of Birmingham, 1980).

'The Study of Theology in Universities' (University of Leeds, 1981).

'Religion and Social Righteousness' (Birmingham University, 1982).

'The Dynamics of Creation' (Society for the Study of Theology, 1983).

'Why Special Training for Black Clergy?' (Advisory Council for the Church's Ministry, London, 1984).

'Pastoral Studies: An Interdisciplinary Activity' (Anniversary Conference, University of Birmingham, 1984).

'Integrating Training for Theology Graduates' (Advisory Council for the Church's Ministry, London, 1984).

'Truth and the Election of God's People' (Carlisle Cathedral, 1988).

'The Nature of a University' (University of Durham, 1989).

'Spirit of Unity – Reconcile Your People' (Commission on Faith and Order, World Council of Churches, Würzburg, FRG, 1989).

'Introduction to Theology: Eight Lectures' (University of Durham, 1989).

'Church, Ministry and Sacraments: Fourteen Lectures' (University of Durham, 1989).

'On Leadership and Priesthood' (University of Newcastle, 1989).

'The Value of Land' (Newcastle City Chaplaincy, 1990).

'Theological Inquiry Today' (Old Guards' Association, Princeton, 1991).

'The Foundation of Cognition and Ethics in Worship' (Durham–Tübingen Consultation, 1991).

'The Religion of America' (Trinity Church, Princeton, 1991).

'On the Public Character of Theology' (Higher Education Chaplains' Conference, High Leigh, 1991).

'Theology and Life's Irreducible Structure' (Polanyi Centenary, St George's House, Windsor, 1991).

'On the Ordination of Homosexuals' (Episcopal Church General Convention, 1991).

'Living in Faith, Living in the World' (Christ Church, Greenwich, 1991).

'The Search for Order and Dynamism in Anglicanism' (Trinity Church, Princeton, 1991).

'Preparing Theology for the 21st Century' (Church of the Redeemer, Bryn Mawr, 1991).

'The Recovery of Christian Faith in Modern Life' (Church of St Michael & St George, St Louis, 1991).

'The Trinity in Language' (Annual Lecture, Scholars Engaged in Anglican Doctrine, Alexandria, 1992).

'Where is Home? Identity and Diaspora in Christianity' (Consultation on Inter Religious Relations, Center of Theological Inquiry, Princeton, 1992).

'The Relationship of the Mainline Churches and Fundamentalism' (Trinity Church, Princeton, 1992).

'Developing Christian Faith for the 21st Century' (St Barnabas Church, Greenwich, 1992).

'The Debate about Ordination of Women' (London, 1992).

'The Future of the Church' (St Barnabas Church, Greenwich, 1993).

'Sin and Confession' (All Saints' Church, Princeton, 1993).

'The Center of Theological Inquiry: History and Future' (Nassau Club, Princeton, 1993).

'Theology, Cosmology and Change' (Society for the Study of Theology, 1993).

'The Future of the Church: An Exploration' (Princeton, 1993).

'The Question of God in "God's Action in the World"' (Consultation on Theology and Science, CTI, Princeton, 1994).

'The Orientation of Life to God' (Princeton, 1994).

'The Situation of Christian Faith Today and a Response' (New York, 1994).

'Dimensions of Interfaith Dialogue' (Consulate General of India, New York, 1994).

'The Roots of Values' (Old Guards' Association, Princeton, 1995).

List of Contributors

Diogenes Allen is Stuart Professor of Philosophy, Princeton Theological Seminary.

Jeremy Begbie is Vice-Principal of Ridley Hall, Cambridge and a member of the Faculty of Divinity, University of Cambridge.

James D. G. Dunn is Lightfoot Professor of Divinity, Department of Theology, University of Durham.

David F. Ford is Regius Professor of Divinity, Faculty of Divinity, and Fellow of Selwyn College, University of Cambridge.

Colin Gunton is Professor of Christian Doctrine, King's College, University of London.

Stanley Hauerwas is Professor of Christian Ethics, The Divinity School, Duke University.

John M. Hull is Professor of Religious Education, School of Education, University of Birmingham.

Ann Loades is Professor of Theology, Department of Theology, University of Durham.

Alistair McFadyen is Lecturer in Theology and Religious Studies, University of Leeds.

Hugh McLeod is Professor of Church History, Department of Theology, University of Birmingham.

Robert Morgan is Lecturer in Theology and Fellow of Linacre College, University of Oxford.

Micheal O'Siadhail is a freelance poet and writer, and a former Professor at the Dublin Institute for Advanced Studies.

Stephen Pickard is Lecturer in Theology at the United Theological College (an institution of the Uniting Church in Australia), Sydney, Australia.

Esther D. Reed is Lecturer in Theology, University of Exeter.

Richard H. Roberts is Professor of Religious Studies, Department of Religious Studies, Lancaster University.

Brian Russell is Bishop's Director for Ministries in the Diocese of Birmingham, and formerly Secretary to the Committee for Theological Education of the Church of England.

Peter Sedgwick was Vice-Principal of Westcott House, Cambridge, and a former Lecturer in Theology at the Universities of Hull and Birmingham.

Peter Selby is the William Leech Professorial Fellow in Applied Christian Theology, University of Durham, and former suffragan bishop in South West London.

Dennis L. Stamps is Curate of St Mary's, Moseley, Birmingham and part-time Lecturer in Theology, University of Birmingham School of Continuing Studies.

Stephen Sykes is Bishop of Ely, and the former Regius Professor of Divinity, University of Cambridge.

Frances Young is Edward Cadbury Professor of Theology and Dean of the Faculty of Arts, University of Birmingham.

Index of Names and Modern Authors

INDEX